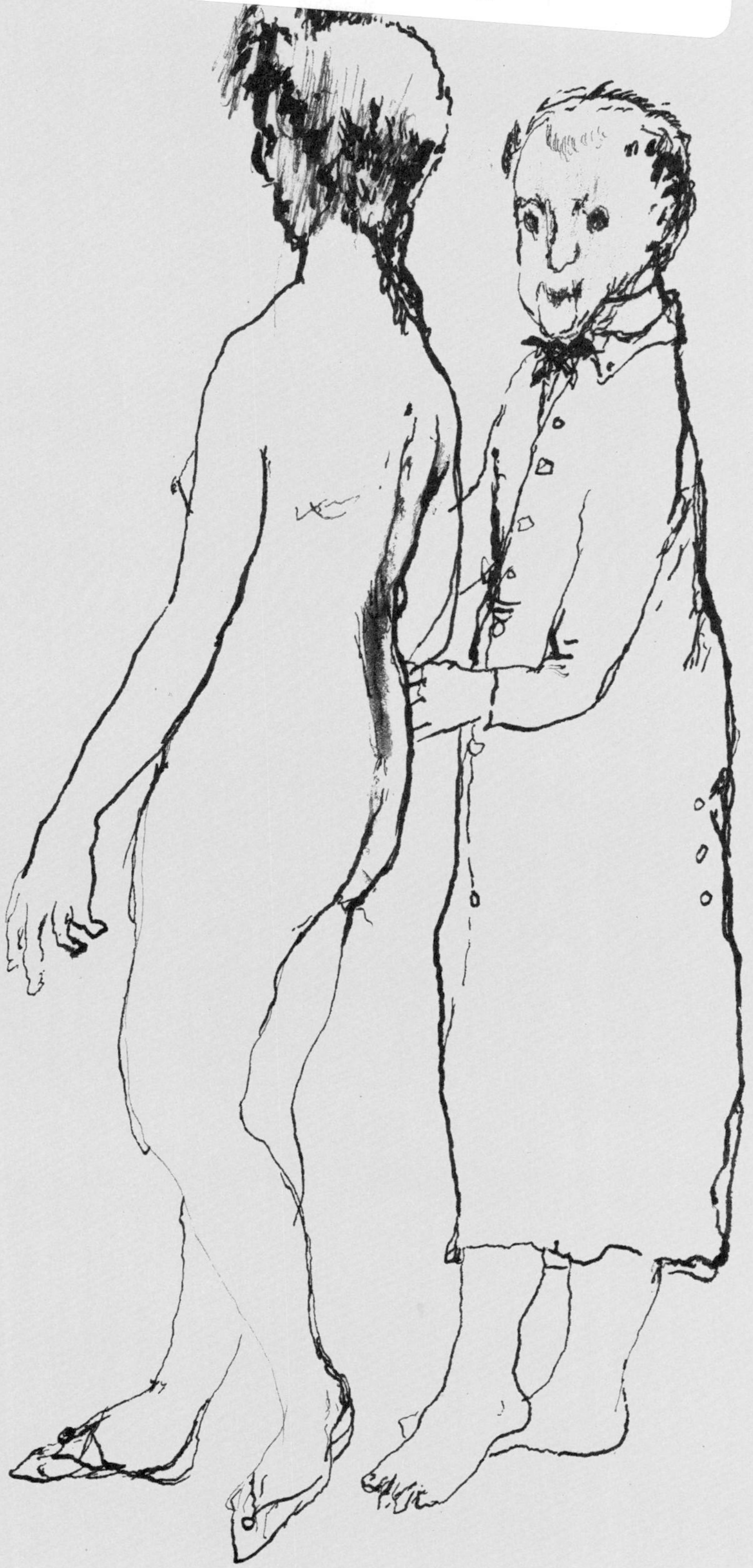

Eugene Ludins

An American Fantasist

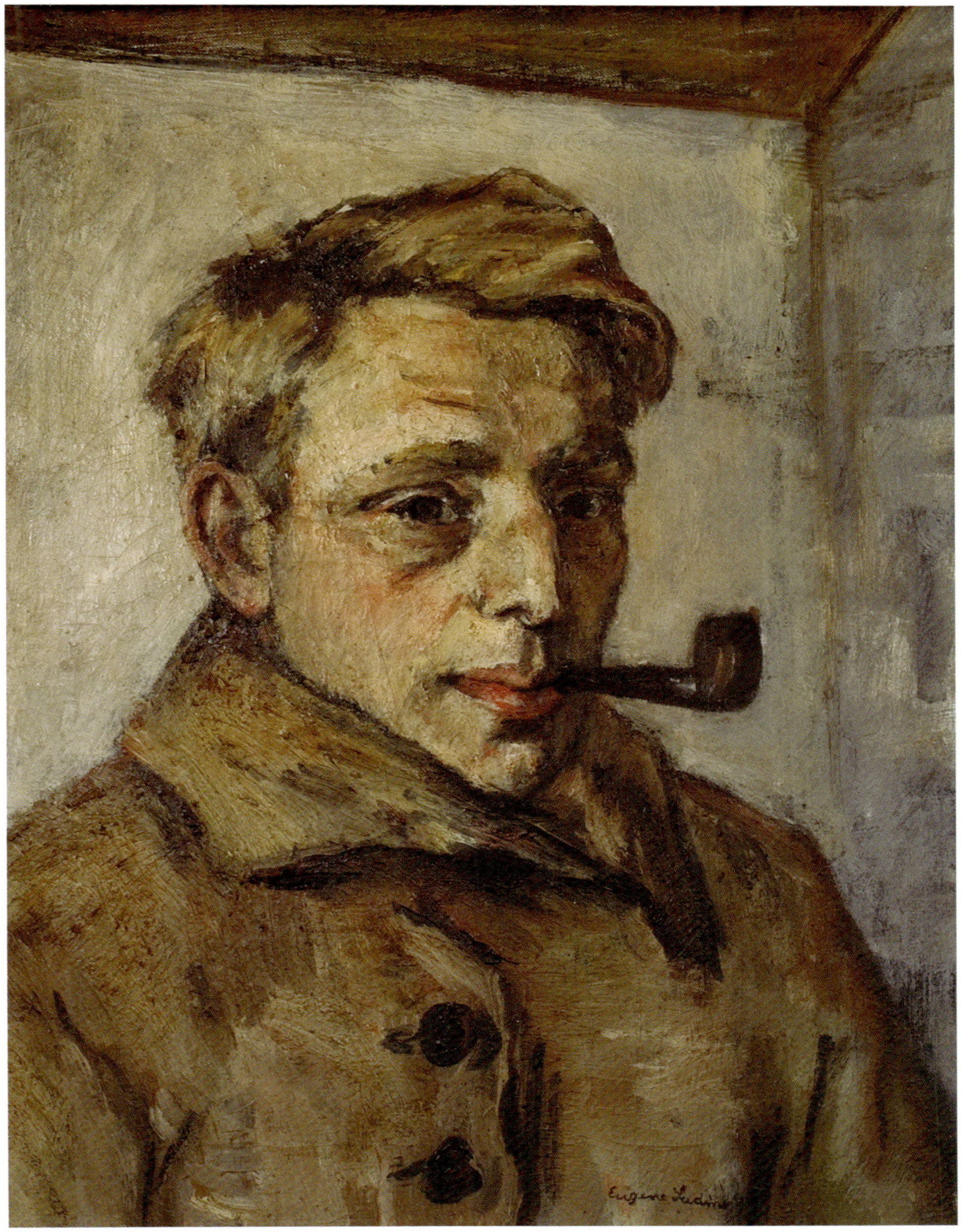

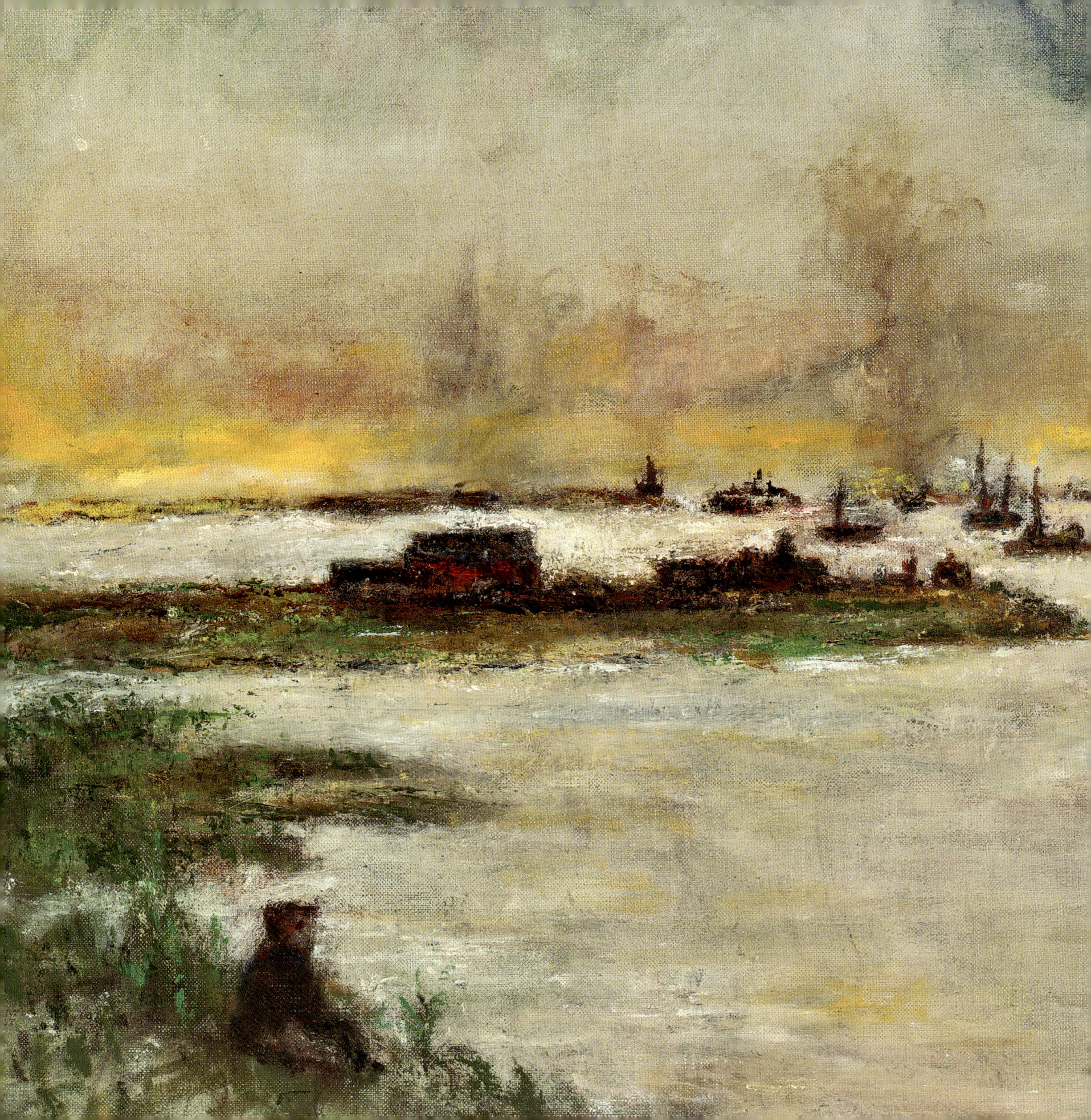

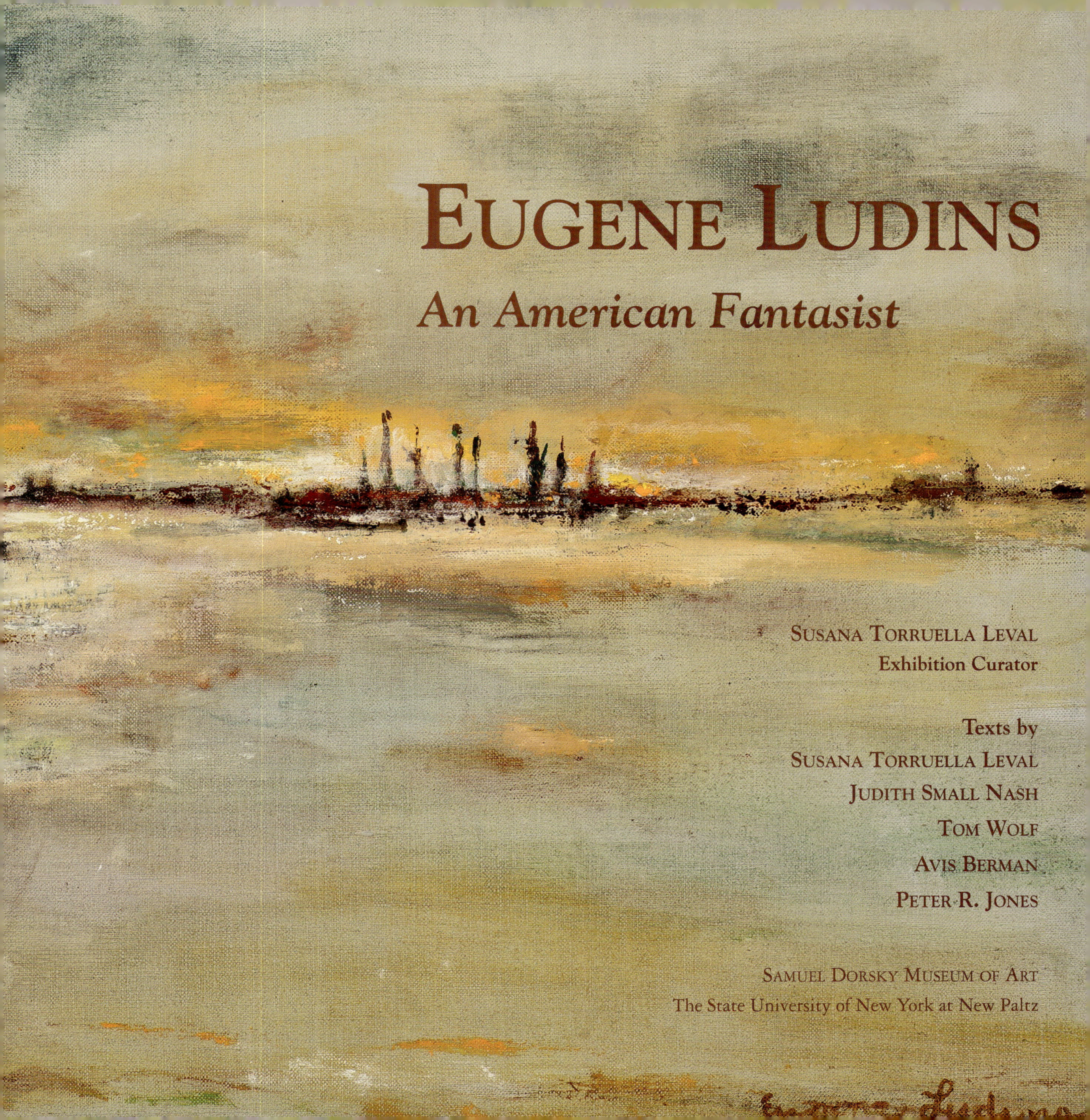

EUGENE LUDINS

An American Fantasist

SUSANA TORRUELLA LEVAL
Exhibition Curator

Texts by
SUSANA TORRUELLA LEVAL
JUDITH SMALL NASH
TOM WOLF
AVIS BERMAN
PETER R. JONES

SAMUEL DORSKY MUSEUM OF ART
The State University of New York at New Paltz

Published in conjunction with the exhibition
Eugene Ludins: An American Fantasist
curated by Susana Torruella Leval,
held from February 11 through July 12, 2012,
in the Morgan Anderson, Howard Greenberg Family, and
Corridor Galleries in the Samuel Dorsky Museum of Art.

Major support for this publication was provided by
Friends of the Samuel Dorsky Museum of Art
The State University of New York at New Paltz
The Estate of Eugene Ludins

With special thanks to:
Peter R. Jones
Judith Small Nash
Abigail Sturges
Emily R. Jones

Published by the Samuel Dorsky Museum of Art
State University of New York at New Paltz
One Hawk Drive
New Paltz, New York 12561

Designed by Abigail Sturges

Printed by Pimlico Book Company

Distributed by the State University of New York Press
www.sunypress.edu

ISBN 978-0-615-45510-5

ENDPAPERS

Couple

1977, ink on paper
9⅜ x 4½ in.
Private Collection
Photo John Kleinhans

Couple

Undated, ink on paper
8⅞ x 4¼ in.
Private Collection
Photo John Kleinhans

PAGE 1: CAT. 1

Self-Portrait with Pipe

c. 1929–31, oil on canvas
20 x 16 in.
Private Collection
Photo Beckett Logan

PAGES 2–3: CAT. 56

Gulf Coast Landscape

1985, oil on canvas
18 x 30 in.
Estate of Eugene Ludins
Photo John Kleinhans

Photo Credits

Janis Conner and Joel Rosenkranz, cat: 25, 26

Wayne Lempka, Samuel Dorsky Museum, SUNY New Paltz, 37

Peter Jones, cat: 4, 8, 12, 21, 34, 40, 59, 62, 65, 68, 69, 71, 73, 74

John Kleinhans, cat: 2, 3, 5–7, 9–11, 13–20, 22–24, 27, 28–33, 35, 36, 38, 39, 41–49, 51–58, 60, 61, 63, 64, 66, 67, 70, 72, 75–80

Beckett Logan, cat: 1, 50

Whitney Museum of American Art, New York, cat: 10

Contents

Director's Foreword

SARA PASTI

The Neil C. Trager Director

CAT. 33

Hiding Places

c. 1949, oil on canvas
40¼ x 39 in.
Private Collection.
Photo John Kleinhans

I was first introduced to Eugene Ludins's work in 2009 by Susana Torruella Leval and Judith Small Nash. Like many artists who may be well known in their own time but become less so with the passage of time and the advent of new artistic styles, Eugene Ludins is an artist whose work and life are worth revisiting.

As you will read in the excellent essays that appear in this catalogue, Ludins was a product of his time, coming of age in a New York City that offered much for young men and women interested in pursuing a creative life. Like many young artists, Ludins studied at the Art Students League, where he developed his skill as a painter. In 1929 he moved to Woodstock, where he connected with the artists, writers, musicians, and other creative people who would shape his art as well as his life. Later, he became a professor and teaching artist in Iowa, though he spent his summers in Woodstock and relocated there permanently when he retired from teaching in 1969.

This is a story not unlike others in which a young artist came to the Hudson Valley to be inspired and then stayed, captivated by the beauty of the region and by its innovative community of artists. In furtherance of its mission to support Hudson Valley art and culture, the Samuel Dorsky Museum of Art is proud to add Eugene Ludins to the list of Hudson Valley artists we have celebrated and whose work has served as an inspiration for our audiences and for the artists of our time.

We are immensely grateful to exhibition curator Susana Torruella Leval and to Judith Small Nash for drawing our attention to the work of Eugene Ludins, and to Peter R. Jones for his early and continuing support of the exhibition. We thank Susana Torruella Leval, Judith Small Nash, Avis Berman, and Tom Wolf for their marvelous essays and Peter R. Jones for the chronology, all of which have brought Eugene Ludins and his time back to life. In addition, we thank Abigail Sturges for her inspired catalogue design, Nancy Chapman for her expert editing, and archivist Emily R. Jones, framing consultant Walter J. Jamieson, Jr., and conservators Barbara Appelbaum and Paul Himmelstein for their contributions to the project.

Finally, we are grateful to the State University of New York at New Paltz and to the Friends of the Samuel Dorsky Museum of Art, which provide ongoing support for the museum's exhibitions and programs.

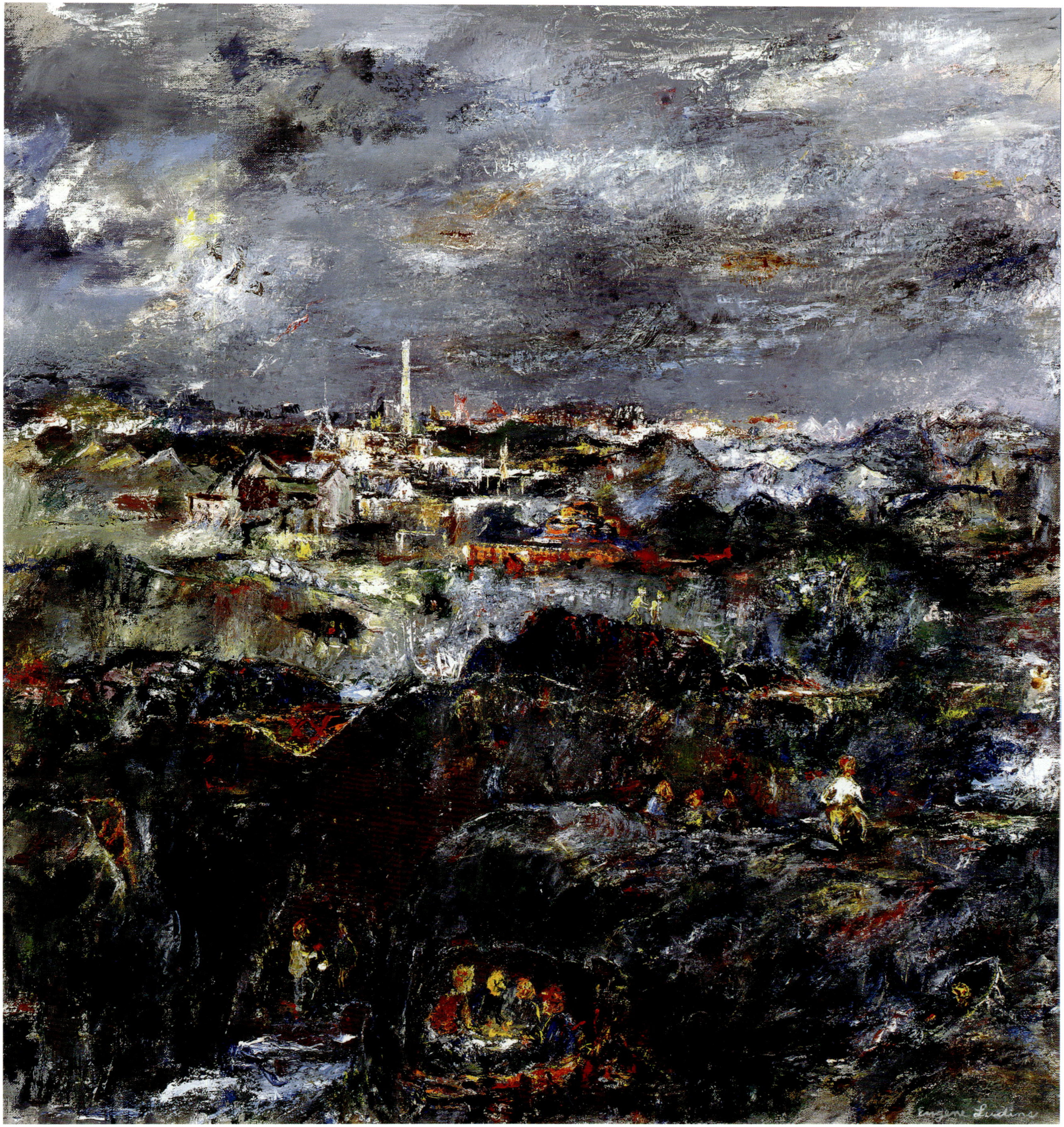
Eugene Ludins

Preface and Acknowledgments

SUSANA TORRUELLA LEVAL

Curator

CAT. 46

Regenerator

1965–75, oil on canvas
39 x 50 in.
Estate of Eugene Ludins.
Photo John Kleinhans

In 1974, my husband and I bought a house in Woodstock and met there an extraordinary generation of artists. Eugene Ludins and his wife, sculptor Hannah Small, became our dear friends. These Woodstock artists were characterized by commitment, talent, vivid personalities, and bedrock values of integrity and civic-mindedness. Ludins and others of the Woodstock group, who worked almost exclusively in a figurative mode, had attained a measure of recognition in the 1930s and 40s, Woodstock's moment in the sun vis-à-vis New York City. They were soon marginalized and largely forgotten by the sweep of abstract expressionism and subsequent "isms" that overtook the New York art world. This exhibition undertakes to bring an exceptionally interesting artist back into view, offering us a second look at his work and his place in Woodstock, a significant regional art center with a unique legacy.

In August 2009, Peter R. Jones, Judith Small Nash, and I envisioned this exhibition during an impromptu meeting at the old Ludins-Small home. Peter Jones's scholarship of Ludins's work provided the foundation for this exhibition, and he has prepared an invaluable chronology. Judith Small Nash, niece of Small and Ludins, provided valuable insights into the selection process and has contributed an interesting essay on the family. Two other key members soon joined us: noted book designer Abigail Sturges, and Emily R. Jones, archivist at the Woodstock Artists Association and Museum, who immeasurably aided my research. Barbara Appelbaum and Paul Himmelstein furnished skillful conservation. Ben Caswell and Barbara Arvanitis provided art handling and transportation. Photographer John Kleinhans and framing consultant Walter J. Jamieson, Jr. completed this exceptional team.

The early, constant support of Sara Pasti, director of the Samuel Dorsky Museum; Brian Wallace, chief curator; Wayne Lempka, collections manager; and trustee Arthur Anderson has been crucial. The exhibition reinforces the Dorsky's mission to champion local and regional arts.

This beautiful catalogue, which will disseminate Ludins's work long after the exhibition, was designed by Abigail Sturges. The rich essays of art historians Avis Berman and Tom Wolf enhance our understanding of Ludins's work and time. The contributions of Nancy Chapman as editor and James Hoff as fact checker were essential to its successful completion.

Sincere thanks to the generous lenders who have made the exhibition possible. They include *Art Times* Collection, Cornelia Seckel and Raymond J. Steiner; Arthur Anderson; Janis Conner and Joel Rosenkranz, Samuel Dorsky Museum of Art; Estate of Jane Jones; Fletcher Gallery; Historical Society of Woodstock; Marilyn and Ira Janow; John Kleinhans and Paula Nelson; Nancy Kline; Abby and Mark Lerner; Peter Mayer; Marc Plate and the Estate of Marion Greenwood; Cornelia and Edgar Rosenblum; John and Elisabeth Small; Abigail Sturges and Daniel Perry; Woodstock Artists Association and Museum; Whitney Museum of American Art; and Jean Young.

Many Woodstockers contributed valuable historical context, hospitality, and lively stories about Eugene Ludins. They include Weston Blelock, artist Manuel Bromberg, Tom Fletcher of Fletcher Gallery, Jean Gaede, Cambiz Khosravi, Nancy Kline, Joanne Margolies of the Historical Society of Woodstock, Tatiana and Anthony Robinson, Cornelia Seckel and Raymond J. Steiner. Visiting the University of Iowa in Iowa City was crucial to understanding Ludins's trajectory. Professors Wallace Tomasini, Virginia Myers, John Beldon Scott, and Sean O'Harrow generously shared their recollections, as did artist Byron Burford.

Professional colleagues and friends have given me valuable guidance and help. I gratefully acknowledge Janis Conner and Joel Rosenkranz, Benita Eisler, Julia Herzberg, Anne Hollander, Dulcy Ross Brainard, Patterson Sims, and Gary Tinterow. My friends Wendy Gimbel, Kathy Preminger, Frederick Seidel, and my daughter India have been wonderfully supportive. Belated thanks also to Arthur Zaidenberg and Tommy Beere, who introduced me to Eugene Ludins. And my love and gratitude to my husband Pierre, for joining me in every step of the way in search of Eugene Ludins—from New York, to Woodstock, to Iowa City and back.

New York and Woodstock, August 2011

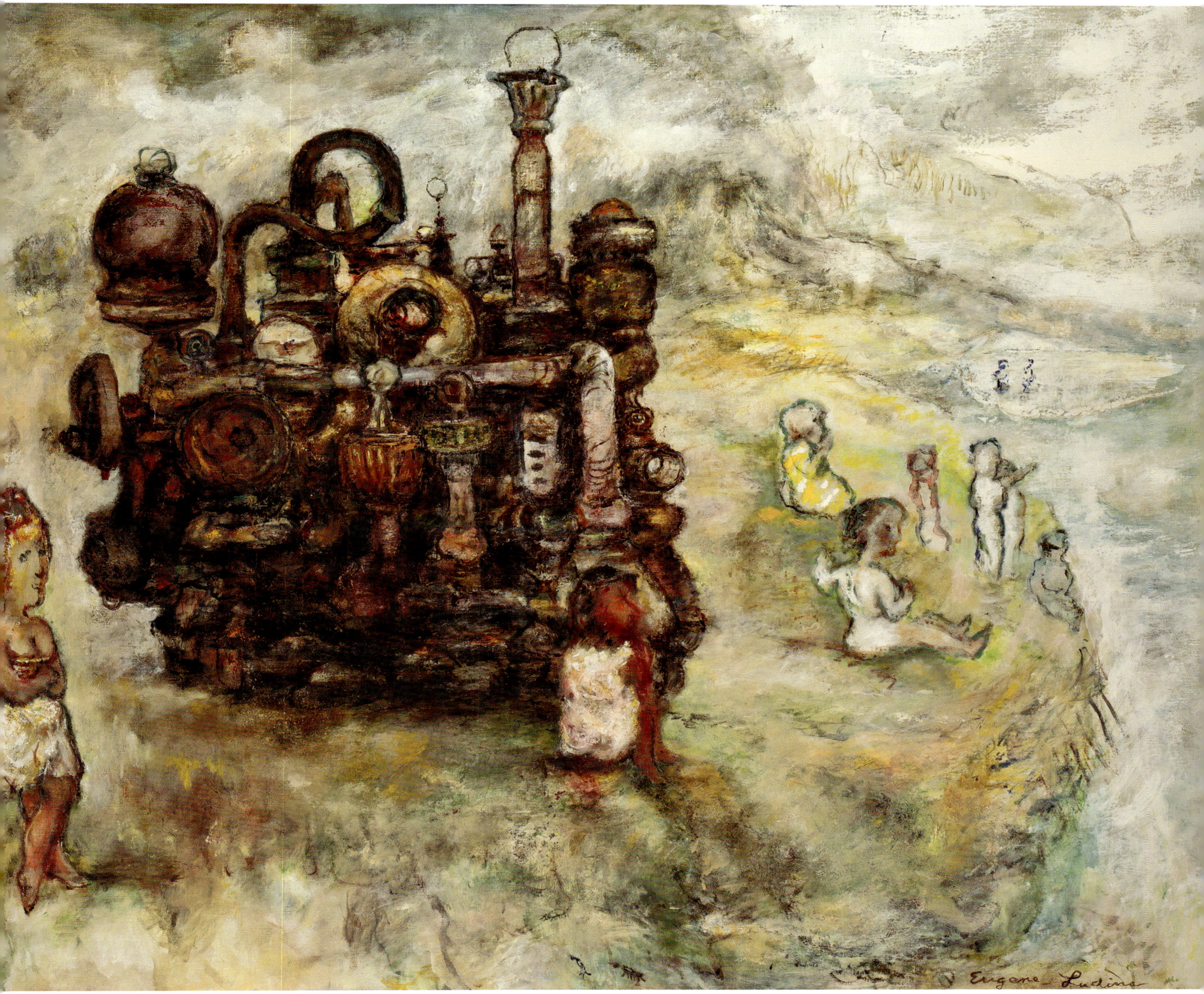
Eugene Ludins

Introduction

PETER R. JONES

Growing up in Woodstock as the son of artists Wendell and Jane Jones, I was close to Gene Ludins and his wife Hannah Small all my life. They were like family because of their deep friendship with my parents. My parents met in Allen Tucker's class at the Art Students League of New York, where Gene was monitor. Gene and my father talked art continually. Once Gene walked my father home to Brooklyn over the Manhattan Bridge, only to have my father walk back to finish the conversation. On Gene's recommendation, my parents spent their first summer in Woodstock in 1928, and after they married and settled in the Maverick; much of Hannah and Gene's courtship occurred in their living room.

As a boy, I remember frequent visits with them. I can still picture Gene getting a Coke—a special treat—for my brother and me in their small kitchen. Gene was my father's dearest friend, and after my father's death in 1956, when I was fourteen, Gene became a father figure for me. Later he would be my teacher in graduate school in Iowa.

When I transferred to the University of Iowa to pursue painting, I stayed with Hannah and Gene. Gene loved to come back in mid-afternoon from his studio on Sundays to watch football. This would be followed by a delicious dinner and the evening shows, particularly Ed Sullivan. I joined this ritual, and even after I found an apartment, we continued the tradition for the next three years.

As a teacher, Gene didn't try to enforce styles or techniques, but dealt with the picture at hand and made suggestions as we painted from the model. I learned from Gene to respect my own students as artists engaged in a noble pursuit. In my first class with him, he suggested that I paint on sheets of brown wrapping paper, which provided a perfect background for quick studies. When I began teaching figure painting at Louisiana Tech thirty years ago, I had big rolls of brown paper donated to recreate that experience for my students. They loved it as much as I had. Gene also taught me how to cut and join my first frame, and he gave me one of his Stanley miter machines.

As Gene grew older, he went to great lengths to ensure the viability of his artistic legacy. In the 1950s, he was one of the first of his generation to build a fire-resistant cinder block storeroom away from his house and studio. In 1994 he built an even better-appointed one. I remember how at age 90, he took me in his little car and drove through the woods down a steep hill, assuring me that there was a road he'd had built to his new storeroom on the edge of his field, which he kept cleared with his walk-behind lawn tractor.

Gene called together the team responsible for this exhibition and catalogue, and in his will he specified that we collaborate to place his work in appropriate locations. Susana Leval and her husband Pierre had been close friends with the Ludinses for many years. As an art historian and past director of El Museo del Barrio, Susana brought strong curatorial skills to the project. Judith Small Nash, Hannah's niece, was a long-time New York art dealer with vast experience. I was the studio painter and university professor responsible for creating the database of work and organizing and digitizing the estate's primary documents. I was able to bring in framing consultant Walter Jamieson, who has known Gene and his work since the 1950s.

Leval and Nash presented the proposal for the Ludins exhibition to the Samuel Dorsky Museum of Art at the State University of New York, New Paltz, where they received the enthusiastic support of director Sara Pasti and her staff. It has been my privilege since to work alongside them in a variety of capacities. We have also relied on the assistance of my archivist daughter, Emily. It is indeed a pleasure and an honor to help present the work of my mentor, teacher, and friend, Gene Ludins.

Legacy
1984, India ink and gouache on paper
8⅜ x 12⅛ in.
Estate of Eugene Ludins.
Photo Peter R. Jomes

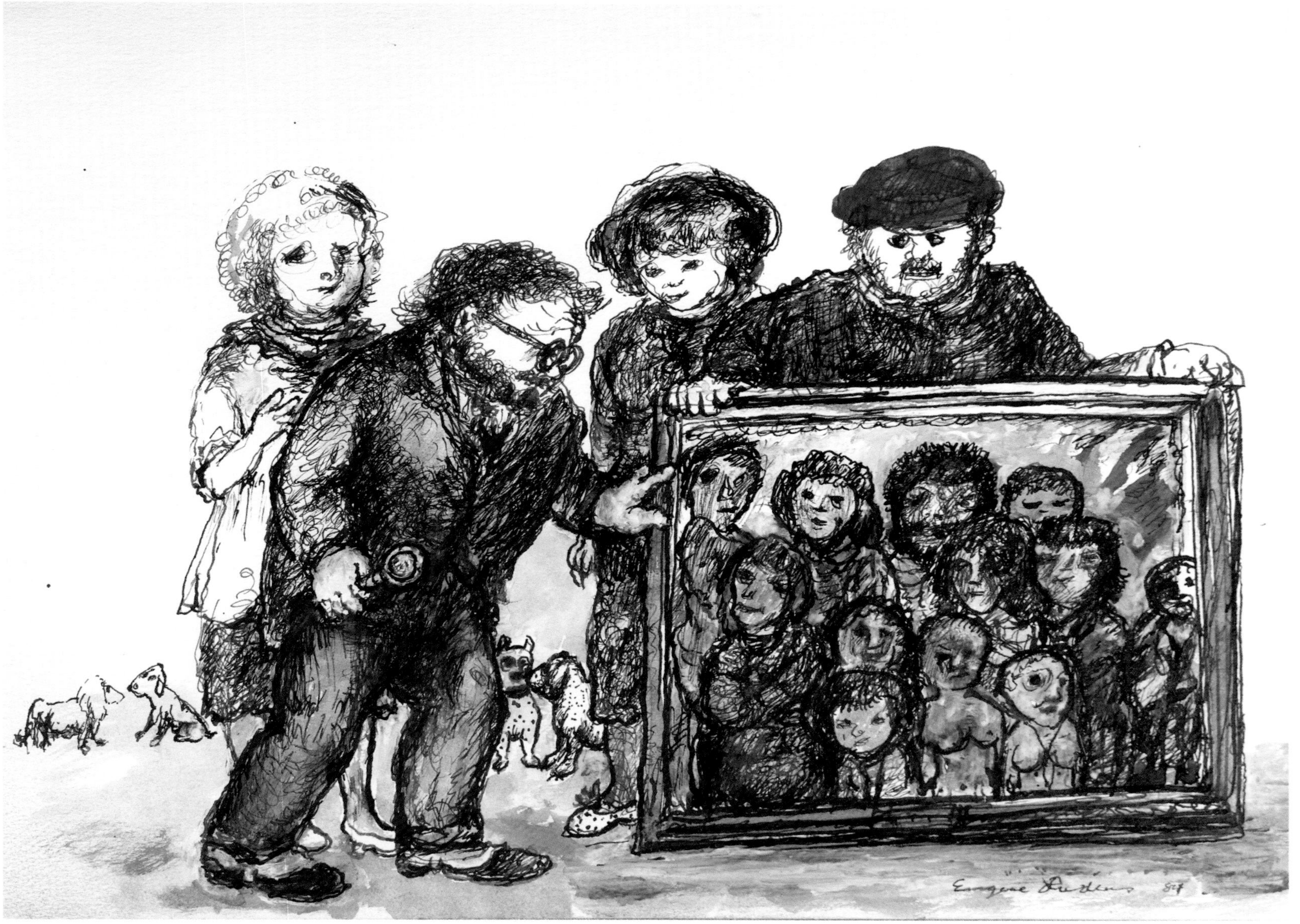

THE WORLD OF EUGENE LUDINS

CAT. 45

Crossing

c. 1960, oil on canvas
38 x 50 in.
Estate of Eugene Ludins.
Photo John Kleinhans

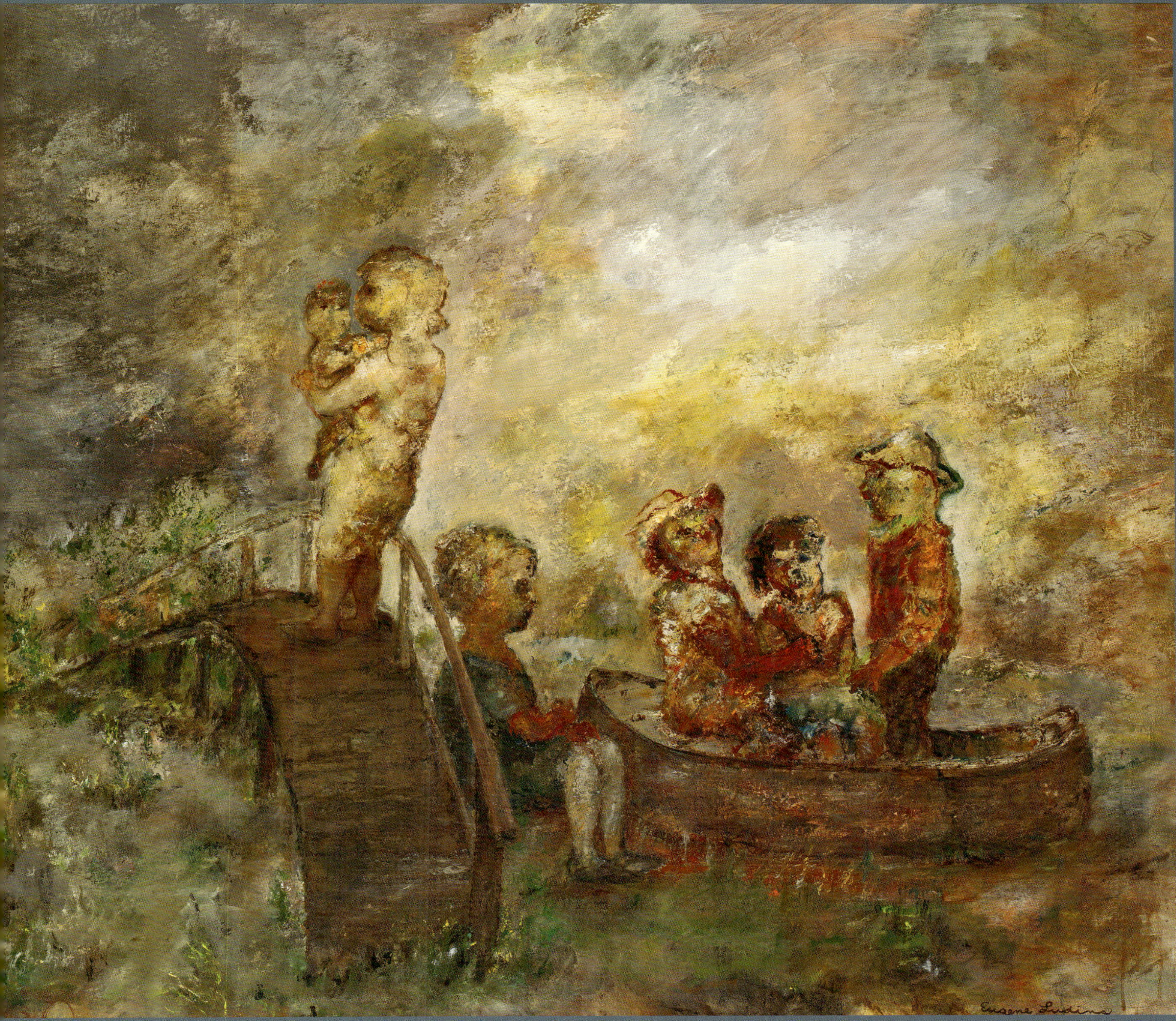
Eugene Ludins

EUGENE LUDINS *An American Fantasist*

Susana Torruella Leval, Curator

THE MAVERICK 1929–34

Looking out of the West Hurley bus window, Eugene Ludins[1] found Woodstock "shockingly beautiful" as he arrived on October 29, 1929 (the day of the stock market crash) to move there permanently. He had "had it with New York."[2] Ludins had some history with Woodstock by then. He had first come to visit his sisters, Ryah and Tima, during the summer of 1923. While enrolled at the Art Students League on Fifty-seventh Street in Manhattan[3] he had often heard about the famed art colony from friends and faculty. During previous summers, he had rented a place in the Woodstock village and began a full-blown campaign to persuade his New York artist friends to move there with him.

Ludins at twenty-five was eager to put into practice the founding values drilled into him at the Art Students League—independence and collegiality. The first independent art school in the nation,[4] the League, in the decades just preceding Ludins's enrollment, had become

> one of the prime movers and shakers in the spirit of artistic change that was taking place on American soil....Even though they would never espouse or endorse any one single style of art, there was hardly a major trend, school, or movement that did not involve League members nor a major figure on the art scene who did not find some nurturing support in its classrooms.[5]

Ludins's teachers at the League—Allen Tucker, Kenneth Hayes Miller, Boardman Robinson, and Walt Kuhn—were men of principle and dedication who practiced what they preached. His favorite teacher was Allen Tucker, whom he referred to as "a great person and a most important influence...inspiring and brilliant."[6] Ludins had become the monitor in Tucker's classes, helping set up and calling the models' poses during life classes (cat. 3).[7] Tucker, in turn, had given him access to the heady world of the Whitney Studio Club,[8] where he had shown *Skating in Central Park* (cat. 5) in 1928. In this three-fold screen, unique in his work, Ludins turns to a well-loved subject of New York painters, printmakers, and photographers since the 1880s, including several well-known skating scenes by William Glackens painted between 1910–12. The New York City setting and the happy activity on the ice follows the conventions of the images of the time—lighthearted bustle of the skaters, framed by snowy hillocks and New York City

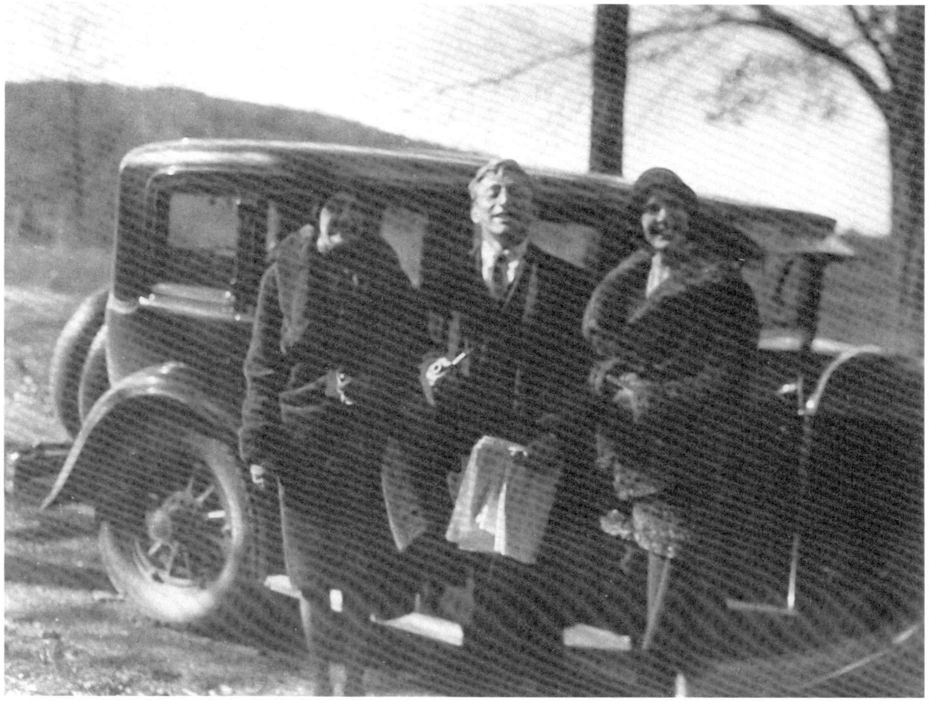

FIG. 1

Left to right, Jane Hays (later Jones), Eugene Ludins, and Mary Holland, Woodstock, c. 1929. Courtesy Estate of Jane Jones. *Photo Wendell Jones*

architecture. Two details presage the mature Ludins. One, the architectural pastiche—real, imagined, and creatively combined—of the iconic New York buildings near the rink on Fifty-ninth Street. The other, the German-looking couple on the lower left of the screen, who stroll along the rink as if invoked from a Berlin street scene painted by German Expressionist Ernst Ludwig Kirchner.

In 1929, Woodstock offered an ideal environment to live out principles of independence and collegiality learned at the League. Ludins was captivated immediately by the exceptional Maverick colony founded by Hervey White just outside Woodstock.[9] It was built on those principles. At White's memorial service in 1944, artist Lucile Blanch said,

> When he founded the Maverick, a colony for the "unbranded" in the arts and crafts, he cast off associations with that which threatened to compromise and hamper his full freedom. No one was invited to come to the Maverick who did not keep his integrity aloof from self-interest or ultimate purpose of profit, social success, triviality and dissipation.[10]

White took a liking to Ludins and offered him a house, charging him rent of $100 a year, *"if you've got it."* Ludins recalled his cabin with delight, especially the big window: "If you were an artist, you got a window."[11] For a young, adventurous artist, living on the Maverick was the epitome of idealistic, bohemian life, a stone's throw from New York City. It was also a rough life—no electricity or indoor plumbing, and only a potbellied stove per cabin for warmth in the then fiercely cold Catskill winters. Somehow, the artists on the Maverick colony survived through the Depression. In the early years of the Maverick, soy sauce and a forty-pound bag of rice, brought from New York's Chinatown, would help feed his neighbors along Maverick Road for a month.[12]

If food was scarce, art and hilarity were plentiful: music, theater performances, and rowdy, costumed festivals at the Maverick; classes at Woodstock's School of Landscape;[13] exhibitions at the Woodstock Art Association; and, a few years later, radical new work at the Sawkill Gallery of Painters and Sculptors. To be "modern" was the highest aspiration, and there were as many modes of pursuing modernity as there were artists, and factions, in the bustling art colony.[14]

Immensely sociable, Ludins jumped into Woodstock's artistic and communal life. He had already volunteered, in the summer of 1929, to help organize that year's Maverick Festival, one of a series of wild, ambitious multi-art festivals.[15] Captured in a humorous photo, captioned "The Committee of Fifty," costumed Maverick revelers mockingly assume the pose of the committee of townsmen who were bent on closing down the festival. Rakishly handsome, Ludins, clad in the garb of a Romantic poet, stands at the far left (fig. 32).

He was a generous neighbor to his fellow artists—Wendell and Jane Jones, Arnold and Lucile Blanch, Eugenie Gershoy and Harry Gottlieb, among others—along Maverick Road. He was handy with tools and always ready to fix anything, or to drive anyone to New York. Soon upon arrival, when all his artist friends were penniless, Ludins earned a substantial sum by making frames for John Carroll,[16] a well-known local painter. Almost immediately, he joined Woodstock's baseball team, founded by New York Realist painter George Bellows,[17] who had died four years earlier.

Ludins's early works in this exhibition capture the scrappy, adventurous, Maverick period of his career. The self-portraits (cats. 1 and 7) of this time show a handsome, self-confident young man with an intense gaze, smoking his ubiquitous pipe. *Self-Portrait with Pipe* (cat. 1) was his first work painted in his new Maverick studio. It can be seen on the shelf above the doorway in the 1931 *Maverick Studio* (cat. 11) a few years later.

FIG. 2

EUGENE LUDINS

Woodstock Landscape

c. 1930, oil on canvas
18 x 22 in.
Estate of Eugene Ludins.
Photo John Kleinhans

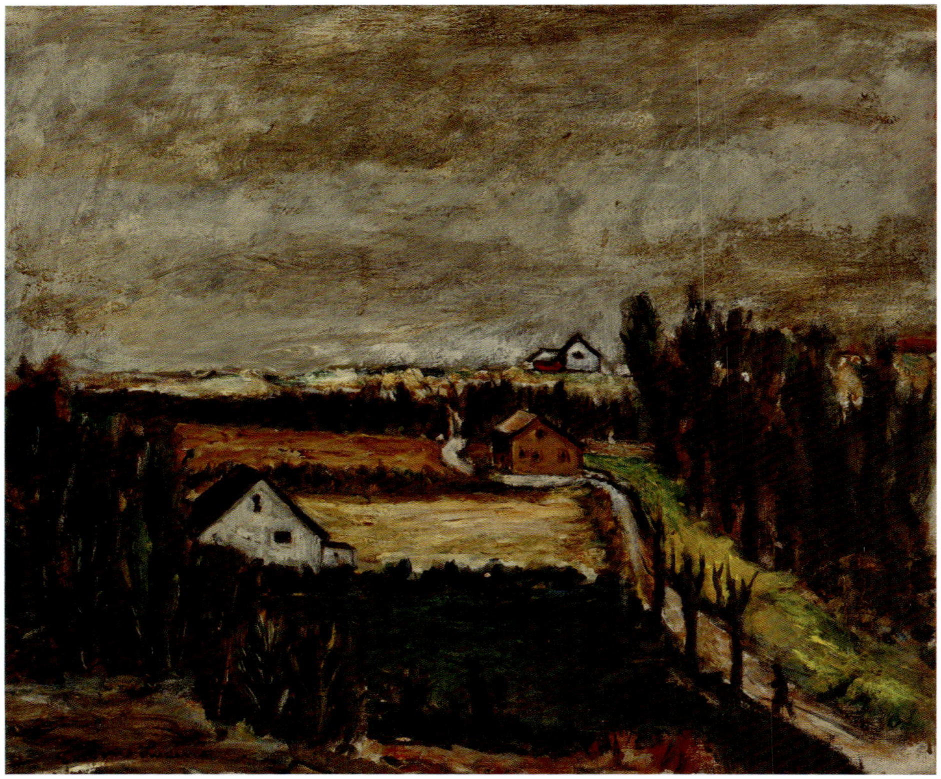

Self-Portrait with Pipe is a clear homage to his artistic hero, Vincent Van Gogh. His best friend, artist Wendell Jones, complained that, as the two friends made the rounds of New York galleries, "Gene stood in front of a Van Gogh at Kraushaar for one hour."[18]

Self-confidence turns into brash sexuality in Marion Greenwood's *Portrait of Gene Ludins* (cat. 6) as he flirts with the wonderful artist, legendary beauty, and free spirit who was painting his portrait. The madcap *Self-Portrait in Roadster* (cat. 8) shows him seated in a Model T Ford, rather than the Pierce-Arrow Ludins brought to the Maverick when his father could no longer afford it.[19] The perilous, teetering raft perhaps alludes to the Arrow's precarious status, given Hervey White's strong disapproval of such a luxury item.

The *Maverick Studio* and *Maverick Kitchen* (cat. 12) interiors distill the simple but heady bohemian life Ludins and his friends found so exciting. Fellow art students Mary Holland, seen asleep on the bed through the studio's doorway, and Jane Hays (later, Jones) became friends at the Art Students League and visited the Maverick during the summers of 1928 and 1929. Jones was then the girlfriend of painter Wendell Jones, Ludins's best friend from the League. The two couples became inseparable. Ludins marveled at "the girls'" adaptability to the rough Maverick life, given their previous New York lives "with all the comforts," and notes they were "just as crazy about the Maverick life as the men." He loved Mary Holland and considered her all important to this period of his life (fig. 1).[20]

Vying with his love of ladies was Ludins's love of baseball. He was described early on as "the best left fielder Woodstock has ever had,"[21] and had joined the ball team as soon as he arrived in town, "one of the few artists in a team of natives."[22] Ludins had been a baseball star at Morris High School in the Bronx and was proud that his team had played in championship playoffs against Commerce High, which featured the young Lou Gehrig.[23] *Third Inning* (cat. 4) is the only known large-scale work about the game he so adored. With runners at first and third, the umpire shows the count as the pitcher and batter square off. Shown at the Whitney Studio Club, *Third Inning* catches the small-town buzz of the Woodstock games, when ladies wore hats and the field offered a fantastic view of the Catskills. In his later Woodstock years, Ludins often referred back to the quandary of his youth—whether to become a ball player or an artist. He also expressed the certainty that he had made the right choice.

The landscapes of the Maverick period were less confident than the portraits. They are tentative, even awkward, and show an eager young painter working directly from the motif, exploring his new surroundings in the *plein-air*[24] tradition. The influence of his Art Students League teachers, clearly visible at this time, was not yet integrated into a mature style. There are sketches of the entrance to Woodstock; of the ever-present Overlook Mountain; streetscapes of Kingston (cat. 13); ferryboat activity in Saugerties (cat. 9) and the Rondout. The most important port between New York City and Albany from the 1830s to the 1950s, the Rondout was a favorite motif.[25] The influence of French modernist Paul Cézanne, revered at the League and in the New York art world since the Armory Show of 1913 and the efforts of Stieglitz's Gallery 291,[26] is omnipresent in Ludins's local landscapes (fig. 2) throughout the thirties.

Landscape (cat. 10), from 1930,[27] is of particular interest as an example of Ludins's studio landscape mode. Big and ambitious in scope, it is a well-composed view of a cement-making plant, such as might have been found north of Kingston, for processing limestone transported through the Rondout. Following Cézanne, Ludins tips up and splays the rising planes: working buildings at the bottom; a series of stepped, verdant shelves in the middle; houses atop the ridge; above, a sky full of exciting movement. Elements of the landscape are based on reality; the limestone quarry rocks behind the crane, for instance, are typical of the area near the Rhinebeck Bridge. But the outsize scale of the chimney, the monumental aqueduct on the right, and the twisting trestle bridge on the upper left are fictional elements, made up for strategic compositional purposes.[28]

Throughout his career, Ludins was torn between two different methods of capturing the natural landscape: the direct out-of-doors mode of sites painted on the spot, and the studio approach, which produced composites of the real and the imagined. In his words:

> I find that wonderfully refreshing, I begin to apply myself to nature. The rest of the time, I work in the studio... pretty much subjective...working out of my head and my memory.[29]

HANNAH SMALL 1932–92

In 1932, Ludins met the most important person in his life—Hannah Small, an accomplished sculptor. Born in New York to an elegant Jewish family, she enjoyed a privileged childhood in New York. Marking time before applying to college, Small registered in 1919 at the Art Students League at age sixteen, missing Ludins by about five years. At the League, she and her close friend Eugenie Gershoy[30] were students of Alexander Stirling Calder. Calder, father to his famous sculptor son, Alexander, was an old-fashioned sculptor and courtly professor who taught traditional methods of modeling and casting. In the course of these years, Small enrolled at Swarthmore College, but she never showed up. Like Ludins, who attended Cornell for one week,[31] she chose instead a life devoted to art.

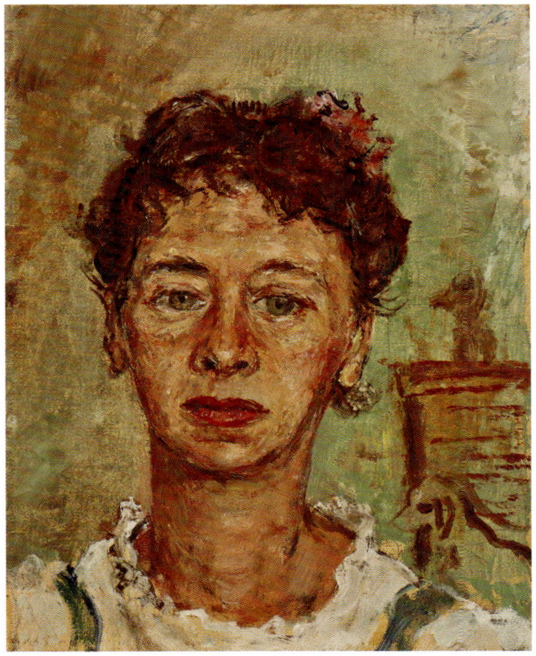

FIG. 3 (CAT. 2)

Portrait of Hannah

1930s, oil on canvas
10 x 8 in.
Estate of Eugene Ludins.
Photo John Kleinhans

After the Art Students League, Small spent a year studying and traveling in England, Holland, and Paris, and another year teaching art to young people in Portland, Oregon.[32] By 1923, Small was married and moved with her painter husband, Austin Mecklem, to the Maverick colony in Woodstock, where her real education in sculpture began. Her neighbor was John B. Flannagan, one of this country's early direct carvers, later recognized as one of the great American sculptors of the period.[33] He became her major artistic influence. In 1924, twenty-one-year-old Small was in and out of Flannagan's studio. She watched him use only a double-bitted ax to carve his powerful image of a "Maverick Horse" from an immense chestnut tree trunk.[34] Commissioned by Hervey White, it still stands in the 1916 Maverick Concert Hall, built by the colony's artists, and serves as a proud symbol of the Maverick.

Direct carving, a vogue in the thirties and a major sculptural movement by mid-century, offered a radically different philosophy of sculpting from the one Small learned at the League. She was captivated by the new dialogue between artist and material:

> When I first get a piece of stone or wood, I study it for awhile. I do not begin with an idea then find material to execute it—I spend time with the particular piece to see what its shape suggests to me. Not only does each piece suggest a specific form, but each piece must also be carved differently. Even pieces of the same material do not carve alike.[35]

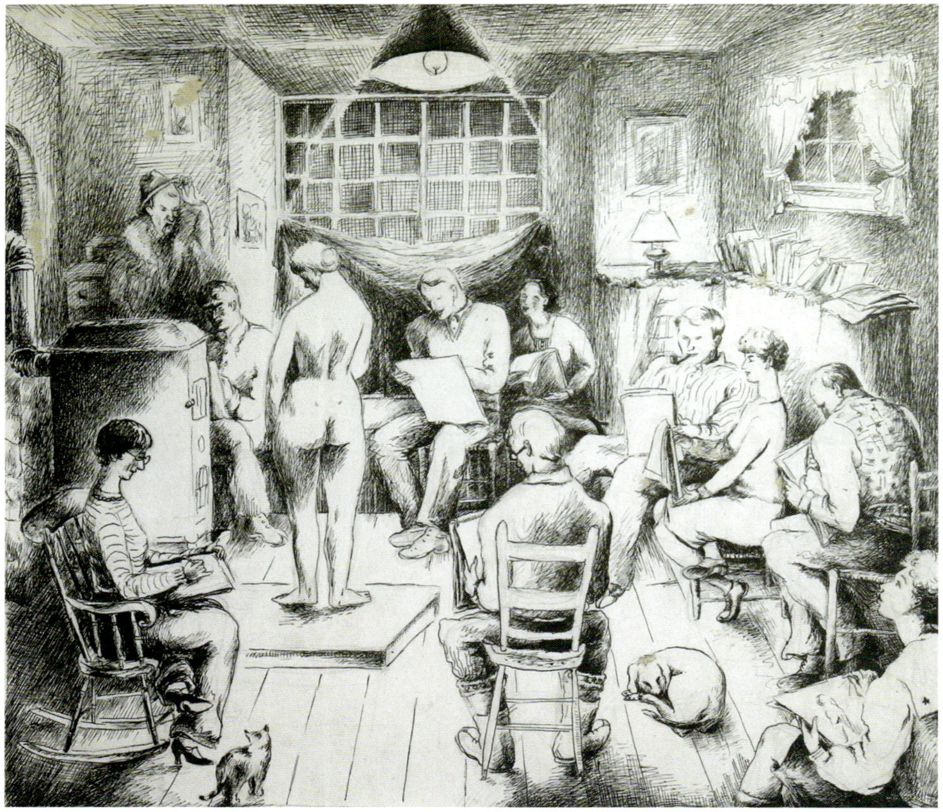

FIG. 4

EUGENIE GERSHOY

Maverick Sketch Class

c. 1935, pen and ink
11¾ x 14⅛ in.
Collection Woodstock Artists Association and Museum. Courtesy of Estate of Jane and Wendell Jones. *Photo Peter R. Jones*

By 1929 Small was working exclusively in the direct mode. She loved its sensuousness and explored a wide variety of woods and stones: ebony, pearwood, mahogany, walnut, ash, basswood, cherry; marbles and alabasters; and bronze. "I like to try new woods and new stones," she commented in 1943."The rarer and the stranger they are, the better."[36] In her later years, and when traveling, she worked in malleable composition stone and *papier mâché*.

Early on, Small's work was noticed and praised. In 1940 she was awarded the prestigious Logan Prize from the Art Institute of Chicago. By 1943, Henry McBride identified her as "one of the new school of sculptors, like Mr. DeCreeft, who are fully awake to the quality of the stone that is carved and vary their styles to suit the occasion."[37] She showed at the Downtown Gallery that year with William Zorach, a well-known sculptor, and almost stole the show:

> And so the veteran sculptor is on view. But further joys are to be had from the chisels of younger ones, much less known and less practiced. Hannah Small...appears as a thoroughly integrated sculptor of fine intelligence with a deeply incised understanding of her mediums and the sculptor's provinces.[38]

During the 1940s and '50s, Small showed regularly in New York galleries, national exhibitions, and a number of Whitney Museum sculpture annuals. Critics praised the contrasts in her work—mass and delicacy, roughness and softness, rhythm and bulk—and identified Mesoamerican and Egyptian sculpture as influences. Scholar and dealer Janis Conner describes the essence of Small's sculptural strategy: "By exaggerating volumes and compressing proportions, Small evokes recognizable feelings of coziness or languor or introspection; but the cool polished stones flow so rhythmically as to leave the realm of the specific to become purified form."[39]

Throughout her life, Small was described as delicate, even fragile, and naturally elegant. As direct carving was associated with strenuous "masculine" activity, many journalists had trouble imagining her at work: "Hannah is five foot one, very dainty, and difficult to imagine hewing rock all day."[40] Raymond Steiner described the sculptor in her studio: "A petite woman with a fragile beauty, there is almost an incongruity between her workspace and her presence....her ready pieces of rough wood or stone seem to act as a foil to her elegant presence. Gentle and soft spoken, one wonders at the metal chisels, files, mallets, in those beautiful hands."[41] Small's slight physical frame and mild manner belied the force of her talent and personality. She had a wicked wit and was well known as a fantastic teller of jokes—many of them dirty—with an amazing repertoire.

Small and Ludins first came together with a bang, on stage, during a dance rehearsal for a 1932 Maverick performance of *Scheherazade*:

> Gene related, "The girls had been rehearsing all Summer...and just for the performance they got a lot of young bucks to come in and be eunuchs and throw the girls around. I said to myself: 'That one's pretty cute!'"
> "I thought he was pretty rough," remarked Hannah.[42]

Notwithstanding "pretty rough," something important had happened. It took, and it lasted a lifetime. The sexy energy and humor of their first meeting characterized their life together, as did unstinting mutual devotion and respect. Writer and friend Nancy Kline remembers their special aura: "Wherever they were, the two of them, was a place of illumination, filled with warmth, gaiety and humor. Hannah and Gene created around them a privileged space."[43]

Yet the beginning of their romantic liaison was complicated, as Small was still married to Austin Mecklem, an elegant, respected painter in Woodstock. Ludins and Small were wracked with concern to deal well with him and to keep the good opinion of the community. Despite the complications, their relationship developed quickly. By June 1933, Small and Mecklem were separated, and she and Ludins moved in together.[44] In July, Small's divorce came through. In the fall, Ludins and Small "ran off to Santa Fe to escape scandal."[45] They returned to Woodstock in 1934 and a year later bought an abandoned summer camp in Zena on Chestnut Hill Road, which served as their lifetime home and respective studios.

An interesting sketch done around 1935 by Eugenie Gershoy, *Maverick Sketch Class* (fig. 4), dating from right after the couple's return from Santa Fe, gives an idea of the close quarters of the tiny Woodstock community. To the right of the nude model, at the back wall, Wendell and Jane Jones are absorbed in sketching and looking at the pose. Clockwise, pipe-smoking Ludins follows, while Small sits bolt upright by his side. Next comes the bowed figure of Austin Mecklem, whose discomfort we can only guess at.

Ludins and Small married three years later on August 9, 1937. The humorous hand-written wedding invitation reads: "Generoso Pope announces the marriage of his mother Hannah Small to Eugene Ludins, August ninth nineteen thirty seven." The card might have been delivered across the fields to Wendell and Jane Jones, their best friends, by the same Generoso Pope, better known as Popey, their beloved English setter (fig. 5).[46] For fifty-eight years, Ludins and Small shared each other's talents, intelligence, wit, and social conscience, working "within talking distance" in side-by-side studios. During a joint interview in 1947, Ludins described their life as: "in each other's hair practically all day long. We're never parted." With characteristic mischief, Small corrected, "We certainly do not work in the same studio. We tried it once."

Small was also a tough critic, and her opinion was all important to Ludins. "Hannah doesn't have to say a word. When she walks into my studio I can tell you without even turning around whether she likes my pictures or not."[47] Critical or not, Small always stood by Ludins, and his work and career came first.

The stately *Family Portrait* (cat. 16) is a key emblem of their relationship and denotes their lifelong bond. It also hints at the complex mix of their distinct family backgrounds. The couple sits in an interior, Small on a wooden bench, and Popey at attention at their feet. Though not symmetrical, the image divides visually, each figure's personality spilling onto a complementary background. Ludins sits very straight, sketchpad on his knee, handsome features full of concentration, his stance the epitome of the passionate Russian artist. Behind him, through the huge window, an open vista and stormy skies lead to adobe constructions. Small, hands primly crossed on her lap, leans forward slightly, her lovely face pensive, perhaps doubtful. Behind her, Vuillard-like wallpaper and an oval-framed family portrait bespeak her bourgeois upbringing. The triple portrait is a moving pictorial document of the beginning of a life—tentative, exciting, full of promise and hesitation. The split imagery might unconsciously hint at Ludins's ambivalent desire for, and resistance to, domestic stability.

Ludin's early portraits of Small (fig. 3, cat. 26) show her sensual beauty, her strength and intelligence, and reveal his compelling attraction to her. After the 1940s, although the portraits of Small end, her presence never leaves Ludins's side in the landscapes he painted until his death. Ludins paints a couple, surrogates for him and Small, into most of his landscapes. The paired figures walk along the shore or sit in harmonious repose within the natural setting. Occasionally, a child walks or plays nearby. The landscapes from the last painting trips of the 1980s, taken as their ailments intensified with age, show a lone figure on the shore.

CREATIVE TURMOIL 1932–36

Despite, or perhaps because of, the romantic turmoil of his relationship to Small, Ludins generated high creative energy

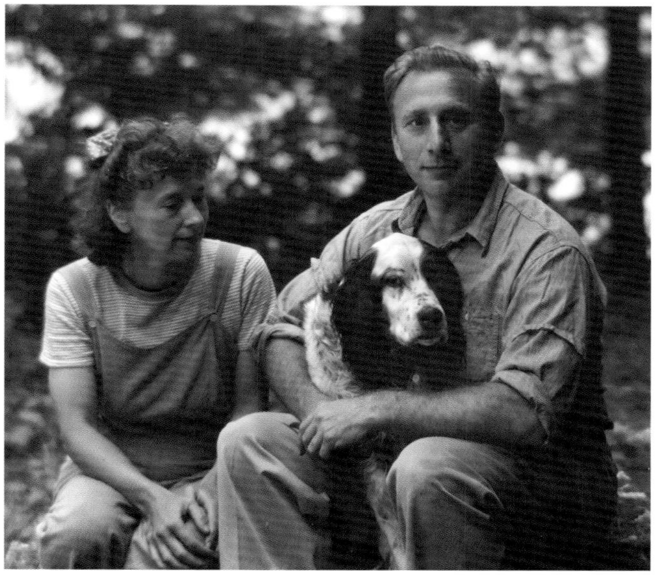

FIG. 5

Hannah Small and Eugene Ludins with Popey. Woodstock, c. 1937.
Photo Peter Juley, Smithsonian

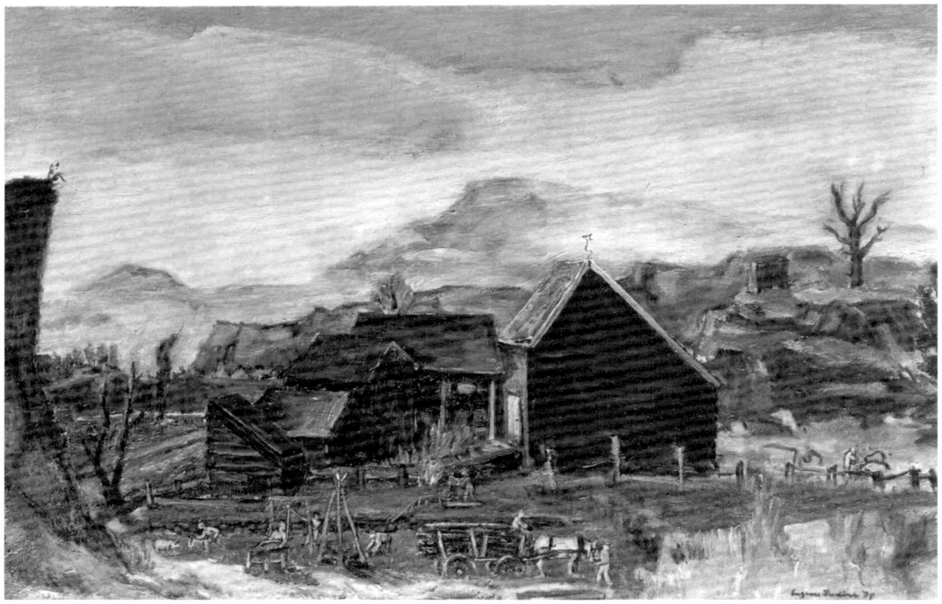

FIG. 6

EUGENE LUDINS

Pig Farm

1930, oil on canvas
Collection Eleanor Rixson. Courtesy Estate of Eugene Ludins. *Photo Stowall Studios, Woodstock*

between 1932 and 1936. In November 1932, he submitted *Mr. Gormley and Mrs. Gormley* (cat. 17) to the First Biennial Exhibition of Contemporary American Painting in the recently opened Whitney Museum of American Art, the first museum dedicated to the art of contemporary, living artists of the United States.[48]

Mr. Gormley and Mrs. Gormley was an interesting choice to send to such an important exhibition. An ungainly couple, a farmer and his wife, stand atop a bluff, looking uncertain and uncomfortable, and hold a white piglet. The picture's scale, the presentation of the large figures, and the drama of the sky suggest ambitious aims. Yet there are major disjunctions in the scale of the elements and uneasy transitions of space on the way to the distant city in the background. The protagonists' stance prompts uncomfortable questions that belie their physical stature: are they really farmers, or urban folks trying to be farmers? There are gaps between the picture's ambitious aims and Ludins's artistic means at this time in his career.[49]

On a larger scale, the Whitney's first biennial presented similarly uncomfortable disjunctions of style and viewpoint. Throughout the exhibition, there is an uneasy sense of artists using outdated means for representing contemporary realities, as well as a tentative exploration of new options available. Artist Manuel Bromberg described the dilemma of his generation during "a very deadly period":

> Our generation was born in the wrong time....stuck in their own moment of no real direction.... [Our art was] a half-assed combination of this and that....[We were] trying to make good paintings....One couldn't find a way to do a figurative thing without running into Picasso or Matisse.[50]

Despite the disjunctions in *Mr. Gormley and Mrs. Gormley*, certain details—the high viewpoint, stormy sky, and abrupt changes in scale—offer clues to a parallel series of large-scale "unreal compositions"[51] that Ludins was working on. One of those studio paintings, *Landscape* (cat. 10), discussed above, had already entered the young collection of the Whitney Museum.

Ludins's first solo show was at the Contemporary Arts gallery in October 1933.[52] Two other major pictures in that show, *Spring Thaw* (cat. 22) and *Game of War* (cat. 20), exhibit the high viewpoint, turbulent skies and shifting scale of his "unreal" studio manner. Lewis Mumford in *The New Yorker* wrote, "Is the air (of another artist's exhibition) too rarefied?...There is better fun among the young... Eugene Ludins, who was recently shown at Contemporary Arts, will bear watching."[53] What Mumford would have observed among Ludins's seventeen paintings in the show was his continuing split between realistic landscapes capturing the "American scene," such as *Pig Farm* (fig. 6), and those painted in the studio in the "unreal" manner which a decade later earned him the admiring designation of "Romantic."

Spring Thaw of 1932 is the epitome of Ludins's "unreal" landscapes. A fantastical cliff rises out of the water, its three tiers displaying puzzling, disjointed activities: carefree skaters on the summit, a raging fire on the second tier, and military exercises, observed by a white piglet, on the ground level. A stream separates the file of soldiers from a group of idyllic nude bathers. Truly sinister activity—sadistic beatings, random violence, a rape—is reserved for the foreground pier. The strange juxtapositions of military movements and social upheaval with pockets of oblivion may well reflect Ludins's awareness of the rising threat of Fascism and disturbing political upheavals in Italy and Germany. Having grown up in a pacifist, progressive Jewish family with socialist leanings, Ludins avidly followed international news of sociopolitical unrest. His family, after all, had fled the fierce anti-Jewish pogroms of 1905 in Russia.

Alongside the menace, *Spring Thaw* has Romantic sources and associations. The cliff itself was a staple of Romantic imagery; in Ludins's work it has possible precedents in Goya, then considered a Romantic artist, and

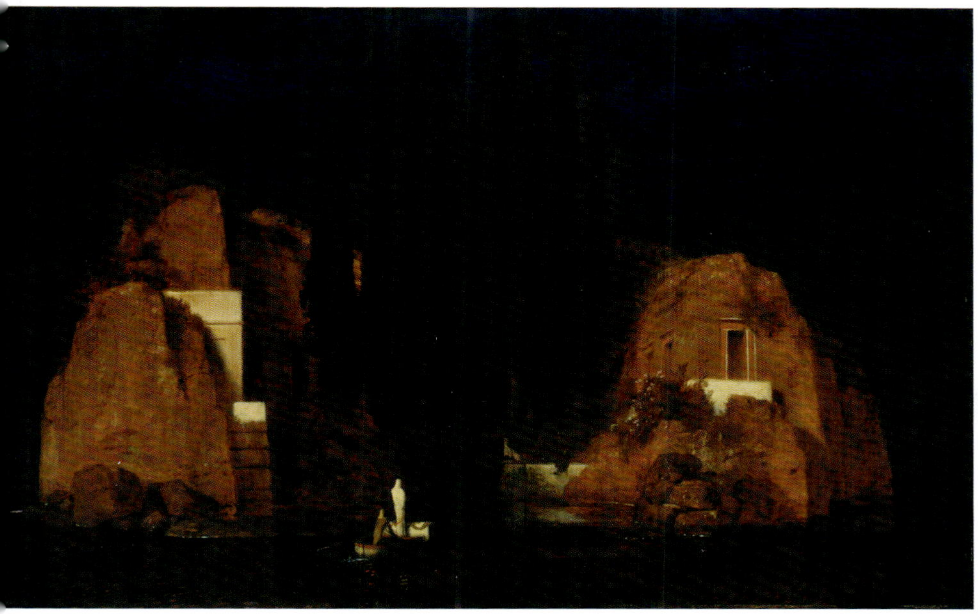

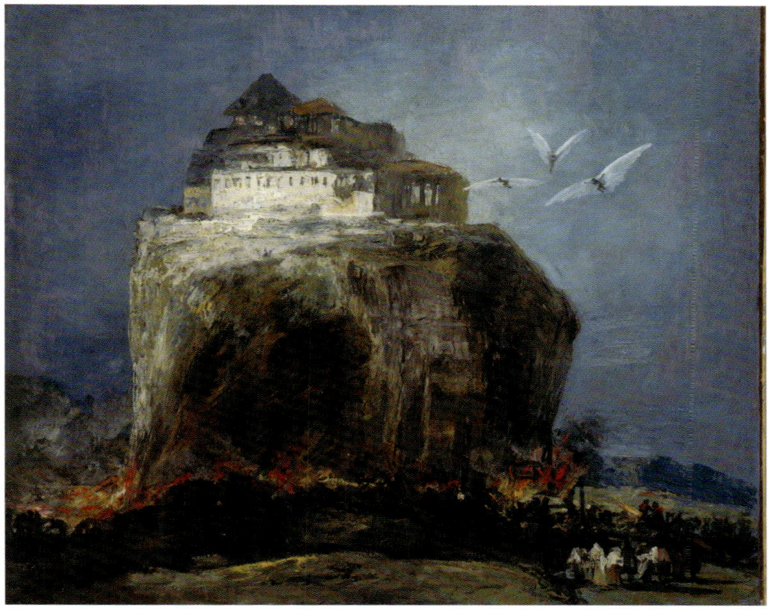

Arnold Böcklin, a Swiss symbolist. Gene would have been introduced to both artists at the League by Allen Tucker, who would conclude his classes by showing illustrated art books. Illustrations of Böcklin's (fig. 7) and Goya's (fig. 8) works were popular and available at the time. More importantly, Ludins would have seen key works by both painters during his frequent visits to the Metropolitan Museum as an art student.[54] The Metropolitan Museum had owned a version of the Böcklin *Island of the Dead* since 1926, and *A City on a Rock*, then attributed to Goya, would also have been on view.

A year later, the glimpses of violence in *Spring Thaw* explode into a full panorama of death and destruction in *Game of War*. Atop a high promontory, a general, his aide-de-camp, and three officers impassively watch a scene of fiery devastation in the valley below—shells explode, planes nose dive, bridges blow up, ships sink. In counterpoint to the figures in full regalia, three high-heeled, white-clad women ritualistically circle a samovar in a nearby tent. Ludins's attention to military uniforms produced hybrid, creative pastiches which drew from different wars and periods,[55] but all lead to a theme that would recur: generals symbolic of abusive power and totalitarian repression. *Game of War* was painted in 1933, the year of Adolf Hitler's election as chancellor of Germany and his immediate suppression of civil liberties.

Not surprisingly, Ludins imagined an overpowering event and rendered it with intense force at a time when his emotions were raw and close to the skin. The year of Hitler's ascendancy had proved emotionally turbulent for Ludins personally: his affair with Small was in full force; Small and Mecklem were divorcing; and the couple had fled to Santa Fe in the fall.

Ludins and Small returned to Woodstock a year later, and in November 1934, Ludins showed his *New Lands* (cat. 19) at the Whitney Museum's Second Biennial Exhibition. It is a perplexing picture, full of purposeless male activity with imperialistic overtones. The men make themselves busy by keeping watch, surveying, waving banners, hauling an immense trunk, and looking plain silly while holding a chicken. The Goyaesque peaks are now snow-capped and dominate a landscape that blends the Hudson Valley and New Mexico. The peak the men are on is split, has steep sides, and straddles a narrow body of water—perhaps a reminiscence of Ludins's trip to Panama, where he was awed by the splitting of cliffs necessary for the Panama Canal's construction. The men look slightly bewildered as they explore new territory—conceivably, Ludins's reaction to his new domesticated state.

For many artists, personal unease ripened into national concern in 1935, as a group of artists, who were to found the American Artists Congress the following year, published

FIG. 7

ARNOLD BÖCKLIN

Island of the Dead

1880, oil on wood
29 x 48 in.
The Metropolitan Museum of Art, Reisinger Fund, 1926 (26.90). Image © The Metropolitan Museum of Art.

FIG. 8

Style of Goya

A City on a Rock

Spanish, 19th century, oil on canvas, 33 x 41 in.
The Metropolitan Museum of Art. H.O. Havemeyer Collection, Bequest of Mrs. H.O. Havemeyer, 1929 (29.100.12). Image © The Metropolitan Museum of Art.

a warning broadsheet about the rise of Fascism and the threat of war. Ludins was one of 110 artist signators who answered the call and donated works to a fund-raising exhibition held in November at the ACA Gallery in New York.[56] The text of the call deplores the dire economic plight of artists, whose income has dwindled to "close to zero"; condemns censorship of free speech, increasing limitations on civil liberties, and rising nationalistic bigotry as "daily reminders of fascist growth in the United States"; and proclaims the need for artists to organize nationally and internationally.[57] The foreword, written by artist-activist Stuart Davis, deplores the isolation of most artists from sociopolitical realities and exhorts them to join the American Artists Congress against Fascism and War and for the Defense of Culture, to be held in New York the following year. Davis distinguishes between the powerful yet purely esthetic impact of the 1913 Armory Show on artists and that of the projected Artists Congress of 1936, which will "move the artists to revaluations in a much more basic manner, as their ideologies will be discussed in their political and economic as well as their cultural and esthetic aspects."[58]

Ludins attended the 1936 congress in New York. Its program reveals the high passions and leftist agenda of political concerns of the moment. Lewis Mumford delivered the Public Session's opening address, which was followed by rousing discourses from important contemporary writers and artists. Their exhortations signaled the need to organize to oppose Fascism and prepare for the possibility of war; to fight rising repression and racism in the United States; to boycott the Berlin Olympics Art exhibition; and, leaving behind ivory towers and personal isolation, "as artists...take our places in this crisis on the side of growth and civilization, against barbarism and reaction, and help create a better social order."[59] The three closed sessions were led by a distinguished array of artists and cultural leaders of the time, addressing the topics "The Artist in Society," "Problems of the American Artist," and "Economic Problems of the Artist." The fourth closed session included reports from José Clemente Orozco and David Alfaro Siqueiros, admired as leaders of the Mexican mural movement as well as for their radical social politics.

At the local level, in Woodstock, hard economic times produced an interesting experiment in 1935, the Sawkill Painters and Sculptors, an artists' collective that Small and Ludins joined. These "somewhat younger members of the Woodstock colony,"[60] an entrepreneurial group, opened a gallery in a wood frame house by the Sawkill stream that ran along main street. The members shared equally in this cooperative venture, taking turns running the gallery and paying regular maintenance costs and monthly exhibiting fees to defray costs. The group's objectives were twofold: "to establish themselves upon a footing of economic independence" and to spread the importance of art to society by placing "a picture in every home." Since 1933, government relief funds had begun to flow into Woodstock from the Roosevelt administration's national New Deal art programs, and the Sawkill member artists wished to show their desire to remain contributing members of society, not merely "on the dole."[61] To meet the second, democratic objective—enabling every member of society to purchase pictures—the gallery charged moderate prices, took minimal commissions, and embarked on an active campaign to turn "butcher, baker, merchantman and chief...bus driver and woodchopper" into art patrons. The gallery ran two successful seasons, at the end of which there were ambitious projects for traveling exhibition tours. These were not realized, as the communities to which the exhibitions were offered could not pay the necessary fees. The Sawkill Gallery experiment ended in 1938.

Ludins's creative activity in Woodstock during this period earned him the 1936 annual Elisha Keith Memorial Prize of $50 at the Woodstock Artists Association for the artist under age 35 "considered to have shown the most promising work during the season."[62] In November of that year, he sent *The True Story* (cat. 15) to the Whitney Museum's Third Biennial Exhibition. Ludins again chose an enigmatic picture to represent him at one of the most important national group exhibitions of the day. In this case, the image combined personal emotional turmoil with an inscrutable allegory about the stages of life. Specifically, *The True Story* refers to the emotional drama around Small and Ludins's romantic affair.[63] It has landed them in a leaky, one-oared boat, about to capsize in a heaving sea. The sky, as often Ludins's do, reflects the human turmoil below, and is a perfect foil for the sea. Small is in charge, in a stately blue dress, but faces an uncertain prognosis, given she has only one oar and a chancy-looking buoy to point the way. She is the only active, decisive member of the miscellaneous all-male crew. Everyone else on board seems paralyzed and isolated, inhabiting a separate world. It is hard not to think of the popular theme of the *Ship of Fools*—a boatful of fools, steered by fools, seeking a fools' paradise. It also recalls the Ages of Man theme, as the seven men seem to represent all ages. Several of them could be self-portraits, in various states of undress; one hides behind Small. The bowed figure at the prow possibly represents Austin Mecklem, Small's first husband.[64] No one knows what to do. It is tempting to see in this misadventure at sea Ludins's homage to Géricault's great rescue painting, *The Raft of the Medusa*. The protagonists of *The True Story* need to be rescued. And Ludins places a luscious clump of white brushstrokes on the horizon, just beyond the boat's prow, in exactly the spot where Géricault's rescue ship appears.

In contrast to the allegorical complexity of *The True Story*, a small *Woodstock Landscape* (cat. 14) from the same year shows the fresh, on-the-spot quality of Ludins's *plein-air* painting mode, distinct from the ambitious studio pictures painted for national exhibitions. A delightful painterly sketch, fluid and unusually free for Ludins, *Woodstock Landscape* suitably captures the Zena site facing Overlook Mountain.

WPA 1937–39

Since 1935, the Federal Art Project of the Works Progress Administration, President Roosevelt's massive initiative to hire unemployed artists for public projects, began to infuse hope, cash, and energy into Woodstock.[65] For a small village, Woodstock enrolled an exceptionally large number of artists in the FAP easel-painting project. Ludins remembered, "At the time, it was the biggest payroll in Woodstock, and one of the biggest WPA art projects in the country."[66]

Painter Karl Fortess expressed the artists' viewpoint:

> It was the first time anybody wanted us to paint anything and pay us for it!...Many Americans forced out of their jobs by the Depression felt ashamed of going on the public dole. But artists found less shame and more pride in going on the dole. For the first time, they felt accepted as essential, functioning members of American Society. They weren't outsiders any more.[67]

But in Woodstock, artists still faced serious barriers to full acceptance. Dating back to the first artist migration to the Byrdcliffe colony in 1903, the inherent tensions between the traditional, religious town fathers and the "freethinking artists"[68] were problematic. Local conservative Republicans, distrustful of the Roosevelt administration's social programs, saw the art programs as a particular waste of public funds. Nationally, communities that had little previous contact with art resisted thinking of artists as workers, comparable to miners, farmers, and machinists. Across the country, artists hired to travel to sites to execute their public works met with resentment and hostility from local communities. Fortess recalls being berated by an angry woman in Alaska, where he and eleven other artists had been sent to capture the New Frontier. "God damned Washington," she yelled. "We need roads...and they send us artists!"[69]

Nevertheless, the FAP got money circulating, and, in Woodstock, artists were unexpectedly able to settle their bills at the grocery markets, hardware stores, and car repair shops. "They found themselves suddenly popular with shopkeepers, even though many of these were Republicans who disapproved of the New Deal."[70] Yet recalling the "wonderful community spirit," Ludins especially remembered one friendly grocer, F.B. Happy:

> I remember none of us had any money, so we all charged and Happy said, "It's okay, pay me when you have it. You can charge anything you want, but don't get fancy and order sardines or anything like that."[71]

Ludins was named supervisor of the Ulster County Federal Art Project in April 1937, four months before his marriage. The appointment immediately became controversial because of Ludins's membership in the Artists Union. He said, "In New York they organized an artists union and we started a chapter up here....It caused a great deal of controversy. The town fathers didn't like it. It was the first union in Woodstock."[72]

Despite the bitter conflict it generated, Ludins's appointment held after a mandated probationary period.[73] In a public letter, Kingston physician H. Lambert Bibby declared his shock over the harassing manner in which the protesters' objections had been voiced, which included invoking "the red herring of Communism." His moving defense of local artists in general, and Ludins in particular, captures the emotional tenor of the moment:

> I have thought of these artists as the front line shock troops in the struggle for greater social and political justice... as a kind of union or base upon which might be built a stronger humanitarian structure. I have thought of these artists as free individuals—free from prejudices motivated by racial or religious or by personal or emotional conditioning—sublimated to a high degree—working in the classless field of art.[74]

Despite the initial controversy and ongoing bad feelings within the community, Ludins's tenure as supervisor in fact proceeded without major incident. One of his last initiatives as Ulster County supervisor was perhaps motivated by the unfulfilled promise, in 1938, of the Sawkill Gallery's traveling exhibition tours. Later that year, Ludins used a decommissioned ambulance to outfit a traveling art show, named it the Art Caravan, and sent it on the road through small towns in New York, New Jersey, and Pennsylvania. The initiative had the grudging approval of town supervisor Albert Cashdollar, who magnanimously donated a first-aid box.[75] The Art Caravan had popular support throughout its tour. The exhibitions, held on the town greens, and their related lectures were well attended and well received, as proven by on-the-spot ballots collected at every stop. In a few cases, the tour had lasting effects.[76] As its managing supervisor, Ludins was proud of its success. In his words: "We were infiltrating with art where art had never been seen before."[77]

Ludins experienced considerable stress during his FAP tenure from the artists' protests, from constant supervisory duties in Woodstock, and from frequent administrative trips to New York. With the exception of the large-scale *Rotten Foundations* (cat. 23),[78] Ludins produced little work during 1937-39 and worried about becoming a bureaucrat. During this time, too, Ludins and Small suffered the personal misfortune of a miscarriage.[79] In July 1939, Ludins was promoted to state supervisor but resigned only three months into the job. He recalled sadly, "By the time I got to Albany, the project had lost its heart and purity."[80]

The Federal Art Program raised complex national issues, still debated, regarding the appropriateness of federal funding of the arts and the place of art in American society. An equally intense debate, generated as soon as the program was created, concerned the quality of the work produced in the national WPA/FAP programs. Despite these unresolved debates about the merits of the WPA art programs, Ludins's generation of artists remembered those years in Woodstock as a golden time. Recalling the collective spirit, camaraderie, and creative intensity it engendered, Ludins mused, "It was a Renaissance and will never happen again."[81]

POST-WPA AND WORLD WAR II 1939–46

The termination of Ludins's WPA/FAP supervisory duties freed him to return to painting. Between 1939 and 1944, he showed actively in national annuals: the Pennsylvania Academy of Fine Arts (1939, 1942); the Carnegie Institute, Pittsburgh (1941 and 1944); the Art Institute of Chicago (1941–42); and the Whitney Museum of American Art (1943–44). He also showed in An American Group, Inc.'s, Tenth Anniversary Exhibition at Associated American Artists in 1940, and in Drawings for Collectors at Williams College in February 1942. Ludins also continued the sociopolitical involvement he had begun at the 1936 American Artists Congress by participating in multiple exhibitions sponsored by artist-members of antiwar societies and organizations: the American Artists Congress (1940), whose motto was "For Peace...For Democracy...For Cultural Progress";[82] the "Artists for Victory" membership exhibitions at the Metropolitan Museum of Art (1942-43); the Carnegie Institute (1945); and the Artists League of America exhibition, "This is Our War," at Wildenstein and Company (1943).

Throughout these years Ludins produced a varied series of enigmatic paintings related to war themes. The series began as early as 1932 with *Spring Thaw* and continued with *Game of War* in 1933 and *New Lands* in 1934, discussed above. These representations of war are not realistic, but rather fantastical pre-World War I "extravaganzas"[83] by turns prescient or puzzling, shot through with intimations of repressive social upheavals and covert military action. A few years later, in 1938, Ludins returns to the war theme in an allegoric vein in *Rotten Foundations*. The ubiquitous Romantic peak rises in the left foreground, and four men use a battering ram against it. To the right, a parapet offers cave-like refuge, a motif that would recur. In the center, an entire city sinks into the Hudson River, as its valley extends a placid backdrop. Towers, silos, churches, buildings, factories, boats are engulfed in the cataclysm, as ten men in the foreground ineffectually try to help. The title implies that the catastrophe is man-made, the ills deeply rooted, and the consequences, beyond the loss of a single city, could signal the end of civilized society.

Ludins struck a similar allegorical note in *Interlude* (cat. 24), a painting shown in the Museum of Modern Art's 1943 exhibition, "Romantic Painting in America." Curator James Thrall Soby included the painting under the rubric of Lyric Painting and described it:

> Eugene Ludins's pictures appear at casual glance to be matter-of-fact and primarily notable for their skillful naturalism. But he is a subtle fantasist as well. The strange activities of the foreground figures in *Interlude*, the mysterious, endless pipe from which emerges a black dog—these suggest a bewitched countryside whose inhabitants have stepped from the ages of a Washington Irving.[84]

Aside from the fact that the animal in the pipe is a little goat, Soby got it right. Ludins's fantasy had again juxtaposed surprising, enigmatic elements: a hulking black form, like a surreal medieval dragon, corrupts the radiant landscape while the locals, in Bruegel-like oblivion, are mesmerized by music. *Interlude* exemplified Ludins's important studio picture and, before MoMA, was shown to critical acclaim at the Carnegie Institute's "New Directions in American Painting" (1941) and at Ludins's solo show at Associated American Artists in 1943.

Guerrillas (cat. 27) and *Heavy Water* (cat. 28) from 1942 exemplify Ludins's unusual approaches to the war theme. *Guerrillas* is another war spectacular, with a cast of thousands, this time the half-frozen soldiers of the Winter War fought between Russia and Finland from 1939-40. Ludins hallmarks recur: distant fires, stormy skies, files of marching soldiers, violent and dangerous actions, and exactitude in depicting the white uniforms and gear, knowledge of which he gleaned from news images. *Heavy Water* locates us in a dangerous fantasy world. The title refers to the Manhattan Project which was developing the atom bomb. Yet the unconcerned natives eat and dance at a country fair, using the sinister nuclear artifact as a musical stage. Action? Denial? Ludins's message is deliberately ambiguous.

In the July–August 1944 issue of *Sidelines*, a publication of the Woodstock Artists Association, a surprising double notice appears: "Eugene Ludins's 'Interlude' has a place in the 'American Romantics' showing at the Modern....Ludins was just accepted by the Red Cross for overseas duty."[85]

A notice published in Woodstock's *Hue and Cry* alongside a profile sketch of the artist smoking his omnipresent pipe, said:

> To say that we miss Ludins is a masterpiece of understatement. His burly strength and masculine good looks have made him one of the pillars of our town. He could always be counted upon to help out. We're sorry that we won't see him cooking his frankfurters at the library fair this summer.[86]

After setting up a plane-spotting program in Woodstock (fig. 9), Ludins, at age forty, had enlisted in the Army Ambulance Corps[87] and was shipped to the Pacific Theater of World War II. He served as a field director of the American Red Cross in Okinawa and experienced one of the largest, bloodiest assaults of the Pacific War, which ended just weeks before the atomic bombs were dropped on Hiroshima and Nagasaki. He later recalled "the nights and days of constant work and bombing and shelling."[88] An explosion left him deaf in one ear.

Ludins must have endured indescribable horrors while fulfilling his ambulance duties in Okinawa. The human toll of the ferocious eighty-two-day campaign, fought in the Ryukyu Islands between April 1 and June 22, 1945, was unimaginable: around fifty thousand Allied casualties, one hundred thousand Japanese dead, one hundred thousand civilians killed or wounded. This battle generated one of the highest losses of life of World War II. Beyond this hideous death tally, the war's devastation of the natural environment was overwhelming. A snapshot in Ludins's family archives taken during this time shows two weary soldiers on a dusty, winding road, traversing a blasted landscape of charred trees and desiccated fields (fig. 10).[89] It was a memory image of devastated nature that was to recur in Ludins's most sinister, ominous landscapes of the next decade.

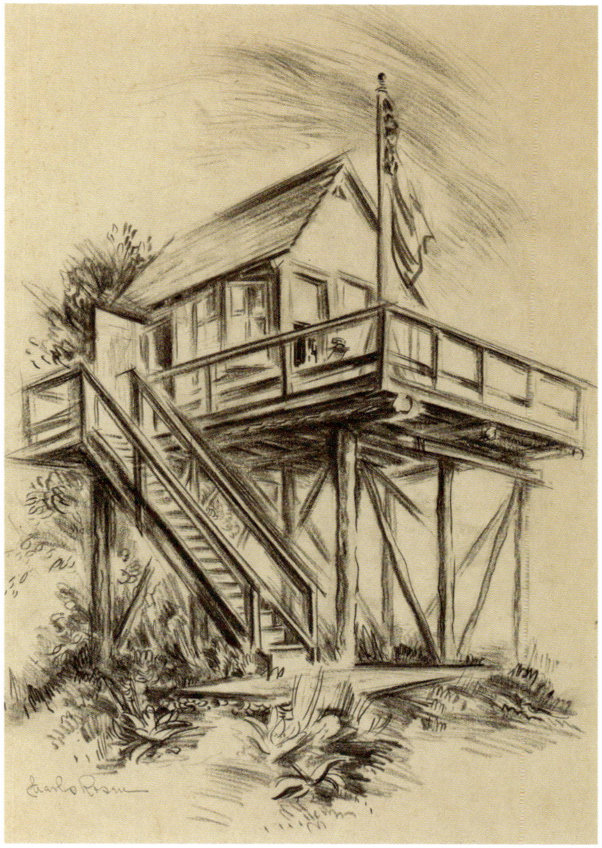

FIG. 9

CHARLES ROSEN

The Woodstock Observation Post

n.d., ink on paper
15¾ x 10¾ in.
Collection Weston Blelock.
Photo John Kleinhans

Despite the surrounding chaos of war and his grueling ambulance duties, Ludins made a few sketches on the ground in Okinawa. In contrast to the dramatic pomp and fantasy of his earlier war scenes, the Okinawa works are simple, modest, on-the-spot sketches, hastily drawn in pen and ink, often enhanced with oil stick. They represent no heroic actions or gestures, no dramatic battles or colorful explosions, but rather the daily grind and tedium of camp

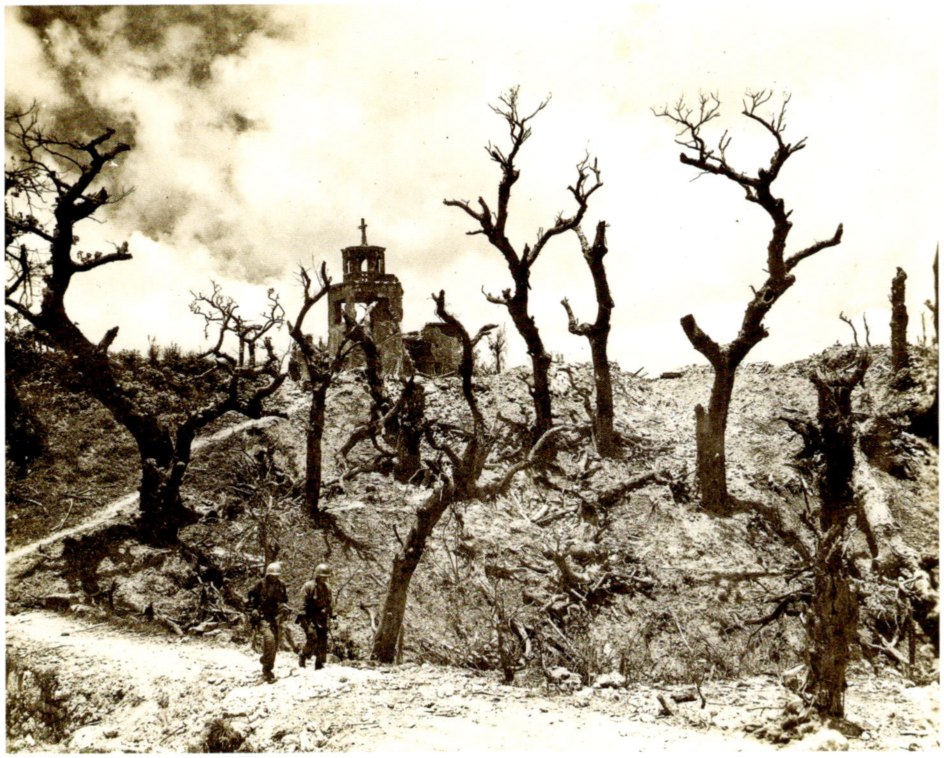

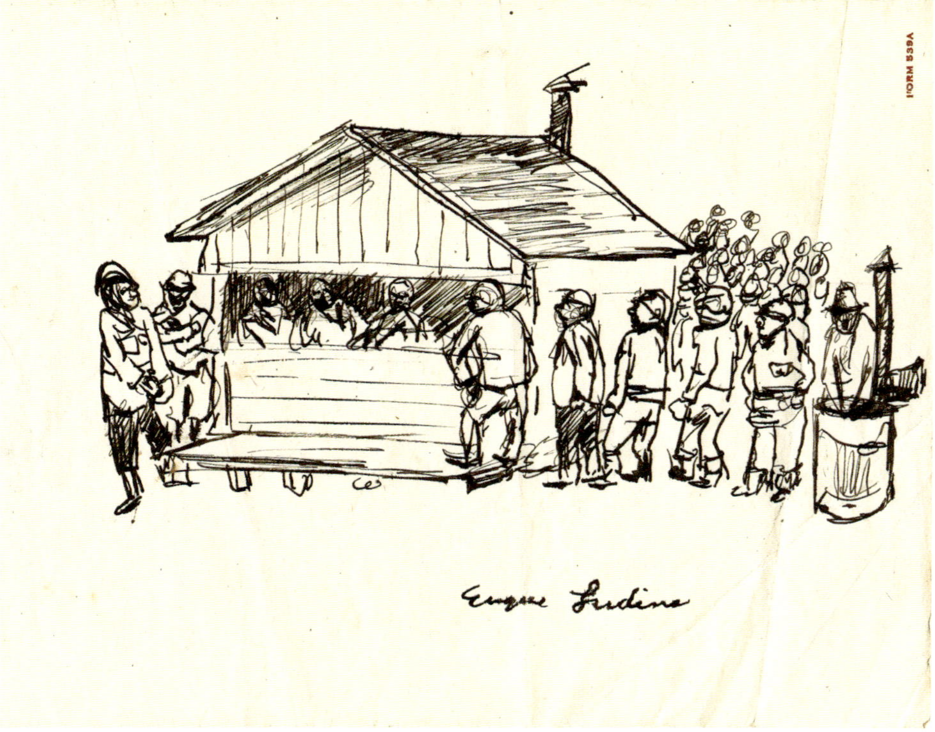

FIG. 10

War Torn Fields

c. 1945–46. Vintage photo courtesy of Judith Small Nash.

FIG. 11

EUGENE LUDINS

Waiting on Line, Okinawa

c. 1945–46, ink on paper
c. 6 x 9 in.
Estate of Eugene Ludins.
Photo John Kleinhans

life near the hospital tents, described in direct, unromanticized terms. Men dig ditches, pitch camp, line up for lunch (fig. 11), and go about the everyday duties of service outside the battle zones. Only two ink sketches attempt "pure" landscapes. They are quickly drawn from a high vantage point but are well laid out, and show color notations. He didn't have time to complete them.

One sketch is notable, that of an awkward, bare-chested young soldier standing motionless in a reverie. We can only guess at his thoughts; perhaps he listens to distant explosions. In this ordinary GI Joe, Ludins finds an anonymous figure, perhaps a farm boy from Tennessee or Illinois (fig. 12). The boy is portrayed with dignity and surrounded by a lyrical landscape. Ludins's memory stored this image of uncertain, anonymous humanity. In fascinating variations—comic, tragic, and the entire range of human emotions—this anonymous, simple hero would recur throughout his future work.

POST-WAR 1946–48

By May 1946, Ludins was back from the service and painting again in full force. In September, he had the first solo show with the Georgette Passedoit Gallery on Fifty-seventh Street in New York City. The critics noted that his work had changed, and they loved it. Distinguished critic Thomas B. Hess wrote in *Art News*:

> Eugene Ludins returned this May from almost two years' service with the Red Cross in the Pacific, and took a vacation driving and painting through the Southeast and Texas. The results of his trip, a series of pleasant, low keyed, unpretentious landscapes…on display at the Passedoit Gallery…almost all constructed on a series of horizontal planes of foreground, hills and sky, but…within his simple schemes…[show] considerable complexity of nuance and architectural strength. They are some of the few American landscapes which achieve representation without illustration.[90]

Howard Devree, in "Two Out of Service," felt Ludins's work "has fully matured. ...This is disciplined romantic work to be reckoned with—at once well realized and spontaneous, realistic but infused with imaginative insight."[91] Robert Coates gave special note to *Carbon Black* (cat. 34), "whose strangely shaped, smoky factory set down in a vivid landscape conveys a queerly disturbing suggestion of eeriness...."[92] To Margaret Breuning, *Carbon Black* confirmed "the artist's ability to seize the emotion of a landscape." She also noticed an "arresting" self-portrait, which was to enter the private collection of Juliana Force, then director of the Whitney Museum.[93] Emily Genauer praised Ludins's "new clarification of color and definition of form,"[94] in which Carlyle Burrows noted "both poetry and realism share in about equal parts."[95]

The positive critical reviews continued throughout 1947, a year in which Ludins had a second solo show at Passedoit and also participated in five major annual national shows: the Carnegie Institute, the Corcoran Biennial, the National Academy of Design, the Pennsylvania Academy of Fine Arts, and the Whitney Museum. Ludins's second Passedoit solo show brought renewed praise from all the major critics who followed his work. But this time critical praise focused on two key elements in his work: a paring down as a means to a more essential vision, and a more expansive integration of figures and background. Emily Genauer wrote, "His color is stronger and clearer, and his compositions are bigger and looser."[96] Carlyle Burrows valued "an expanded mood of personal expression in the painting of figures in landscape which are infinitely more robust and substantial. ...The compositions are more imposing in concept...[and show] a vigorous painterly grasp of the essentials....His color has a jewel-like effect."[97]

Ludins's entry to the 1947 Whitney Annual of Contemporary Art was *Birds*, an uneasy confrontation with ten birds and six people who stare intensely at the viewer against a distant city. Burrows singled it out in his review as "imaginative" and included it in the "romantic" group of works revealing "an imaginative trend in art."[98] The 1947 Whitney Annual, intended as a snapshot of the contemporary art scene in the United States, presented an unwieldy variety of work.[99] It included 162 paintings: 122 from New York, and 40 from 17 other states. Then as now, the critics reviewing the exhibition faced an impossible task. Even an experienced reviewer like Carlyle Burrows strained to create multiple straightforward and hybrid categories to encompass the works: realistic, transforming realism, expressionist, modern, traditional, poetic, romantic, imaginative, semi-abstract realism, romantic representationalism. With approval and relief, he noted 1947's greater variety in contrast to the previous year's overrepresentation of surrealism and abstraction.

Howard Devree, however, in his end-of-year review of the art season, underscored the emergence of abstraction. He noted:

> Increasingly, the evident use of an abstract approach in painting, particularly as coupled with the steady advance of expressionism...the distinctly American genius: Something quick, free, personal, vigorous...The war years interrupted an influx of the tired and extreme productions of Europe and brought many of the best European artists to this country....One...can hardly doubt that the next decade will give us great cause for pride.[100]

FIG. 12

EUGENE LUDINS

G.I., Okinawa

c. 1945–46, ink and oil pencils on paper
c. 9 x 6 in.
Estate of Eugene Ludins.
Photo John Kleinhans

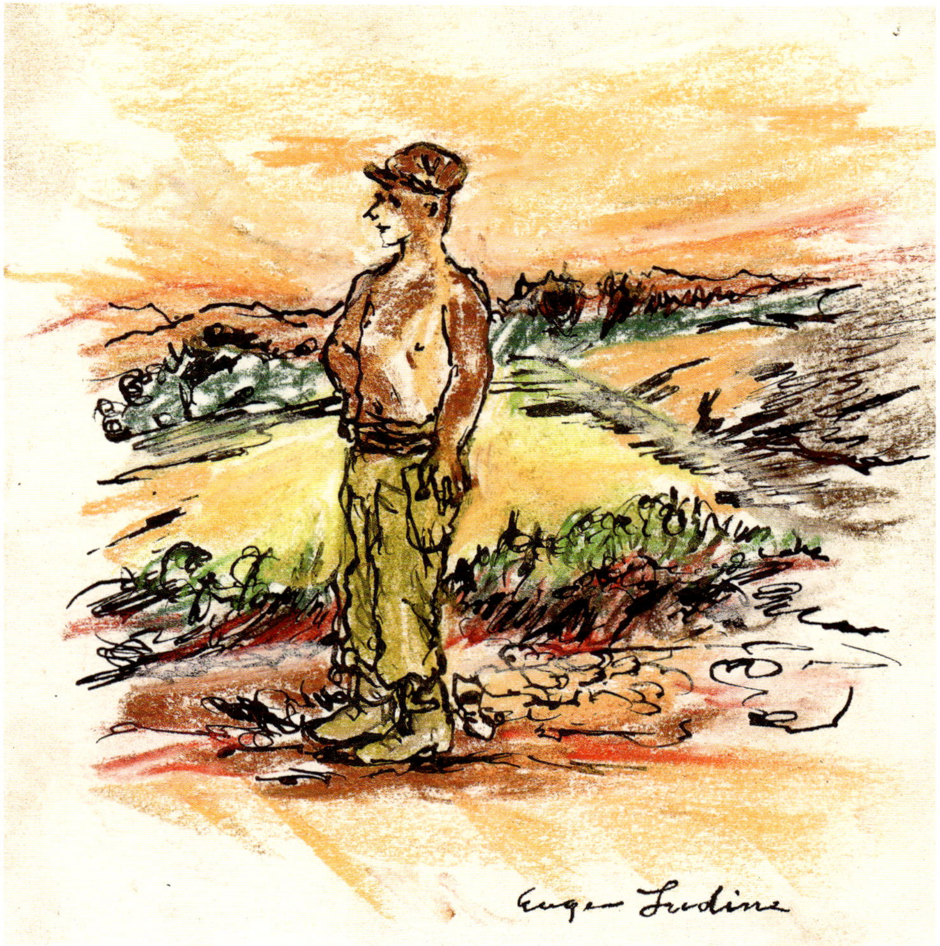

Indeed, a major new current of abstraction was taking shape in New York that would sweep aside all other art movements, change the face of art in the United States for many decades, and effectively shift the center of Western-world art from Paris to New York. While Carlyle Burrows barely mentioned abstract art in his 1947 Whitney Annual review, Emily Genauer was closely watching a different group of artists, one for whose style she coined the word "archaism": "pictures which artists have been developing around archaeological and hieroglyphic symbols."[101] This group—comprising Adolph Gottlieb, Theodoros Stamos, Mark Rothko, and Mark Tobey—was later to be recognized as the first to launch Abstract Expressionism, then in its embryonic stage. Also participating in the 1947 annual were two other key protagonists of the emergent movement. One was an on-and-off Woodstocker, Philip Guston, who, with his *Porch No. 2* submission, began a transition to abstraction. The other was Jackson Pollock, whose entry, *Galaxy*, one of a series of four, was his earliest drip painting.

This movement toward a new form of abstraction—distinct from the early European varieties revealed at the Armory Show of 1913, or the later home-grown varieties that flowed from them—seemed inevitable. Abstract Expressionism was to affect Ludins's generation most directly. His generation of artists had come of age under the influence of "modern" teachers with passionate allegiances to painting the human figure from life, capturing the lyric immediacy of European *plein-air* landscapes in an American context, and dignifying humanity through scenes of daily life. Within a few years, the total sweep of Abstract Expressionism would marginalize the earlier generation as outdated, undervalue and undermine their careers, and unravel their support system of museums, galleries, and critical champions. The remarkable artistic talents of the AbEx group, bringing, as Devree predicted, "great cause for pride" to New York and the United States as the new world center of art, launched an explosive burst of energy to the art world and market[102] and pushed all other contemporary art into obscurity.

Ironically, as the Abstract Expressionist tsunami formed, Ludins reached new assurance and depth in his figurative work. His war experience had provided heightened gravity and emotional power from which he could project a new sense of humanity. From that dimension, Ludins produced memorable figure paintings for the next thirty years.

The Valley (cat. 30) was one such painting. Howard Devree had praised it when it was shown at Ludins's 1947 Passedoit solo:

> a scene behind the levee on the lower Mississippi, or two powerful figures symbolizing drab life and silhouetted in motionless resignation against a busy industrial scene. This is spirited and moving work...Ludins paints with a Romantic sense of humanity, with sympathy, with ruggedness, with kindly humor.[103]

At the Pennsylvania Academy of Fine Arts 1948 Annual Exhibition, *The Valley* won the Temple medal for the "best oil without regard to subject." Critic Aline Louchheim described it as a "romantic landscape and figure piece."[104] The two anonymous protagonists are Giotto-like in their physical heft and quiet dignity. They look impassively as the industrial boom changes their world, passing them by. Another picture of the period, *Faith* (cat. 29), offers a similar layering of still figures against an active background. A curious trio—two tense, possibly angry, women and a relaxed, pipe-smoking man—stare out at us against the backdrop of a gigantic black machine. Unlike the menacing pipeline in *Interlude*, this homemade machine seems harmless, puffing a white, billowy fabric from a chute and sporting a red cap. A red high-heeled shoe sits amidst its levers, gears, belts, and drive shafts. Yet the looming black presence presages something, and it's not entirely good. There will be surprises.

The personages of *The Valley* and *Faith* await their uncertain fates passively, and they initiate a key narrative in Ludins's work—vulnerable, powerless humans at the mercy of life's uncertainties and the control of others. In the decade to come, this story—which will focus on the events of the McCarthy and Cold War periods—will gain force in Ludins's work.

IOWA 1948–69

In 1948, at a high point of his critical recognition in New York and nationally, Ludins accepted a post as visiting assistant professor at the University of Iowa in Iowa City. Jobs were scarce, and the Iowa University Art School was renowned. It was particularly proactive in recruiting professional artists previously employed by the WPA to teach the swelling number of students registering after the passage of the GI Bill in 1944. Emil Ganso, Fletcher Martin, and Philip Guston were Woodstock artists associated with WPA programs who preceded Ludins in the Iowa Art School faculty. Ludins was made associate professor with tenure in 1951.

Since 1882, Iowa's School of Art and Art History had a distinguished history and, during the twenties, a particularly innovative one. Since 1922 the art school had accepted creative work in lieu of honors theses and was a national pioneer in offering graduate arts degrees. The "Iowa idea," developed under artist educator Charles A. Cumming, united major practicing artists and art historians in one faculty and, in 1936, moved them into a Palladian-style building on the bank of the Iowa River. In 1938, art historian Lester Longman reinvigorated the Iowa idea by combining the Art History and Studio Art departments, so that renowned regionalist artist Grant Wood (1934–41) and internationalist art historian Horst W. Janson (1938–41) taught for a few years under the same roof. By the time Ludins arrived, these major figures had left, but the faculty continued their legacy with pride.

Ludins and Small adapted quickly and happily to Iowa. They arrived in the full maturity of their careers and immediately loved the stimulating company of like-minded colleagues and the intense creative activity around them. Lynda Caspe, a painter and sculptor who attended the art school during the mid-sixties, remembers it as an "oasis" where the whole university community "knew art and understood what it was to be an artist."[105] The faculty was collegial, and Ludins was already friendly with one colleague from Woodstock, painter Stuart Edie.[106] Small was recognized as a fine sculptor and, although not on the faculty, was given a place to work in the sculpture studio of Professor Humberto Albrizzio.[107] Small and Ludins were sociable and outgoing, and Ludins was a good cook. In the Woodstock tradition, he and Small entertained constantly at their tiny home on Melrose Court just across from the Hawkeye football stadium.[108] Their Saturday night after-game parties were especially lively and crowded.

Ludins as Teacher

Ludins loved being a professor and considered himself a natural teacher (fig. 13). He often expressed pride and delight at having been awarded a professorship at a good university despite having only a high school education. His method of teaching was direct and personal:

> Gene had enormous presence and authority in the classroom. He taught one on one and dealt with each individual painting as a work in progress. With a marvelous eye for what was fresh and vital, he was open minded about everything but slickness and superficiality. He treated his students as serious people involved in a serious endeavor, and his students loved him.[109]

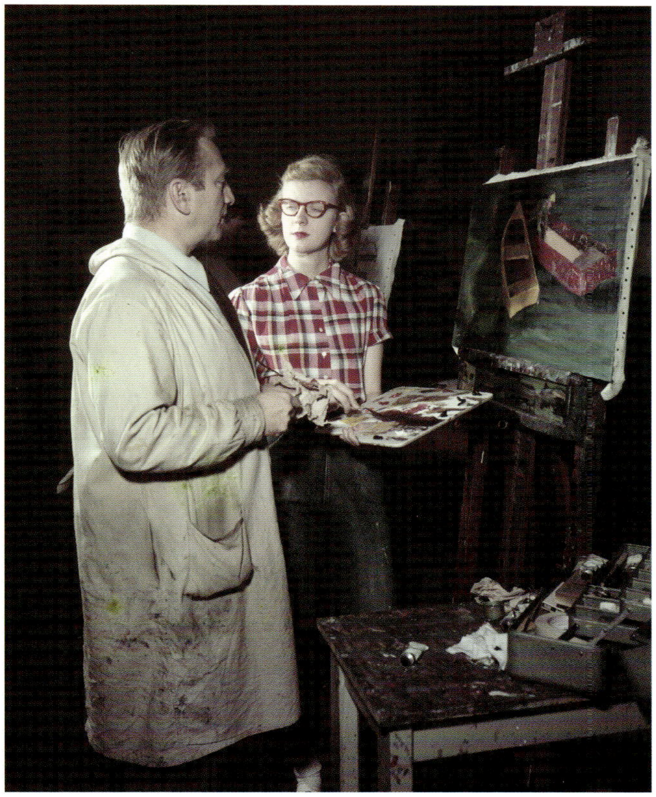

FIG. 13

Photo of Eugene Ludins and student Barbara Nichols, University of Iowa. Courtesy of the *Des Moines Sunday Register*, from article December 16, 1951.

One such student was Virginia Myers, now professor of printmaking at Iowa, who came in 1955 to study with well-known printmaker Mauricio Lasansky. She also took painting lessons from Ludins and recalled him with admiration and fondness as an especially caring teacher. One day, noting that she was struggling to make ends meet, he asked how she intended to make a living. She replied she would make frames if she had a miter box. Not only did he lend her his, but, declaring himself "an old picture framer,"[110] Ludins taught her how to make fine frames, and, vital to her future career, how to apply gold and silver leaf.

Ludins continually debated with himself whether painting could be taught. His teaching method was undoubtedly influenced by his beloved Art Students League teacher Allen Tucker, who had declared, "...no one can teach painting—it has to be learned....A good teacher can help you to learn, and the teacher has the advantage of personal contact, and, if he is able, a great deal should be got from that personal contact."[111] Many years later, with typical puckish humor, Ludins recounted the strategies he would use to encourage less promising students as he went around and stopped in front of their paintings for a ten-minute review. He would point to a spot on an otherwise weak canvas, and say: "I'm so glad you did that!"[112] It invariably started a good conversation and imparted something valuable.

Ludins's philosophy of artmaking is hard to pin down. Three years of teaching clarified his ideas, and, though loath to make declarations about art,[113] Ludins agreed to talk briefly at a conference on Art in Liberal Education:

> I believe every artist has at some time had a sudden flash of insight which has solved impossible art problems.... I guess all this is usually called inspiration....To me the validity of the intuitive process...is one of the most important things we can sell our students. Most of them are accustomed to seeking the reasons for any act. They are not accustomed to trusting their intuition....I believe we are justified in filling them with all the knowledge of the formal elements of art that we know, but of warning them that that is only a weapon which they must have in order to be ready for those moments of insight with which they might make their own art.[114]

Ludins loved the life of a teaching artist: "We can lead two lives and each enhances the other. We can concentrate on our teaching load part of the time and shift to an environment without distractions for our creative world."[115] By the mid-sixties, Ludins was allowed to concentrate his classes on Thursdays and Fridays, so he could paint five days straight in uninterrupted solitude at the expansive faculty studios. To the end of his life he remembered the huge, beautiful skylights of the Faculty Art Building.

The Iowa Landscapes

The life Ludins and Small led in Iowa fell into a rhythm that lasted twenty years. Each week consisted of intense teaching and painting for Ludins, sculpting for Small. Often, during weekends, they went on short painting and sculpting excursions to Mississippi river towns—Dubuque, Guttenberg, and McGregor, Iowa; Prairie de Chien, Wisconsin; and Nauvoo, Illinois. During spring break, they took long, luxurious creative trips through the Gulf Coast in a studio-outfitted wagon. Favored sites on the coast ranged from Mobile and Bayou La Batre, Alabama; Biloxi and Gulfport, Mississippi; and Cameron Parish, Louisiana, to sites around Houston and Corpus Christi, Texas, with a particular fondness for Fulton and Aransas. Spring trips to Texas often included excursions into Mexico.[116] Small would set up a sculpting studio in the motel room, modeling or working in *papier-mâché*, while Ludins painted landscapes in the rear of the wagon.

Influenced by the surrounding countryside, Ludins's realistic Iowa-period landscapes, such as *Aransas Pass* (cat. 40) and *Dubuque* (cat. 41), present a more expansive vision, broader stretches of sky, and a lighter palette. The horizontal format of *Aransas Pass*, its earthy palette and lush handling, capture perfectly the activity of the bustling channel Ludins loved. In Ludins's painting of *Dubuque*, one of his favorite cities on the Mississippi, the city rises jewel-like from the surrounding marshy fields, capped by a luminous sky. Many of the Iowa and Gulf Coast landscapes continue Ludins's habit, set early on with his *Landscape* (cat. 10) of 1930, of creating "composites"[117] of real, site-specific elements and images that are remembered or imagined.

Ludins loved good machines. A Cézannesque portrait of a farm machine on a Woodstock field from the 1930s, *Farm Machine* is an early example of many such tributes. The Iowa period gave new stimulus to his passion. *New Machine* from 1955 straddles the mechanical, animal, and human worlds as the machine's elephant-like extensions embrace a young family. Its hybrid mechanical parts recall the whimsy of the machine in *Faith* and looks forward to those that will cohabit with humans in the Arcadian pastorals of the 1960s. In 1992, Ludins recalled a lovely memory of Iowa machinery:

> It was so wonderful in Iowa....On a moonlit night you would see four tractors abreast, covering 200 feet...all their lights on...back and forth, 10 mile ride each way... planting or harvesting...[118]

Beyond his love of machines, Ludins found beauty and variety in the Iowa landscape, recalling Tucker's reminder to his students: "The thing that we speak of as beauty does not have to be sought in distant lands....It is here close about us or it is nowhere."[119]

Describing his methodology for painting landscapes, Ludins expressed trust in the intuitive process, as he did for teaching:

> Picking the spot to paint in advance rarely works...on returning...I find that the place has gone dead. The light and my mood have changed. The horse decided to move or the guy sitting on the fence went home....In any case the magic is gone....Up to a certain point in the painting I am quite literal in putting down the objects and relationships as I see them, at least the ones I've decided to use... which originally excited me enough to draw me to the particular spot...at a later point—usually when the canvas

has been well covered and all the main elements suggested—the real painting and fun begins. Here I let go. The landscape as it exists and as I first saw it no longer interests me—mountains and fields and buildings are moved or wiped out and the canvas begins to exist as a thing of itself with a life of its own....wonderful things happen. Problems and troublesome spots take care of themselves and click into place....I have come to depend on having the "punch line" supplied me—not that it always happens....When it fails to happen I go home thoroughly beaten, carrying another dud....[120]

Ludins sustained a remarkably high level of quality in his work during the Iowa years. Wherever it was exhibited, it met the elevated critical expectations set in 1946–48. He was a painter in full command of his means, and Iowa allowed him to grow his skills to match its expansive, creative setting. The realistic *plein-air* landscapes painted during weekend trips offered emotional relief from a remarkable series of intense "problem pictures"[121] which he painted in the Iowa studio throughout the 1950s.

Ludins showed six of these "problem pictures" in his solo show at the Des Moines Art Center in 1955, and they caught the imagination of Frederick Dwight Kirsch Jr., then the center's director, who described them as:

> major paintings...six ironic fantasies which suggest the results of modern "civilization"—the products of impending or past wars, catastrophes; the dump heaps of the machine age; and especially the anonymous, homeless, underprivileged little people. Ludins' commentaries in paint are thought-provoking because of the depth of his conceptions and the sympathy he has for his fellow men.[122]

Ludins's "Little People"

Who are they, Ludins's "little people," alluded to above? Woodstock art writer Tram Combs described them well: "The people look a bit confused about who and where they are, but are looking around and getting on with the lives they've been given. It all adds up to a quotidian theatre of absurdities. All works imply narratives, but certainly no clear ones!"[123] In 1962, George Shane, art critic of the *Des Moines Art Register,* had also associated Ludins's characters with an absurdist vision, Beckett's: "...crowds waiting idly and apprehensively in open fields for something ominous to happen, perhaps for the advent of Godot, to aggravate their puzzled anxiety."[124]

Perhaps Ludins's characters hint at a national temperament? German artist George Grosz, a keen observer of humanity and a strong influence on Ludins's drawings, generalized in a letter to a friend: "When I compare it with Europe or Russia, I prefer America. It's a wonderful land.... The people are like big children—not weighed down like we theoretical Europeans."[125] In the end, perhaps Wallace Tomasini, a Ludins colleague from Iowa, had it right: "Gene's little people, grown up children....Little figures, doing strange things....all himself of course."[126]

Ludins's Drawings

Nowhere can we observe Ludins's "little people" better than in his drawings, a medium he excelled in (fig. 14). Ludins had his first solo show of drawings in 1958 at the Passedoit gallery. It was a revelation. Howard Devree wrote:

> He has taken selective shots at various human foibles, particularly those of our own generation's befuddlement. The psychiatrist's couch, visiting dignitaries, red tape, the esthetic dance for amateurs, shore leave...come in for good natured spoofing in a somewhat ribald manner. ... his animals ...are almost human...But his expressive little drawings are never bitter—rather do they raise a hearty smile at various aspects of our complex quotidian life.[127]

The critic of *Arts* magazine saw European roots in the drawings, specifically in the art of George Grosz, and an

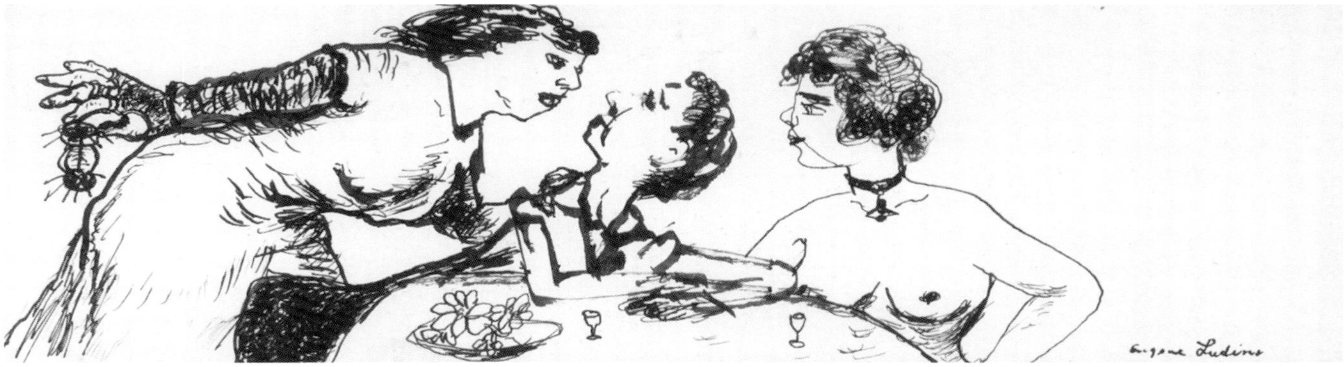

FIG. 14 (CAT. 69)

Showdown

Undated, ink on paper
2 x 9 in.
Collection Nancy Kline.
Photo Peter R. Jones

almost un-American quality in the character of their satire. He was perplexed by Ludins's "awkward and lumpy animals, to go with the bunchy, motley people," but loved "the thinning, then thickening, then wavering" quality of Ludins's line.[128] In 1983 Ludins had a solo show of drawings at Louisiana Tech University, and in 1984, a collection of his drawings was published in Woodstock.[129] In the book's preface, Woodstock writer Heywood Hale Broun praised the character of Ludins's line: "His large hands, bent from bashings in his baseball-playing days, can shape a line with the errant grace of a hummingbird in honeysuckle."[130] Broun also loved, and understood, the flash of inspiration behind the drawings:

> Eugene Ludins sees the world with a vision which is fantastic, comic, fearsome and forgiving....He is a man who dances through fields of banana peels, unwilling to give up his jaunty skip for the tentative tiptoe of common sense....he asks us to come running out on a tightrope with him....He offers, not lessons, but visions, visions of rickety glory, visions of what Rene Dubos called "Despairing Optimism."[131]

Fellow Woodstock artist and dear friend Petra Cabot shared Broun's love of Ludins's imagination: "He approached life with an attitude about humanity that was both tender and funny. He accepted 'man the huddler'—who huddles together with love against the miseries of mankind. He saw the humor in life."[132]

On the occasion of the book's publication, Ludins, then age eighty, revealed thoughts about his drawing process to Tram Combs, Woodstock art critic:

> When I draw, I don't start with an idea, but just start and let it develop....I find drawing natural....I make art regularly six or seven hours a day, painting. Drawing is a relaxing activity. I draw to relax after a hard day of painting.... I listen to music and draw simultaneously.[133]

Ludins was most himself as a draftsman. Drawing released his natural penchant for fantasy and his skill as a keen observer of human nature. As he aged, his mordant wit and generous, empathic view of humanity spilled out in a bounty of drawings and sketchbooks. In his last years, he was rarely without a pen in his hand, a pad on his knee. His drawings place human beings at the center—in all their splendor, silliness, nobility, confusion. They appear pell mell, unmediated by paint, untrammeled by principles of composition or perspective.

All forms of humanity parade through Ludins's drawings: lovers, fat ones, skinny ones, nudists, acrobats, beauties, cripples, dancers, doctors and patients, artists, musicians, umpires, sword swallowers, hunchbacks, aunts, generals, and dirty, scruffy, hairy young and old men. He catches them dancing, trembling in fear, dining, singing, strolling, huddling in terror, racing horses, attempting insane acrobatic stunts, selling sweetbreads, and preparing for death in a duel. Their inscrutable actions are sometimes loving, sometimes violent. Ludins has a special eye for the quirks of sexual behavior. He delights in poking gentle fun at the foibles and vanities of his protagonists, male and female, at their most vulnerable—during lovemaking, caught with their pants down.

Ludins's animals are fitting companions for the motley human crew. Weird hybrids—killer bees, singing dogs, buzzard-like birds, scrawny falcons—watch humans with amusement or partake in their weird, quixotic doings: dogs wear flowery hats and ornaments on their tails, a fish looks up from its serving dish, giant ants bear witness to orgies.

"Problem Pictures" of the 1950s

The "anonymous, homeless, underprivileged little people" Kirsch noted are at center stage not only in Ludins's drawings. They also emerge as the protagonists of his most compelling figure paintings, the "problem pictures" of the

FIG. 15

EUGENE LUDINS

Maze

1955, oil on canvas
30 x 42 in.
Estate of Eugene Ludins.
Photo John Keinhans

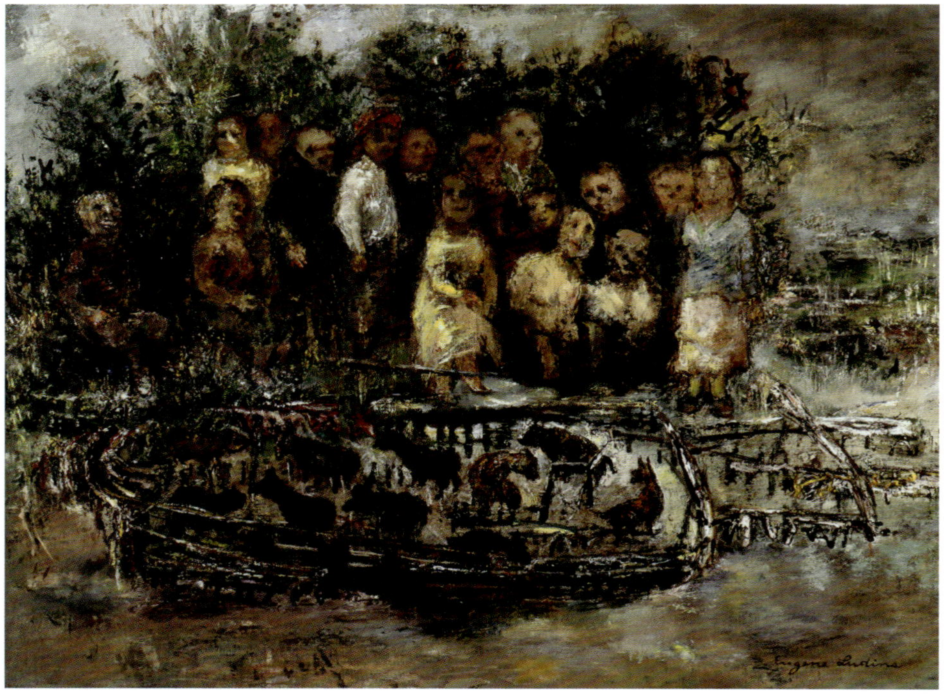

1950s. These works share a common topic: a helpless, anonymous populace at the mercy of figures of power and authority. Through the war-related pictures of the 1930s and '40s, with various degrees of seriousness, Ludins ridiculed totalitarian generals and military leaders, as well as aggressive male types with tyrannical and pompous potential. During the 1950s, the works track world events. The villains—corrupt, greedy politicians, world leaders, or public figures—are no longer visible in the paintings. Yet the deadly consequences of their actions are everywhere. They hold humanity in their grip, poison the air they breathe, and cast suspicion on all human contact.

In *Sum* (cat. 32), five of Ludins's "little people" huddle by a huge billboard/blackboard that presages a dark future—or no future at all. The half-visible calculations may be prescient signs of the looming H bomb,[134] or may signal the ordinary man's helplessness for lack of access to knowledge and influence. The six *Intruders* (cat. 31) aboard the wooden boat face a dubious fate as they go ashore on a desolate marsh thick with hyena-like dogs. The men's staring, mask-like faces, one of them Asian, prompt the question: are they predators or victims?

The anti-Communist investigations of Senator Joseph McCarthy reached a peak in 1953 and created an atmosphere of intimidation and mistrust reflected throughout the works of this period. *Suspicion* (cat. 36) and *Al Fresco* (cat. 37) induce feelings of dread and discomfort as groups of people cluster expectantly in toxic, devastated landscapes. The hellish picnic in *Al Fresco* takes place against the noxious ruins of a destroyed city.

The global menace of the H bomb and the international conflicts of the Suez Canal crisis and the Korean War added to the dismal national mood. Everywhere in Ludins's pictures of this time, humans seek shelter in vain. *Hiding Places* (cat. 33) alludes to the national obsession with protective bomb shelters during the 1950s. Under a menacing sky, nothing is what it seems: figures dissolve into foliage, caves melt into mountains, mountains swallow up crumbling cities. There is no hiding place. Humans and animals share bewildered paralysis and a common fate in *Maze* (fig. 15); the only difference between them is the encircling fence. In pictures of the time, like *Footbridge* (fig. 16), row upon row of hushed, shadowy people find themselves stuck on urban walkways, multilevel structures, pier ends, and jerry-built reviewing stands. They have no say in their own lives.

In *Oil Riches* (cat. 39), veiled, turbaned figures stand motionless amidst a forest of oil rigs. They confront us, stunned, expressionless, pawns of the exploitative forces that have destroyed their land. Amidst the devastation, there is beauty, and even hope: flowering bushes grow amidst the charred ruins under a radiant sky. Writer Glenway Wescott noted Ludins's ability to create a mood through "his eerie portrayal of twilit cities in fragmented color and crusted surfaces, pictorially equivalent to the dream-world of a poet."[135]

Ludins is occasionally humorous. In *High-Level Conference* (cat. 38), he re-envisions the complex international

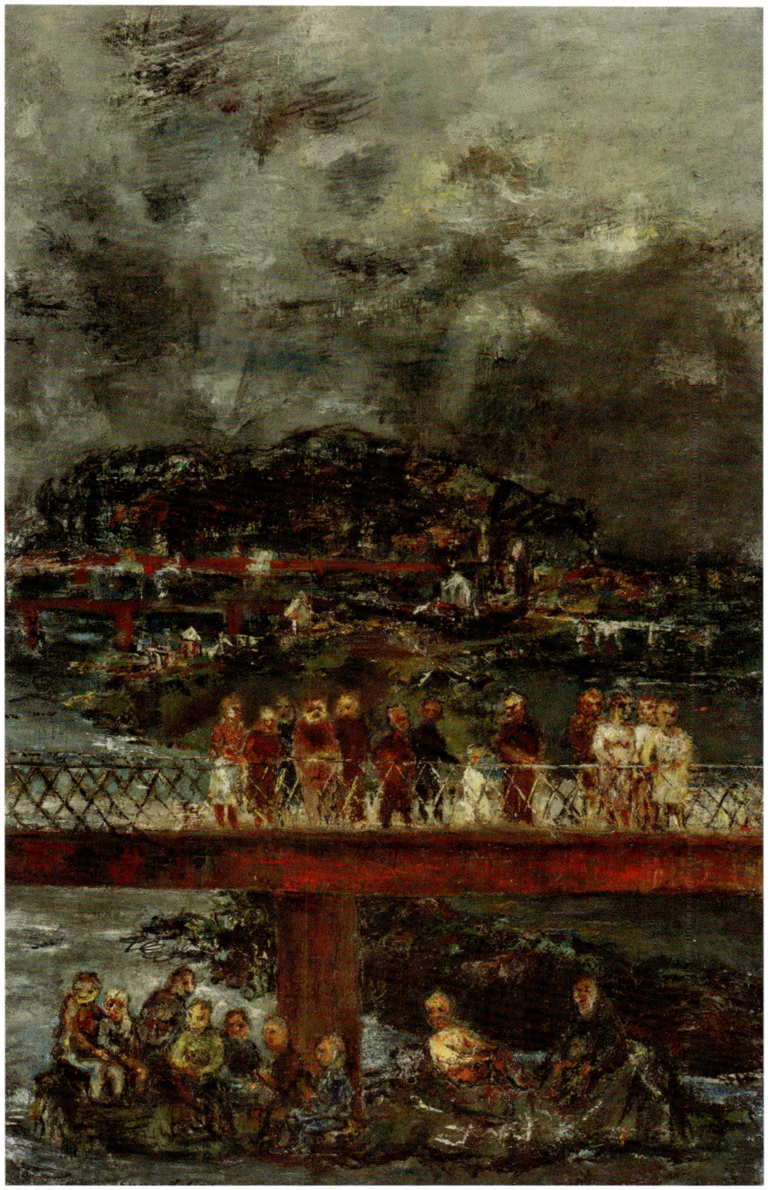

FIG. 16

EUGENE LUDINS

Footbridge

1951, oil on canvas
34 x 22 in.
Estate of Eugene Ludins.
Photo John Keinhan:

negotiations of the Suez Canal crisis of 1956. He suggests that world-famous personages—Israel's foreign minister Golda Meir and a gentleman attired like Sir Anthony Eden, prime minister of England, in relaxed conversation at a table on the far right—share a common fortune with anonymous fellow humans who share their desert tent.

The Pastorals of the 1960s

The imaginative vein of Ludins's studio pictures of the 1950s found their sources in the testing ground of world events. During the sixties, he turned to a radically different inspiration, the Arcadian pastoral, and modified it to his eccentric artistic vision. Ludins matches the large-scale "problem pictures" of the Cold War era with a parallel production of pastorals, which return to the romantic fantasist spirit noted by early reviewers.

To Space (cat. 48) of 1961 provides a fascinating transition from one genre to another. Its subject clearly refers to the United States-Soviet "race to space," then at a peak moment. Russian astronaut Yuri Gagarin was the first human to orbit the earth on April 12 of that year, prompting President Kennedy, amidst the raging Cuban Missile Crisis, to commit himself to land a U.S. astronaut on the moon. Ludins slyly refers to both crises, making his space ship look like a missile, yet mocking the missile's sinister function by adding ridiculously decorative curlicues around its base. Two couples nearby seem torn between fear and desire. In the far distance, twin church spires oddly echo the missile. What connections is Ludins implying? The couples in *To Space* seem poised on the edge of an otherworldly zone of luminous skies and carefree pursuits. The pastorals of the 1960s transport us to that transcendent world.

Monument (cat. 44) locates us in just such a radiant world of light and color, suspended in time. Although the figures are still and expectant, the previous sense of menace is gone. In its place is a peaceful stasis, a harmonious limbo, free of anxiety and, perhaps, emotion. Figures group together and pass each other, but each is isolated in his or her own world. Ludins's beautiful skies reach a peak of luminescence. A passion and trademark throughout his career, the sky seemed the only place where Ludins let loose, foregoing overpainting or retouching. In the pastorals, the sky's glow expands into an all-encompassing ether that his characters populate.

Arcadia, the land to which pastorals ultimately refer, has its source in the name of an ancient tribe from the Peloponnese peninsula where, far from the sea, they led a shepherd life. Ancient Greeks mythologized Arcadia as a land of pure idyllic bliss, far from the bustle of cities. They also complicated its original Utopian concept by the addition of minor gods (Pan and Dionysus); a huge cast of nymphs, satyrs, fauns, dryads, etc.; dangers (Cyclops); and even death. Renaissance artists in the seventeenth century, such as Guercino and Poussin, reintroduced the idea of death into the paradise garden.[136] Ludins knew his art history well, and would have been aware of the joys and dangers of Arcadia.

Meadow (fig. 17) introduces a humorous note into the Arcadian paradise. Humans will have to share it, not with sheep, but with bulls. Also, all human types, in different combinations, are allowed into the garden: a bourgeois couple, arm in arm; a pudgy couple sitting on the hill; two solitaries, a few yards apart; and an absorbed dreamer, hands in his pockets. There will be machines, too, in the garden. *Regenerator* (cat. 46) presents us with one quirky model, clearly related to the earlier one in *Faith*. The citizens of Arcadia on the sloping bank barely take notice, preoccupied by something across the luminous lake. The title implies a positive role for the machine. A black-skinned woman seems comfortable with it and sits close by it. An aging ballerina on the far left looks doubtful.

Pastoral (cat. 49) introduces the theme of love, and with it, hints of Watteau's *Pilgrimage to the Island of Cythera* and Matisse's *Bonheur de Vivre*, well-known allegories of love in natural settings. Ludins loved Watteau, and the reflecting stream, the shape of the hillock on the front plane, and the luminous golden bowl of the sky invoke the spirit of the rococo painter's masterpiece. Seeing these pastorals, a teasing faculty colleague in Iowa called Ludins "the last surviving 18th century painter."[137] Carlyle Burrows, reviewing Ludins's last exhibit in New York in 1962, praised the pastorals' delicate sensibility:

> emphasis is less on realities, more on poetry and atmosphere. Figures play in an atmosphere of dense but warm and radiant color. If they appear as fireflies in the night, or as blossoms dotting a hillside, they are gay, warm-hearted and mysteriously human too.[138]

With *Crossing* (cat. 45), the shadow of death enters the garden. The mood is elegiac as a ghostly mother carrying a baby crosses over a bridge to infinity; the trio in the boat embark on a water excursion. An earlier work, *Excursion* (cat. 35), provides an interesting comparison. Although *Excursion* implies separation and an indeterminate destination beyond a fantastical city, the passengers seem earthbound, the voyage finite. The characters in *Crossing*, by contrast, seem untouchable, approaching a transcendent state that mirrors their sublime setting.

Throughout his life, Ludins painted self-portraits to touch base with himself. Two self-portraits from the fifties and sixties document the transition from the self-assured, lighthearted guy of the 1940s (cat. 25) to a mature man with a realistic measure of himself. *Self-Portrait* (cat. 58) is as transparent and free as any work Ludins painted. Yet the mood is anything but free. We see a jowly older man questioning himself in clear-eyed self-assessment. *Self-Portrait* (cat. 59) is another superb self-reckoning. Here he seems wiser, more at peace with the process of aging. We glimpse the humor and emotional range of the painter who could produce lyrical landscapes, ominous "problem pictures," comical drawings, and joyful pastorals.

Ludins's twenty-year tenure in Iowa spanned a fascinating and increasingly tumultuous period in the New York art world. He arrived in Iowa when the stylistic and philosophical debate within the faculty was still fairly equally split by the parameters of the 1913 Armory Show: the choice between variations of figurative or non-objective work, the choice between looking back to Europe or searching for a new "American" idiom.

In recognition of the Iowa Art School's advanced pedagogical philosophy, Peggy Guggenheim in 1951 gave the university the remarkable *Mural* by rising star Jackson Pollock. Beyond its power and beauty as a work of art, Pollock's *Mural* also signaled the imminent ascendancy of the Abstract Expressionist movement. AbEx's "big picture" and its concomitant ethos of larger-than-life artist-heroes soon obliterated the primacy of figurative and realist painting in the United States. The movement achieved a quick and powerful takeover of the art world, with the help of professional curators, museum directors, critics, and dealers. This sweep was to wound Ludins's generation permanently, casting them as backward-looking anti-modernists. The movement also ushered in a dizzying series of trends and "isms"—pop art, minimalism, conceptualism, performance, feminism, photorealism, neo-expressionism, globalism, post-minimalism, neo-realism, and many more, which continue to consume the art world's attention to this day.

David Hockney's residency in 1964 brought signs of change to Iowa, but 1968 brought revolution as well. Visionary conceptual artist Hans Breder founded the Intermedia program, an internationally minded experimental program that explored the boundaries between the arts, between media, between genres, and between sociopolitical and cultural worlds. Its studies drew from all the university disciplines in the arts (music, film, dance, theater, literature, poetry) as well as anthropology, psychology, and communication studies. Intermedia, which Breder ran until the year 2000, was centered on collaborative process. Its "anti-products" were performances, rituals, and ephemeral site-specific installations. Robert Wilson, world famous avant-garde theater artist, was a visiting artist in 1970. These harbingers of the twenty-first century came to Iowa just as Ludins and Small headed back to Woodstock.

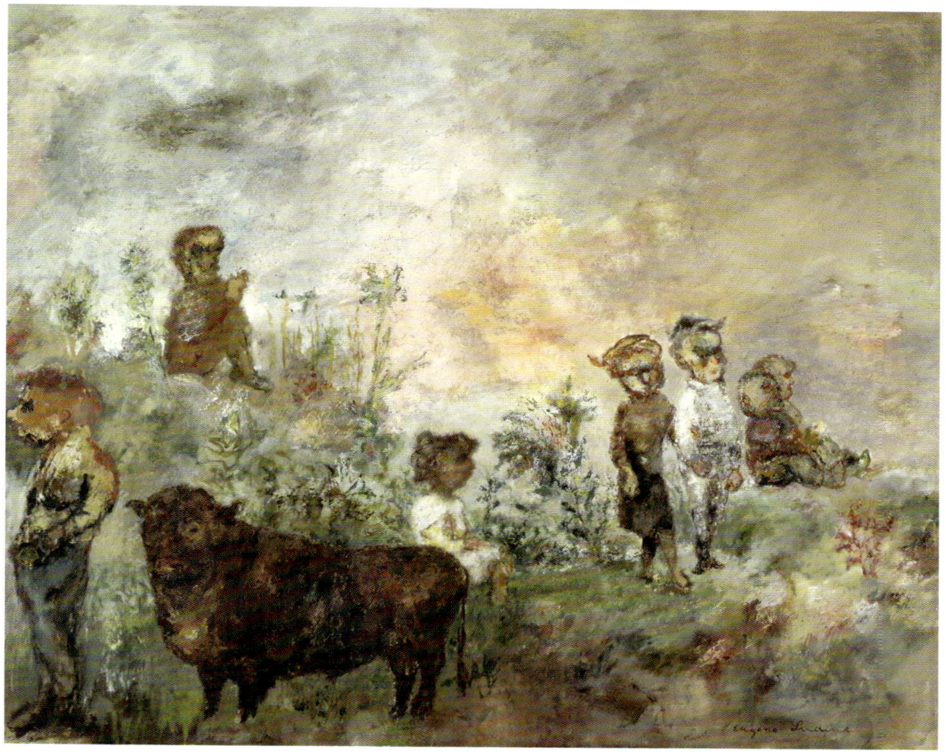

FIG. 17 (CAT. 47)

Meadow

1960s, oil on canvas
40 x 50 in.
Estate of Eugene Ludins.
Photo John Kleinhans

RETURN TO WOODSTOCK 1969–96

In 1969, Ludins retired from teaching, and the couple returned to Woodstock for good. In some senses, they had never left. In the preceding Iowa years, as soon as classes ended, Ludins and Small would hasten to Woodstock for the summer. Beloved members of the arts community, they were eagerly awaited. "Summer wasn't official until they arrived," said artist Jane Jones, their dear friend. Ludins was continually involved in the Woodstock Artists Association, serving five terms as chair of the board.

During the late forties and early fifties, he had formed part of the organizing committees of four important art conferences held at the Woodstock summer home of the Art Students League in 1947, '48, '50, and '52. The first three conferences, sponsored by the Woodstock Artists Association and Artists Equity, drew highly distinguished art world personages—artists, art historians, the directors of all the major museums, dealers, educators—from New York City and across the United States. Sam Hunter reviewed the second conference, titled Art Now, in 1948:

> In what has already proved a national forum of importance for the arts, a representative group of artists, educators and intermediaries assembled last weekend at Woodstock to iron out their knottier esthetic and economic differences and plead a more effective social role for the artist...in effect a lively protest against the socially and self-imposed isolation of the artist.[139]

During the Sunday session of this conference, a minute of silence was observed in honor of Juliana Force, who had died the day before.[140] The death of Woodstock's greatest patron and strongest champion in the New York art world, along with the rise of Abstract Expressionism, marked the waning of Woodstock's star.

When Ludins and Small returned from Iowa in 1969, the world had changed, and so had Woodstock. In 1968, student protests had broken out throughout the world. Anti-Vietnam War protests in the United States were at their highest intensity. The civil rights, black power, and feminist movements raised competing voices. The summer they returned, the Woodstock Festival, "Three Days of Peace and Music," was to change the town's dynamic forever. Tourists poured in on the recently built New York State Thruway, looking for the music. Visual art no longer held a place of honor. From the New York art world's point of view, "Woodstock became obsolete."[141]

In New York City, the art market, stoked by the quick succession of movements—-Abstract Expressionism, Pop Art, color field painting, lyrical abstraction, minimalism, conceptual art—began a whirlwind of escalating prices and over-consumption, occasionally interrupted by recessions, that continues to this day. Leo Castelli, legendary New York art dealer, was a key ringmaster of the ferocious hyperconsumerism that swept the New York art world of the seventies, following the country's disenchantment over Watergate and Vietnam.[142]

Ludins, like other Woodstock artists of his generation, was bewildered by this market phenomenon. For them the New York market began to reek of "selling out," creating with an eye to whatever the art market demanded at the moment. Ludins nonetheless kept in close touch with the New York art world of the seventies, making frequent trips to check out new exhibitions and visit his favorite museums, the Metropolitan and the Whitney. He was intent on understanding the new movements, and his dinnertime conversations would often start with: "What about the tires in the well of the Whitney?"[143] or questions about the meaning or relevance of David Hockney's swimming pools in his 1988 retrospective at the Metropolitan.

Until 1962, Ludins had shown regularly in New York City, requiring special dispensation from his Iowa teaching duties. A decade later, he attempted to find a New York gallery that would represent him. But the time was over for most artists associated with figuration and social realism. Also, Ludins's work was too quirky to benefit from subsequent revivals of WPA art. His aspiration to be a player again in the New York art gallery life was not to be.

During the 1990s, a measure of success came to Ludins—not as a painter, but as a frame maker. Already in 1928, a letter from Wendell Jones had announced, "Gene is going to make frames for a living."[144] As soon as he moved to the Maverick, Ludins survived by making frames for established artist John Carroll, who trained him and gave him his first miter machine. During his teaching years in Iowa, students interested in frame making, such as Virginia Myers, had immediate access to his instruction, and even his formula for making gold leaf. Ludins recalled that his students teased him about the difference between the exactitude with which he spoke about frame making, and the vagueness of his expression about painting. "Frame-making is a craft and can be taught,"[145] he explained. Around 1989, through the agency of dealers Janis Conner and Joel Rosencranz, Ludins's frames came to the attention of Julius Lowy, head of a well-known frame and restoring company, who bought a group of them. In 1992, some were auctioned, and an article in *New York Magazine* noted the sale of a Ludins frame for $6,500.[146] William Adair, master gilder and frame conservator and historian, included two Ludins frames in his 1995 exhibition, "The Frame in America, 1860–1960."[147] Given the nature and timing of the tribute, success might have seemed bittersweet, but Ludins, then almost 91, was delighted.

Despite the ups and downs of his final years, Ludins continued to do until his death what he had done every day since age 25. He went into the studio to paint. He and Small continued to take painting and sculpting trips in their studio-outfitted van. The early trips roamed far—Texas and New Mexico in 1974; Canada and Nova Scotia in 1975. As they got older, they remained on the East Coast, and increasingly explored Maine. Ludins took his last landscape painting trip at age 89, in 1993, the year after Small died.

The Gulf and New Mexico landscapes of the 1970s, such as *Navigation Boulevard* (cat. 52) and *Red Hills* (cat. 51), like those painted in Iowa, continue to offer expanded vistas of terrain and sky. The bustle of the port subsides, the scope of vision widens. A decade later, the panorama of the waterscapes *Aransas* (cat. 53) and *Coastal Landscape* (fig. 18) sweeps the whole canvas, edge to edge. All motion stops. The boat in *Fishing Boats* (cat. 55) is a reflection of the lone artist on the shore, who has come to say goodbye. Infinite space meets infinite sky in *Gulf Coast Landscape* (cat. 56) and *Wells, Maine* (cat. 57). The artist prepares for death, and a sense of the sublime.

CONCLUSION

Who was Eugene Ludins, the source of such visions?

The question puzzled critics throughout Ludins's sixty-year career. The individualistic character of his work made it difficult for critics to categorize his work or pin him down to any school or style. The different critical labels—Romantic, fantasist, Surrealist, imaginative, Expressionist, poetic—all converge on the imagination as the source. Perhaps, to the end, Ludins followed his teacher Allen Tucker's directive: "The affair of the painter is to exercise and develop his creative imagination."[148] Perhaps Howard Devree's 1947 description of a "distinctly American genius...something quick, free, personal, vigorous..."[149] applies.

At Ludins's death in 1996, friends and fellow artists recalled his talent, his humanity, his charm and humor. Genius of sound engineering and longtime friend Ed Villchur summarized his life: "Gene has had many careers: baseball player, painter, professor of art, framemaker, Red Cross worker during the War."[150] A local art reviewer's headline added the categories of "spotter" and "administrator."[151] Yet all who knew Ludins agreed he was an artist first and foremost and agreed with artist Manuel Bromberg's emphasis: "He was a very, very dedicated artist.... He was almost the prototypical artist, working every day."[152]

Like all creative people, Ludins suffered moments of self-doubt. Addressing a non-artist friend, he mused: "When you finish a project, you know whether or not it's a success. As an artist, I never know."[153] His life and art were of a piece, and in both he aspired to meet the high moral expectations that Allen Tucker placed upon his students: "To be one's self, to be honest with one's self, to do as one thinks, to follow one's own vision and to develop that talent, that vision, continually all one's life, is the way to learn to paint."[154] Ludins's moving last *Self-Portrait* (cat. 60) shows signs of this lifelong toil. The existential struggle of making art, the uncertain labor of wrestling with his "problem paintings," the whimsical output of his drawings, gave his work its inexplicable edge and humanity. Always a mocker of self-important pretense, throughout his life Ludins insisted, "I am not an artist. I am a painter."

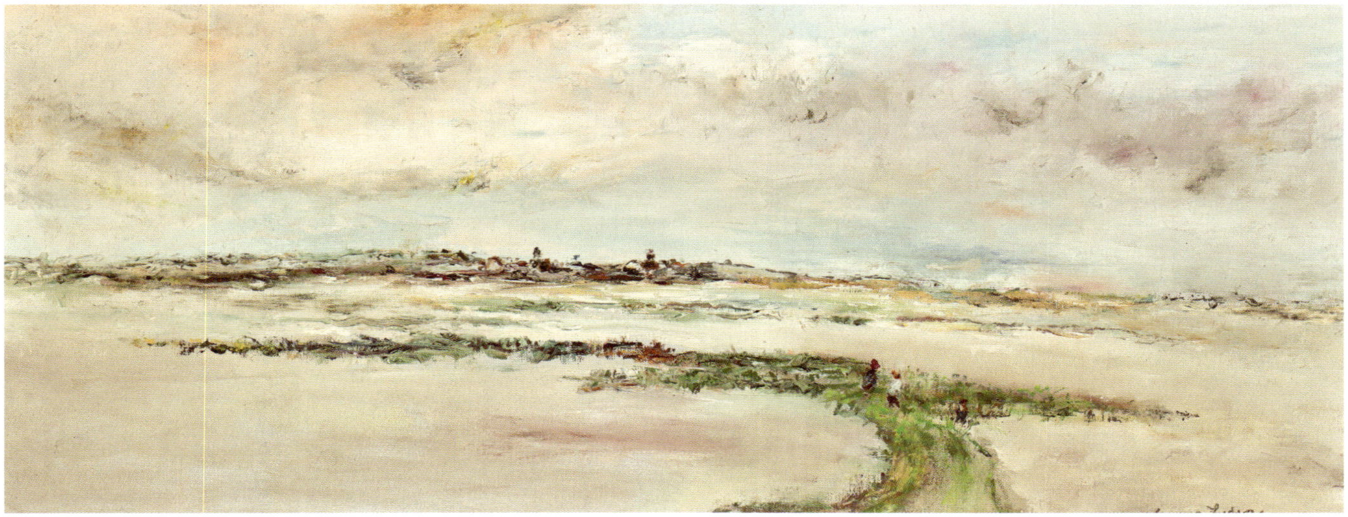

FIG. 18 (CAT. 54)

Coastal Landscape

1983, oil on canvas
12 x 30 in.
Estate of Eugene Ludins.
Photo John Kleinhans

Notes

1 Born Eugene David Ludschinski in Mariupol (Ukraine), Russia, 1904. Detailed biographical information about Eugene Ludins is contained in this catalogue in the essay, "Eugene Ludins: Early Influences," by family member Judith Small Nash, as well as in the biographical chronology by Peter R. Jones.

2 This and the previous quote are among Eugene Ludins's recollections during "A Small-Ludins' House," a video interview of Ludins and Small conducted in 1987 by Woodstock documentary producer Cambiz Khosravi. Filmed at the Small-Ludins home, Chestnut Hill Road, Woodstock, New York.

3 Art Students League records show Ludins enrolled at the school from 1924–27. His teachers were Allen Tucker, Boardman Robinson, Kenneth Hayes Miller, and Walt Kuhn. He was known at the school as Gene Ludins.

4 Steiner, *The Art Students League of New York*: A History, p. 41.

5 Steiner, ibid.

6 Ludins, letter to Susan Geller, June 29, 1974, Ludins's estate archives.

7 Art Students League records. My thanks to archivist Stephanie Cassidy and collection curator Pam Koob for their assistance.

8 See the Avis Berman essay in this catalogue, "Alliances and Activism: Eugene Ludins's Social and Cultural Networks." Thanks to the Tucker connection, Ludins showed at the Whitney Studio Club in 1925, '26, '27, and '28 while he was a student at the Art Students League. This was an unusual opportunity for someone still in art school, as the Studio Club was then the site of high visibility and artistic innovation and offered young painters the unprecedented opportunity to exhibit next to the major artistic figures of the time.

9 Founded in 1902, the Maverick colony was a splinter off Byrdcliffe, itself already an important art colony. See Tom Wolf's essay, "Woodstock, 1929," in this catalogue for a full account of the relationship between the Byrdcliffe and Maverick colonies.

10 Lucile Blanch, eulogy at Hervey White's funeral, Memorial Program, October 23, 1944.

11 Ludins, recollection in "Woodstock: From Plough to Easel," a one-hour documentary of the Maverick conducted in 1987 by Cambiz Khosravi, Woodstock documentary producer.

12 Ludins's oft-told recollections to the author throughout twenty years (1976-96) of fascinating conversations at dinner in Woodstock.

13 As early as 1906, the Art Students League started a summer program for landscape painting in Woodstock, led by distinguished painter Birge Harrison. The Woodstock school's philosophy was inspired by the French Barbizon School, which since the 1830s encouraged painters to work out of doors directly from nature.

14 Tom Wolf, art historian who specializes in this period in Woodstock and the Hudson Valley, addresses this period/year's artistic activity in "Woodstock, 1929" in this catalogue.

15 The photograph is in Tom Wolf and William B. Rhoads, *The Maverick: Hervey White's Colony of the Arts* (Woodstock: Woodstock Artists Association and Museum, 2006), 20. Fig. 9. Catalogue of exhibition by the same name, curated by Josephine Bloodgood and Tom Wolf.

16 Ludins interview with Cambiz Khosravi, "A Small-Ludins' House," 1987.

17 George Bellows, American painter, was part of a radical realist group which broke with academic realism and elegant, turn-of-the-century aestheticism to paint gritty scenes of New York City life. Bellows was a beloved figure in Woodstock. He founded its baseball team and lived there from 1920 until his death in 1925.

18 Wendell Jones letter to his wife-to-be Jane Hays, about 1928. Jones's estate archives.

19 For a fuller account of this incident, see Avis Berman's essay in this catalogue.

20 Ludins, in a taped interview with Raymond J. Steiner and Cornelia Seckel, Woodstock, August 11, 1992.

21 Anon., cited in "Painters Prepare for Hobby Show at Woodstock Shop," *Kingston Daily Freeman* (May 27, 1947), 12.

22 Culp, "Work Project," in conjunction with Woodstock Historical Society's exhibition by the same title. *Woodstock Times* (August 22, 1985).

23 Ludins, in a taped interview with Raymond J. Steiner and Cornelia Seckel, Woodstock, August 11, 1992.

24 Just before his death, Hervey White expressed his belief in *Sidelines* 1, no. 1 (June–July 1944), that the Art Students League's landscape school "saved the situation," helping Woodstock remain relevant as "an artist colony for the present day."

25 I am grateful to Marita Lopez Mena, former director of the Maritime Museum at Rondout, and Allyne Lange, its curator, for discussing these sites with me and sharing their expert knowledge of the Rondout's history.

26 Photographer Alfred Stieglitz was a major force in bringing European modernism to New York and the U.S. through his Little Galleries of the Photo Secession at 291 Fifth Avenue, New York. He introduced Paul Cézanne to America in a solo exhibition in 1910. Ludins's wife Hannah Small was Stieglitz's cousin.

27 *Landscape* entered the collection of the recently founded Whitney Museum of Art in 1931. See essay by Avis Berman in this catalogue for Ludins's amusing story of its acquisition.

28 I thank geologist John Small for helping me identify real elements in the painting based on the geology of the region. John Small is a nephew of Hannah Small.

29 Interview with Ludins and Small conducted by Cambiz Khosravi, videographer, at the Small-Ludins home, Chestnut Hill Road, Woodstock, 1985.

30 Gershoy would also move to Woodstock and become one of the early settlers of the Maverick. She married artist Harry Gottlieb and, although they moved to New York City, she remained Small's lifelong friend.

31 Ludins said he stayed at Cornell "just long enough to see the first football game of the season." Ludins, quoted in Mary Bragiotti, "Married to the Arts," 3.

32 Anon., "Work of Hannah Small, Woodstock Sculptor," *Kingston Daily Freeman* (March 4, 1938).

33 John B. Flannagan (1895–1942), acclaimed American sculptor, led a troubled life and committed suicide at age 47.

34 Small often recounted this experience to the author during dinners in Woodstock in the seventies and eighties. See the website of the Maverick Concerts for Hannah Small's narration and an image of the Maverick Horse.

35 Hannah Small, quoted in Steiner, "Profile on: Hannah Small."

36 Anon., "Work of Hannah Small, Woodstock Sculptor," *Kingston Daily Freeman* (March 4, 1938).

37 Henry McBride, review, *New York Sun* (February 26, 1943).

38 Maude Kemper Riley, "Art Exhibitions: Time, Space and the Sculptor," *Cue* (March 6, 1943), 24.

39 Janis Conner, "Hannah Small Ludins," essay written for joint exhibition of Eugene Ludins and Hannah Small, Woodstock Artists Association, 1995. I thank Janis Conner and Joel Rosenkranz for generously making available the materials about Small's professional life, upon which this section is based. Their gallery represented Hannah Small from 1989–92.

40 Bragiotti, "Married to the Arts," 3.

41 Steiner, "Profile on: Hannah Small," 9. Steiner, a writer, was a friend of Small and Ludins in Woodstock. Through their publication, *Art Times*, Steiner and his partner Cornelia Seckel since 1984 have documented the work of many artists from Woodstock and the Hudson Valley region.

42 Bragiotti, "Married to the Arts," 3.

43 Nancy Kline, writer and friend of Ludins and Small in Woodstock since childhood. Statement written for Ludins's memorial gathering at Edward Villchur's home, Woodstock, July 20, 1996.

44 Small sent a hand-written calling card to dear friends Wendell and Jane Jones inviting them to visit. The text, "Mr./Mrs. Eugene Ludins perfectly at home from June second, nineteen thirty-three," emanates tongue-in-cheek propriety.

45 Ludins and Small, throughout their later years, delighted in thinking that "running off to Santa Fe" had been necessary to quell the "scandal" created by their liaison. Their Woodstock friends, reminding them of the free-wheeling social attitudes of the artistic community, teased them that the scandal and opprobrium were only in their own minds.

46 Note card, hand-written pen-and-ink on fine stock, Ludins's estate archives. Popey was named after Generoso Pope, a media mogul. According to Woodstock lore, Popey was accustomed to delivering mail to the Joneses.
47 Previous three quotes from double interview in Bragiotti, "Married to the Arts," 3.
48 Catalogue, "First Whitney Biennial of Contemporary American Painting," listed on p. 9, illustration #50, Gallery III. It is noteworthy that in that same gallery were showing well-known figures such as Allen Tucker (Ludins's teacher at the Art Students League), Edward Hopper, George Luks, Guy Pène du Bois, Isabel Bishop, and Ernest Lawson, as well as artists related to the Woodstock community such as Georgina Klitgaard, Yasuo Kuniyoshi, Henry McFee, and Alexander Brook.
49 I thank Americanist curator and art historian Patterson Sims for his insightful viewpoints on Ludins's work against the general background of American art during this time.
50 Manuel Bromberg, interview with the author at Bromberg's home in Woodstock, November 4, 2010.
51 Wendell Jones, letter to Jane Hays, his wife-to-be, 1931–32, Jones's estate archives. Jones, Ludins's best friend, writes that he is worried about Ludins: "The more I thought about it, the worst I felt about his unreal compositions....My idea was that being alone has made him self-conscious, and he can't look at nature any more." Perhaps *Mr. Gormley and Mrs. Gormley* was Ludins's reaction to his friend's advice, and an attempt to hew more to the realistic "American scene" style prevalent among so many artists then.
52 Catalogue of the exhibition, Contemporary Arts gallery, October 9–28, 1933. A total of 17 pictures were shown, including *Mr. Gormley and Mrs. Gormley* and realistic landscapes such as *Red Barns* and *Maverick Farmhouse*.
53 Mumford, "The Art Galleries," the *New Yorker*, IX (December 9, 1933). Reprinted in *Mumford on Modern Art* in the 30's, edited and with an introduction by Robert Wojtowicz (Berkeley and Los Angeles: University of California Press, 2007). Clipping from Ludins's family scrapbook.
54 The picture has now been demoted to "the style of Goya" category, but in Ludins's time would have been labeled "by Francisco de Goya y Lucientes." Phone conversation with Gary Tinterow, head curator of 19th, 20th, and Contemporary Art Department, Metropolitan Museum of Art, June 12, 2011.
55 I express my gratitude to Ann Hollander, art historian specializing in the history of costume, for the hours she spent generously exploring the sources of Ludins's uniforms. The most credible inspiration for helmets and other details of his mostly imaginary military uniforms was from Kaiser Wilhelm II's reign during World War I.
56 Catalogue from exhibition, American Artists Congress.
57 Ibid.
58 Stuart Davis, "Foreword," catalogue from exhibition, American Artists Congress.
59 Peter Blume, "The Artist Must Choose."
60 All quotes in this paragraph from Nancy Schoonmaker, "The Sawkill Experiment." This is perhaps the only known article about this collective initiative of which Small and Ludins were founders.
61 "On the dole" is an English colloquial term originally referring to any charitable gift of food, clothing, or money, usually distributed through a church. Here, in its early-twentieth-century use, it refers to funds received through government public assistance programs, specifically the Federal Art Program beginning in Woodstock then.
62 Anon., "Eugene Ludins awarded Keith Memorial Prize," no reference, n.d. Clipping in Ludins's family scrapbook.
63 Ludins discussed this picture in detail with Peter Jones, confirming the personal sources of its inspiration.
64 I thank artist Sarah Mecklem, Austin Mecklem's daughter, for generously sharing her impressions of this painting and its sources.
65 Avis Berman's essay in this catalogue recounts Ludins's role as WPA supervisor of Ulster County in full detail.
66 Ludins, quoted in Culp, "Work Project: Art Exhibit Captures Spirit of Woodstock in the Depression Era."
67 Karl Fortess, quoted in Martin, "Art of the WPA: A Legacy of Hard Times."
68 Rose, *The Vanishing Village*.
69 Karl Fortess, quoted in Ludington, "For Area Artists, WPA Became Stroke of Luck."
70 Martin, "Art of the WPA," 5.
71 Ludins, quoted in Alexander, "WPA Painter Ludins Recalls Early Woodstock Days."
72 Horowitz, "Depression Art."
73 Avis Berman's essay in this catalogue offers a full discussion of Ludins's Artists Union activities and the conflict they generated around his appointment.
74 Letter from Dr. H. Lambert Bibby, quoted in Judson P. Philips, "Artfully Speaking," *The Overlook* (May 7, 1937).
75 Ludins's reminiscence in Culp, "Work Project." Ludins also recalled bitterly that the only work of art from the FAP that the conservative Town Board accepted during his tenure was a weathervane.
76 The Art Caravan tour resulted in the creation of a small museum in Ellenville, New York.
77 Ludins, quoted in Horowitz, "Depression Art," 29. Ludins's pride is also evident in the Art Caravan report, written to Geoffrey Norman, assistant regional supervisor, FAP, and found in the estate archives and the Woodstock Artists Association and Museum archives. Ludins's report, slightly expanded, was published as "Art Comes to the People," Francis V. O'Connor, ed., *Art for the Millions* (Boston: New York Graphic Society, Ltd., 1973), 232–33.
78 *Rotten Foundations* was shown at the 134th Annual Exhibition of Painting and Sculpture at the Pennsylvania Academy of Fine Arts, Philadelphia, Pennsylvania, January-March 1939. The picture is discussed later in the text.
79 Although Small spoke to the author only once about this incident, it became clear, over time, that it had been a sad and major event in her life. According to Janis Conner, scholar and Hannah's dealer, the miscarriage occurred just as the news reached her that she had won the prestigious 1940 Logan Prize for Sculpture. Small was wonderful with children, and maternities were a lifelong theme for her. Many of Ludins's landscapes show a ubiquitous couple with a child, who is sometimes carried by the female, but most often depicted walking or playing nearby.
80 Ludins, quoted in Culp, "Work Project."
81 Ludins, quoted in Martin, "Art of the WPA," 5.
82 Ludins's sister Ryah, a good artist and successful printmaker, also showed a watercolor in this exhibition. In my experience, Ludins was reserved about his sisters.
83 William Alden Jewell, "Exhibitions," the *New York Times* (October 15, 1933).
84 Soby and Miller, *Romantic Painting in America*, 44.
85 Chase, "Below the Belt," *Sidelines* (July–August 1944).
86 The *Hue and Cry* (July 14, 1945).
87 His teacher Allen Tucker had served in the same capacity in World War I.
88 Ludins, in a letter to C. B. Berendt, whom he addressed as "Slim." The two had helped in evacuation efforts "on the beach at Okinawa." Letter dated October 27, 1948, Ludins's estate archives.
89 I thank Judith Small Nash, who made family scrapbooks and photographs available to me.
90 Hess, "Exhibition Review."
91 Devree, "Two Out of Service."
92 Coates, "The Art Galleries: Old Myth and Modern Paintings."
93 Breuning, "Eugene Ludins Paints in Full Command." The little self-portrait referred to has an interesting story, courtesy of Avis Berman. Juliana Force had wanted to buy it from Small, but Ludins was away at war and she feared he might not return, so she did not sell it. When

Ludins returned, the couple gave it to Mrs. Force. It is illustrated on a coffee table in Mrs. Force's living room in a 1947 issue of *House and Garden*. Its present whereabouts are unknown.

94 Genauer, "Two One-Man Exhibits at ACA."

95 Burrows, "In the Art Galleries" (September 29, 1946).

96 Genauer, "Ludins More Dashing."

97 Burrows, "In the Art Galleries" (November 30, 1947).

98 Burrows, "Whitney Museum Annual."

99 *The Annual and Biennial Exhibition Record of the Whitney Museum of American Art, 1918–1989*, 11. The Whitney Annual was begun in 1932. Since 1973, annuals and biennials were combined into the Whitney Biennial we know today.

100 Devree, "Signs and Portents: The Year in Retrospect and a Glance at Currents Running Strongly."

101 Genauer, "Abstractions Spread Over City in Many Exhibits." Despite the title of the piece, Genauer mentions Ludins among a group of "top-notch items" in the show.

102 Woodstock artist Manuel Bromberg commented during a phone interview on October 4, 2010, with the author that Abstract Expressionism had launched "merchandising" in art.

103 Devree, "An American Gamut."

104 Louchheim, "Ludins Oil Judged 'Best' at Art Show."

105 Lynda Caspe, interview with the author, New York City, January 4, 2011.

106 Stuart Edie, also associated with WPA programs, was appointed to the Iowa faculty the same year as Ludins. Painter Byron Burford, a faculty colleague, remembers the "Woodstockers" as an "orthodox" duo "unto themselves." Recollection to the author during an interview at Burford's home, Iowa City, March 12, 2011.

107 Iowa alumnus James Born, who took sculpture classes, remembered Small working daily in the Albrizzio sculpture studio. Seeing her great skill, he often asked her for advice, believing her to be faculty. Author's interview with James Born, CAA conference, Iowa alumni breakfast, February 14, 2011. Yet Wallace Tomasini, director of the Art School in Iowa between 1971–94, said of Small: "She never made an attempt to teach. Iowa was his [Ludins's] world." Interview with author in Iowa City, March 11, 2011.

108 Wallace Tomasini, interview with the author, Iowa City, March 11, 2011.

109 Painter and art historian Peter Jones's recollections at Ludins's memorial gathering, home of Edgar Villchur, Woodstock, July 20, 1996. Jones was Eugene Ludins's student in Iowa from 1964–67, wrote the chronology in this catalogue, and is a curatorial advisor to this exhibition.

110 Virginia Myers, interview with the author, Studio Arts Building, Iowa City, March 11, 2011. Myers credits Ludins's introduction to metallic foils as important to her subsequent invention of the Iowa foil printer in 1986, which has led to creative uses of foil imaging in contemporary printmaking.

111 Tucker, *Design and the Idea*, 12–13.

112 Ludins, in lively discussions with the author over twenty years of dinners in Woodstock, 1976–96. Ludins was particularly interested in comparing how teachers' strategies for reviewing works in the classroom compared with those of curators when visiting artists' studios. By and large, he did not admire the curatorial profession.

113 "There's enough mumbo-jumbo written and said about art," Ludins is quoted in Steiner, "Eugene Ludins's Art Addresses Man's Ridiculous Pomp."

114 Ludins, talk delivered at Art in Liberal Education conference at Bard College, Annandale-on-Hudson, New York, July 12–14, 1951.

115 Ludins, quoted in anon., "Show Continues this Month at Art Building: Ludins's Paintings on Exhibit Here," *Iowa City Press Citizen* (November 4, 1961). The exhibition showed twenty-five oils and some drawings and opened in the Art Gallery of the recently inaugurated Art Building. From there it traveled to New York City to be shown at the Krasner Gallery in February 1962. It was in fact Ludins's last solo show in New York. Clipping from Ludins's family scrapbook.

116 My thanks to Peter Jones for his experiential and scholarly knowledge of these travel routes.

117 Again, thanks to geologist John Small, whose extensive knowledge of the Gulf region helped me better understand Ludins's "composite" Gulf landscapes of the 1950s.

118 Ludins, interview with Raymond Steiner and Cornelia Seckel, Woodstock, August 11, 1992.

119 Tucker, *Design and the Idea*, 81.

120 Ludins, "Landscapes," Chapter 9, 58–60.

121 Ludins would refer with delight to his studio "problem pictures" that made him think about difficult subjects and current world events.

122 Kirsch, "Eugene Ludins," solo exhibition brochure. Kirsch was an essayist, lecturer, teacher, and artist and was named director of the Des Moines Art Center in 1950.

123 Combs, "Art Pair."

124 Shane, "Art Critics Laud Ludins and Bouche." Shane's title refers to Stuart Preston's review of Ludins's joint exhibition at the Krasner Gallery in the *Sunday New York Times*, January 1962.

125 George Grosz, in a 1932 letter, in McCloskey, *George Grosz and the Communist Party: Art and Radicalism in Crisis*, 151. Grosz lived in New York from 1933 to 1959, during which he taught intermittently at the Art Students League. He was an artist-in-residence at the Des Moines Art Center during the 1950s.

126 Wallace Tomasini, professor of art history, is director of graduate studies, Art History Division, of the University of Iowa. He was director of the Art School from 1971–94 and a friend of Ludins and Small. Interview with the author, Iowa City, March 11, 2011.

127 Devree, "Art: Satiric Drawings; Eugene Ludins Spoofs Modern Foibles."

128 All quotes in this paragraph from critic "A.V." (author's name unknown), "Drawings at Passedoit Gallery," *Arts* (February 1958).

129 Broun, *Drawings, Eugene Ludins*.

130 Broun, Preface to *Drawings, Eugene Ludins*.

131 Broun, ibid.

132 Petra Cabot, quoted in Werthamer, "Noted Woodstock painter Eugene Ludins dies at 92," 8.

133 Combs, "The Draughtsman and the Drawings."

134 On January 31, 1950, President Truman announced his support of the development of the first hydrogen bomb. On November 1, 1952, the United States detonated the first H bomb, vaporizing an atoll on the Pacific Marshall Islands. The Soviet Union detonated their H bomb on November 22, 1955.

135 Glenway Wescott, president of the American Academy of Arts and Letters, Exhibition of Work by Newly Elected Members and Recipients of Honors and Awards, May 26–June 19, 1960.

136 This concept is best expressed in Guercino's [Giovanni Francesco Barbieri] *Et in Arcadia Ego*, 1618–22, at the Galleria Nazionale d'Arte Antica, Rome, and in Nicolas Poussin's *Et in Arcadia Ego*, 1637–38. Louvre Museum, Paris.

137 Wallace Tomasini, interview with the author, Iowa City, March 8, 2011.

138 Burrows, "Around the City with Art."

139 Hunter, "Roundup at Woodstock."

140 Berman, *Rebels on Eighth Street: Juliana Force and the Whitney Museum of American Art*.

141 Manuel Bromberg, interview with the author at Bromberg's home, Woodstock, New York, November 4, 2010.

142 Cohen Solal, *Leo and His Circle: The Life of Leo Castelli*, 371.

143 Ludins in conversation with the author and her husband Pierre Leval during many dinners in Woodstock over twenty years. Ludins was a great conversationalist with wide-ranging interests in the arts. Here, he is referring to Allan Kaprow's installation at the Whitney, during which Kaprow, a pioneering performance artist, filled the well of the museum's entrance space with rubber tires, reconstructing a 1961 piece originally created in Pasadena.

144 Wendell Jones, letter to his wife-to-be, Jane Hays, about 1928. Jones's estate archives.

145 Ludins, according to Virginia Myers, interview with the author, Studio Arts Building, Iowa City, March 11, 2011.
146 Robin Raisfeld, "Picture Frames," *New York Magazine* (May 11, 1992), 49.
147 Adair, "The Frame in America, 1860–1960," 10, 19.
148 Tucker, *Design and the Idea*, 82.
149 Devree, "Signs and Portents: The Year in Retrospect and a Glance at Currents Running Strongly."
150 Edgar Villchur, recollections at memorial gathering for Ludins at Villchur's home, Woodstock, July 20, 1996.
151 Twine, Tinker, "Eugene Ludins Exhibition," *Woodstock Times* (June 26, 1994).
152 Manuel Bromberg, Woodstock artist, in Werthamer obituary notice, "Noted Woodstock painter Eugene Ludins dies at 92."
153 Edgar Villchur, recalling Ludins's words to him during Ludins's memorial gathering at Villchur's home, Woodstock, July 20, 1996.
154 Tucker, *Design and the Idea*, 16.

Selected Bibliography

Books and Articles

Alexander, Gary. "WPA Painter Ludins Recalls Early Woodstock Days." *Kingston Daily Freeman*, October 21, 1994.

The Annual and Biennial Exhibition Record of the Whitney Museum of American Art, 1918–1989. New York: Soundview Press, 1991.

Berman, Avis. *Rebels on Eighth Street: Juliana Force and the Whitney Museum of American Art*. New York: Atheneum, 1990.

Blume, Peter. "The Artist Must Choose." In *First American Artists Congress*. New York: American Artists Congress, 1936.

Bragiotti, Mary. "Married to the Arts." Joint interview with Eugene Ludins and Hannah Small. *New York Post Weekend Magazine*, November 22, 1947, 3.

Breuning, Margaret. "Eugene Ludins Paints in Full Command." In *The Art Digest* 21, no. 1, October 1, 1946. Clipping from Ludins family scrapbook.

Broun, Heywood Hale. Preface to *Drawings, Eugene Ludins*. Woodstock: The Overlook Press, 1984.

Burrows, Carlyle. "In the Art Galleries." In the *New York Herald Tribune*, September 29, 1946. Clipping from Ludins family scrapbook.

______. "In the Art Galleries." In the *New York Herald Tribune*, November 30, 1947. Clipping from Ludins family scrapbook.

______. "Whitney Museum Annual." In the *New York Herald Tribune*, December 7, 1947. Clipping from Ludins family scrapbook.

______. "Around the City with Art." Review of Ludins show at Krasner Gallery, New York. In the *New York Herald Tribune*. February 4, 1962.

Chase, Mabel. "Below the Belt." In *Sidelines* 1, no. 2, July–August 1944. Editorial Board of the WAA Bulletin Committee, Woodstock, New York.

Coates, Robert M. "The Art Galleries: Old Myth and Modern Paintings." In the *New Yorker*, October 5, 1946. Clipping from Ludins family scrapbook.

Cohen Solal, *Annie. Leo and His Circle: The Life of Leo Castelli*. New York: Alfred Knopf, 2010.

Combs, Tram. "The Draughtsman and the Drawings: An Interview with a Veteran Woodstock Artist." In *Woodstock Times*, August 2, 1984.

______. "Art Pair." Exhibition review of joint Ludins-Small show at Petrucci Gallery, Saugerties, New York. In *Woodstock Times*, October, 8, 1987.

Culp, Marguerite. "Work Project: Art Exhibit Captures Spirit of Woodstock in the Depression Era." Exhibition review in *Woodstock Times*, August 22, 1985.

Devree, Howard. "Two Out of Service." In the *New York Times*, September 29, 1946. Clipping from Ludins family scrapbook.

______. "An American Gamut." In the *New York Times*, November 30, 1947.

______. "Signs and Portents: The Year in Retrospect and a Glance at Currents Running Strongly." In the *New York Times*, December 28, 1947.

______. "Art: Satiric Drawings; Eugene Ludins Spoofs Modern Foibles." In the *New York Times*, February 5, 1958.

Genauer, Emily. "Two One-Man Exhibits at ACA." In the *New York World Telegram*, September 28, 1946. Clipping from Ludins family scrapbook.

______. "Ludins More Dashing." In the *New York World Telegram*, December 6, 1947. Clipping from Ludins family scrapbook.

______. "Abstractions Spread Over City in Many Exhibits." In the *New York World Telegram*, December 6, 1947. Clipping from Ludins family scrapbook.

Hess, Thomas B. Exhibition Review. In *Art News* XLV, no. 8, October 1946. Clipping from Ludins family scrapbook.

Horowitz, Mikhail. "Depression Art." In *Kingston Daily Freeman*, August 18, 1985.

Hunter, Sam. "Roundup at Woodstock." In the *New York Times*, September 5, 1948.

Louchheim, Aline. "Ludins Oil Judged 'Best' at Art Show." In the *New York Times*, January 25, 1948.

Ludington, Callaway. "For Area Artists, WPA Became Stroke of Luck." In *Poughkeepsie Journal*, July 31, 1988.

Ludins, Eugene. "Landscapes " In *The Art of the Artist: Theories and Techniques of Art by the Artists Themselves*, compiled by Arthur Zaidenberg. New York: Crown Publishers, 1951.

Martin, Eleanor. "Art of the WPA: A Legacy of Hard Times." In the *Times Herald Record Sunday Magazine*, July 5, 1987.

McCloskey, Barbara. *George Grosz and the Communist Party: Art and Radicalism in Crisis: 1918–36*. New Jersey: Princeton University Press, 1997.

Mumford, Lewis. "The Art Galleries." In the *New Yorker* IX, December 9, 1933. Clipping from Ludins family scrapbook. Reprinted in Mumford on Modern Art in the 30's, edited and with an introduction by Robert Wojtowicz. Berkeley and Los Angeles: University of California Press, 2007.

Raisfeld, Robin. "Picture Frames." In *New York Magazine,* May 11, 1992.

Rose, Will. *The Vanishing Village*. New York: The Citadel Press, 1963.

Schoonmaker, Nancy. "The Sawkill Experiment." In *Magazine of Art*, June 1937.

Shane, George. "How S.U.I. [State University of Iowa] Is Taking Over World Leadership in the Field of Art." In *Des Moines Register*, December 16, 1951. The photograph on p. 29 showing Ludins with a painting student is an outtake from this article, courtesy of the *Des Moines Register*.

______. "Art Critics Laud Ludins and Bouche." In *Des Moines Register*, February 13, 1962.

Steiner, Raymond J. *The Art Students League of New York: A History*. Saugerties, New York: CSS Publications, Inc., 1994.

______. "Profile on: Hannah Small." In *Art Times* 1., no. 2, September 1984, 8-9.

______. "Eugene Ludins's Art Addresses Man's Ridiculous Pomp." In the *Sunday Kingston Daily Freeman*, July 29, 1984.

Tucker, Allen. *Design and the Idea*. New York: The Arts Publishing Corporation, 1930.

Werthamer, Cynthia. "Noted Woodstock Painter Eugene Ludins dies at 92." In *Kingston Daily Freeman*, May 23, 1996.

Archives and Exhibition Catalogues

Adair, William. *The Frame in America*, 1860–1960. Exhibition at Federal Reserve Board Building, Washington, D.C., January 24–March 17, 1995.

Archive, Estate of Eugene Ludins, Woodstock, New York.

Archive, Woodstock Artists Association and Museum, Woodstock, New York.

Exhibition Catalogue, *Exhibition, American Artists Congress*. ACA Gallery, November 10–23, 1935.

First Whitney Biennial of Contemporary American Painting. Catalogue from exhibition held at the Whitney Museum of American Art, November 22, 1932–January 5, 1933.

Kirsch, Frederick Dwight, Jr. "Eugene Ludins." Catalogue of Ludins's first solo exhibition, Contemporary Arts gallery. October 9-28, 1933. Foldout solo exhibition brochure, Des Moines Art Center, March 16–April 17, 1955.

Soby, James Thrall, and Dorothy Miller. *Romantic Painting in America*. New York: The Museum of Modern Art, 1943.

Wolf, Tom, and William B. Rhoads. *The Maverick: Hervey White's Colony of the Arts*. Catalogue for exhibition by the same name, Woodstock, New York: Woodstock Artists Association and Museum, 2006. Curated by Josephine Bloodgood and Tom Wolf.

EUGENE LUDINS *Early Influences*

JUDITH SMALL NASH

Born in 1904, Eugene Ludins's long life spanned most of the twentieth century. As Herman Melville famously wrote, "Whereas great geniuses are part of the times, they themselves are the times, and possess a corresponding coloring." Gene's life and work were to reflect vividly the galvanic changes of his time.

Other essays in this catalogue will be discussing Eugene Ludins as a mature artist, but as Gene's niece by marriage, I am going to address the formative influences that helped to create the man and the artist.

Gene's parents, David and Olga Ludschinski, were secular Russian Jews from Mariupol, a Ukrainian port city on the Sea of Azov. Mariupol was home to about five thousand Jews in 1904 and was considered a cosmopolitan, European-oriented city. Its Jewish population, however, could not own land or other property. Gene's parents, who considered themselves part of the local urban intelligentsia, would have found this prohibition particularly difficult. Gene's father was born in 1866 and came of age during the surge of revolutionary thought in Russia. He first traveled to the United States in 1891 and explored the idea of communal living then in vogue by working at Woodbine, an agricultural colony in New Jersey, where he honed his skills as a builder. In later life he wrote movingly about this time.[1]

David returned to Russia to marry Olga in 1892. They had five children—Ryah, Tima, Laura, George, and Eugene. Laura died in infancy. The others all went on to have remarkable careers. According to Tima Ludins,[2] "David and Olga nurtured their children's curiosity, proclivities, and ambitions."

By 1905, it would have become impossible to sustain that nurturing atmosphere within a Jewish family in Russia. As a result of the disastrous defeat suffered by Czarist forces in the Russo-Japanese War of 1904–05, long-simmering discontent roiled the country. It culminated in the first Bolshevik uprising and led to catastrophic anti-Jewish massacres across Russia.

David and Olga moved their young family to the security of the New World. They weren't alone in this; the early twentieth century was the height of mass immigration from Europe and Russia to America. By 1905, New York had the largest Jewish population in the world. The new immigrants needed housing, and David's skill as a contractor and builder assured his family's financial future. They all became citizens in 1911.

The family settled into a middle-class life on Jennings Street in the Bronx. When Gene was two years old, the house burned down, almost trapping his brother George.

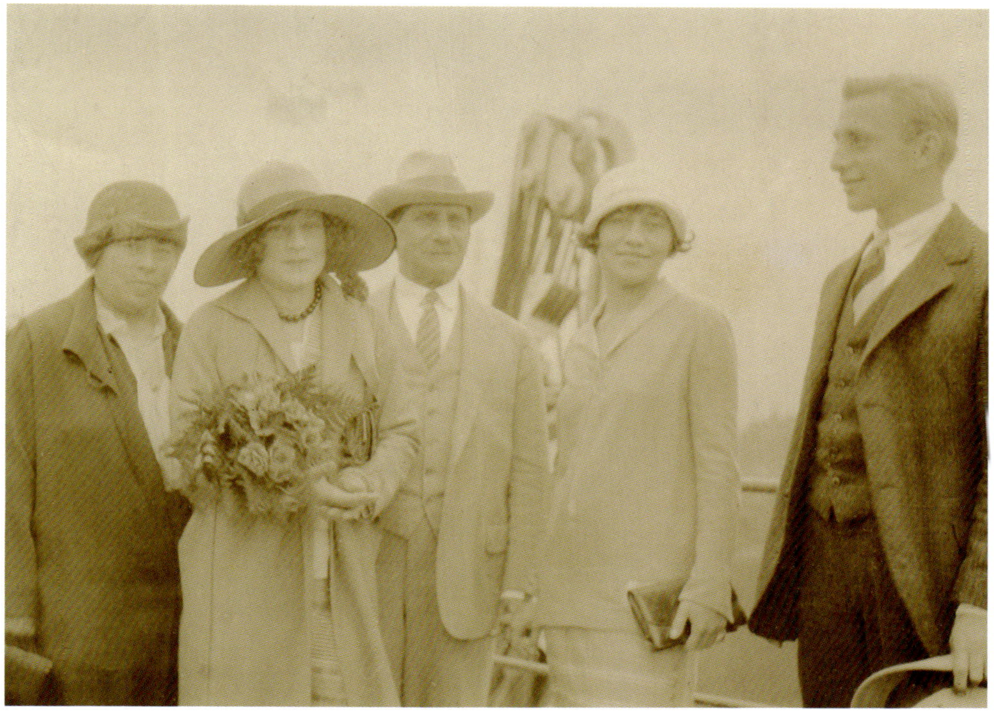

FIG. 19

Gene (far right), embarking on one of his ocean voyages, 1924 or 1925. Left to right, his mother Olga, sister Ryah, father David, sister Tima. Collection of author.

Later, Gene would often include fiery images in his paintings. The family then moved to Morris Avenue, and in 1910, to Charlotte Street near Crotona Park.

In that first decade of the twentieth century, New York was a very different city from the one we know today. Electricity and indoor plumbing were still a rarity in most homes. Central heating would not replace coal fires until after 1913, when diesel fuel would begin replacing coal, both in homes and for transportation. Automobiles would not replace horses for the majority of people until the Model T came on the market in 1908. It was a patriarchal society that valued self-improvement, discipline, religion, and obedience.

The first decade of the new century, however, was also a time of tremendous change in social thought and the sciences and arts, leading Virginia Woolf to insist,[3] "On or about December 1910 human nature changed."

At this time, industrialization and the move away from the agrarian-based pioneer communities to the cities was at its zenith. With this shift came the push to better workers' conditions. Unions began to gather strength, education became available for all, and the government challenged corruption in its own bureaucracy and in private industry. The year that Gene was born, Theodore Roosevelt went to court against J. P. Morgan, exerting the rights of a national government to rein in rampant capitalism. Women were gaining strength in their fight for equal rights, although it was not until 1920 that they were finally allowed to vote. Change was in the air. Much of it came from established citizens, but the new immigrants added a special energy and a fresh viewpoint. New York City was the exhilarating hub of this change.

The Ludins family in the Bronx would have absorbed the new momentum by reading the newspapers that were now available morning and evening throughout the city, espousing myriad causes in ink or cartoons or photography. Monthly self-help magazines targeted women and children. There was also the lecture circuit. And one could attend meetings at town or union halls or in clubs and theaters, which hosted orators such as Eugene Debs of the Socialist Party; Robert La Follette, the future leader of the Progressive Party; and suffrage leader Carrie Chapman Catt. These reformers, among many others, discussed the new ideas that would lead to protection of child laborers, food safety laws, establishment of national parks, and the first challenges to racial and sexual discrimination. To take part in this progressive era must have been exciting for the Ludins family after their restricted life in Russia. It would

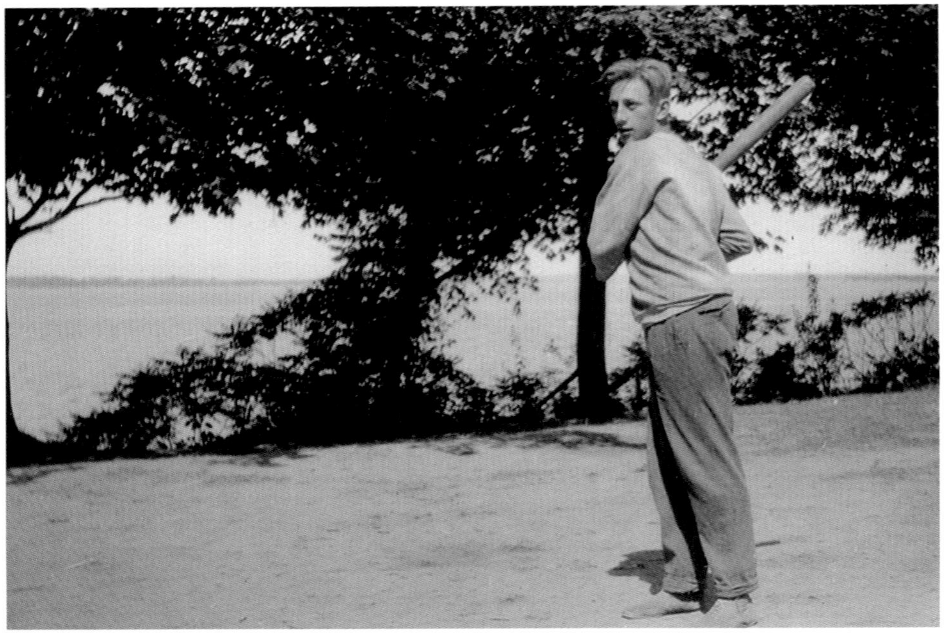

FIG. 20

At Camp Jened, Gene demonstrating his favorite pastime. Collection of author.

prove to have the strongest meaning for Gene's older sister, Tima, who became a teacher and lifelong political activist.

More importantly, for the future artists in the family, Gene and Ryah, it was a time of equally progressive movement in the arts and sciences. The Wright Brothers had made their historic first flight the year before Gene's birth. The year after, Albert Einstein published his theory of relativity. The next year, Upton Sinclair's *The Jungle* was published. This exposé of Chicago's meat industry was the most influential book of the era. The decade saw the publishing of Gertrude Stein's *Three Lives* and Ezra Pound's "Personae," among many other seminal works of literature. In music, Arnold Schoenberg introduced atonality in composition, challenging the classicists. If atonal music did not appeal to them, the Ludinses could have gone to the theater to see the operettas of Victor Herbert and Gilbert and Sullivan. Scott Joplin was introducing ragtime. Ellen Terry and Maude Adams graced the stage. George Bernard Shaw was writing serious plays, and works of the late Henrik Ibsen were shown in New York to acclaim. America would soon have its first towering playwright, Princeton dropout Eugene O'Neill, who would so convincingly portray our national ethos.

While two of the Ludins children, Gene and Ryah, became serious artists, the art scene in New York during their early childhood was insular and tied to the Victorian ideals of the previous century. Americans had always hung discreet family portraits on their walls beside equally discreet landscapes. Late in the nineteenth century, newly rich Americans traveled to Europe to shop, carting back vast amounts of treasure to adorn their new mansions. Henry James, in *The Golden Bowl*, published in 1904, examined the frenzied collecting of the era. The orgy of acquiring art led to the establishment of the first museums in the city. The Ludins children could have seen dinosaurs in the Museum of Natural History and, across Central Park, the galleries of Greek marbles and brown-toned Old Masters on view at the Metropolitan Museum of Art.

If one was aware of it, far more interesting art was happening seventy blocks south of the Met in Greenwich Village, where the vibrant bohemian scene was in full flower. It was home to the young artists, dealers, and collectors who would challenge the established criteria of art in the country.

Nowhere were the sweeping changes occurring in the art world more evident than in the work of the Ashcan school. Led by Robert Henri, the group included, among others, George Bellows and John Sloan. Most came from Philadelphia, where they had been newspaper illustrators and cartoonists. Influenced by their journalistic backgrounds and by the progressive thinking around them, these artists chose to portray realistically the raw vitality of everyday American life.

Art, like life, doesn't evolve in a vacuum. Americans at this time were beginning to see what Europeans and Russians had created since the Old Masters put down their brushes.

The Impressionists and Post-Impressionists such as Picasso, Braque, and Matisse had been on view in Europe since before the turn of the century. The Fauves and German Expressionists were challenging literal art by exposing their emotional attitudes in their work. In Russia, the Constructivists were beginning to dismantle Realism.

In 1908, in New York, Alfred Stieglitz showed Matisse and Picasso for the first time at his Gallery 291.[4] But most Americans did not learn about the "new art" until 1913, when the famous Armory Show was held. The exhibition included many of the best American and European artists. While provoking shock and dismay, it was a sensational hit in New York. Forty thousand people viewed it there and another two hundred thousand viewed it on tour. It forever burst apart the insular bubble that art traditionalists inhabited. Gene was too young to have appreciated the Armory

Show, but he greatly benefited from the revolution it launched.

In his earliest photographs, Gene is always wearing a football or baseball uniform (fig. 20). He is already robust, red-headed, and strong-faced, with charisma and charm radiating from wicked green-flecked eyes. "Take Me Out to the Ball Game," written in 1908, could have been Gene's theme song in his teens. He was wild about baseball. While attending Morris High, he played in Crotona Park and dreamed of becoming a professional player like the heroes of the day, Ty Cobb and Babe Ruth. There is no record that he had any intellectual pursuits. On vacations and in the summer he worked for his father, picking up the mechanical and carpentry skills that would later aid him as an able frame maker. He developed a love of machinery that was often reflected in his paintings. With his sisters, he sketched and drew cartoons. We have a record of his drawings from programs he designed for Camp Jened in the Catskills, where he was a counselor for three summers (fig. 21).

Gene was ten when World War I broke out and thirteen in 1917, when the Bolshevik Revolution, under the leadership of Lenin and Trotsky, transformed the world's political and social climate. In its aftermath in the nineteen-twenties, a new, optimistic spirit rose in America.

Cities expanded. "Bedroom communities" and suburbs flourished. People wanted the newest home appliances and faster cars, powered by the new fuels, to take them on the new roads. Automobile registration rose from eight million to twenty-three million by the end of the decade. By 1929, more than two-thirds of American families had electricity, and more than ten million homes had the new miracle—radio—making current events instantly available. With radio came advertising. Lucky Strike cigarettes, Listerine, canned foods, manufactured clothes, and home décor were now "must haves." American heroes no longer embodied social change, morality, and virtuous self-improvement but were popular idols, like film stars Charlie Chaplin and Mary Pickford.

At the same time, an ultra-conservative backlash was sweeping the country. There were tremendous setbacks, often violent, for labor unions. The Ku Klux Klan grew strong in anti-civil rights persecution. In 1921, two Italian immigrants, Sacco and Vanzetti, were put on trial in Massachusetts. Although there was no convincing evidence against them, they were convicted because they were immigrants and had anarchistic political beliefs.

This fear of radicalism, or "the Red menace," led to anti-immigration movements, especially against Russian Jews. The Palmer Raids arrested ten thousand supposed Bolsheviks. In Albany, New York, the Lusk Commission pursued New York's Russian Jews, and in 1921 alone, twenty-one thousand were deported, a sad reverse immigration.

Gene was seventeen in 1921. His progressive family would have been deeply affected by these events. It is likely that his future liberal left-leaning political views would have taken root during this time, as they did for many artists and writers of that decade. This was certainly the case with his sister Tima, the political activist and teacher.

Gene still dreamed of being a professional ball player, and for a time he played in the upstate New York Farm Team of the American League. When this didn't work out for him he tried college, but he left after one week. He then joined his sister Ryah in classes at the Art Students League, and there he finally found his métier. Ryah went on to become an accomplished muralist under the influence of the famous Mexican mural artists Siqueiros, Orozco, and Rivera.

For Gene, his four years (1924–27) at the League were crucial, as he started to learn the painter's craft.

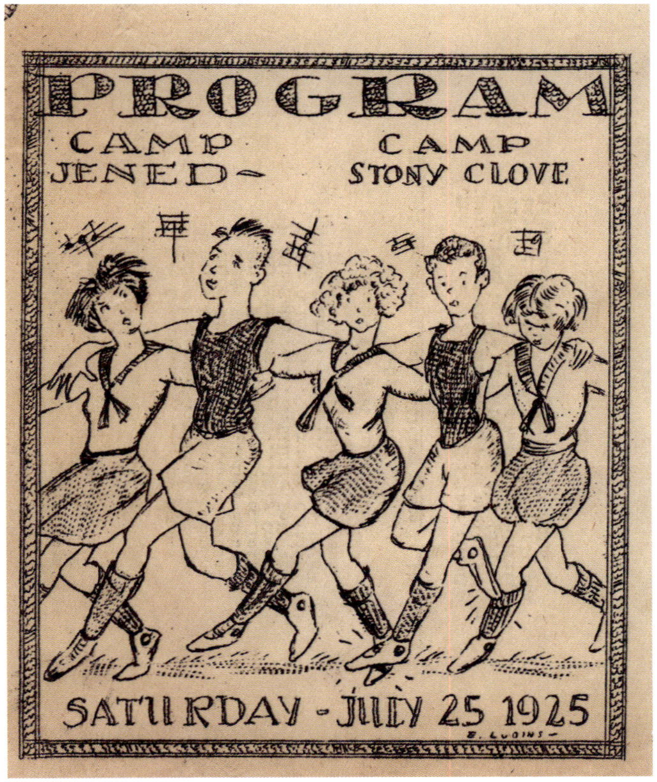

FIG. 21

Gene's drawing for the program for the midsummer show. The Fast family ran Camp Jened for boys and Stony Clove for girls. Estate of Eugene Ludins.

The Art Students League, established in 1875, was modeled on the French art school, the Académie Julian in Paris, where many of the Impressionists had studied. The teachers were usually artists of the strict academician tradition. When Gene was a student, however, the League was much under the influence of Robert Henri and his followers of the Ashcan school. Although Henri had been a pupil of Thomas Eakins, the Realist painter, he moved beyond Realism, absorbing the technique and philosophy of the Impressionists and Post-Impressionists. "Forget detail, capture the spirit and be yourself," was his approach to teaching art, he would tell his students. They were still quoting Henri when I attended classes there thirty years after Gene.

During Gene's years at the League, other instructors were Allen Tucker, Boardman Robinson, and Walt Kuhn, all respected artists of the period. Gene always spoke warmly of Allen Tucker, who greatly influenced his development. All the teachers at the League encouraged their students to explore the expanding New York art world outside its walls.

Gene spent many hours at the Met absorbing the technical skills of the Old Masters. Delacroix, Courbet, Goya, Brueghel, Dürer, were all echoed faintly in some of Gene's later work. He also saw the Met's newly acquired Manets and Cézannes. It was Cézanne about whom Matisse would say, "Cézanne was almost a God."[5] Later, Gene applied Cézanne's technique of dividing a canvas into three separate sections to increase the focus and intensity in his own work.

Vital for an art student, the work of the new giants was on view downtown in galleries, clubs, and the Whitney Studio Club. Ludins would have seen the energetic American artists Marsden Hartley, Arthur Dove, Georgia O'Keeffe, John Marin, Charles Demuth, and Edward Hopper, to name a few. At the galleries he would have seen Picasso, Matisse, and the many other European catalysts of change.

Gene took a break from his easel in 1924–25 while he went to sea as an assistant steward on ships (fig. 19) that traveled between New York and San Francisco (the *S.S. Kroonland*) and between New York and Bremerhaven (the *S.S. Republic*). From those experiences he developed a life-long love of ships and the sea. The Germany he visited was trying to recover from the disasters of World War I. This was the era of the Weimar Republic, a brief period of democratic rule before Adolf Hitler's rise to power in 1933. The arts were flourishing, and it is possible that Gene would have seen the works of George Grosz and Max Beckmann in Hamburg. The satiric drawings of Grosz were echoed in Gene's own drawings.

In the summer of 1920, Robert Henri vacationed in Woodstock as a guest of George Bellows and Eugene Speicher, who had established homes in the quaint village in the Catskills near the Hudson River. Gene would have heard of Woodstock's charm from his teachers. Not only was Woodstock hospitable to artists, but the surrounding scenery had drawn landscape painters to the area since the early nineteenth century.

There was also the lure of the two idealistic compounds of Byrdcliffe and the Maverick. Utopian art colonies had existed in America since the turn of the century in Woodstock, Taos, and Aurora, to name a few. They were inspired primarily by the English Arts and Crafts movement and by John Ruskin's "less is more" theory.

Gene started visiting Woodstock in the mid-1920s and moved there permanently in 1929, just as the stock market tumbled and the deep Depression of the 1930s was beginning.

Gene was drawn toward the Maverick colony, he often said, "because no one had any money and…it didn't seem to matter." Much has been written about Hervey White and the Maverick so I will write no more here, other than to quote Gene from an interview he gave in 1985,[6] speaking about his early days on the Maverick. He said, "I'd go to Hervey and say, What should I read? And he'd say, *War and Peace*. So I read that, and then I'd go back and say, what should I read now? And he'd say, *Crime and Punishment*…." Between the strong influence of White and the older, intellectually curious artists, writers, musicians, and actors that Gene met in Woodstock, he started to mature as a man and an artist.

Life wasn't always so cerebral for him. He played baseball on the team organized by George Bellows in Woodstock. He learned to cook. Omelets and spaghetti were his specialties. He helped paint sets and design costumes for the Maverick Theater. That is where he met his future wife and life-long artistic partner, the sculptor Hannah Small.

It is impossible to write about Gene without including Hannah. Where Gene was temperamental, boisterous, vital, and physically strong, Hannah was petite, delicate, and cerebral with a quiet, wicked sense of humor that was often hidden behind her refined manners.

Hannah's background was very different from Gene's. She was born in New York in 1903 to a wealthy family that had been in the country since the 1840s. They had immigrated from Holland and England and had been financially secure and socially prominent for generations.

Hannah used to talk about having great-uncles on both sides of the Civil War. She was brought up in the family brownstone on West Seventieth Street, in a luxurious, cloistered Victorian atmosphere. She was surrounded by nannies and German governesses, as were her three brothers, including my father, John. One of his complaints was that the nannies made him wear embroidered lace dresses until he was seven years old.

Their father, Eugene Small, was a cousin and close friend of Alfred Stieglitz. The Small and Stieglitz families summered at their adjacent properties on Lake George, where Hannah would have met the artists, writers, actors, and political figures who visited Stieglitz. Among them was Georgia O'Keeffe, whom Hannah disliked intensely.

For a woman of her background, it would have taken a great deal of courage and tenacity to pursue a career in the arts, much less to become a sculptor, which was considered a man's profession. Hannah also attended the Art Students League, but she registered in 1919 and missed Ludins by about five years.

Hannah married the artist Austin Mecklem and they joined the Maverick Colony in the mid-1920s, living a very different life from the one she had known on Seventieth Street. As a wedding present, her parents had given Hannah a small island on Lake George, with an old shack on it. When time with family became claustrophobic, Hannah and her friends would row out to the island to escape them. Gene used a rowboat as an image in some of his more inexplicable paintings.

Hannah often said that she fell in love with Gene the first time she saw him at the Maverick Theater. Their relationship got off to bumpy start since she was married and Gene had other women in his life. When they both realized that they wanted to be together, they knew that divorce would not be easy or socially acceptable. They also faced disapproval from Hannah's family, who, although Jewish themselves, shared the prejudices against Russian Jews that were prevalent at the time. No matter; they escaped to Santa Fe for a year, returning to Woodstock after the scandal had died down. They eventually married in 1937.

By that time, they had purchased property on Chestnut Hill Road (fig. 22), with a charming old house and two generous outbuildings that would serve as their studios for the next fifty-odd years. There, they settled into a close, loving partnership, sharing many generous times with friends, family, their community, and, above all, creating many vital works of art.

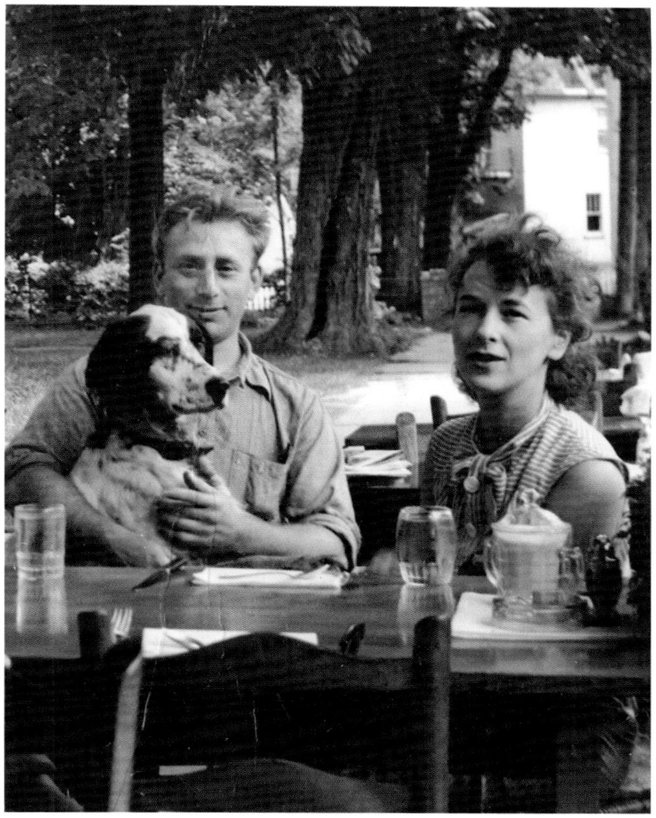

FIG. 5

Hannah, Gene, and Popey. Collection of author.

Notes

1 David Ludins, "Memories of Woodbine," *The Jewish Frontier* (June 1960).
2 Joan Lefkowitz, *Tima Ludins, A Life on the Left*, thesis, University of California, San Francisco, n.d.
3 Christine Stansell, "Virginia Woolf," *American Moderns* (Princeton, New Jersey: Princeton University Press, 2000), 1.
4 Sue Davidson Lowe, *Stieglitz, A Memoir/Biography* (New York: Farrar, Straus and Giroux, 1983).
5 Anthony F. Janson, *History of Art* (New York: Harry Abrams, 1981), 782.
6 Karl Fortess, "Interviews with old Woodstockers and Mavericks," courtesy of the Woodstock Library, 1985; see also Jim Reed, Woodstock Winter Roundtable, courtesy of *The Woodstock Times* (1981), and "Interview," *New York Post* (Nov. 11, 1947).

WOODSTOCK, 1929

Tom Wolf

When Eugene Ludins moved to Woodstock in 1929, he entered the life of an art colony that had been established more than a quarter of a century earlier. One hundred miles from New York City, it benefited from a rich interchange with the metropolis while maintaining its own unique culture. In the 1920s it was the rural equivalent of Manhattan's bohemian Greenwich Village, and many artists, writers, and cultural thinkers traveled back and forth.

At the beginning of the twentieth century, though, Woodstock was a small, tranquil farming town—until a handful of people intentionally transformed it into an artists' colony. The metamorphosis was led by the extraordinarily wealthy, idealistic Ralph Radcliffe Whitehead.[1] Born into a family that made its fortune with a textile factory during the Industrial Revolution in England, Whitehead studied at Oxford with the great critic and aesthetic philosopher, John Ruskin. There he absorbed many of Ruskin's concepts that would define the Arts and Crafts movement. Among them were a respect for the handmade as opposed to the mechanically manufactured and a faith in the value of living close to nature, as opposed to struggling in polluted and congested urban centers.

During a visit to Florence, Whitehead met and fell in love with Jane Byrd McCall, an aspiring artist from a prominent Philadelphia family, who also knew Ruskin personally and admired his ideas. Ralph and Jane courted and, after he divorced his first wife, married in 1892. The Whiteheads moved to Montecito, near Santa Barbara, California, where they built a mansion overlooking the ocean and nurtured dreams of bringing together a group of artists and craftsmen to live creatively in a beautiful and healthful natural setting.

After about six years, frustrated by their lack of success in achieving this goal, they resolved to find a new location and make their ideals a reality. For help with this project they enlisted two colleagues: Hervey White, an energetic, impoverished young writer who had met Whitehead at Jane Addams's Hull House in Chicago, and Bolton Brown, an ambitious artist from New York, who was the first art teacher at Stanford University in California. The group resolved to explore parts of the United States looking for an ideal site. While the Whiteheads and White traveled around Virginia and the Carolinas, Brown, an experienced mountain climber (a peak in the Sierra Nevada is named after him) hiked through the Catskills. He had an epiphany when he

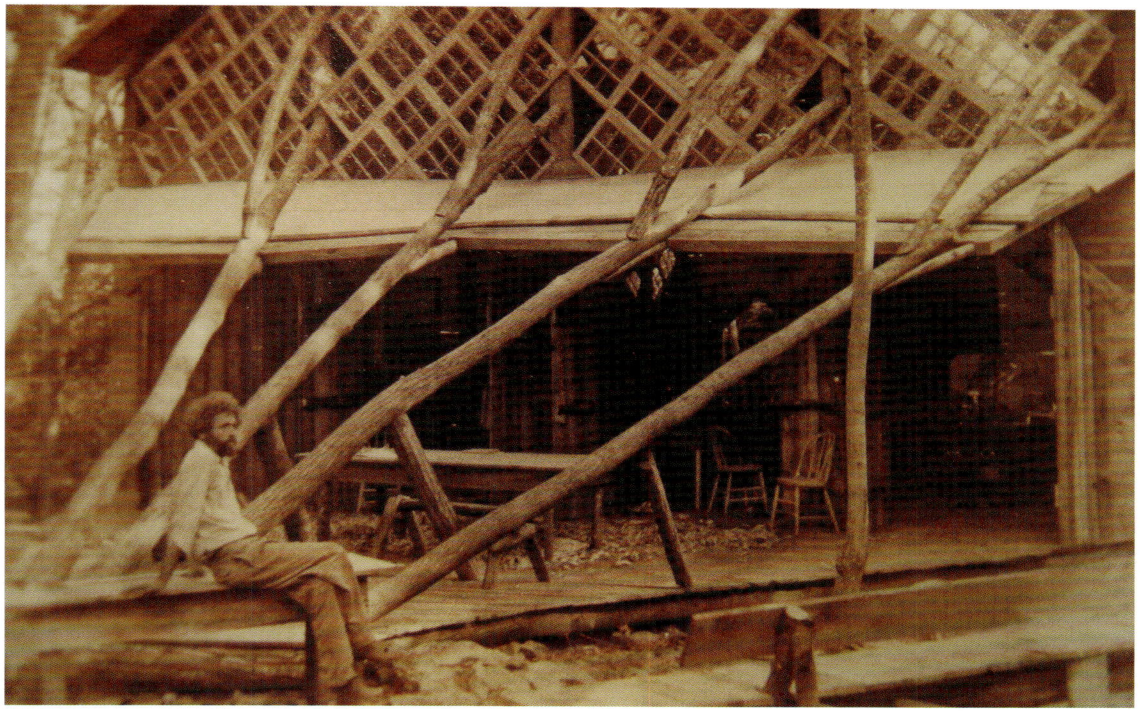

FIG. 23

LOUIS E. JONES

Hervey White at the Maverick Concert Hall

1919, postcard. Private Collection.

ascended Overlook Mountain and looked down at the peaceful town of Woodstock in the valley below, and he immediately telegraphed the others that he had found the place.

Whitehead promptly visited, was convinced, and directed Brown to negotiate with the local farmers to sell him their property. He then hired Brown and White to supervise the building of close to thirty houses and studios on the mountain. By 1903 the colony, named Byrdcliffe, was inviting artists and craftsmen to live and work there. Byrdcliffe's crafts studios included a forge for metalworking, a ceramics studio, and facilities for weaving and furniture making. There was an airy, well-lit space for lessons in painting and drawing, an art students' dormitory with individual studios attached, and a large residence for the head painting instructor and his family. Among the first of these instructors was Birge Harrison, a well-traveled and highly respected landscape painter whom the Whiteheads knew in California. Having spent years in Paris and in French art colonies, Harrison brought the nineteenth-century tradition of *plein-air* landscape painting to Woodstock.

Perhaps Byrdcliffe did not fulfill the most idealistic goals of its founders, but it forever transformed the town of Woodstock from a farming village to an artistic center. One of the impediments to the success of the colony was that few of the buildings were winterized, and the Whiteheads returned to California most winters, discouraging the colony from being active year around. And although Whitehead was very generous about paying the bills, he was also the final decision maker. Consequently independent-minded artists and intellectuals at Byrdcliffe were reluctant to settle there permanently. But the art seed had been planted, and when the Art Students League in New York decided it needed a rural summer locale for teaching landscape painting, it accepted the recommendation of John Carlson, who had studied with Birge Harrison at Byrdcliffe, and in 1906 the Art Students League opened its new branch in Woodstock, with Harrison as its first instructor.

Harrison's popularity, coupled with the interest in outdoor landscape painting at the time, brought scores of young art students to Woodstock, some of them permanently. Meanwhile, conflict arose between Hervey White and Whitehead, who were diametric opposites. (White once described the Englishman as "the most reserved person I had ever met.") So White split from his patron, scraped together a little money, and with a friend bought land a few miles from Byrdcliffe to open his own colony, the Maverick—

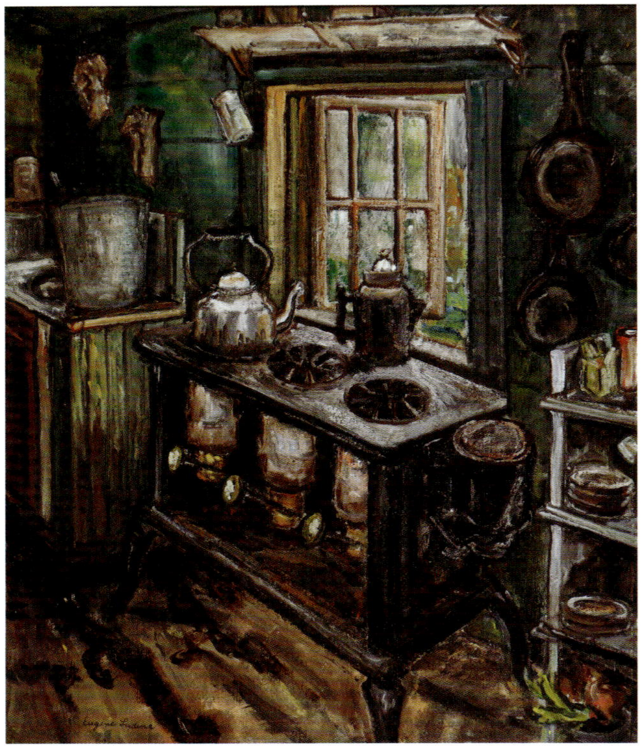

FIG. 24 (CAT. 12)

Maverick Kitchen

c. 1931, oil on canvas
30 x 26 in.
Estate of Eugene Ludins.
Photo Peter R. Jones

which is where Gene Ludins lived once he moved to Woodstock.[2]

White's approach to his colony was low budget, improvisational, and communal. He was generous, charismatic, and egalitarian, and consequently people were willing to help him with his projects. He invited sympathetic people to stay on his property and often built cheap, simple dwellings for them. Soon after some musicians showed up he had them putting on concerts, which led to the building of the extraordinary Maverick Concert Hall in 1916 and the start of the Maverick Sunday chamber music concerts (fig. 23) . John Cage debuted his famous 4' 33" there in 1952, and these concerts still go on today.

After the musicians, artists began to arrive. Ludins spent several summers in Woodstock before permanently moving there, encouraged by painter Arnold Blanch, who has been called "the unofficial mayor of Woodstock" because of his zeal for recruiting artists to the colony.[3] A group of artists lived at the Maverick colony, including Harry Gottlieb, Eugenie Gershoy, Arnold and Lucile Blanch, John Flannagan, Wendell and Jane Jones, Carl and Helen Walters, and Ludins's future wife, the sculptor Hannah Small, with her first husband, Austin Mecklem. Friends of theirs were frequent visitors.

The Maverick enterprise included a theater in addition to the music hall, and starting in 1915 a raucous and uninhibited Maverick Festival took place at the end of every summer, on the night of the full moon in August. Ludins sometimes helped out by directing traffic at the festival; for income he made frames for the more established artists.[4]

According to advertisements in local newspapers, the biggest-selling items in Woodstock at this time were electric radios and General Electric refrigerators. But admirers of Ruskin, like White and Whitehead, were skeptical of modern technology, and the Maverick residents were proud of the hardy lives they led, dedicated to art, without amenities like electricity and running water. Ludins's two paintings of the interior of his Maverick cabin illustrate the austere living conditions these artists embraced. The diagonal composition of his *Maverick Kitchen* centers on the iron stove which holds its fuel stored below the burners (fig. 24). A big bucket stands between the kettle and the sink, ready to fill them with water carried in from a distant pump outside. The kettle's spout points out the window to the greenery of nature around the humble cabin.

His second interior, *Maverick Studio*, is full of the tools of the artist and encodes a romantic message: his self-portrait, perched above the door, seems to stand guard over his girlfriend sleeping in the next room (fig. 25). A dog dozes blissfully below, warmed by the fire that glows in the fireplace at the right edge of the painting. As there is no gas or electricity in this artist's abode, the fire and the kerosene lamp perched on the bureau at the left, in front of the artist's palette, are powered by fuel that is brought in from the outside. The bright surrounding landscape is glimpsed through the window in the bedroom; Ruskin's ideal of a life fulfilled by making art in the midst of nature has been achieved.

In the early days of Byrdcliffe, Whitehead would not allow automobiles in the colony, but he eventually relented and bought a fancy one.[5] White did not like them, either, and on Saturdays Maverick residents would often walk five miles to town to shop at the lively market fair at the village green. Ludins eventually inherited an old Pierce-Arrow from his father, and a car is the subject of his comic self-portrait where he parodies the image of a dashing man sitting jauntily at the wheel of his convertible, confronting wide-open spaces (fig. 26). Ludins with a little smile sits in his car before one of his typical scumbled, painterly skies, but his automobile is motionless, stuck on a towing platform with a chain ready to pull it out of the picture.

The Maverick and the Art Students League lured more and more young artists up from New York City, and in 1919 a group of artists bought land in the middle of town and created the Woodstock Art Association (later to be renamed Woodstock Artists Association) to show work by Woodstock painters. During the populous summer months, the association held four or five exhibitions that would be reviewed in New York papers plus the two summer newspapers that were published in Woodstock: the *Hue and Cry*, established in 1923, and its rival, the *Woodstock Bulletin*, established in 1928. In addition, the year Ludins moved to the Maverick marked the debut of the Woodstock Playhouse, which competed with the Maverick by presenting plays and concerts during the busy summer months. On days when there were no performances, movies were shown in the Fireman's Hall. The colony was so active that Martin Schütze, a scholar who taught at the University of Chicago and was part of the Byrdcliffe colony from its earliest days, wrote in 1929,

> ...in the recent history of Woodstock the development from the purely agricultural to the most modern stage of social life, which in general history requires hundreds and thousands of years, has been telescoped into a period of less than one generation, so that each of us has, day by day, seen the fundamental forces of human history actually at work.[6]

Schütze was in a contemplative mood because 1929 was a turning point for the Woodstock art colony, even though no one was yet aware of the stock market crash that would mark the onset of the Depression later that year. Key father figures of the Woodstock colony died in 1929, defining the end of a generation. First, the founder, Ralph Radcliffe Whitehead, died on February 23, seventy-five years old and heartbroken because of the tragic death at sea of his older son, Ralph Jr. Then in May the beloved Birge Harrison, teacher of many of the artists who settled in the colony, died at age seventy-four. In addition, an influential contingent of painters in Woodstock were friends of Robert Henri, the inspiration for the Ashcan School. He also died that year, in July at age sixty-four. Henri's democratic ideal of painting all aspects of life around him inspired his colleagues and disciples, who were among the most important artists in the country at the time. Most famous of them was George Bellows, who lived the last five years of his short life in Woodstock, where Henri spent the summer of 1921 with him. Henri's many students included Andrew Dasburg, a modernist who was one of the founders of the Woodstock Art Association, and Bellows's close friend, Eugene Speicher, who was the most celebrated artist in Woodstock when Ludins moved to the colony.

Although several of its founding fathers died in 1929, Woodstock's vitality as an art colony persisted. Yasuo Kuniyoshi, who was fast becoming one of the most respected painters in the United States, bought land and built a house in Woodstock that year. He joined several other successful artists who had residences both in the colony and in New York City, which was accessible by

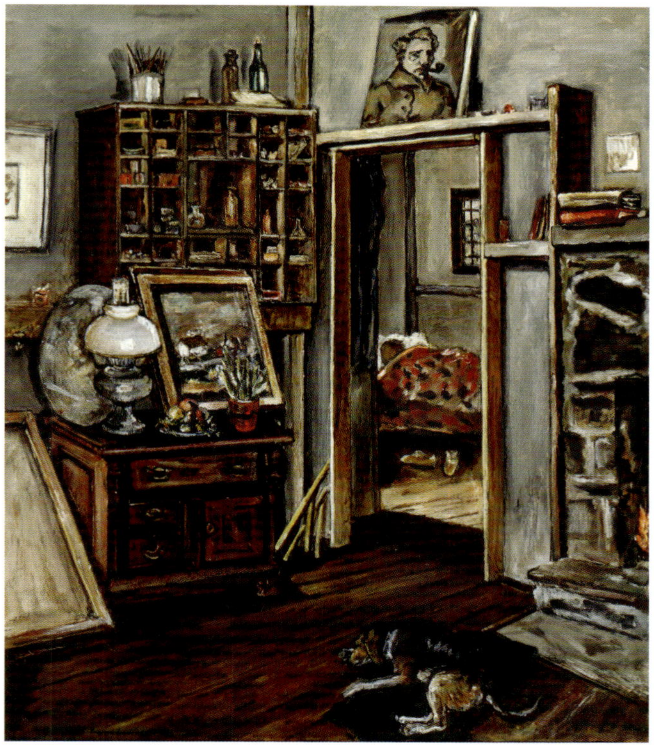

FIG. 25 (CAT. 11)

Maverick Studio

1931, oil on canvas
36 x 32 in.
Estate of Eugene Ludins.
Photo John Kleinhans

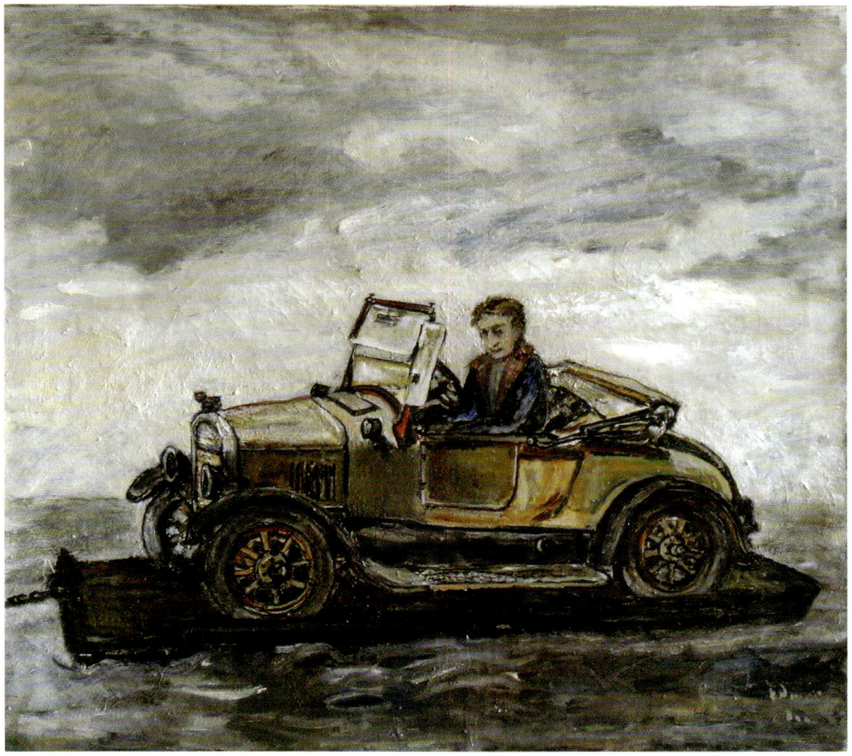

FIG. 26 (CAT. 8)

Self-Portrait in Roadster

Early 1930s,
oil on canvas
28 x 32 in.
Estate of Eugene Ludins.
Photo Peter R. Jones

motoring twelve miles to Kingston and from there taking a five-hour boat trip to Forty-second Street in Manhattan.

By that time Woodstock had a strong sense of its uniqueness, and there was concern in the local press that its popularity as a tourist site would dilute its distinctive artistic character. A new country club with a golf course was built, plus new restaurants and the second theater. During the 1929 season the Maverick Theatre presented Eugene O'Neill's *Emperor Jones* and the Woodstock Playhouse featured *Rain*, adapted from a Somerset Maugham story by Woodstock resident Clemence Randolph. Often the two theaters competed for audiences by importing lightweight comedies from Broadway. The local press frequently invoked images of "Babbitts" overrunning the colony and turning it into a "Main Street," referring to Sinclair Lewis's popular novels about unimaginative, materialistic small town-Americans.[7] This attitude could become smugly elitist, as when a writer in the *Hue and Cry*, complaining that Woodstock's two theaters showcased too many popular Broadway plays, argued "An auditorium seating twenty-five Woodstockers of high rank as artists commands more respect than an auditorium bulging with several hundred

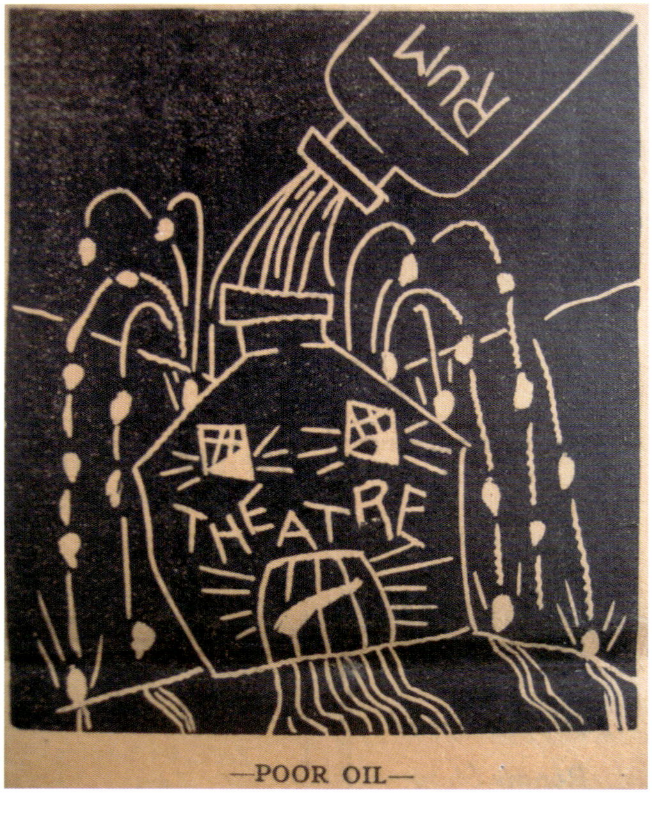

FIG. 27

"Poor Oil," from the *Hue and Cry*, August 24, 1929. Collection of author.

Kingston clerks and Saugerties merchants" (referring to two neighboring towns).[8] More tolerant Woodstockers observed that the influx of curiosity seekers was good for the local businesses, and artists who wanted solitude could retreat to the less frequented outskirts of town.[9]

There were also tensions between the local inhabitants, referred to as "natives," who were there before Byrdcliffe, and the more bohemian artists who lived in their midst. But as Woodstock historian Alf Evers has pointed out, the newcomers brought economic energy to a town that had depended on exporting bluestone for New York City sidewalks, an obsolete income source since bluestone was being replaced by concrete as the material of choice.[10]

The symbol of artistic Woodstock was the Maverick Festival, which in 1929 was in its fourteenth year and becoming more crowded and controversial each season. In 1929 an estimated six thousand people visited it.[11] The festival had acquired a reputation for uninhibited bacchanalian behavior. People were encouraged to come in costumes (for half-price admission), which could get pretty wild, and the partying sometimes lasted through the night. And although Prohibition was now law, it was customarily ignored at the festival as well as in the everyday lives of the artists. Ludins served home-brewed applejack (an apple brandy) to guests.[12] The *Hue and Cry* made fun of Prohibition, stating in its inaugural issue of the 1929 season, "we must be distinctly Wet," and criticizing "local grocers who run out of oranges, limes and lemons on Saturday afternoons. . ." It published a comic print in its 1929 Maverick Festival issue showing the theater being swamped by a downpour from a giant bottle of rum (fig. 27).[13]

Such levity provoked a reaction from less frivolous-minded citizens, and before the 1929 festival a letter appeared from a "Committee of Fifty" urging "all good thinking people" to take action against "wild parties, nude bathing, indecent dress and indecent behaviour."[14] The Committee of Fifty turned out to number about four, led by Reverend Todd, and the festival, which was organized around a Gay Nineties theme, was relatively tame.[15] But the influx of outsiders, the scrutiny from the police, the notoriety, the continued opposition from church leaders, and the effort of sponsoring the event all weighed on Hervey White, and he held only two more galas. The last one, on a much smaller scale, was in 1931.

Tensions between locals and artists, between culturati and tourists, between conservative moralists and free-thinking liberals were compounded by bigotry. In the early 1920s the Ku Klux Klan had a brief moment in the town

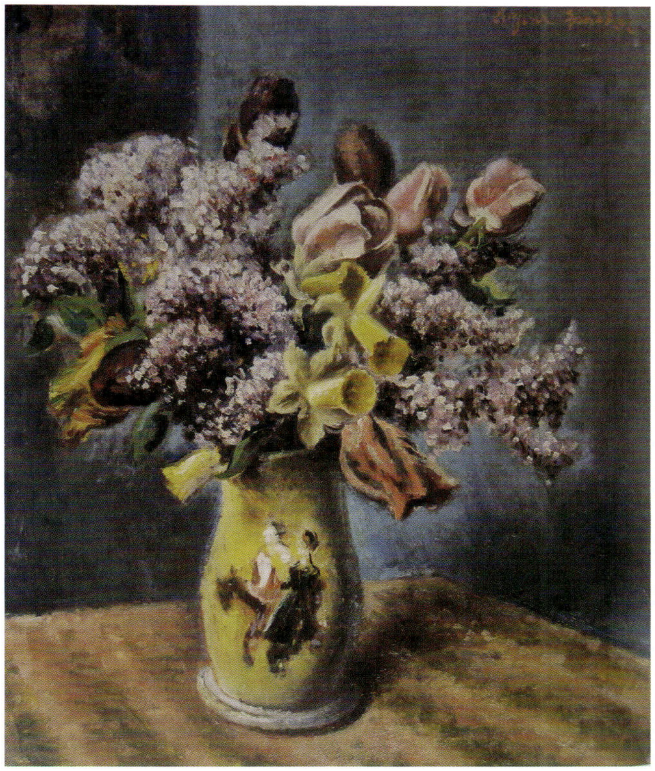

live in what was in effect his extended family; it seems as though his prejudice was abstract and did not apply to the people he actually knew.

Regardless of these undercurrents, artists continued coming to Woodstock for the art. The center of the art world was the Woodstock Artists Association. In 1929, its tenth year, it hosted five art exhibitions over the summer. In an article for the *Hue and Cry* in August, Carl Eric Lindin, who replaced Birge Harrison as the president of the association, called for tolerance between the "radicals" and the "academics." Lindin and others felt that the progressive group had taken over, leaving the traditionalists, like John Carlson, Harry Leith-Ross, and Orville Peets, reluctant to show at the association. From today's point of view many of the "radicals" look quite conservative, but in their day they gained that reputation because they were younger than the traditionalists, and they incorporated varying degrees of European modernism into their art. In the early teens the aggressive modernists in Woodstock were led by Andrew Dasburg, who had encountered Cubism in Paris; Konrad Cramer, who had known members of the Blaue Reiter group in Germany; and

FIG. 28

EUGENE SPEICHER

Lilacs and Tulips

c. 1930, oil on canvas
22½ x 19½ in.
Woodstock Artists Association and Museum Permanent Collection, gift of Cecile Forman, 1978-09-02. *Photo by Ben Caswell*

during which they burned a cross, but there was little support for their endeavors.[16] Some of the artists, including Ludins, were Jewish, and anti-Semitism was a fact of life in the colony since its origins. Ralph Whitehead's main hesitation about settling in Woodstock was that he had heard that the Catskills were full of Jews.[17] A popular feature of the *Hue and Cry*, punning on the name of the local village of Bearsville, was "The Barzevil Bue-Gull." This satiric column was written by Ned Thatcher, a metal craftsman affiliated with Byrdcliffe who was admired for the ingenious mechanical devices he manufactured for Maverick plays and festivals. Mocking the native residents, he wrote his column in the persona of a semi-literate yokel, Iddie Fletcher. The column included verses that parodied Yiddish-accented English and incorporated bigoted puns, for example calling the Catskills the "Kikeskills."[18] He could be pretty insulting to women, too. Even the saintly Hervey White wrote and published a couple of anti-Semitic tracts.[19] Ludins in later years hesitatingly described him as "even a little bit fascist ...he wasn't even anti-Nazi....He was very strange politically. Well, he was completely nonpolitical."[20] But White welcomed several Jewish artists to the Maverick, to

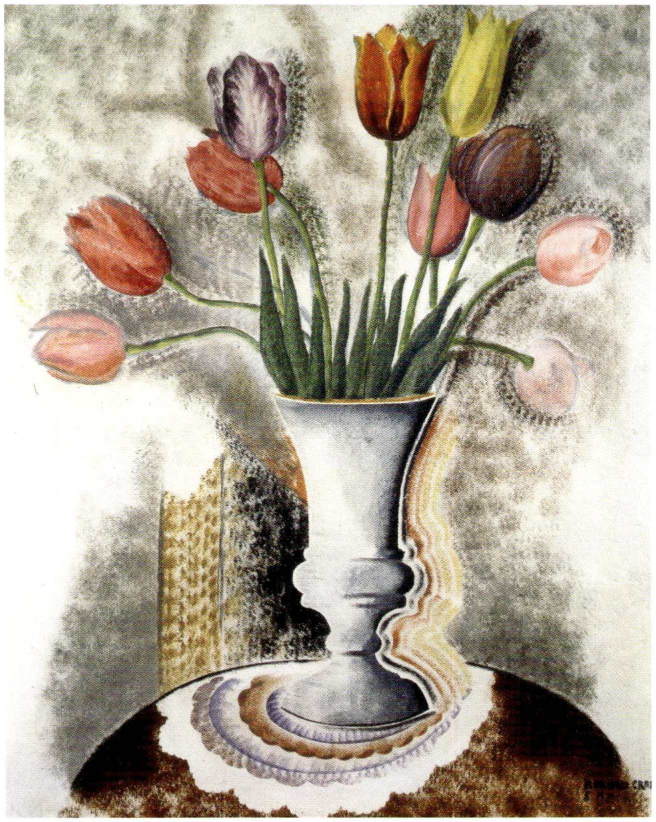

FIG. 29

KONRAD CRAMER

Tulips

1929, oil on board
24 x 20 in.
Photo courtesy of Gerald Peters Gallery, New York.

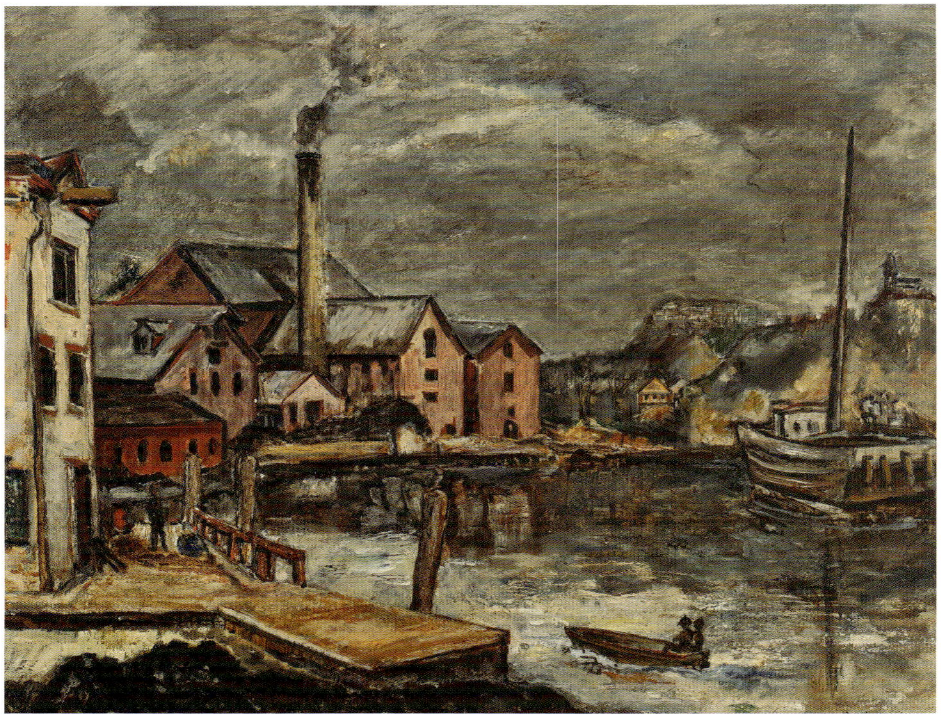

FIG. 30 (CAT. 9)

Saugerties Pool

1930, oil on Canvas
24 x 30 in.
Private Collection.
Photo John Kleinhans

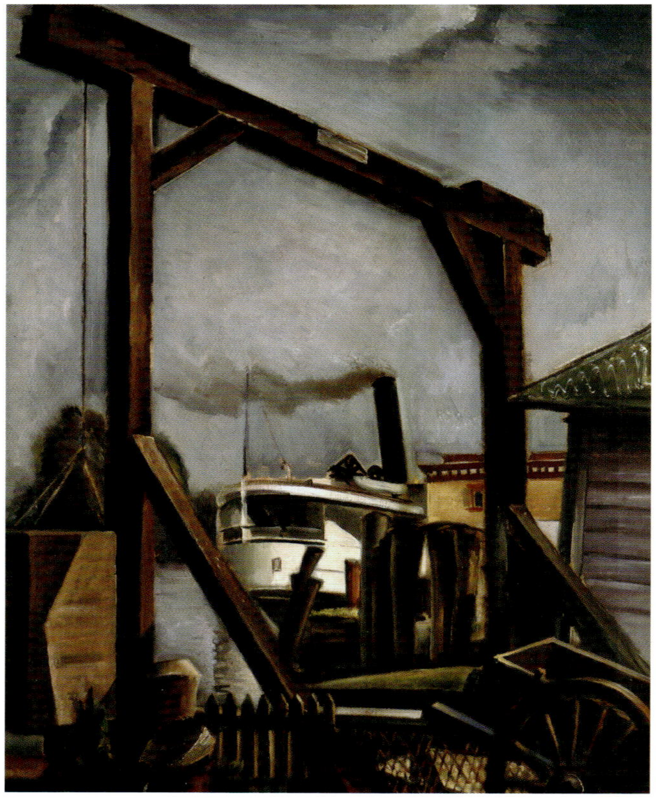

FIG. 31

CHARLES ROSEN

Steamboat Landing

c. 1929, oil on canvas
30 x 24 in.
Collection of Jim's of Lambertville Gallery, Lambertville, New Jersey.

Henry Lee McFee. By 1929 Dasburg had moved to New Mexico, McFee's style had grown more conservative (and was greatly admired), and Cramer remained as the radical, practicing a decorative version of Cubism.

Genuine European modernism was represented by the sculptor Alexander Archipenko, who was on the board of the Woodstock Artists Association in 1929. He traveled a lot, though, and seems to have been fairly aloof from the local art scene. The painter who represented the pinnacle of success in the Woodstock art world in 1929 was Eugene Speicher. A regular exhibitor at the Artists Association, he was nationally esteemed and the winner of many prizes. His still life *Lilacs and Tulips*, a beautiful, domestic subject confidently rendered (fig. 28), shows why. The strongly modeled vase is firmly located on a corner of a table clearly defined in perspective, and each tulip and daffodil has its own firm structure that plays against the flurry of Impressionist strokes that animate the clusters of lilacs. Konrad Cramer's modernist *Tulips*, from 1929, is considerably more edgy, with its abdication of perspective; the multiple contours on the right side of the vase and the grey echoes of the tulips in the background make it seem to vibrate futuristically (fig. 29). At the same time its rigid centrality, shared with Speicher's painting, evokes American folk art, which progressive American artists admired at the time. Cramer's artist wife, Florence, dealt in folk art out of her Woodstock shop, which was also one of the few places people could find books about avant-garde artists like Picasso.

Ludins showed repeatedly in the 1929 Artists Association exhibits and was often both criticized and encouraged by the critics: "Eugene Ludins' emotional landscape, rich in color but confused in execution, shows promising originality."[21] Esteemed *New York Times* critic Edward Alden Jewell likened his work to that of Chaim Soutine because of its painterly energy.[22] His *Saugerties Pool* is typical of his art in this period—a softly brushed realist scene with personal inflections (fig. 30).

Many Woodstock painters, from Birge Harrison on, explored the local landscape for subjects; its picturesqueness and variety were part of what drew them to the region. They liked to drive to nearby towns with docks, like Saugerties and Kingston, to find harbor scenes, which provided images of working-class labor and industrial modernity, plus a range of visual effects, from geometrical architecture to watery reflections. Charles Rosen's painting *Steamboat Landing* is an example from a Woodstock artist who had a remarkable career. He was a successful Pennsylvania Impressionist who renounced this style and moved to Woodstock in 1920 to become a modernist (fig. 31). His harbor scene is dominated by powerful geometries, intersecting each other and half obscuring the glistening steamboat in the center of the composition.

While Rosen fragmented his imagery and blocked the viewer from visually entering the space, creating a majestic play of near-abstract forms, Ludins was more welcoming. In his *Saugerties Pool*, we gently enter the scene from the lower right, as a towering funnel releases its dark smoke into the air at the left. The large boat opposite the smokestack is a sailboat, a reminder of pre-industrial times. And, unlike most of the harbor scenes painted by Woodstock artists in these years, this one includes two small figures with whom we can empathize. They sit close to each other as their little boat glides into the harbor. This tiny couple, plus the artist's soft touch, humanizes the scene in a way consistent with Ludins's other works. Neither an academic nor a modernist, he was an individualist, steering his own path, making art about the human condition rather than making art about art.

When Ludins moved to Woodstock in 1929, it was a peak time in what became a disastrous year. The colony was thriving artistically and economically, spurred by the burgeoning stock market. In its first issue of the summer season, the *Hue and Cry* published a warning:

> Things are booming. Nowhere can that pyramiding increment of wealth be better observed than in our own village. Who would have guessed, surveying the row of broken-down Fords in 1925, that four brief years would endow us so heavily with Packards, Lincolns, Pierce Arrows and Dusenbergs?
>
> Yessir, we're in a boom, and the only fear is that someone's going to fall down. "Buy til it hurts," is the H. Morton Robinson slogan. But By-bye is what the banks will be saying if by any chance the boom gives these bozos the go by.[23]

The stock market crash in October took a while to affect people, but by 1930 things started looking grim; because of the economy, Ludins lost framing jobs he had been promised. In the coming years of the Depression, the situation in Woodstock would change drastically, and Ludins would take on a new role, working with government programs to try to help his fellow artists.

Acknowledgments

Much of what I have written here is derived from the work of Alf Evers, who always gave me great encouragement to pursue this research. For their valuable help with this essay I would like to thank Susana Leval, the guiding force of the Eugene Ludins exhibition project; Avis Berman, Franklin Riehlman, Amy Raff at the Woodstock Public Library, Jeanette McDonald at Bard College, Reagan Upshaw at Gerald Peters Gallery.

Notes

1 The history of the origins of Woodstock as an art colony has been told many times, including most importantly, Evers, *Woodstock*; Smith, *Woodstock*; Marling, "Introduction"; and Tom Wolf, "Historical Survey."
2 White, *Autobiography*, 102. I quoted this in my "Byrdcliffe's History," 22, the major study of Byrdcliffe.
3 Sally Avery in conversation with the author, c. 1985.
4 Cambiz Koshravi interview with Eugene Ludins and Hannah Small, typescript courtesy Cambiz Koshravi, 1985.
5 Evers, *Woodstock*, 444.
6 Martin Schütze, the *Woodstock Bulletin* 2, no. 7 (September 1, 1929).
7 For example, the article titled "Babbitts Buzz About," in the *Woodstock Bulletin* 2, no. 5 (August 1, 1929), states "Being composed of many individualists, Woodstock has seemed to resent the intrusion of MAIN STREET tactics during recent years; many of our workers in the arts desire some seclusion and solitude..."
8 "Broadway Actors Broadway Plays," the *Hue and Cry* 7, no. 5 (July 27, 1929).
9 Hughes Mearns, *The Woodstock Bulletin* 2, no. 7 (September 1, 1929), 4.
10 Evers, *Woodstock*, 349–56.
11 "A Teapot Tempest," *Art Digest* (October 1, 1929).
12 Cambiz Koshravi interview, 1985.
13 "Prelude to Another Season," the *Hue and Cry* 7, no. 8 (June 29, 1929).
14 Quoted in "Four Men Sign Letter as 'Committee of Fifty,'" the *Woodstock Bulletin* 2, no. 8 (September 15, 1929).
15 Reviewing the 1929 festival, the *Woodstock Bulletin* quoted several newspaper accounts. The raciest, in the *New York Journal*, titled "Police Chase Art Colony Revelers," cited some on-stage "displays of feminine anatomy." Most accounts, though, agreed with Sheriff Houst, quoted in the *Herald Tribune*, who described it as "extremely quiet." The *New York Sunday News* wrote, "the festival was discovered to be just about as sinful as a Thursday night meeting of the Ladies Aid Society." The *Woodstock Bulletin* 2, no. 8 (September 15, 1929), 1–2.
16 Evers, *Woodstock*, 493–94.
17 Wolf, "Byrdcliffe's History," 23.
18 "Barzvil Bue-Gull," "The Boobs Guide to the Maverick," the *Hue and Cry* 2, no. 10 (August 30, 1929).
19 Cambiz Koshravi interview; Wolf, "Hervey White's Maverick Colony and Its Artists," 23.
20 Cambiz Koshravi interview, 1985.
21 I. E. P., "Atelier and Classroom," the *Hue and Cry* 7, no. 4 (July 20, 1929).
22 Edward Alden Jewell, "Art Progresses Steadily in Rip Van Winkle's Country," the *New York Times* (September 1, 1929), X7.
23 "Little Deep Stuff," the *Hue and Cry* 7, no. 1 (June 29, 1929). Henry Morton Robinson was a writer who lived on the Maverick.

Selected Bibliography

Evers, Alf. *Woodstock, History of an American Town*. Woodstock, New York: Overlook Press, 1987.

Marling, Karal Ann. "Introduction." In *Woodstock, An American Art Colony, 1902–1977*. Poughkeepsie, New York: Vassar College Art Gallery, 1977.

Smith, Anita. *Woodstock, History and Hearsay* (1959), 2nd ed. Woodstock, New York: Woodstock Arts Publications, 2006.

White, Hervey. *Autobiography*. Papers of Hervey White, Special Collections, University of Iowa, Iowa City. n.d.

Wolf, Tom. "Byrdcliffe's History," In *Byrdcliffe, An American Arts and Crafts Colony*. Herbert F. Johnson Museum of Art, Cornell University. Ithaca, New York: Cornell University Press, 2004.

______. "Hervey White's Maverick Colony and Its Artists." In *The Maverick: Hervey White's Colony of the Arts*. Woodstock, New York: Woodstock Artists Association and Museum, 2006.

______. "Historical Survey." In *Woodstock's Art Heritage, The Catalog of the Permanent Collection of the Woodstock Artists Association*. Woodstock, New York: The Overlook Press, 1987.

ALLIANCES AND ACTIVISM

Eugene Ludins's Social and Cultural Networks

Avis Berman

As a young and footloose artist, Eugene Ludins consistently alighted in the right place at the right time. Whether accidental or planned, his early decisions unerringly brought him close to the center of an equally youthful American art world, a burgeoning coalition of artists, patrons, and private and public organizations intent on forming an environment more inclusive of uncredentialed artists than the establishment had been in the past. In whatever art community he landed, Ludins made the most of his opportunities, yet he was never a careerist. Indeed, he was quite the opposite: often he seemingly went out of his way to create uningratiating paintings, challenging viewers to understand and accept them. But his professional instincts coalesced with an authentic social conscience and a genuine passion for participation. He readily joined his fellow artists to initiate cooperative action, which not only shaped but gave resonance to his artistic trajectory. Through his choices of schools, mentors, and residences, as well as his own attributes of concern and leadership, Ludins built a solid reputation among museums and galleries and helped pilot the Woodstock art colony through the economic abyss of the 1930s.

Born in Russia in 1904, Ludins was one of five children of Jewish immigrants who attained a comfortable, middle-class life in America after David Ludins, their father, became financially successful as a builder and contractor in New York. It was a family in which the children were encouraged, and artistic talents were not suppressed. Eugene's sister Ryah (1898–1957) became a painter, and Eugene's ambition to be an artist was supported as well. After high school and a brief and unsuccessful try at college,[1] he was allowed to go to art school. As a city resident, Ludins had easy access to several important and venerable art schools—Pratt Institute, the National Academy of Design, and the Art Students League of New York. Both Pratt and the academy's school were extremely conservative in practice and attitude. In contrast, the League was lively and liberal, and Ludins chose to study there. In the mid-1920s, the League's instructors were working professional artists with substantial or up-and-coming reputations: John Sloan, Guy Pène du Bois, Walt Kuhn, and Thomas Hart Benton were some of the more prominent teachers at the school. It was clear that ambitious students were drawn there, too—Fairfield Porter, James Brooks, John Graham, Isabel Bishop, and Jack Tworkov attended the League at the same time as Ludins.

Ludins's instructors at the League who influenced him most were Allen Tucker, Boardman Robinson, and Kenneth

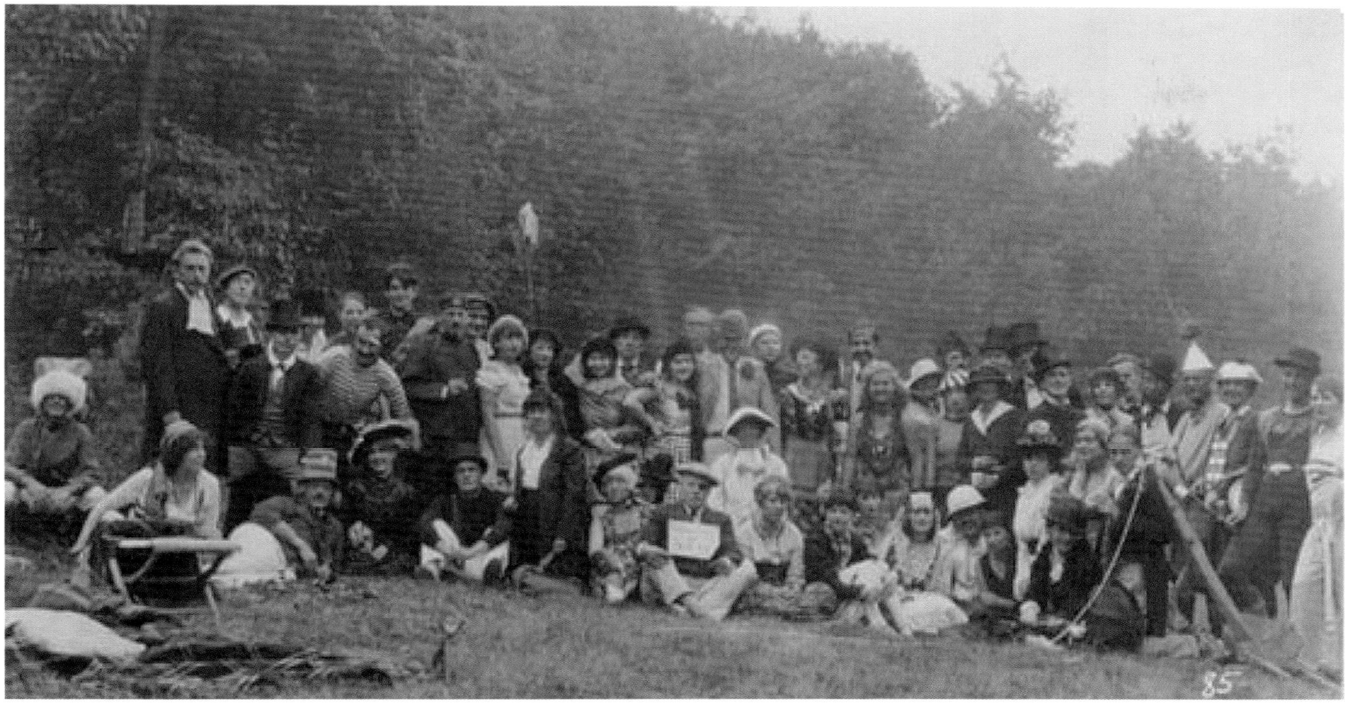

FIG. 32

Maverick revelers, Woodstock, 1929. Ludins is standing on the extreme left. The Gaede/Striebel Archives, Center for Photography at Woodstock Permanent Print Collection. On extended loan to the Samuel Dorsky Museum of Art, State University of New York at New Paltz.

Hayes Miller.[2] Because of his own interest in landscape, Ludins became closest to Tucker, a portraitist and landscape painter whose use of intense color, pulsating forms, and undulating brushstrokes showed his indebtedness to the innovations of Monet and Van Gogh. Tucker was an old friend of Robert Henri and Ernest Lawson, both members of The Eight and fighters for artistic independence against exclusionary exhibition policies that favored academic artists. Through these connections, Tucker moved into the thick of progressive art movements.[3] In 1910 he was in the Independent Artists exhibition, and he was a charter member of the Association of American Painters and Sculptors, the artists' group that organized the Armory Show. He began teaching at the League in 1921, and Ludins eventually became the monitor for his class.[4]

Whereas Tucker was an open-minded liberal, Boardman Robinson, who taught drawing and painting at the League from 1919 to 1930, was an avowed socialist. Robinson, who worked as a cartoonist for *The Masses*, *The Liberator*, and *The New Masses*, went to Europe to report on World War I with the radical journalist John Reed, and he illustrated the book that resulted. The forceful line and expressionist distortions in his drawings as well as his left-wing political sympathies were compatible with Ludins's own emerging sense of social engagement.

Kenneth Hayes Miller, an urban genre painter, was best known for his images of middle-class women in workaday interactions. Miller, who taught at the League from 1911 to 1951, was one of the school's most popular instructors, and many of Ludins's future friends in Woodstock, including Arnold Blanch, Lucile Blanch, Yasuo Kuniyoshi, and Katherine Schmidt, were also his students.

With the reputations of its teachers and the variety of its pupils, the Art Students League was a fertile incubator for any young mind, but in Ludins's case, the progress of his career was immeasurably enhanced by his instructors' firm enmeshment with the Whitney Studio Club, one of the predecessor organizations of the Whitney Museum of American Art. The brainchild of the sculptor and art patron Gertrude Vanderbilt Whitney and the woman who directed all of her art activities, Juliana Rieser Force, the Club was founded in early 1918 in Greenwich Village as a place for young artists to meet, relax, and exhibit their work. In addition to established artists, those just starting out and even pupils at the League were asked to join because its teachers were so close to Whitney and Force. John Sloan, who had received his first one-person show in 1916 at the Whitney Studio (an exhibition space begun by Whitney and Force in 1914 that existed concomitantly with the Club) and had painted Force's portrait that same year, announced the Club's existence in his classes. Dorothy Varian, a Sloan student and another future Woodstock resident, learned about it from him and became one of the first to be affiliated with the Club. Similarly, Miller, who was given a solo show at the Club in 1918, encouraged his large following of students to sign up.

Allen Tucker was as intimately connected to the Whitney art organizations as any artist in its history. He exhibited at the Whitney Studio in 1914, had a one-person exhibition at the Club in 1918, and was a trusted art advisor to Force and Whitney. He was known for his generosity to other artists, and his word was enough to guarantee admission to the Club: it was he who made it possible for Ludins to join. Ludins himself admitted that he became a member

> through friendship, through personality. It happened that Allen Tucker... liked me very much. Forbes Watson [an art critic and Force's lover] was his best friend and Forbes Watson had a great deal of influence. That's how I got into the Club. I had accomplished nothing at that time. I was just a student.[5]

Ludins became a member of the Whitney Studio Club in 1925, the same year as Edmund Archer (another Tucker student) and Karl Free, two painters who were hired as assistant curators when the Club was reorganized as a museum in 1930.[6] Although it was true that Ludins had no standing as an artist then, Force and Whitney were willing to encourage any young person with a hint of merit. Indeed, the women were insistent on helping unheralded artists who did not have dealers and were not yet accepted by officialdom. They were inclusionary and fallible, extending sympathies to a broad spectrum of aesthetic stances. Whitney and Force were champions of artists without prospects. Accordingly, their influence on American art in the 1920s cannot be overestimated. The Museum of Modern Art had not been born, the Metropolitan Museum of Art was a closed brotherhood, the National Academy of Design was in the hands of reactionaries, the government gave no help to living artists, and society at large placed no value on their work. For the young and uncredentialed, the Whitney Studio Club, where their pictures were bought and their exhibition careers born, was their only hope. Woodstock painter Lucile Blanch, whom Force sent to Europe, said of her,

> She was interested in our opinions and differences of opinion, and you could never get away with hedging with her. ...She would quicken bodily when the discussion heated up. She allied herself with our generation, and we bloomed because of her and her connection with Mrs. Whitney. Otherwise who knows what our destinies may have been.[7]

Ludins was one of those artists who directly benefited and bloomed. His paintings were in the 1925, 1926, 1927, and 1928 members' annuals held at the Club, and thus he established an exhibition record. He also would have seen the one-person shows given to fellow members Andrew Dasburg, John Flannagan, Jan Matulka, Glenn O. Coleman, Reuben Nakian, and Stuart Davis.[8] More important, Ludins came to Force's attention. As the dispenser of Whitney patronage, she was an indispensable ally.

Because he had entered the Whitney circle, even Ludins's eventual decision to leave New York City did not have dire consequences for his career. After finishing his studies at the League, he began visiting Woodstock, New York, during the summers of 1927 and 1928. Woodstock, a small town in the Catskills, was the headquarters of a well-publicized artists' colony that began its life in 1902, when a small group of idealists established a commune for painters and artisans who would attempt to live by the social and aesthetic ideas proposed by John Ruskin and William Morris. The colony was given a great boost four years later, when the Art Students League opened a summer school there. Because of its rural setting and cheapness—the founders built primitive cottages for artists, who were allowed to live there rent free or for a nominal sum—the area began attracting creative residents. By 1923, well before Ludins arrived, more than one hundred artists lived in the Woodstock area at least part of the year, and myth making was already rampant. As a local writer boasted, "To the map where we find Sèvres, Barbizon, Bayreuth and Kelmscott [is] now to be added—Woodstock."[9]

A principal—and willing—object of this self-advertising was Force, who started spending weekends at Woodstock in the early 1920s. She usually stayed with well-off artists like Eugene Speicher or Charles Rosen and embraced their impecunious colleagues. Thereafter, most of them showed at the Whitney Studio Club. Many of the artists in the colony had talent or promise, and Force would have had to be obtuse and mistaken to ignore them all. However, a Woodstock address did seem to ensure privileged treatment.[10] Because Force was one of the rare persons who did buy art, her visits there resembled an imperial processional. When she was about to arrive in town, the powerful Woodstock grapevine passed along the news, and the invitations would pour in.

The sculptor Hannah Small, who would wed Ludins in 1937, preceded him to Woodstock because she lived there with her first husband, Austin Mecklem, to whom she was married from 1923 to 1933. Recalling the excitement that Force's visits brought, Small said,

> In those days, we had a wonderful telegraph operator and postmistress who took a personal interest in all the artists. As soon as she knew Mrs. Force was coming, she'd get into her Model T and drive madly through town, waving the telegram and blowing her horn. As we ran outside, she would yell, "Mrs. Force is IMMINENT!" That would be the signal to bring out our work. We were all very poor, and the ones who grabbed her first often got the best of it.[11]

In an essay tracing the art colony's history, Karal Ann Marling stated, "While Woodstock was not the creation of the organization, the national prestige of Woodstock modernism in the decade just prior to the Depression rested heavily on Mrs. Force's enthusiastic support."[12]

On October 29, 1929, the day the stock market crashed, Ludins moved permanently to Woodstock. Arnold Blanch had persuaded Hervey White, one of the original founders of the Woodstock colony, to build Ludins a small cabin that would join the other houses for artists on the grounds of White's farm on the southern slope of Ohayo Mountain. This area of town became known as the Maverick, and it was where the youngest and poorest of the artists lived in pine-board shacks without electricity, heat, running water, or plumbing until they could afford a place with basic comforts. In Ludins's words,

> I got fed up with New York, and I'd been coming here summers, living in town, and I suddenly got the idea that this is where I wanted to live. Arnold Blanch got me to meet Hervey, and Hervey said, "We'll build you a house." Well, the houses they built were pretty primitive, made out of old slabs and things, but they all had beautiful studio windows and a nice fireplace. So he had this house built for me where I wanted it, he asked me how I wanted it and I told him, and then he came over as I was moving my stuff in, and he said to me, "Now Gene, this is a business proposition. Starting today you owe me a hundred dollars a year. That is, if you have it." That was typical of him.[13]

Ludins was not alone on the Maverick, and the homesteading spirit of White's colony appealed to his sense of camaraderie (fig. 32). Besides Arnold and Lucile Blanch, his early neighbors were Harry Gottlieb and Eugenie Gershoy, Carl Walters, Flannagan, and Austin Mecklem and Hannah Small. Ludins himself was joined by Mary Holland, a young artist who lived with him for about two years and whose sleeping figure is visible in the bed in Ludins's painting, *Maverick Studio* (fig. 33). The winters were especially harsh in the rough Maverick cabins, and the deprivations only worsened with the onset of the Depression. But Force made several buying trips to Woodstock to alleviate the artists' plight. In October 1930, Ludins said, "Hermon More [a summer resident of Woodstock whom Force had appointed as head curator of the Whitney museum] and Mrs. Force came up one day, and the door was locked, so they climbed through the window and bought a picture. They left a note."[14] *Landscape* (fig. 34), the canvas that Force purchased, is an uneasy blend of local and fantastical elements. The foreground seems to depict the Rondout, a Hudson River port that was part of the city of Kingston, whereas the background features an imaginary Roman aqueduct and terraced hills.

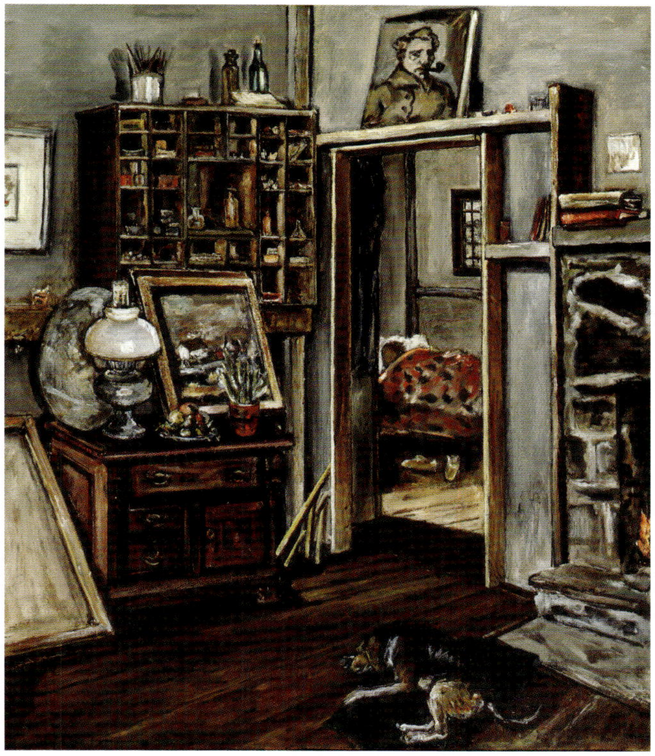

FIG. 33 (CAT. 11)

Maverick Studio

1931, oil on canvas
36 x 32 in.
Estate of Eugene Ludins.
Photo John Kleinhans

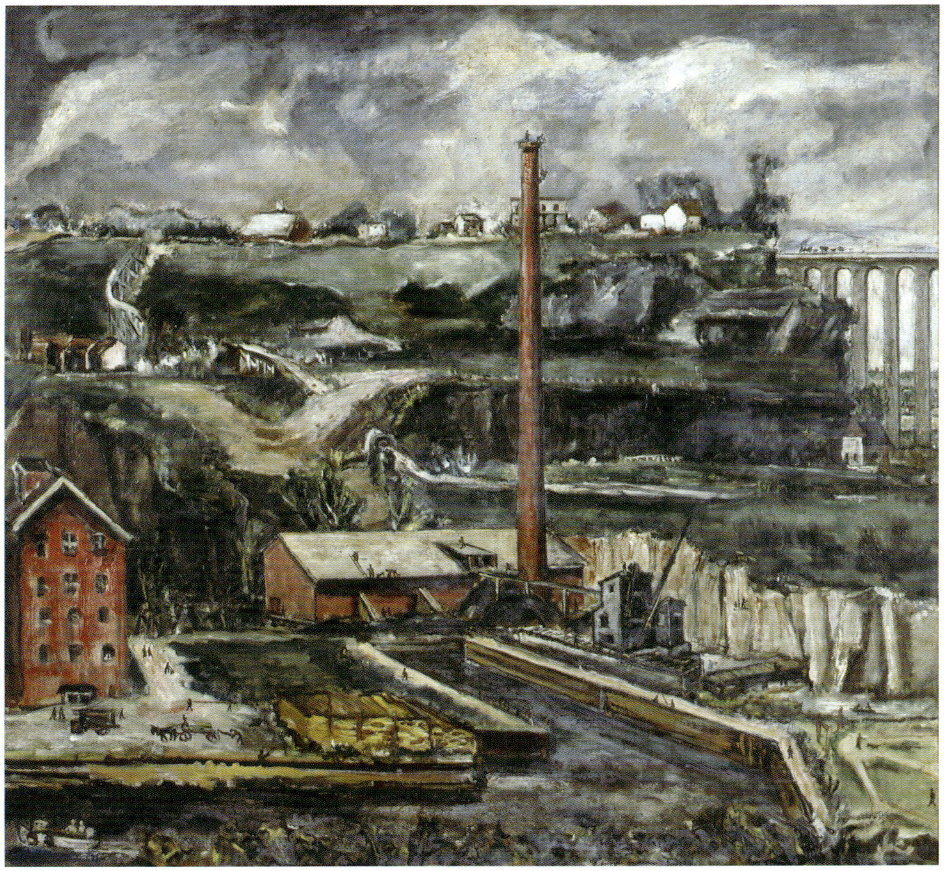

FIG. 34 (CAT. 10)

Landscape

1930, oil on canvas
30¼ x 33 in.
Whitney Museum of American Art, New York; purchase (31.286).

Landscape was Ludins's first museum sale, and the $250 that he received for the painting would have kept him going for several months. As the Depression wore on, Force found other ways to help him. Ludins's father gave him a luxurious Pierce-Arrow car that he could no longer afford,[15] and with it he became an informal car service for Force. As Ludins recalled, "When she wanted to come to Woodstock, she would send me a note to come and get her. She paid me wonderfully for that. Then she'd forget her bag and she'd write to me to make a trip to New York with her bag and I was paid for that. That sort of thing was very graciously done all the time."[16] Through occasional errands from Force and Ludins's own skills as a carpenter—he became a skilled frame maker and made frames for wealthier artists like Speicher and Murray Hoffman—he was able to eke out a living during his first years in Woodstock.

In 1932 Ludins and Hannah Small fell in love with each other. Small left Mecklem to be with Ludins, and her divorce became final in July 1933. The couple made a brief visit to Lake George, New York, where Small's family—wealthy German-Jews who were cousins of Alfred Stieglitz—had summer property.[17] Afterward they left for Santa Fe, New Mexico, for a one-year stay. In Ludins's and Small's retelling of their story in later life, they represented themselves as "running off to Santa Fe" because they "felt it wouldn't be seemly to re-appear in Woodstock immediately after the divorce," although their bohemian friends would have taken the scandal in stride and accepted them, especially after Mecklem found happiness with an art student who became his second wife in 1936. When Small lived in Santa Fe, she was known as Hannah Ludins, even though she and Ludins were not married—and would not be—until August 9, 1937. The couple represented themselves as married, and would continue to do so, presumably for respectability as well as convenience, in both Santa Fe and Woodstock, for the next four years.

Within a few months of Ludins's and Small's arrival in Santa Fe, the annals of American art patronage were forever transformed. Many artists were destitute or on the verge of it because their services were the first to be dispensed with in a moribund economy. On March 4, 1933, Franklin D. Roosevelt took office as President of the United States, and he was determined to pass legislation designed to bring economic recovery to the Depression-ravaged populace. At first, no provision was made for artists in the alphabet soup of jobs, agencies, and other relief measures of the New Deal, but by the end of 1933 the unprecedented first effort to put artists on the national payroll and keep them in their chosen profession was initiated. A short-term experiment lasting from December 1933 to June 1934, the Public Works of Art Project (PWAP) was set up to aid nearly four thousand artists working in all genres in all sections of the country. Artists were paid a set sum of money a week; in return, they gave the work they produced to the federal government. In Santa Fe, Small was put on the project, and she carved two sandstone sculptures that were allotted to the Santa Fe Public Library. They remain there to this day. Ludins, however, was not accepted, because, Small recalled in 1938, "His paintings showed no understanding of the [New] Mexican landscape, we were told."[18]

Despite his rejection by art officials in Santa Fe, Ludins was a fervent New Dealer who understood the larger political situation. He saw that artists—who are historically resistant to hierarchies and authorities—needed to take innovative steps and band together for a better chance at survival. Ludins and Small returned to Woodstock during the fall of 1934. Small, who owned a small island in Lake George (a present from her parents), sold it so that she and Ludins could move off the Maverick and have a larger and more comfortable place to live. In January 1935, Small bought a house and land in Zena, a wooded area within the boundaries of Woodstock, which the couple kept until their deaths.

In March 1935, shortly after settling in Zena, Ludins and Small, along with their friend Wendell Jones and four other artists, started a cooperative gallery called the Sawkill Painters and Sculptors. All seven pooled their money to rent a house on Tannery Brook, in the center of Woodstock, and close by the more established Woodstock Artists Association. The gallery opening in June featured a number of Maverick artists' paintings, sculptures, and works on paper. Paintings were offered for as little as $15.00.[19] Within two weeks of the opening, eighteen sales had been made; by the end of the year, sixty exhibitors were on the roster, and more than eighty works had been sold.[20] The Sawkill group recorded a second successful season in 1936, and Ludins was lauded in the press as one of the gallery's outstanding exhibitors. That year the Woodstock Artists Association awarded Ludins its annual Elisha Keith Memorial Prize for being the colony's most promising artist under thirty-five. The Sawkill venture was so successful that it was able to launch traveling exhibitions and hire someone to publicize them. The gallery's viability led to the ultimate local seal of approval—it was absorbed by the Artists Association in 1938. Moreover, the cooperative's effectiveness instructed Ludins and other artists in the virtues of collective action.

A month after the Sawkill Painters and Sculptors opened for business, a speaker from the New York City Artists' Union visited Woodstock. Ulster County artists and craft workers were invited to a mass meeting on July 24, 1935, to organize and lobby for jobs and money for unemployed artists. More than one hundred artists attended, and the Ulster County Artists' League was formed, with Harry Gottlieb as temporary chair. (Gottlieb was shortly to move to New York City.) The purpose of the union was to provide jobs for all artists, and when an executive committee was named to write a constitution and membership regulations, Ludins was on it.[21]

The second major government relief project—the Federal Art Project of the Works Progress Administration (WPA/FAP)—was inaugurated in August 1935, and Ulster County artists, who resided primarily in Woodstock, were first hired in November. Because there were so many artists, the Woodstock project was second only to New York City in volume. During its early years, there were as many as fifty-five artists on the payroll, which was larger than the employment totals of some entire regions in the South and Midwest. The project supervisor was the painter and muralist Judson Smith; he was in charge of hiring and firing and making sure that project artists were meeting their monthly quotas of work. The artists' monthly salaries varied between $77.00 and $84.70, and approximately forty artists were employed.[22] Ludins was hired as a non-relief artist in 1935 and was represented in a local FAP exhibition in October 1936.[23] Small, however, was not considered eligible for inclusion. It was highly unusual in a two-artist family for both to be allowed jobs, and the choice was almost always decided in favor of the man. Furthermore, since economic relief was a paramount factor in being selected for employment, Small was considered too well off to qualify, because she had a private income of $60.00 a month.[24]

Eventually, because of Small's income and his occasional sales from frame making, Ludins was dismissed from the project when the quota of non-relief artists was cut. Ironically, if he had pressed the matter by revealing that he and Small were not legally married and the property they owned was not in his name, he might have been able to pass the means test and could have continued on the FAP.

Unlike the PWAP, which was designated a temporary measure from the outset, the FAP was indefinite in tenure, but there was no guarantee of steady appointment. Payroll allocations were irregular, and the number of employed positions arbitrarily rose and fell according to budgetary instability and constant sabotage by Republican politicians bent on curtailing the WPA's cultural programs by cutting their funding. Because of these political issues, artists were often dismissed for what they considered unfair or irrational reasons, and then re-appointed when monies were processed. As Ludins recalled, negotiating became imperative:

> When it [the FAP] started, the government was so anxious to put money into circulation that ... [it] would hire indiscriminately. There were no relief standards. So anybody who was an artist who wanted a job would get one. Then it began to constrict, and money got short. Then it became a question of who do you save, the artists or the needy? Who goes and who doesn't? Well, this is where collective bargaining came into it. It got very tough. Who do you fire, the good artist or the guy with ten kids?[25]

In 1936 the Ulster County Artists' League ceased to exist, and a successor organization took its place. The Ulster County Artists' Union, which was affiliated with the national Artists' Union (founded in New York City in 1933), was dedicated to applying pressure to the WPA administration to sustain and expand government employment to needy artists through demonstrations, delegations, and petitions.[26] By June 1936, its new president was Ludins, whose previous history in obtaining economic gains for his peers meant that he was adept at stating less articulate artists' cases with force and tenacity. (Not surprisingly, the reorganized union's other officers were also in the Sawkill group.[27]) And Ludins had further credentials of militancy when it came to artists' welfare. He was one of the original one hundred ten artists who signed the published call for the first meeting of the American Artists' Congress, which took place from February 14-16, 1936, in New York City, with about three hundred sixty artist-delegates attending.[28]

In early June 1936, as Ulster County's union president, Ludins requested national authorities in Washington to place a destitute artist on the project who had fulfilled residence requirements.[29] In August, he and several other artists in the union met with Audrey McMahon, the flinty FAP director of the New York region, and Judson Smith to demand that Woodstock artists be paid the same as those in New York City and receive workman's compensation.[30] In December 1936, McMahon was ordered to lay off non-relief personnel because Congressional appropriations were running out. Union artists in New York City responded with a sensationally publicized (especially by Republican newspapers in New York and Ulster County) strike; in Woodstock, Ludins and three other artists not on relief were dismissed from the FAP.[31] After he was laid off, Ludins bought a car, and he and Small left for a few months in Mexico and the American Southwest. This display of affluence, as well as his deserting the scene for a pleasanter climate, angered some Woodstock artists, even ones in the union.[32]

On March 4, 1937, Judson Smith submitted his resignation as supervisor of the Ulster County FAP and hoped to be gone within a month. The job of supervisor was taxing, and Smith had not been able to do his own work while he held it. McMahon needed to find a successor immediately, and she offered the job to painter John W. Taylor, but he declined.[33] Recently returned from Mexico, Ludins, her second choice, accepted the position. McMahon saw no inconsistency in selecting him as a government administrator despite his presidency of a union that was usually her adversary. In fact, Ludins's familiar presence in her office boosted his candidacy. McMahon knew that he was devoted to the economic advancement of the Woodstock colony, had analyzed his manner of negotiating grievances, and sized him up as a good leader. Furthermore, Ludins had been on the FAP himself for more than a year, so he had experienced the anxieties and uncertainties of government employment from the artist's side.

But if McMahon harbored no bitterness for past clashes, the artists of Woodstock were another story. Twenty-one of thirty artists then on the Ulster County FAP[34] immediately protested Ludins's appointment and demanded his ouster. They announced their opposition in a letter to McMahon that was reprinted in the April 1, 1937, issue of the *Ulster County News* and the April 2 issue of *The Overlook*. The letter was signed by one Gus Schrader, the chief accuser and chair of the anti-Ludins faction. In attacks that went on for weeks, Schrader and his followers said that Ludins was unfit for the office, but they would not state why, nor would they divulge the names of the other signers of the letter. Ludins believed that envy was involved. "I think it had to do with some jealousy, because of the money that went with it," he recalled.

> I was on the project, but I got fired because I was too rich. But when I was appointed—the workers on the project got $18.00 a week, and I got $50.00 a week, plus driving expenses. ... The thing was that one of ... [their own] had been pushed ahead. And particularly one who had stuck his neck out—on that union thing. I led that union thing. I started it.[35]

Union partisanship was a more potent danger to Ludins than he noted. After McMahon appointed him, the jubilant officers of the Ulster County Artists' Union telegraphed their endorsement to her, and reactionary elements in the local community—townspeople and artists alike—erroneously concluded that the telegram led McMahon to give him the job. The citizenry of Woodstock in general was hostile to the local artists' union because it borrowed aggressive labor-union tactics and because they were sure it was Communist-controlled. There is no question that the national Artists' Union and the Artists' Congress were initiated and heavily supported by members of the Communist Party (then a legal political entity in the United States), but Communist artists did not dominate the union, nor did the Party "exercise a sinister or politically subversive influence" on it.[36]

As the head of the Ulster County Artists' Union, Ludins personified a Communist threat to poor and provincial townspeople in a conservative Republican area, and it hardly seemed to matter that he resigned from the union as soon as he agreed to become supervisor. Ludins obviously had left-wing sympathies, as did many artists and intellectuals who were disillusioned with a system that had held out so little economic promise to them.[37] And, as a Jew, he would have been particularly outraged by Nazi policies toward Jews and Communists—he probably saw Russia as a bulwark against Fascism. But Ludins was not a Communist, and he was too independent to be a "stooge"[38] for a Communist-front organization, as his enemies alleged.

More savage in their denunciations of Ludins than any reactionary locals were Schrader plus Emmett Edwards and John Nichols, Schrader's two primary partners in persecution. Both Nichols and Edwards had reputations as anti-Semites.[39] Nichols, who had been in the Sawkill group, was materially helped by Ludins's entrepreneurial skills and had been an officer in the defunct Ulster County Artists' League. Schrader, the ringleader, had the most to lose with Ludins in charge. He was deeply insecure, because an excellent case could be made that he shouldn't have received government relief as an artist at all. Before living in Woodstock, Schrader had been a carpenter, and when he moved to the colony in the early 1930s, he made a living as a house-painter and repairman. By his own admission, his first foray into fine art occurred when he found some abandoned paints and brushes and painted a picture on some old oilcloth. Schrader then took a painting class with Judson Smith, and he bartered the fee by painting Smith's house and having his wife work for Smith as a part-time secretary. This ten-week class was his entire art training. Nevertheless, Smith put Schrader on the FAP in 1936. Schrader justifiably feared that Ludins would deem him to be unqualified compared to the other deserving professionals without jobs.[40]

In contrast, most of the more competent artists on the project, such as Karl Fortess, Roland Mousseau, Paul Fiene, and Austin Mecklem, were in favor of Ludins becoming supervisor. McMahon, who remained loyal to Ludins, arranged a meeting in Woodstock on April 12, 1937, at the Woodstock Artists Association between Ludins and his foes. The non-union members of the project had chosen a committee of five to represent them at the meeting. It consisted of Schrader, Nichols, Edwards, Harold Clum, and Grant Arnold. Mary Hunt and Ned Thatcher, two other artists against Ludins, also attended.

The Schrader contingent declined to make their objections public, and the confrontation ended with McMahon, who required a police escort for her physical safety, remaining committed to her choice. For appearance's sake, she made Ludins's appointment provisional. But McMahon held her ground and, after a month's probation, the job was his.

In the meantime, Schrader, Nichols, and Edwards were busy trying to halt the inevitable with unsubstantiated allegations. On April 19, 1937, they wrote jointly signed letters to all important WPA officials, calling Ludins's potential investiture "a dangerous situation." They alleged that on "the recommendation of the Communist led Ulster County Artists Union, a Communist agitator and organizer who is in constant communication with the New York Communist organizations has been appointed as supervisor" over massive protests.[41]

Judson P. Philips, who wrote a weekly column called "Art-fully Speaking" for *The Overlook*, was disgusted by the smear campaign and disillusioned by the behavior of the artists involved. Although he had initially been anti-union, he declared,

> Only out of this mess two figures have appeared who are still clothed with dignity, and these two figures are Judson Smith ... and Eugene Ludins....
>
> In the face of treachery on the part of friends [Nichols] who led him to believe that he had their support, in the face of a concerted opposition to his appointment which has laid him open to a shocking amount of unbridled rumor and abuse, in the face of the dilatory tactics on the part of the New York office which on the surface appear to have left him holding an untenable position without adequate support, Mr. Ludins has shown a high degree of coolness, of good sense, of reserve. ... He has restrained some of his more ardent supporters ... from staging a counter attack of any sort.
>
> .... The artist is an interpreter of life and of nature, and I think I always expected a larger and more human view of things from him than I did from the ordinary man in the street. If one has any illusions about the position of the artist in society, Woodstock is the place to get over them. It seems that here, at least, the artist has a greater capacity for pettiness, for jealousy, for envy, for gossip, than the ordinary man.[42]

For her part, McMahon wrote a detailed report to Holger Cahill, the national director of the FAP, on the controversy, and Cahill discussed it with Harry Hopkins, the director of the entire WPA and one of Roosevelt's chief advisors. Both men agreed that appointing Ludins as project supervisor for thirty days was the right tactic. In a brief note to his aide, Cahill concluded, "I see no reason for all the fuss."[43]

After his thirty-day probation was over, Ludins quietly took up his position and went to work. He processed paperwork, distributed supplies, conferred with artists about the assignments that were due, guided them toward assignments that would fit specific locations, collected them, and found tax-exempt institutions that would hang them. This last duty—allocation—was one of the most onerous because it was inseparable from politics. In Hudson, New York, a beloved high school principal had just died, and Ludins ingeniously devised a role for a project artist. As he remembered,

> I told them [the educational authorities] we were equipped to paint a portrait of this fellow, and that it would cost them $7.00—the cost of the frame and the paint and the canvas. They held a meeting and said, 'We'll let you know.' I drove all the way to Hudson and back at my own expense to present the case. I had to go there five times! They finally accepted it. It was a great success, finally. But it was a Republican community, and they were god damned if they were going to.... When I got up there to deliver it, the janitor met me. I unwrapped it and showed it to him, and he wept. It was so touching to him, the spitting image of this great man. But that was the situation at the time—Roosevelt was hated, and everything he touched was hated. It was a political situation.[44]

While Ludins still had to face jobless artists and members of his former union, who never stopped pressing for permanent and expanded employment, he was also able to hand out a plum assignment. Twelve American artists were chosen to spend six months in Alaska producing landscapes for the Department of the Interior, and three of them were from Woodstock. Ludins liked to joke that he "exiled" Fortess, Mecklem, and Mousseau to the Arctic, but these jobs were prestigious ones with a higher salary, and it did not go unnoticed that the three painters chosen were Ludins's close friends and supporters.

In June 1937, four artists had to be laid off to meet a 25 percent reduction in payroll. Ludins was supposed to select them, but, because his position was still precarious, McMahon made the cuts to protect him.[45] Thus Ludins avoided accusations of revenge after McMahon chose Schrader, who was on the non-relief quota, for dismissal. But John Hurt, another fired artist, retaliated with red-baiting and America-First rhetoric. He complained to Washington that the Ulster County FAP was run "for the benefit of the Red party." He branded Ludins "a Red dictator" and called a German-born artist still on the project "one of the Red group." Hurt's own family, he noted, had served "in every war this nation has ever had.... [f]rom 1776 on down."[46] Because the atmosphere in Woodstock remained poisonous, McMahon in New York and officials in Washington continued to shield Ludins whenever they could. They dealt not only with the hate mail, but also with the many pleas and complaints made by Ulster County artists dismissed from their jobs or about to lose them.

Ludins did not paint much during his tenure as an FAP administrator, because his duties left him no time for sustained concentration on his own work, but it is tempting to speculate that *Rotten Foundations* (fig. 35), created in 1938, is a symbolic distillation of local chaos as well as a warning of global corruption and conflict. Ludins shows us a divided population living in caves of small-minded isolation amid explosions of resentment in a mire of shifting sands. The scene might stand for the turbulence in his own life as much as a meditation on the implications of the Spanish Civil War and the rising imperialism of Germany.

In May 1938 Holger Cahill traveled to Woodstock to announce that funds for the Ulster County FAP that were supposed to expire in July would be extended for the rest of the year. He made the trip to shore up Ludins and deflect future agitation. However, Ludins, as well as other WPA personnel, had to face the continuing gibes and complaints by Woodstock natives that artists were malingering bums idling at government expense. Perhaps he presciently sensed that educational programs aimed at lay people rather than creative work satisfying art professionals would be received more positively, especially in the rural sections of the county. In the summer of 1938, Ludins conceived the Art Caravan, a compact circulating teaching and exhibition unit that he later characterized as the highest achievement of his tenure as a supervisor (figs. 36–38). In some ways, the original idea was rooted in yet another enterprising instance of self-help by the Sawkill Painters and Sculptors, but its practicality and impetus for social betterment were pure Ludins. The Art Caravan was, most importantly, participatory. If the populace couldn't come to see the art FAP workers produced, the art would come to them.

Under Ludins, the Sawkill Painters and Sculptors had devised a roving art unit by stocking a trailer that one of its members owned. The trailer went to nearby Ellenville and several other upstate towns to attract new audiences.[47] The Sawkill group's outreach was for commercial purposes, but Ludins saw that it could be adapted for the FAP. A portable exhibition could heighten public awareness of the WPA, integrate artists into the community, and encourage interest in the arts in places where no one had ever seen an original piece of art, let alone an exhibition. Ludins proposed a clever and economical design. An old World War I Army ambulance was refitted to carry sixty works of art, folding standards on which to hang paintings, screens for

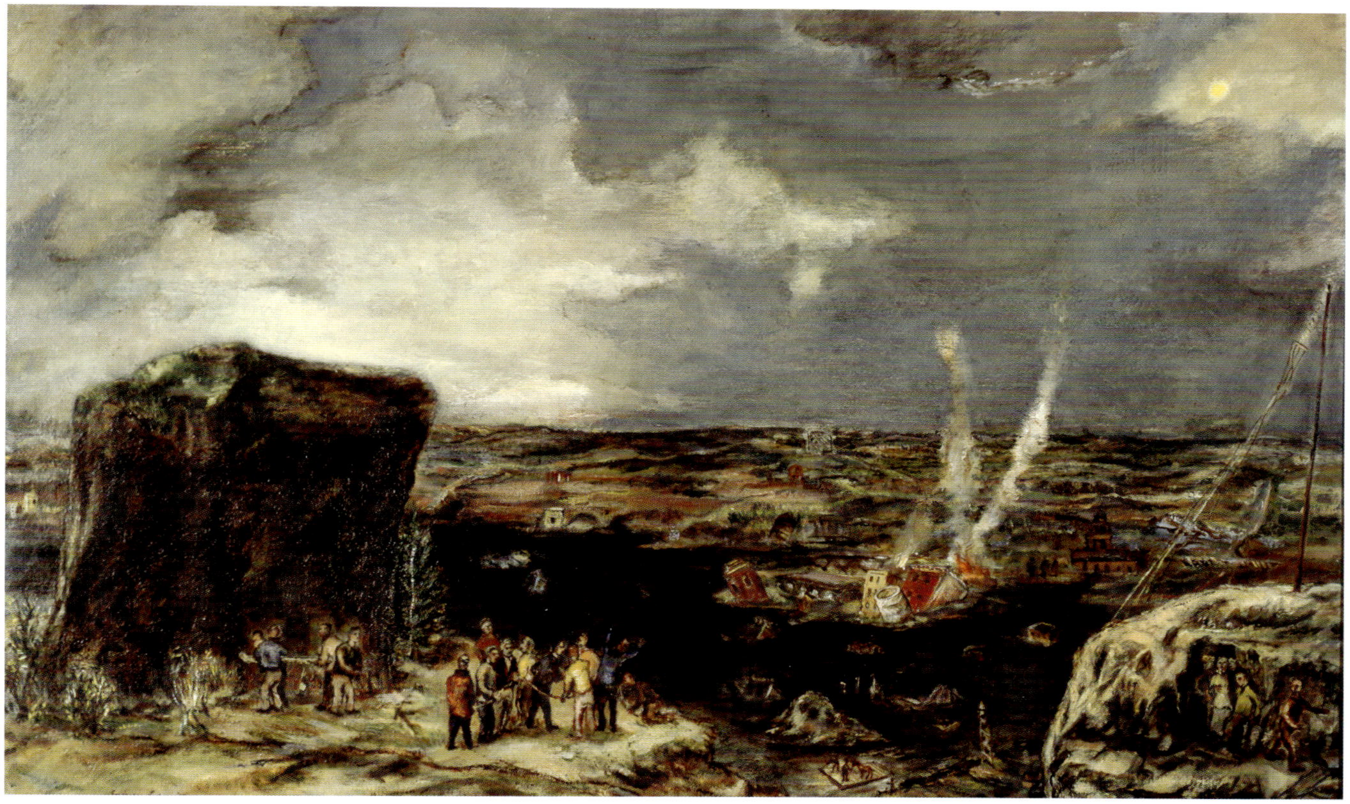

FIG. 35 (CAT.23)
Rotten Foundations
1938, oil on canvas
30 x 50 in.
Estate of Eugene Ludins.
Photo John Kleinhans

works on paper, boxes for displaying sculpture, movie projectors, films, slides, and other paraphernalia (fig. 36). "The entire exhibition," Ludins explained, "could be unloaded from the truck and set up in little more than an hour."[48]

The caravan made rounds of visits to small towns within a reasonable distance from each other. The truck would be unpacked at a square, school, or library, and the works of art would be on view for the day, weather permitting (figs. 37–38). At night, there would be a lecture and discussion, after which the caravan would depart for the next town.[49] Two men operated the caravan; one drove and set up the exhibit, and the other gave talks to passersby during the day and the formal lecture indoors at night.

From September 1938 to January 1939, the caravan toured with Ludins and Judson Smith, who had returned to the FAP in May 1938. They made trips to Albany, Saranac Lake, Potsdam, and Canton, New York, before the winter weather made touring and outdoor shows impossible. Smith then resigned again from the project. When the caravan resumed its travels in April 1939, Smith's successor was the artist and author Kaj Klitgaard, who was Ludins's personal choice. Klitgaard, an articulate and sophisticated man, was an excellent explainer and lecturer, and he was given the title of traveling supervisor. Before long, Ludins no longer went on the tours. He trusted Klitgaard and, besides, he still had his regular tasks as a supervisor. From May through July, Klitgaard filed detailed narratives on the popularity, reception, and utility of the caravan, and recommendations for future programs, while on a twenty-four-city tour that took him through New York State, New Jersey, and eastern Pennsylvania. Along with the exhibitions, the caravan also ignited enthusiasm for community art centers and extension galleries, which FAP administrators hoped would soon become a reality.

In February 1939, Ludins was offered the job of New York State supervisor for the entire Hudson Valley area, which gave him jurisdiction over a third of the state.[50] This reclassification was a byproduct of bureaucratic infighting during which Republican officials successfully began dismantling the FAP by moving it from the federal

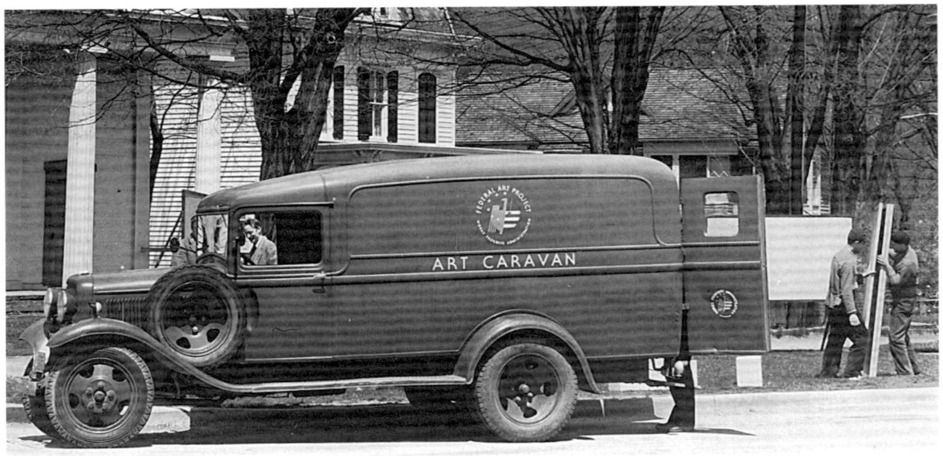

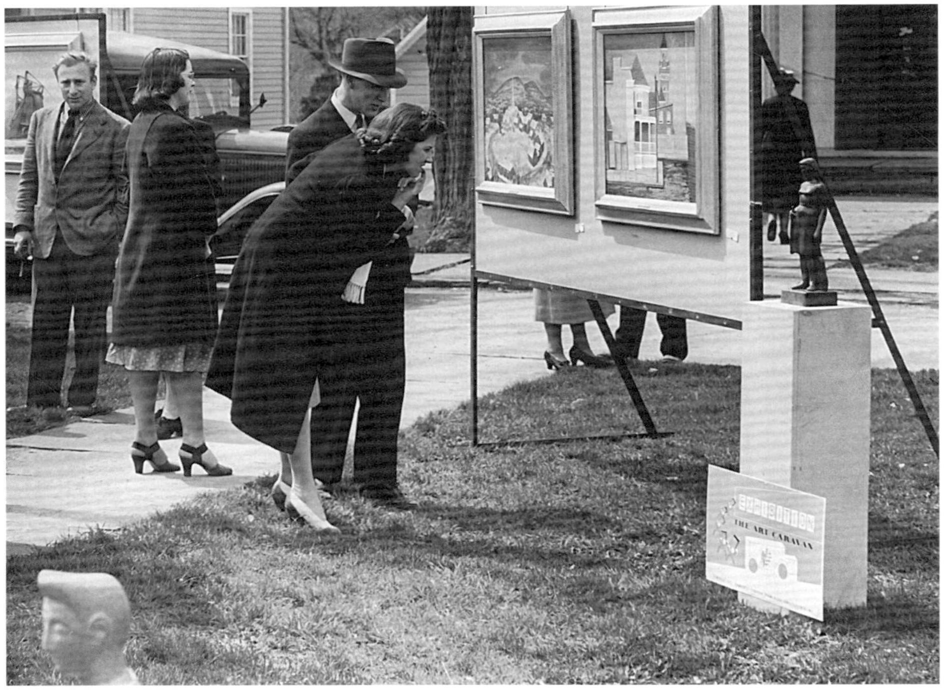

FIG. 36

The Art Caravan on Woodstock's Village Green. Estate of Eugene Ludins.

FIG. 37

Ludins on the extreme left viewing the caravan's traveling exhibition on the Woodstock Green. Estate of Eugene Ludins.

Democratic administration to the Republican state jurisdiction. Under state authority, any art project had to have a guaranteed 25 percent local sponsorship before the state would provide the rest of the appropriation. (Before, when the projects were under federal control, the government contributed 100 percent of the money for artists' salaries and materials.)

Ludins thus had to plead with local businesses, churches, and other institutions for aid, largely in vain. Most Ulster County politicians thought that the art projects were a waste of taxpayers' money; as a result, the relief funds shrank and more artists were laid off. Because they equated artists with Communist radicals, the municipal office holders in Woodstock remained opposed to artists receiving government salaries, despite the fact that their paychecks were spent in local stores. Even the community-minded Art Caravan was disdained. When solicited for help, Woodstock's town supervisor "gave a first-aid box to the ... traveling art show," Ludins stated. "That was the only gesture the town made."[51]

Ludins did not agree to accept the supervisor job until July 1, and he did so with the proviso that he would serve no more than six months. He wished to return to painting, and the working conditions were deteriorating almost daily. But he acceded to McMahon, who needed him to help keep the FAP alive. As she wrote to Washington, "I believe that he [Ludins] will be so valuable to us ... that I hope you will support me in my decision that it is better for us to have him for six months than not at all."[52]

Ludins, however, barely lasted eight weeks, let alone six months. He had to work in Albany rather than out of his house in Woodstock, a change he hated. Then he had to help preside over a humiliating public examination of Emmett Edwards, a chronically slow worker in arrears of paintings owed to the project. Ludins had shielded him for months, despite Edwards's antagonism toward him when he was first appointed in 1937. Edwards prevailed, but the dispute won the artists no friends among state authorities already persuaded that "chiseling" was widespread, and Edwards blamed Ludins for his public ordeal for the rest of his life.[53] In July and August, nineteen other artists received pink slips. On August 1, after a grueling week of twelve-hour days touring Long Island with the Art Caravan, Kaj Klitgaard was terminated because funds were exhausted. The caravan—Ludins's proudest legacy—was unceremoniously retired. Not even McMahon, its other champion, could save it.

The Art Caravan disappeared into history, but the idea behind it is occasionally revived and freshly appraised. In March 2011, Eric Fischl announced a privately funded two-year program for dispatching six specially outfitted eighteen-wheel trucks to cities and towns across the country. Carrying a cargo of art, music, literature, and movie equipment, the rigs are designed to function as portable galleries and performance spaces. "America doesn't usually turn to its artists for help," Fischl commented, "but I actually think it's something that artists do very well."[54]

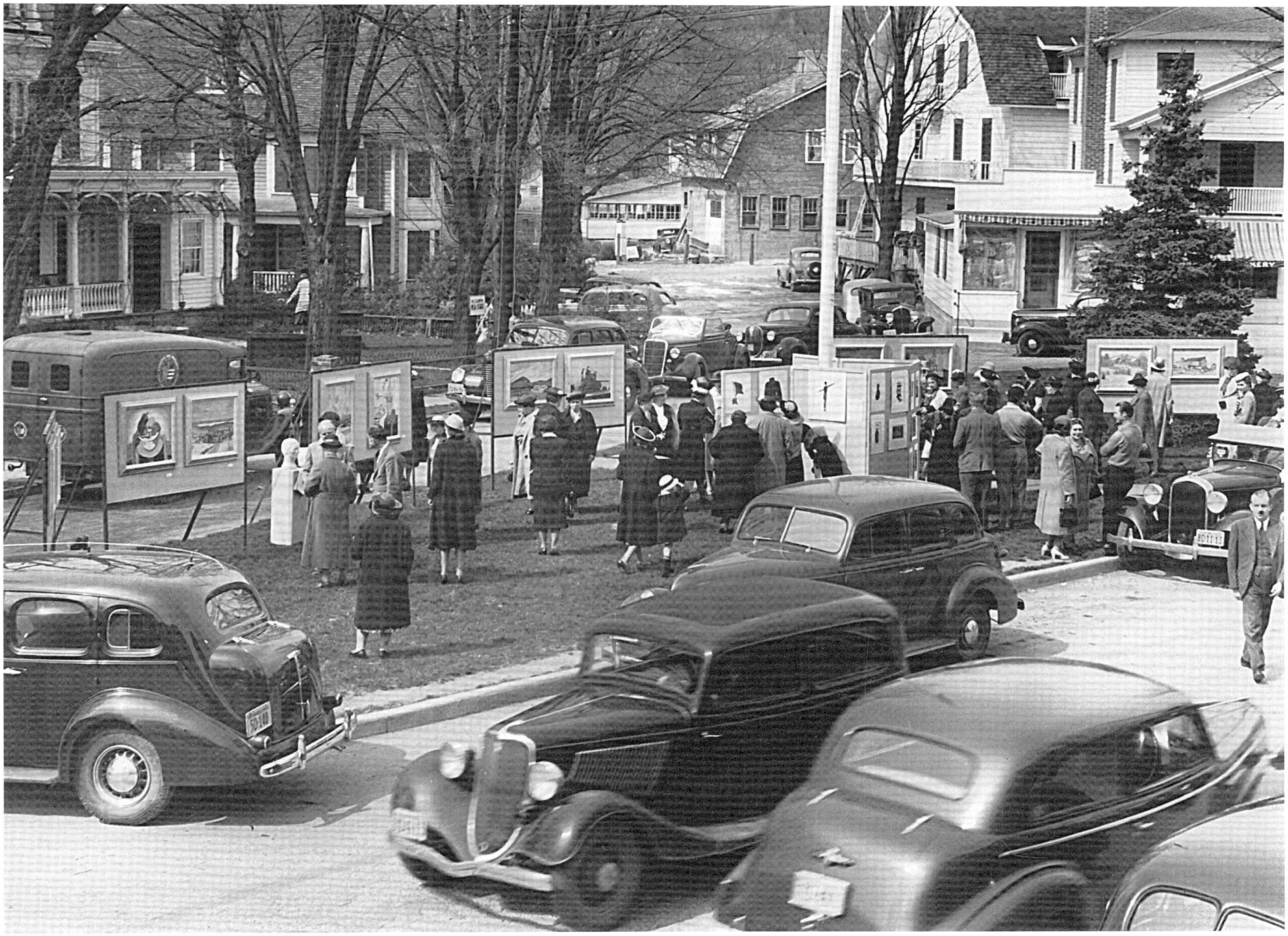

FIG. 38

Viewing the exhibition on the Woodstock Green. Estate of Eugene Ludins.

As for Ludins, neither the curtailment of the Art Caravan nor the paucity of artists to supervise was the final blow. His boss in Albany wanted to put some cronies who were not artists on the project as a quid pro quo for political patronage, and on October 1, 1939, Ludins resigned in disgust. "That was too much," he said. "It had nothing to do with art."[55]

During the 1940s, Ludins continued to paint and exhibit, and in World War II he served in the Pacific as field director for the American Red Cross Ambulance Corps. When he returned, it was as a respected elder of the colony. In 1947 he was elected chair of the Woodstock Artists Association's Board of Directors, and one of his duties was to judge the work of other artists. Less than ten years after Ludins had been execrated for doing his best to assist and evaluate his peers, he was lionized for doing the same thing at Woodstock's most historic art institution.

Acknowledgments and Notes

I am delighted to thank several people without whom I could not have prepared this essay. First, I must commend the warmth and tenacity of Susana Torruella Leval, a trusted friend and the most patient colleague an author could have. Similarly, I am enormously indebted to the generosity and meticulousness of Peter R. Jones, whose knowledge of Eugene Ludins's life and career is matched only by his care and accuracy in sharing it. Emily Jones, the archivist at the Woodstock Artists Association, unstintingly extended herself in locating information on Ludins and other Woodstock artists for me. I also wish to thank Lisa N. Peters, who discussed Allen Tucker's work with me at length; her recent research on the artist, which I have cited below, has educated me.

1 Ludins lasted a week at Cornell University. See Mary Braggiotti, "Married to the Arts," *New York Post* (November 22, 1947).
2 Ludins also studied with Walt Kuhn, but he considered him a poor teacher and an unpleasant personality, and thus he did not respond to him.
3 Unless otherwise stated, all biographical information about Allen Tucker is drawn from Lisa N. Peters, *Allen Tucker: The Force of Emotion—A Post-Impressionist Rediscovered*.
4 Through being Tucker's monitor, Ludins met his best friend and future Woodstock neighbor, Wendell Jones, according to Peter Jones, his son.
5 Ludins, interview with Avis Berman, July 2, 1978.
6 Ludins, interview with Berman, July 2, 1978; Juliana Force and American Art: A Memorial Exhibition, 67, 68.
7 Avis Berman, *Rebels on Eighth Street: Juliana Force and the Whitney Museum of American Art*, 231.
8 *Juliana Force and American Art*, 65.
9 Richard LeGallienne, quoted in Marling, *Woodstock: An American Art Colony, 1902–1977*.
10 Berman, *Rebels on Eighth Street*, 230–231.
11 Hannah Small, interview with Berman, July 2, 1978.
12 Marling, *Woodstock: An American Art Colony*, 1902–1977.
13 Ludins, interview with Karl Fortess, 1985, Woodstock Public Library.
14 Ludins, interview with Berman, July 2, 1978; Juliana Force, letter to Ludins, October 30, 1930; and Ludins, letter to Force, November 1, 1930, Whitney Museum of American Art Archives.
15 David Ludins was a builder and contractor, but there was no call for his services once the Depression set in. He could not maintain such a car, but his son, whose primary expenses were groceries and kerosene for lighting and cooking, could. Thus Eugene Ludins was left in the humorous position of living in an unheated shack while owning a luxurious car. He built a garage to shelter the vehicle, much to the consternation of Hervey White, for whom conspicuous consumption was anathema.
16 Ludins, interview with Berman, July 2, 1978.
17 Small was also related to the American academic sculptor Moses Ezekiel (1844–1917).
18 Quoted in "Work of Hannah Small, Woodstock Sculpture," *Kingston Daily Freeman* (March 4, 1938); "Paintings, Sculpture in Library to Be Shown Sunday," *Santa Fe New Mexican* (July 14, 1934).
19 Gary Alexander, "WPA Painter Ludins Recalls Early Woodstock Days," *Kingston Freeman* (October 21, 1994).
20 Ernest Brace, "Construction Ahead: The Summer in Woodstock, 1935," *American Magazine of Art*, 28 (November 1935), 678; Marling, "Federal Patronage and the Woodstock Colony," 126–128. Dr. Marling's dissertation is an exhaustively researched chronicle of Woodstock patronage and politics, and I have gratefully relied on her documentation of the subject to support my own arguments and conclusions.
21 Marling, "Federal Patronage and the Woodstock Art Colony," 104, 121.
22 Ibid., 135.
23 Ludins showed a landscape painting and a watercolor titled *Catskill Farm* in an exhibition of the Ulster County Federal Art Project on view from October 15–31, 1936, at the Woodstock Art Gallery, according to a

brochure of the exhibition in the Eugene Ludins files, Woodstock Artists Association and Museum Archives.

24 Ludins, interview with Fortess.

25 Ibid.

26 Monroe, "The Artists Union of New York," 206.

27 Marling, "Federal Patronage and the Woodstock Colony," 138.

28 Monroe, "The American Artists Congress and the Invasion of Finland," 15. The congress, chaired by Stuart Davis, aimed to defend artists' interests through collective action. Those interests were defined as improving the economic plight of artists, protesting the suppression and destruction of art works, racial discrimination and the suppression of civil liberties, and sounding the alarm against the growing threat of Fascism in Italy and Germany. Some of the other artists who signed the call were Ivan Albright, Peggy Bacon, Peter Blume, Paul Cadmus, Adolf Dehn, Aaron Douglas, Harry Gottlieb, William Gropper, Yasuo Kuniyoshi, Edward Laning, Doris Lee, Louis Lozowick, Isamu Noguchi, Boardman Robinson, Andrée Ruellan, Ben Shahn, Raphael Soyer, Niles Spencer, and John W. Taylor.

29 Ludins, letter to Holger Cahill, June 6, 1936. roll DC 87, AAA.

30 Marling, "Federal Patronage and the Woodstock Colony," 141.

31 Ibid., 152, 154.

32 Ibid., 179.

33 Audrey McMahon, letter to Cahill, April 22, 1937, roll DC 87, AAA.

34 That Ludins supervised fifty-five artists—a figure that crops up in the literature —has never been substantiated by primary documentation and seems erroneous. However, Smith may have supervised that many people. In 1937, as the protest to McMahon shows, there were thirty artists on the Ulster County project and, although numbers fluctuated, in 1938 approximately thirty-two were registered. Ludins never supervised as many artists as Smith did in 1935–36. Not only were the appropriations lower, but a number of Woodstock artists, including those who qualified for mural work, such as Wendell Jones, Doris Lee, Georgina Klitgaard, and Charles Rosen, were on two other government art projects that he did not manage. See Francis V. O'Connor in his introduction to *The New Deal Art Projects*, 3, for an explanation of the various and concurrent government projects. Also, because the rules were more stringent on the New York State projects than on the ones in New York City, Woodstockers like Dorothy Varian, Eugenie Gershoy, and Arnold Blanch took advantage of Manhattan residency and got on the FAP there.

35 Ludins, interview with Fortess.

36 O'Connor, *Art for the Millions*, 26.

37 Monroe, "The Artists Union of New York," 133.

38 Judson P. Philips, "Philips Interviews 26 Artists," *The Overlook* (April 30, 1937). "Stooge" was the word Schrader applied to Ludins.

39 Audrey McMahon, letter to Cahill, April 22, 1937, roll DC 87, AAA; Marling, "Federal Patronage and the Woodstock Art Colony," 197.

40 "Schrader's Faith in Americans," *Kingston Daily Freeman* (February 10, 1938); Michael Walsh, "Woodstock Artist Gus Schrader," *Woodstock Times* (April 6, 1978). Walsh's article is based on an interview with Schrader, who said that as soon as the economy picked up again before World War II, he went back to the building trade. He did not devote time to painting again until the 1970s. The earlier article also reports that his only art study was the one course he had with Smith.

41 Gus Schrader, Emmett Edwards, and John Nichols, letter to Harry L. Hopkins, April 19, 1937, roll DC 87, AAA.

42 Judson P. Philips, "Art-fully Speaking." *The Overlook*, April 9, 1937.

43 Holger Cahill, undated [April 1937] note to Tom [Thomas C. Parker], roll DC 87, AAA.

44 Ludins, interview with Fortess.

45 See, for example, "Chichester Reinstated on Project," *The Overlook* (July 16, 1937).

46 John Hurt, letter to Aubrey Williams, July 17, 1937, roll DC 87, AAA. Hurt was reinstated later in the year and Schrader in 1938.

47 Marling, "Federal Patronage and the Woodstock Colony," 254.

48 Ludins, "Art Comes to the People," 233.

49 Ibid., 232. Photographs, newspaper articles, reports, statistics, correspondence, and this essay about the Art Caravan and its travels in 1939 were collected by Ludins in a scrapbook that is now in the collection of the Woodstock Artists Association and Museum Archives. Most of the information on the caravan is drawn from this source.

50 "Eugene Ludins to Supervise Larger Area," *The Overlook* (February 10, 1939).

51 Quoted in Marguerite Culp, "Work Project: Art Exhibit Captures Spirit of Woodstock in the Depression Era," *Woodstock Times* (August 22, 1985).

52 Audrey McMahon, letter to Thomas C. Parker, June 23, 1939, roll DC 87, AAA.

53 See Marling, "Federal Patronage and the Woodstock Colony," 281–289, for a complete recounting of this contretemps.

54 Randy Kennedy, "Culture, Rolling into Towns on Big Rigs," the *New York Times* (March 30, 2011).

55 Ludins, interview with Fortess.

Selected Bibliography

Books, Articles, and Dissertations

Berman, Avis. *Rebels on Eighth Street: Juliana Force and the Whitney Museum of American Art.* New York: Atheneum, 1990.

Brace, Ernest. "Construction Ahead: The Summer in Woodstock, 1935." In *American Magazine of Art*, 28, November 1935.

Ludins, Eugene. "Art Comes to the People." In *Art for the Millions: Essays from the 1930s by Artists and Administrators of the WPA Federal Art Project*, Francis V. O'Connor, ed. Boston: New York Graphic Society, 1973.

Marling, Karal Ann Rose. "Federal Patronage and the Woodstock Colony." Ph.D. dissertation, Bryn Mawr College, 1971.

Monroe, Gerald M. "The Artists Union of New York." Ph.D. dissertation, New York University, 1971.

______. "The American Artists Congress and the Invasion of Finland." In *Archives of American Art Journal*,15, no. 1, 1975.

O'Connor, Francis V. Introduction to *The New Deal Art Projects: An Anthology of Memoirs*, Francis V. O'Connor, ed. Washington, D.C.: Smithsonian Institution Press, 1972.

______. Introduction to *Art for the Millions: Essays from the 1930s by Artists and Administrators of the WPA Federal Art Project*, Francis V. O'Connor, ed. Boston: New York Graphic Society, 1973.

Archives and Exhibition Catalogues

Juliana and American Art: A Memorial Exhibition. New York: Whitney Museum of American Art, 1949.

Marling, Karal Ann Rose. *Woodstock: An American Art Colony, 1902–1977.* Poughkeepsie, New York: Vassar College Art Gallery, 1977.

National Archives Record Group 69. WPA central correspondence files, New York State, roll DC 87. Archives of American Art, Smithsonian Institution (AAA).

Peters, Lisa N. *Allen Tucker: The Force of Emotion—A Post-Impressionist Rediscovered.* New York: Spanierman Gallery, 2010.

PAINTINGS

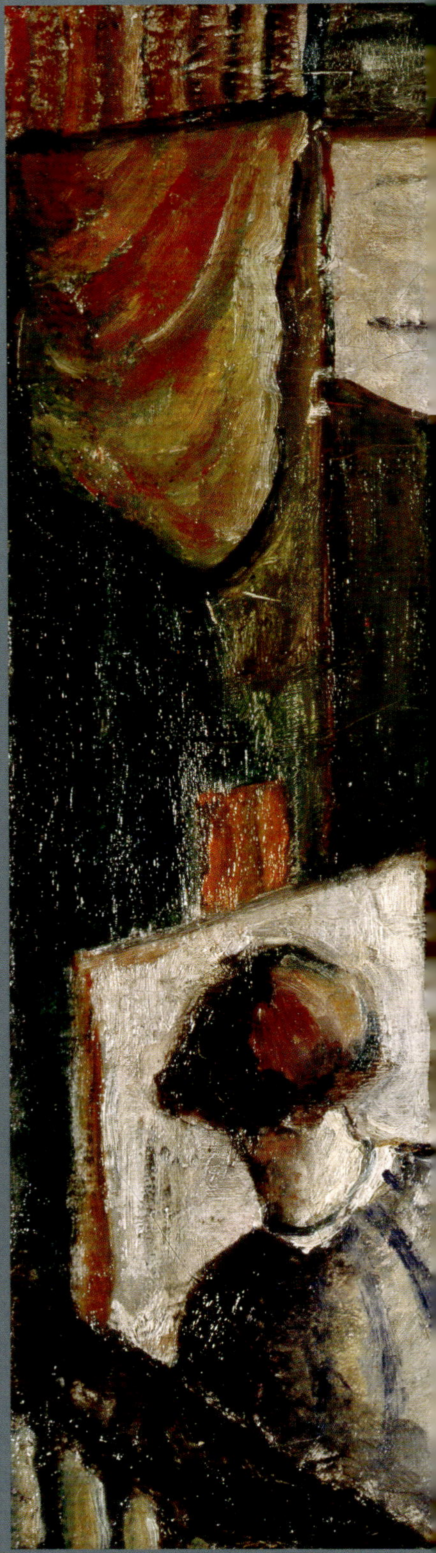

CAT. 3

Art Class

1924–27, oil on canvas
16 x 22 in.
Estate of Eugene Ludins

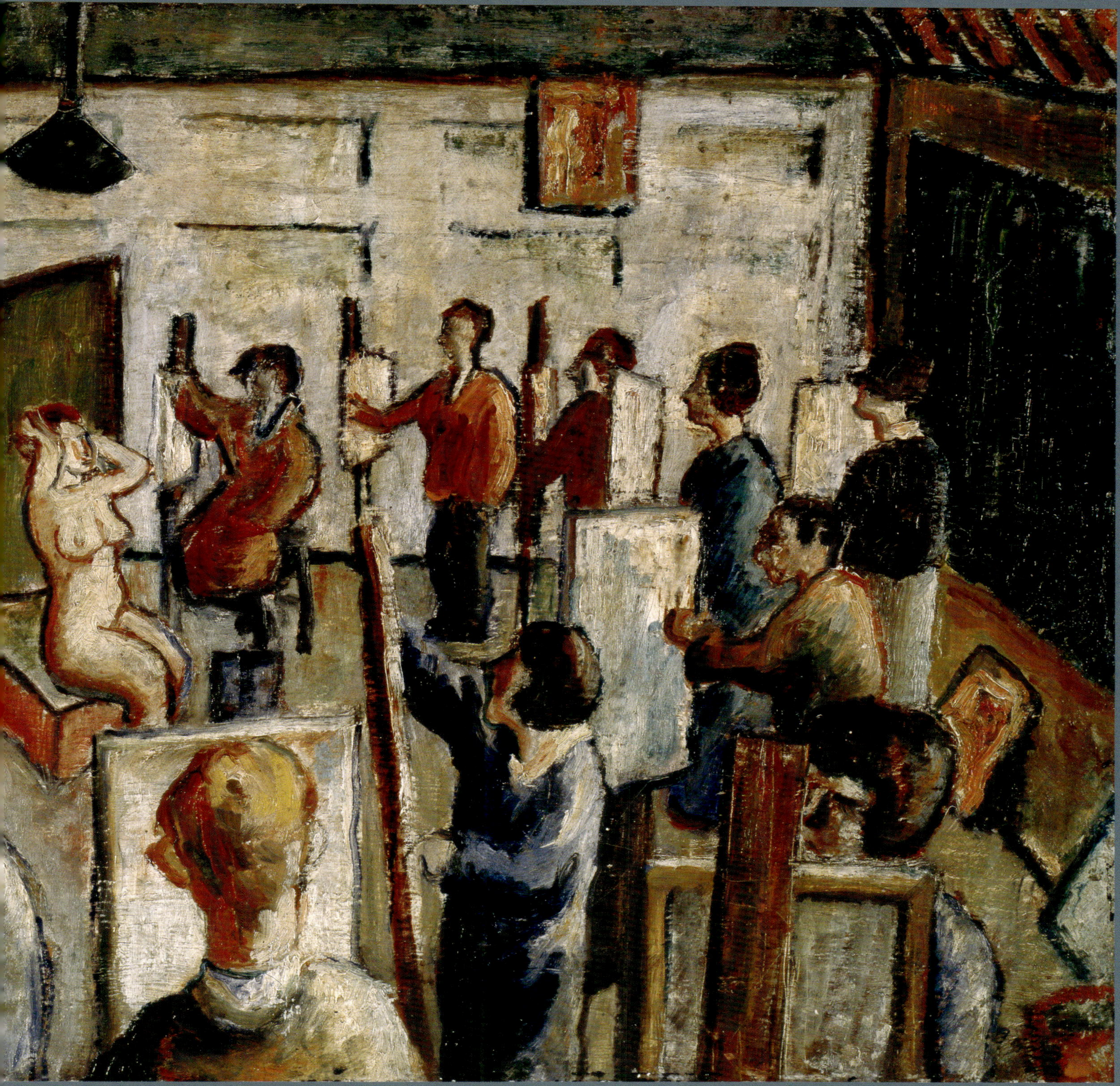

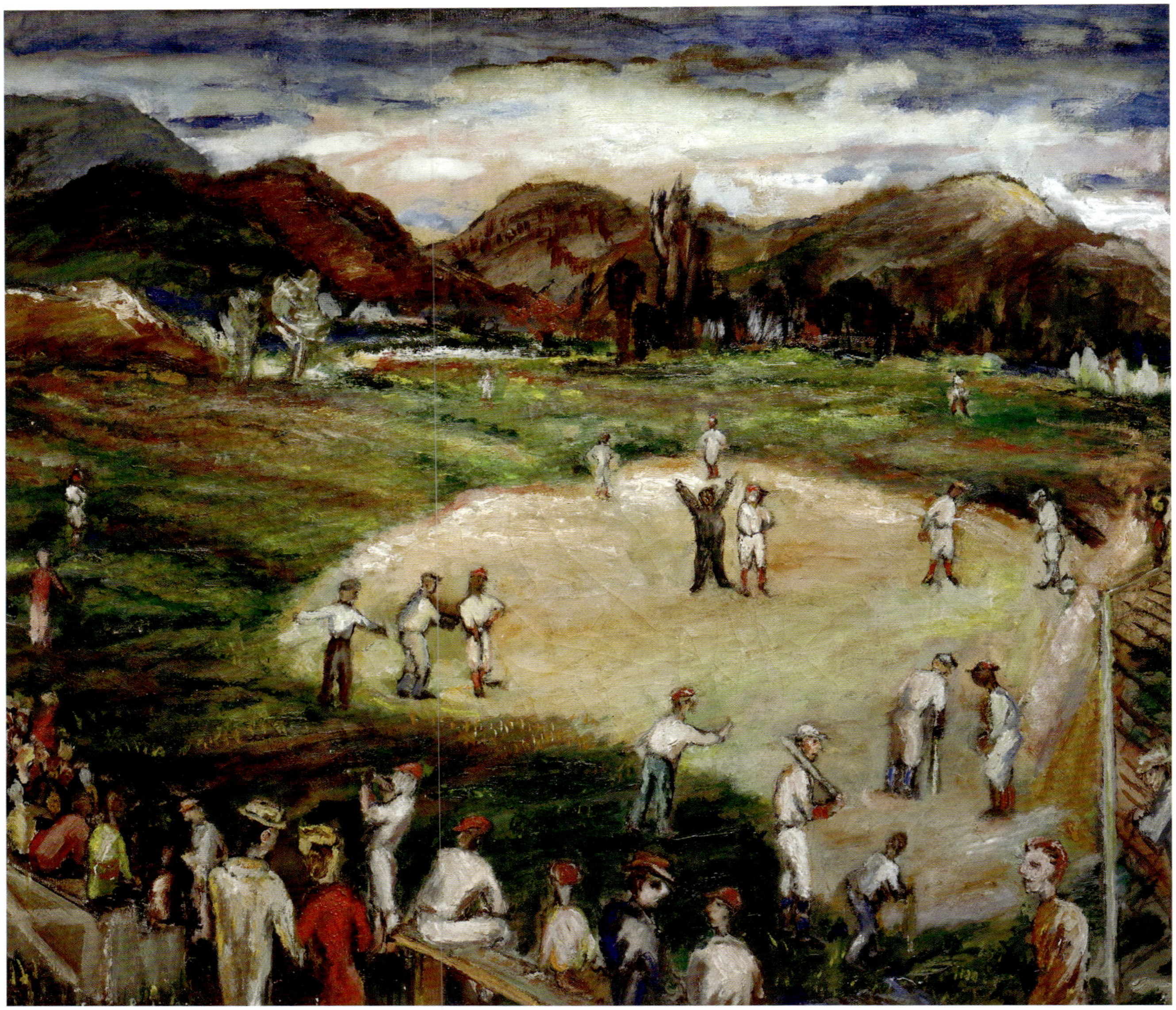

CAT. 4

Third Inning

1928, oil on canvas
30 x 40 in.
Private Collection

CAT. 5

Skating in Central Park

1928, oil on canvas, screen,
three panels
57 x 23½ x 3 in. each
Estate of Eugene Ludins

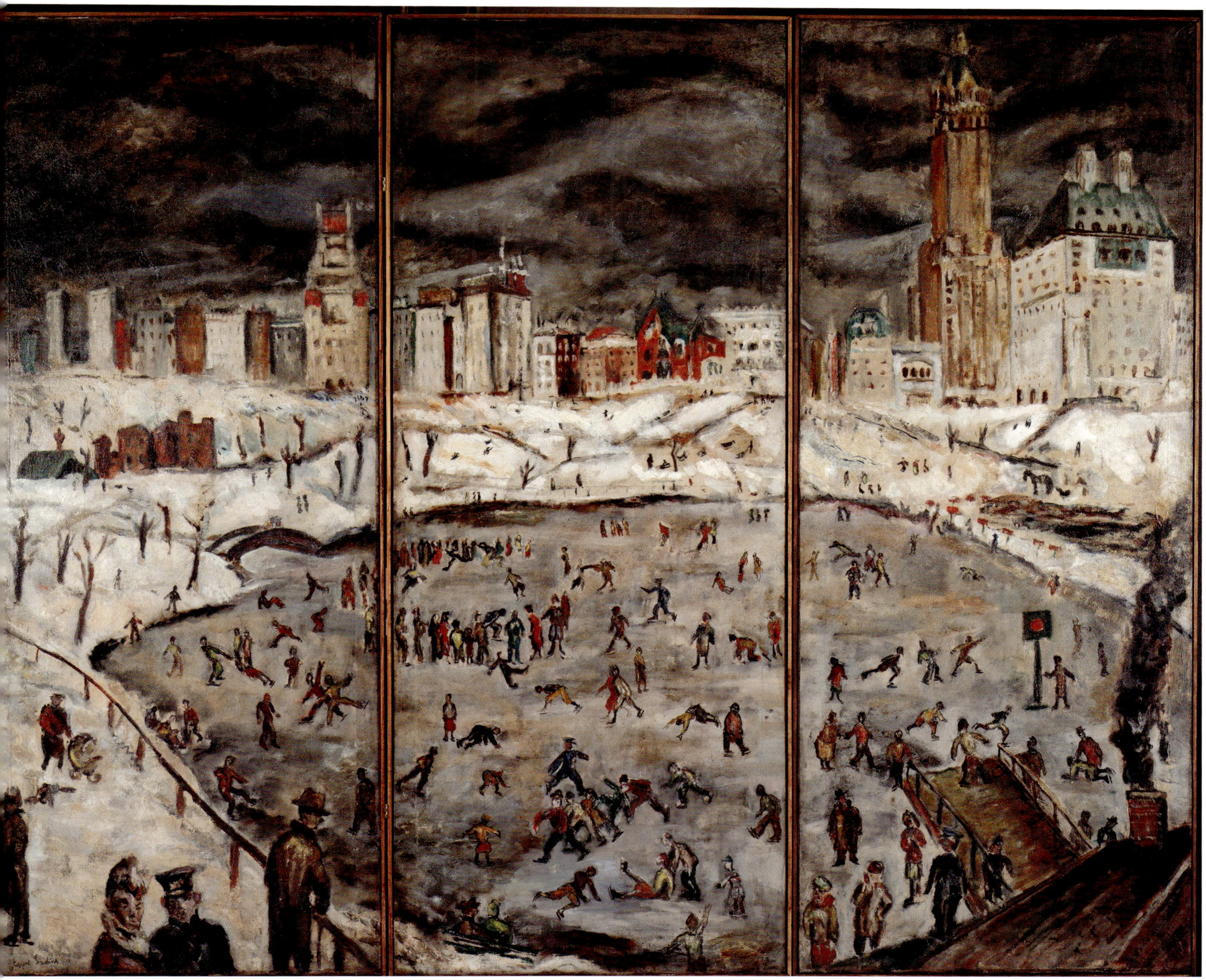

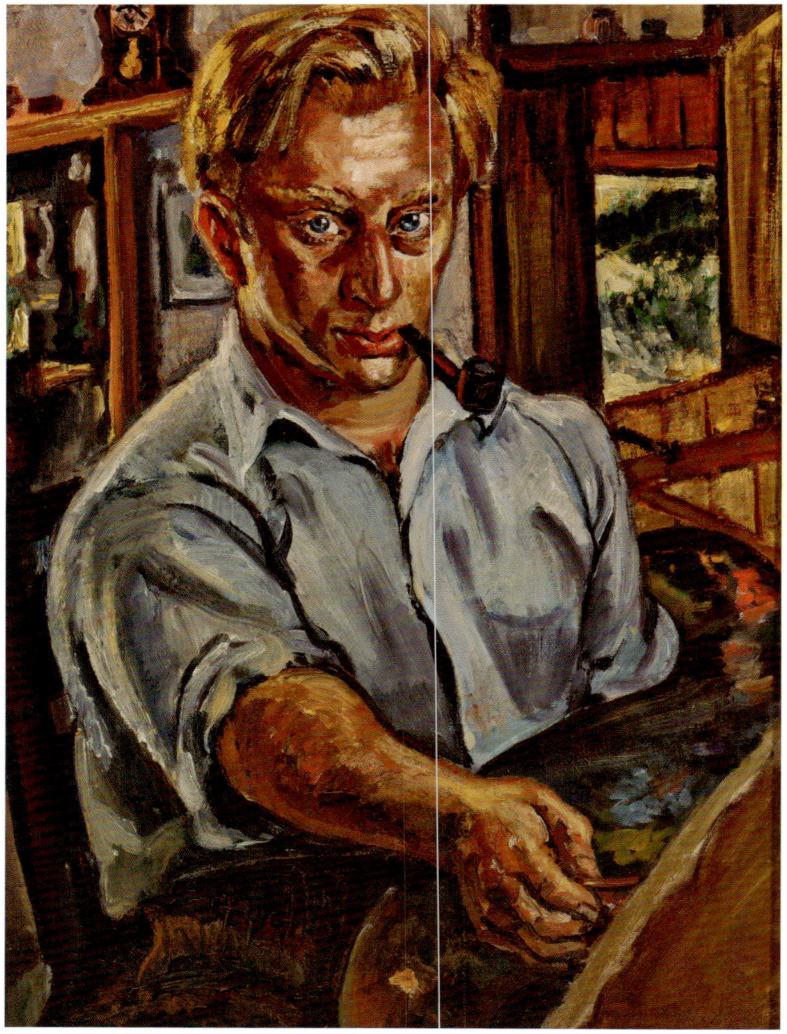

CAT. 6

MARION GREENWOOD

Portrait of Gene Ludins

1929, oil on canvas
30 x 20 in.
Estate of Marion Greenwood

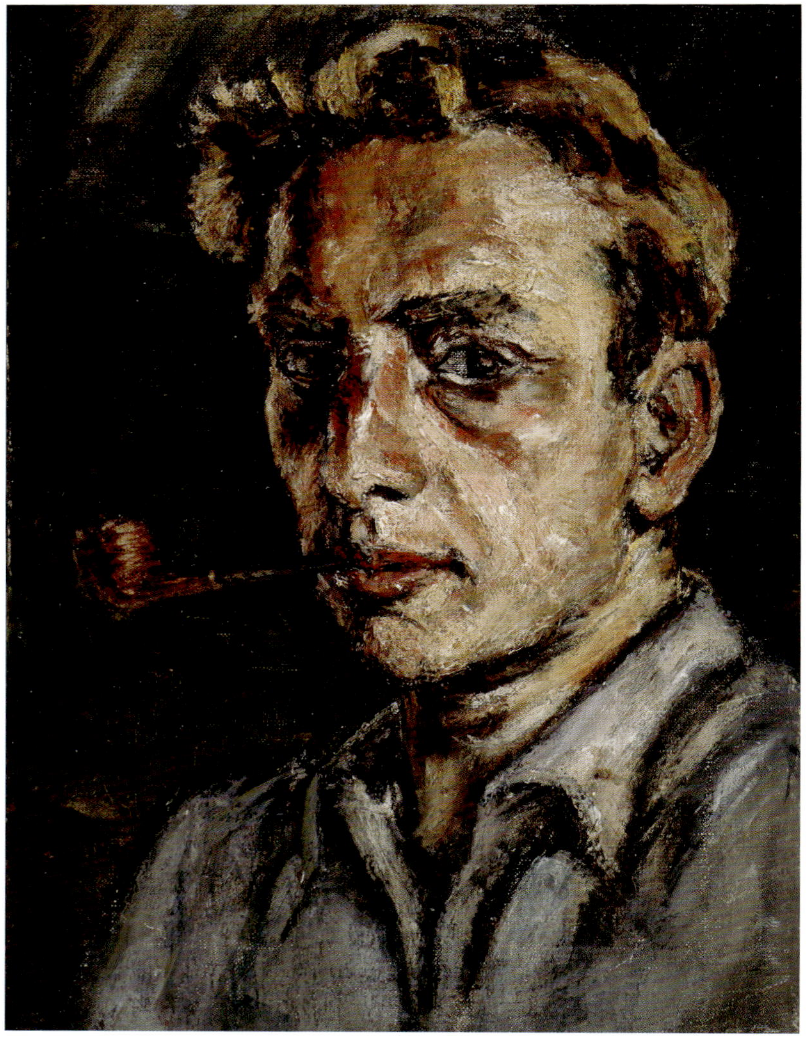

CAT. 7

Self-Portrait with Pipe

Early 1930s, oil on canvas
16 x 12 in.
Estate of Eugene Ludins

CAT. 8

Self-Portrait in Roadster

Early 1930s, oil on canvas
28 x 32 in.
Estate of Eugene Ludins

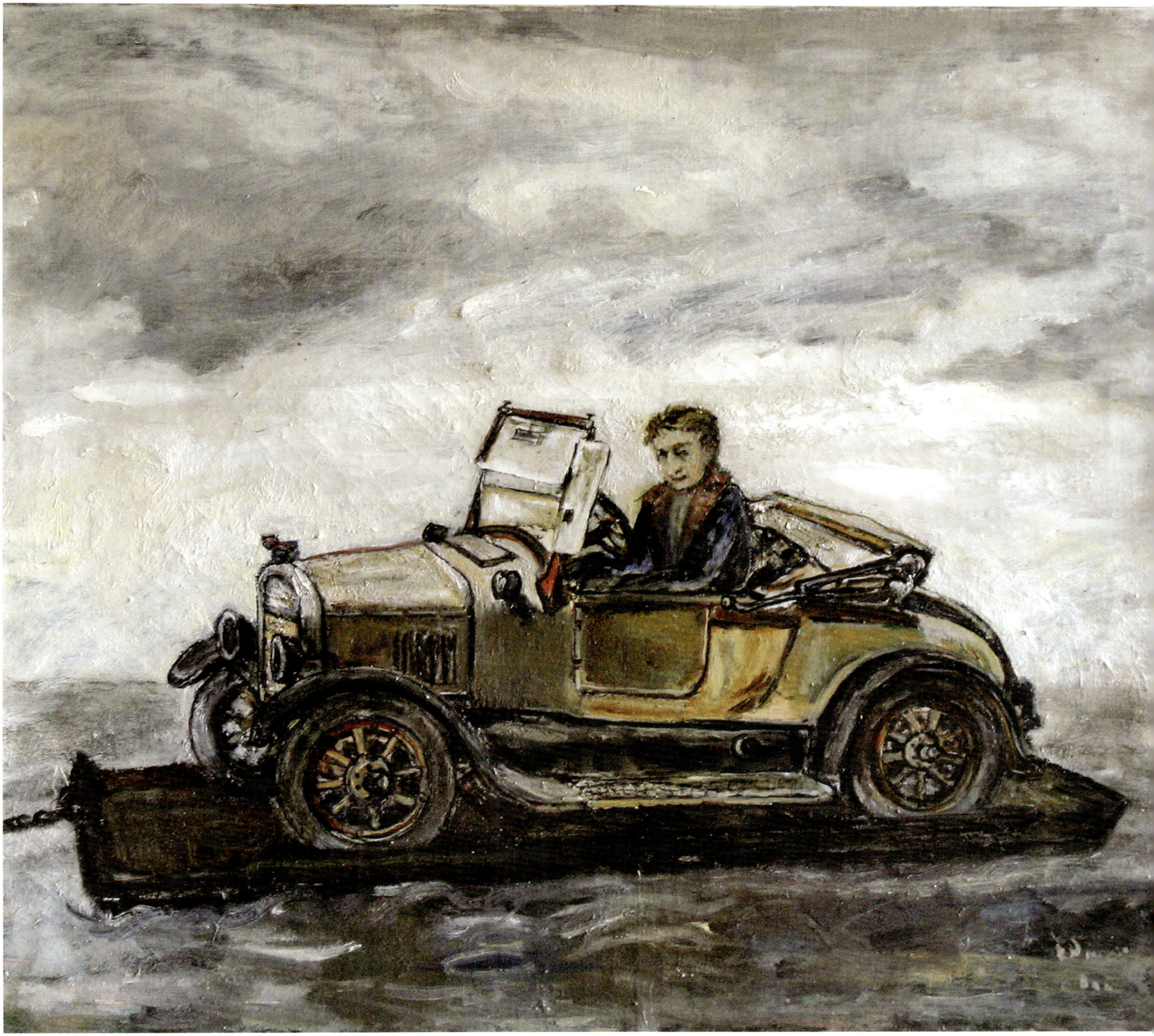

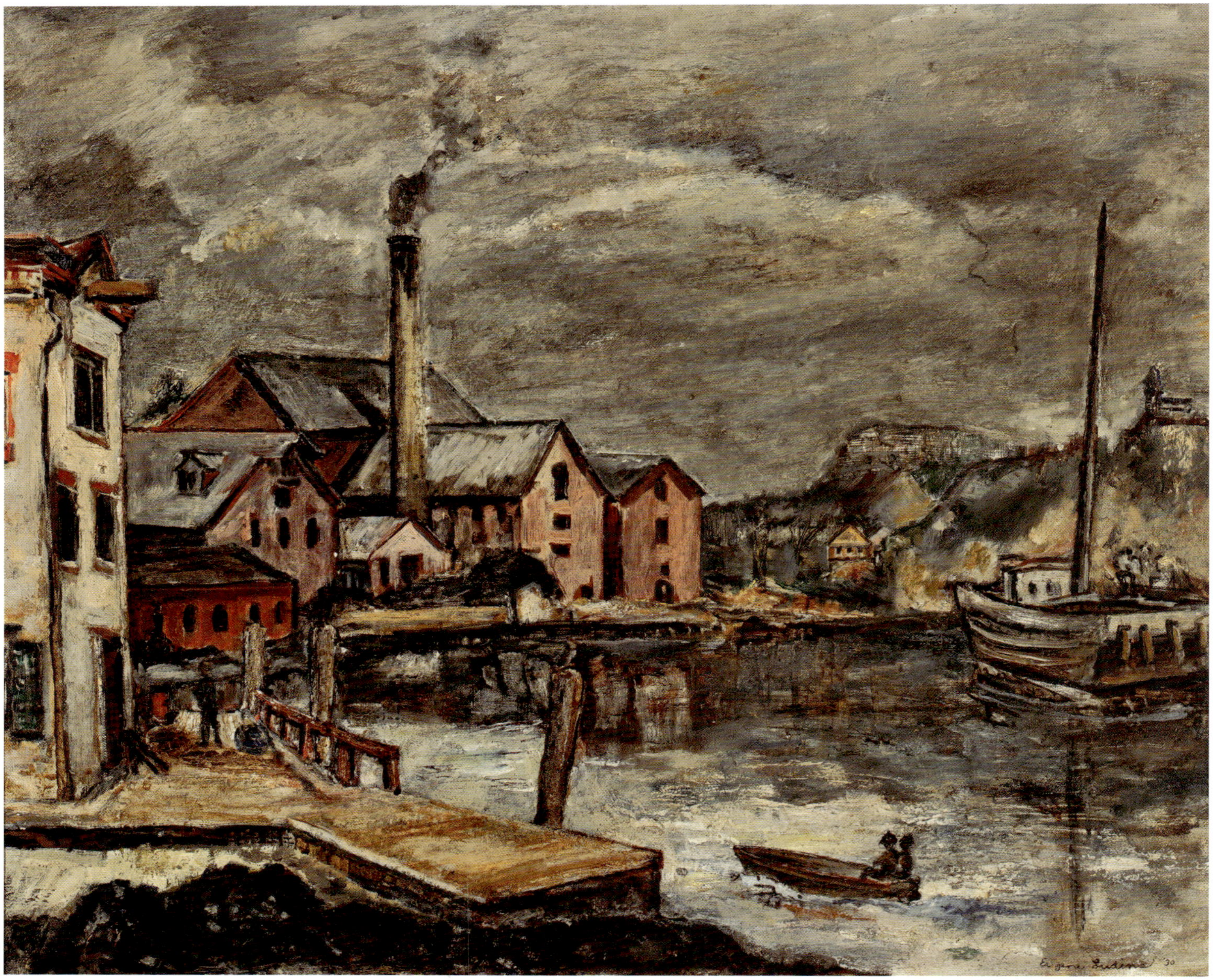

CAT. 9

Saugerties Pool

1930, oil on canvas
24 x 30 in.
Private Collection

CAT. 10

Landscape

1930, oil on canvas
30¼ x 33 in.
Whitney Museum of American Art,
New York; purchase (31.286).

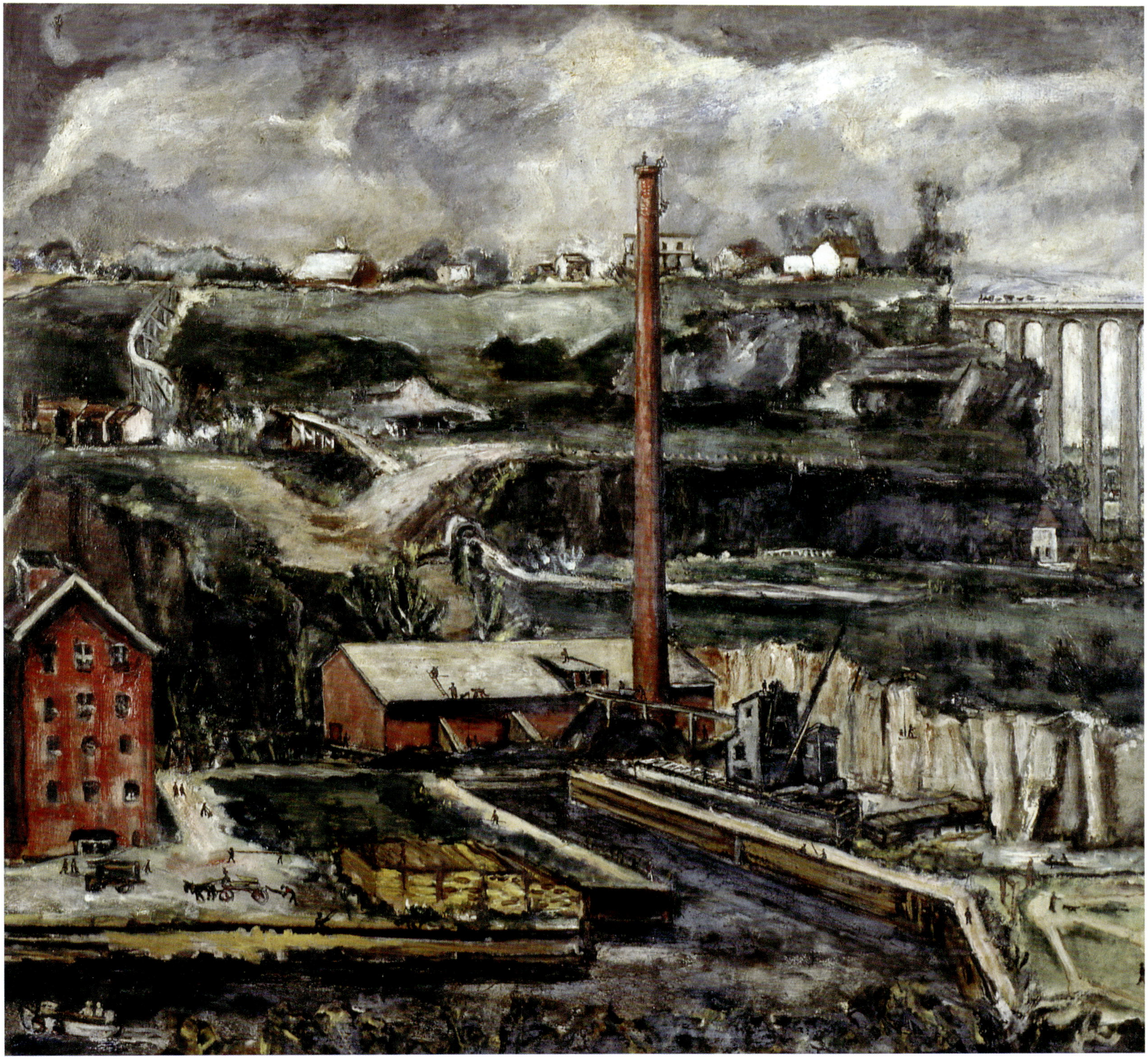

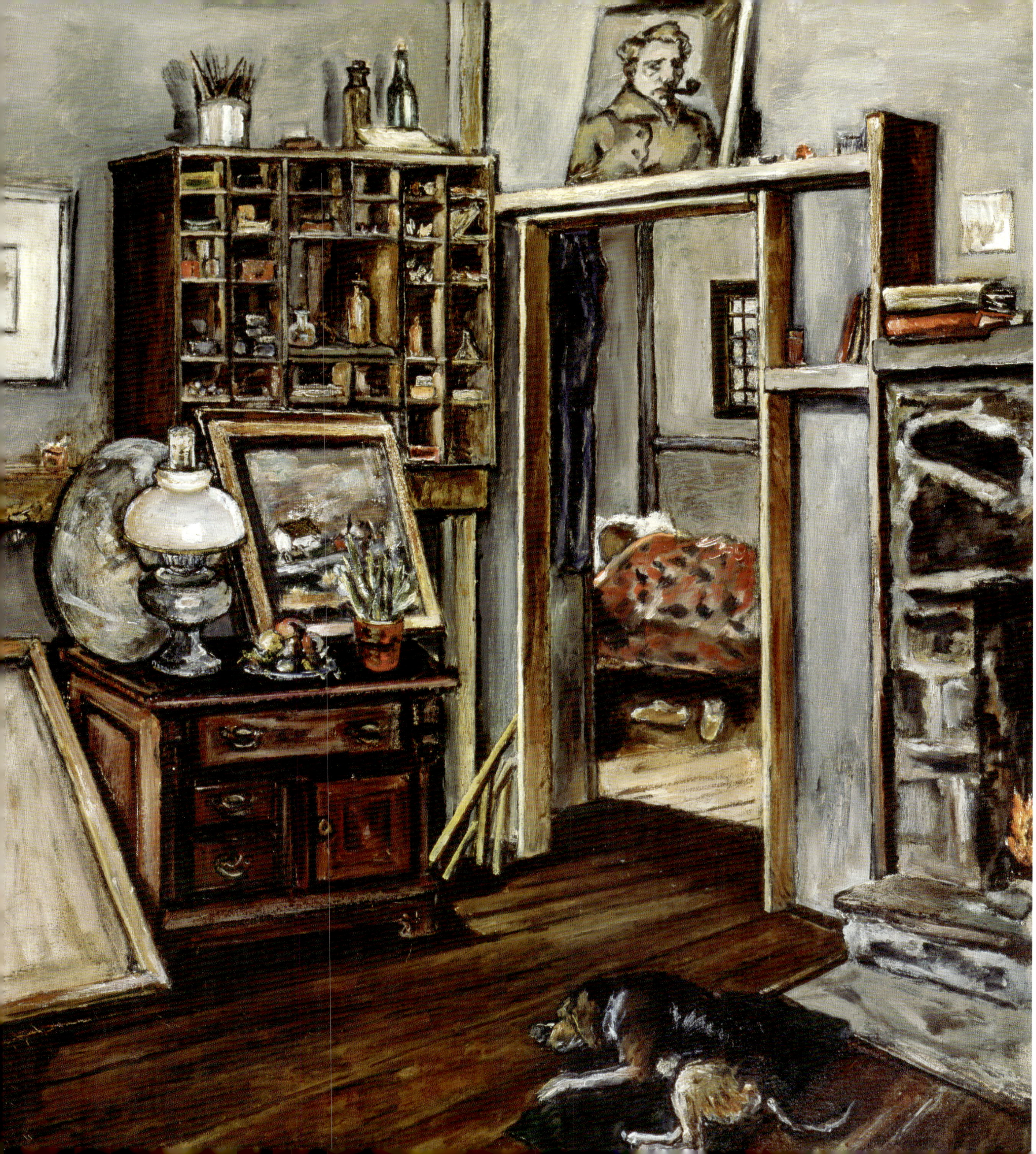

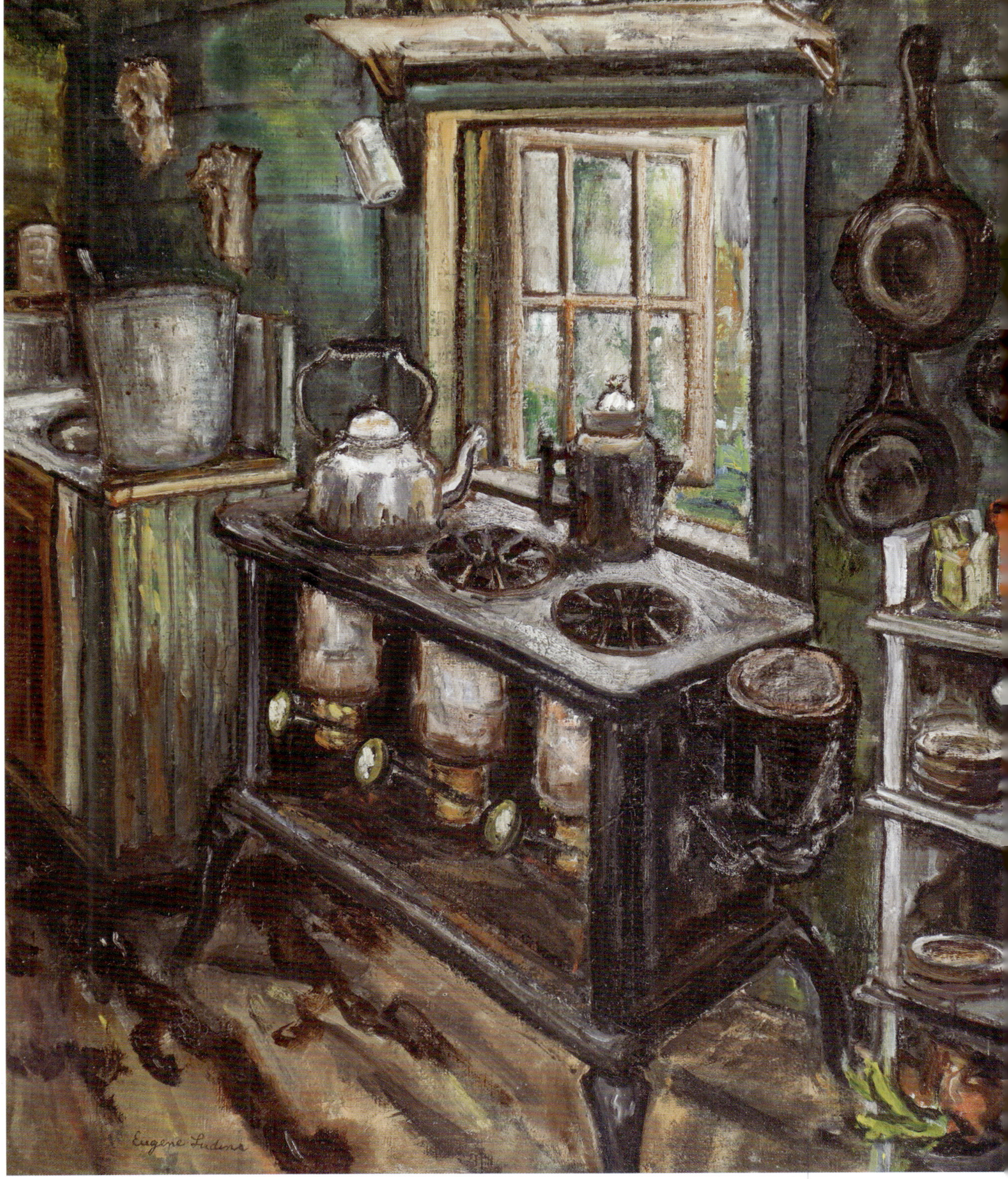

CAT. 11

Maverick Studio

1931, oil on canvas
36 x 32 in.
Estate of Eugene Ludins

CAT. 12

Maverick Kitchen

c. 1931, oil on canvas
30 x 26 in.
Estate of Eugene Ludins

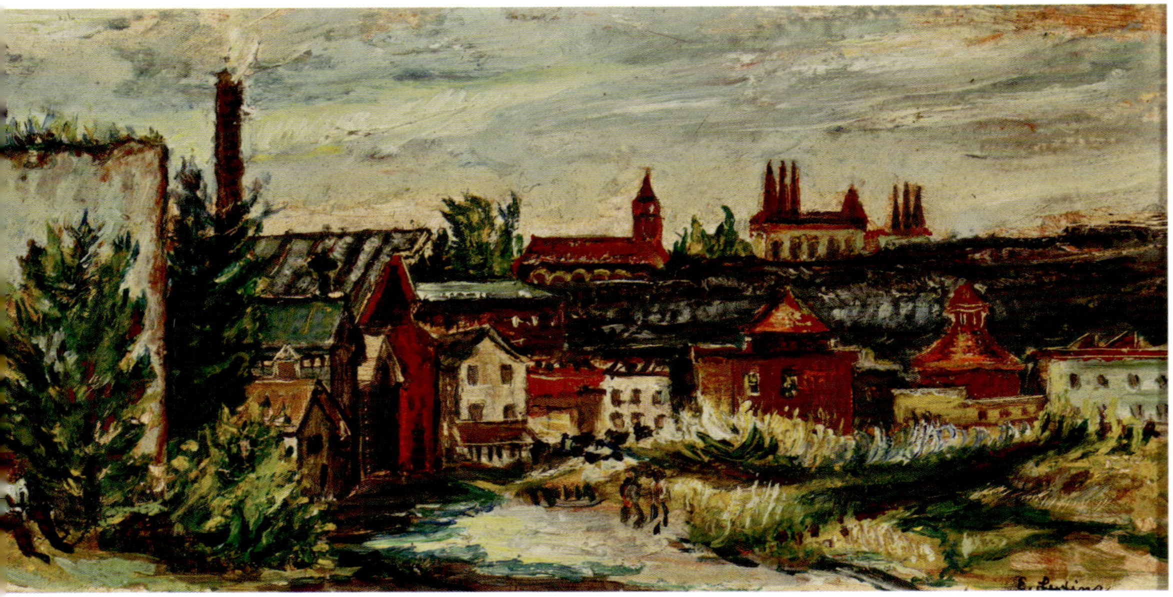

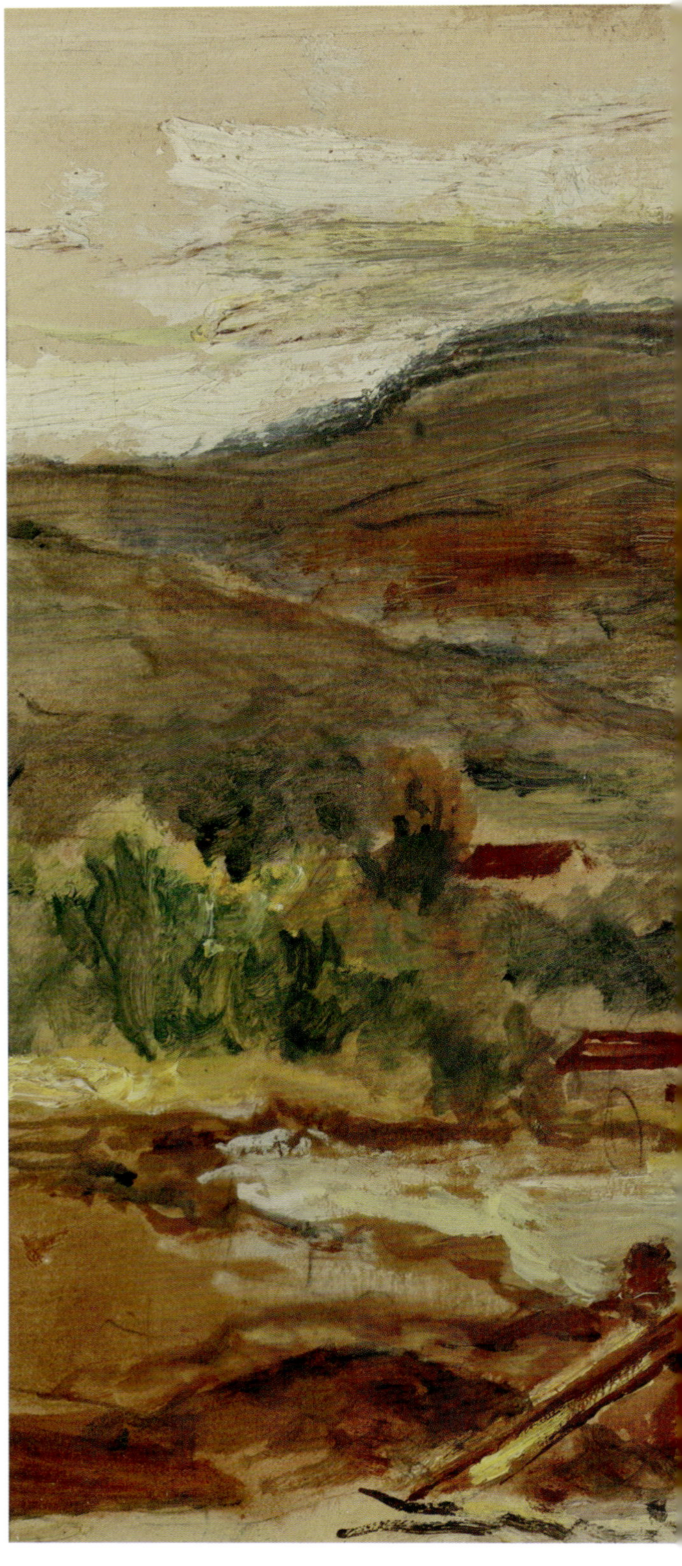

CAT. 13

View of Kingston

c. 1931, oil on panel
5 x 11 in.
Collection Jane Jones

CAT. 14

Woodstock Landscape

1936, oil on canvas
6.5 x 11.5 in.
Historical Society of Woodstock

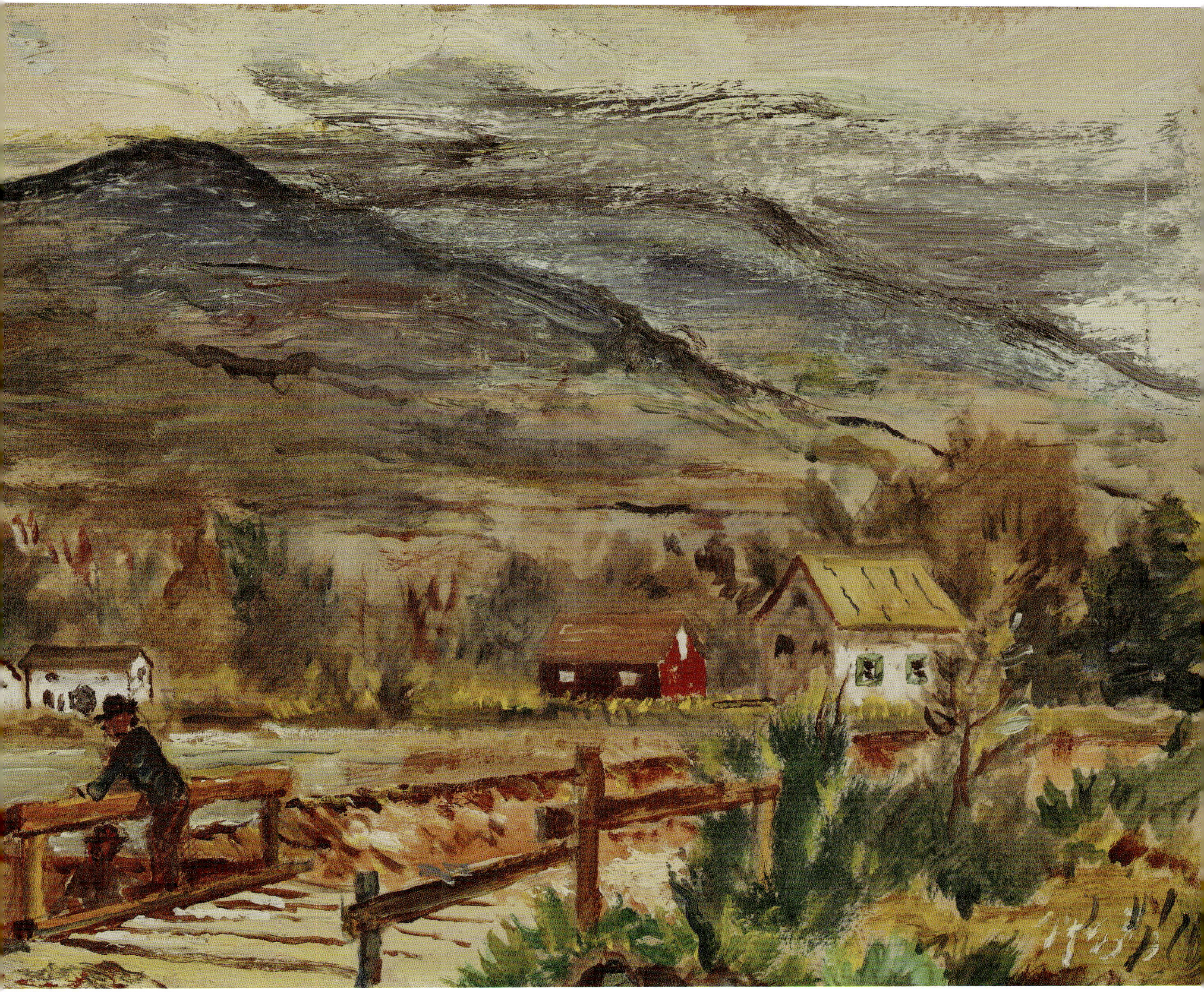

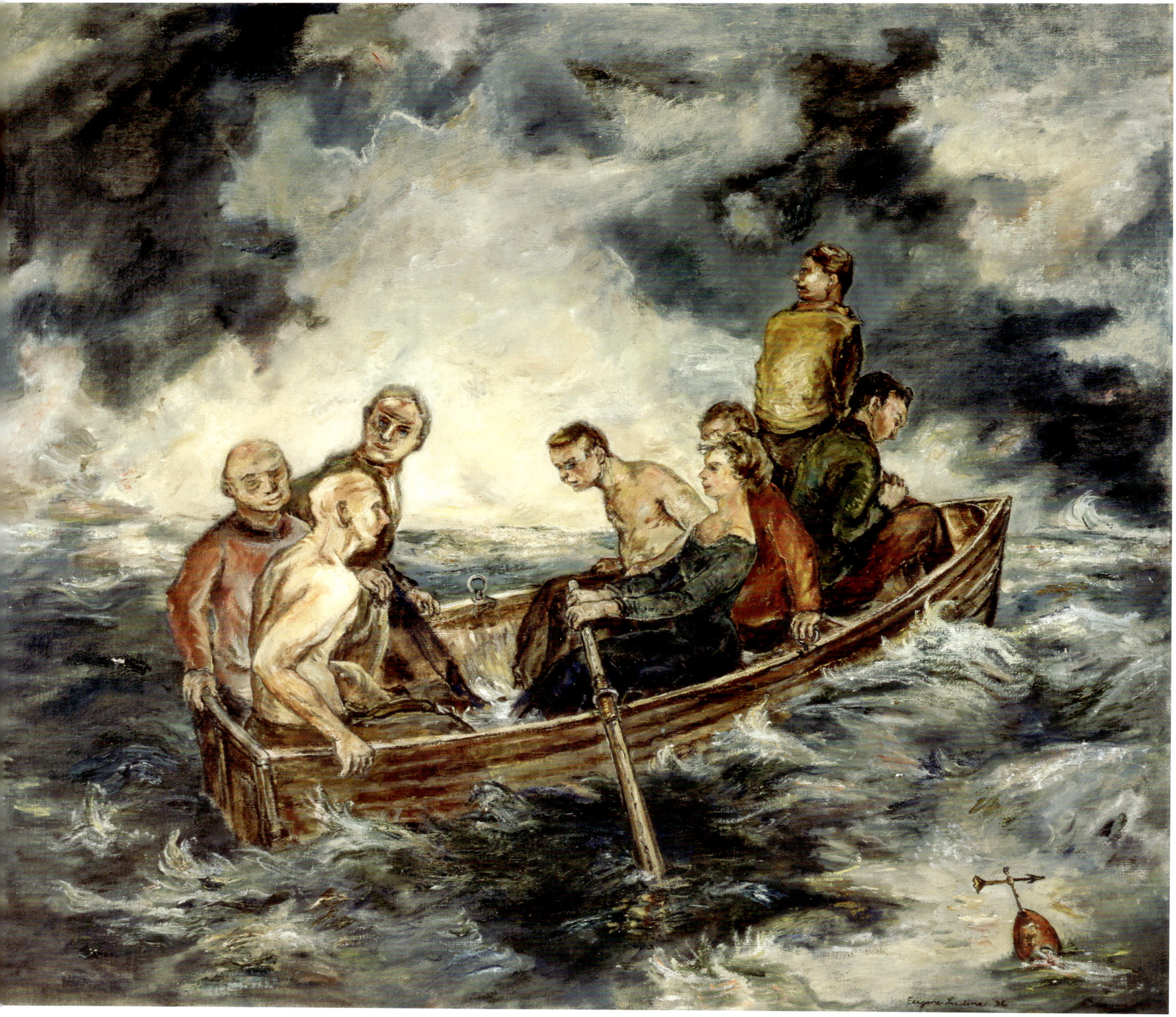

CAT. 15

The True Story

1936, oil on canvas
34 x 42 in.
Estate of Eugene Ludins

CAT. 16

Family Portrait

1934, oil on canvas
54 x 46 in.
Estate of Eugene Ludins

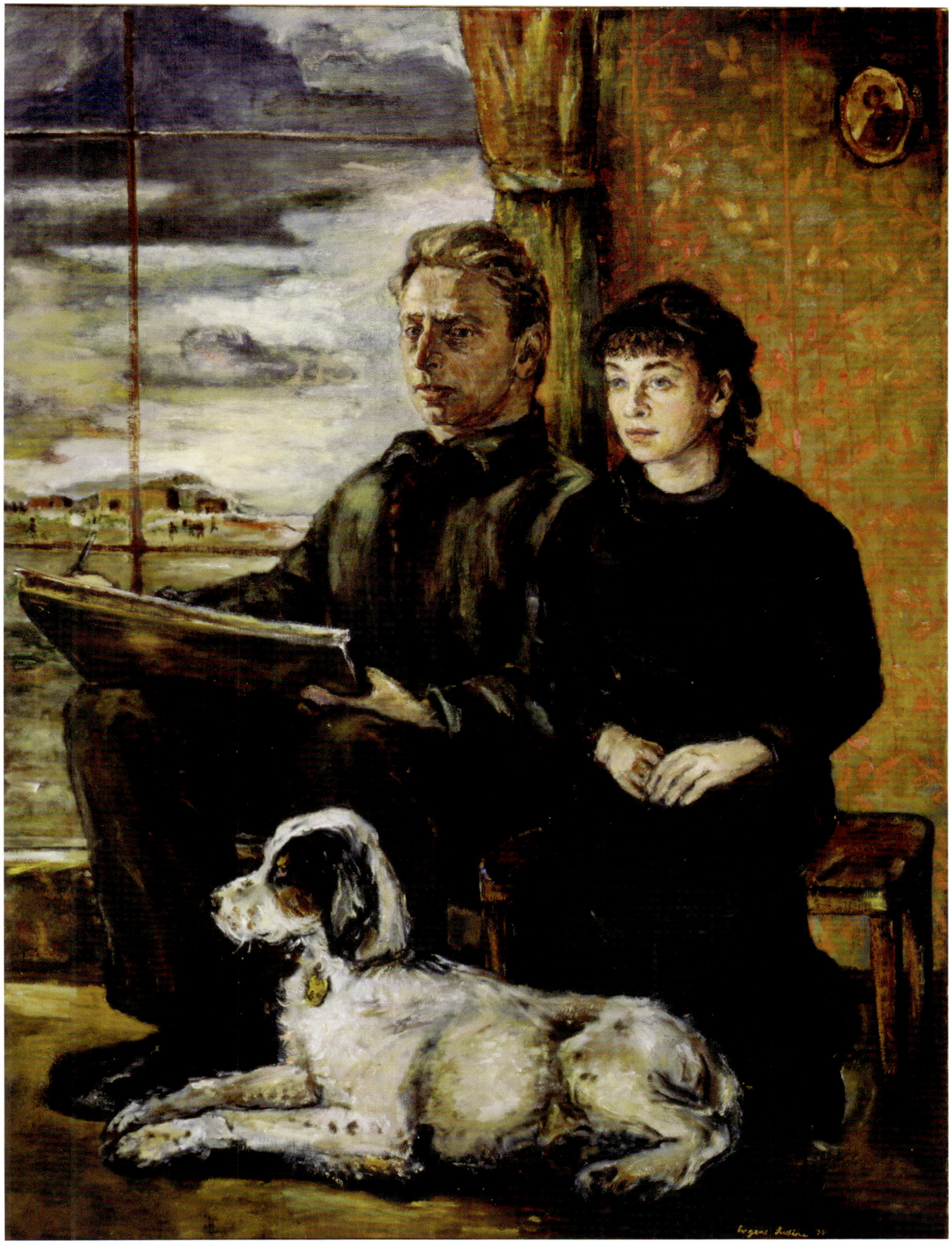

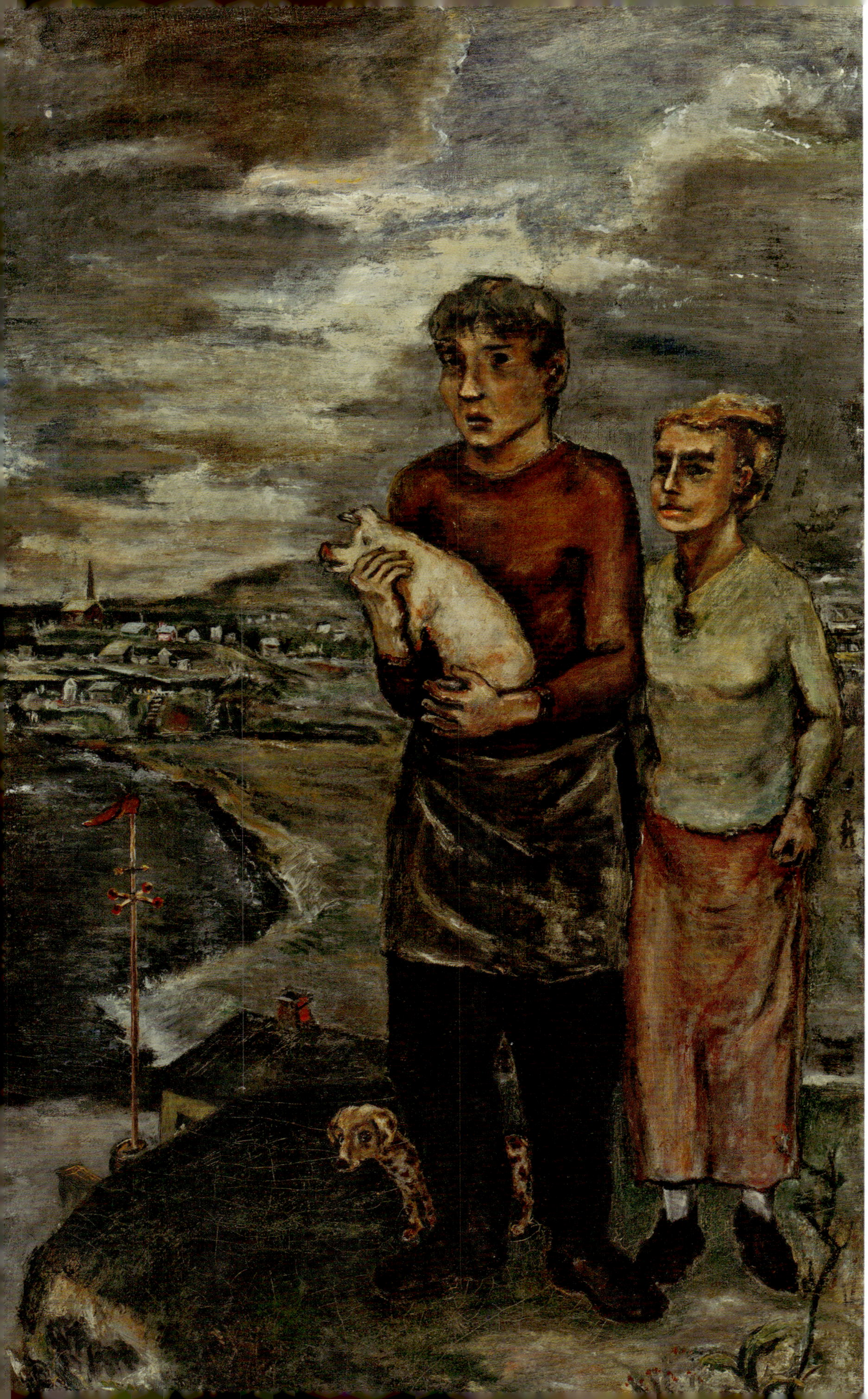

CAT. 17

Mr. Gormley and Mrs. Gormley

1932, oil on canvas
30 x 22 in.
Private Collection

CAT. 18

Self-Portrait in Winter

c. 1940, oil on canvas
31 x 19 in.
Collection John and Elisabeth Small

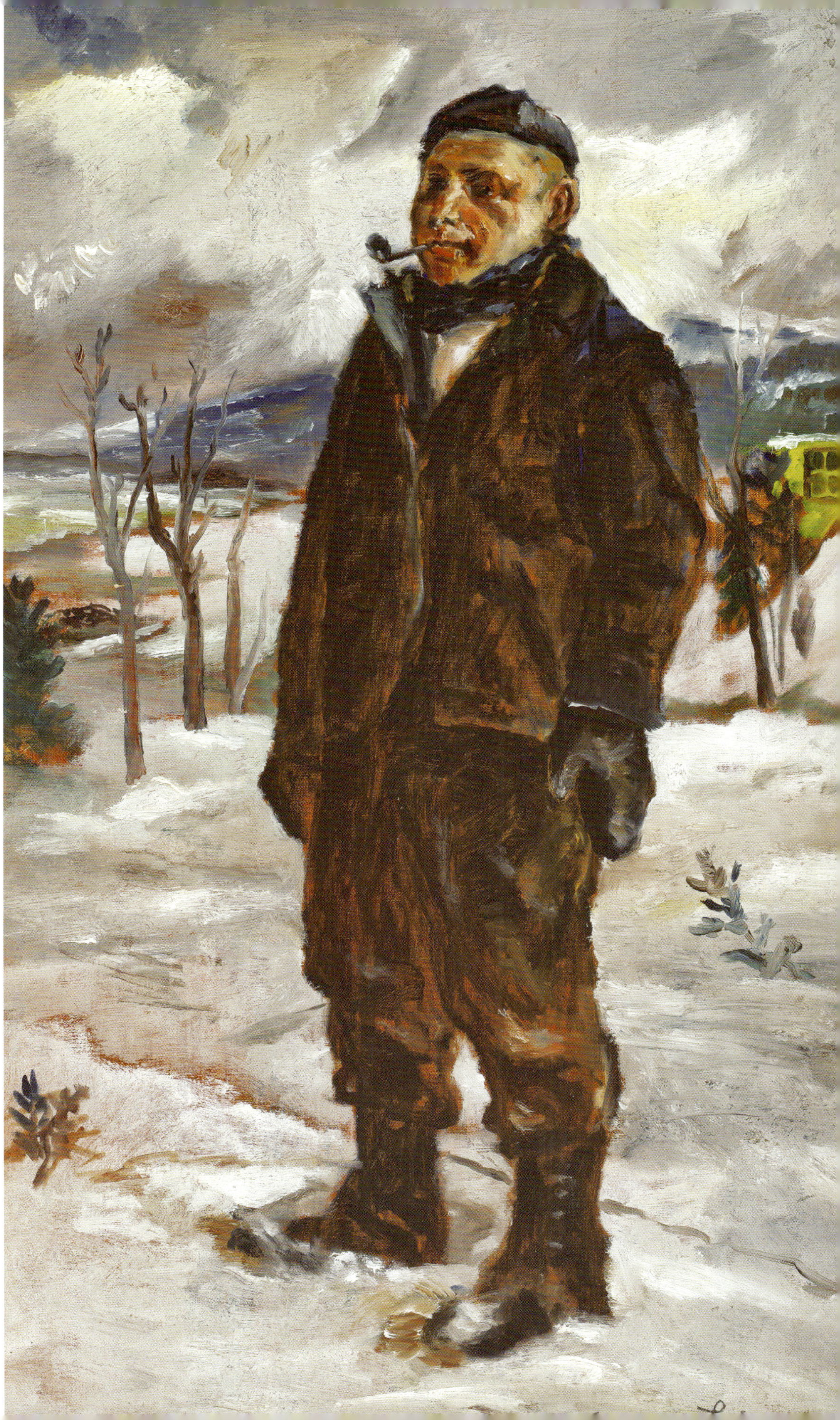

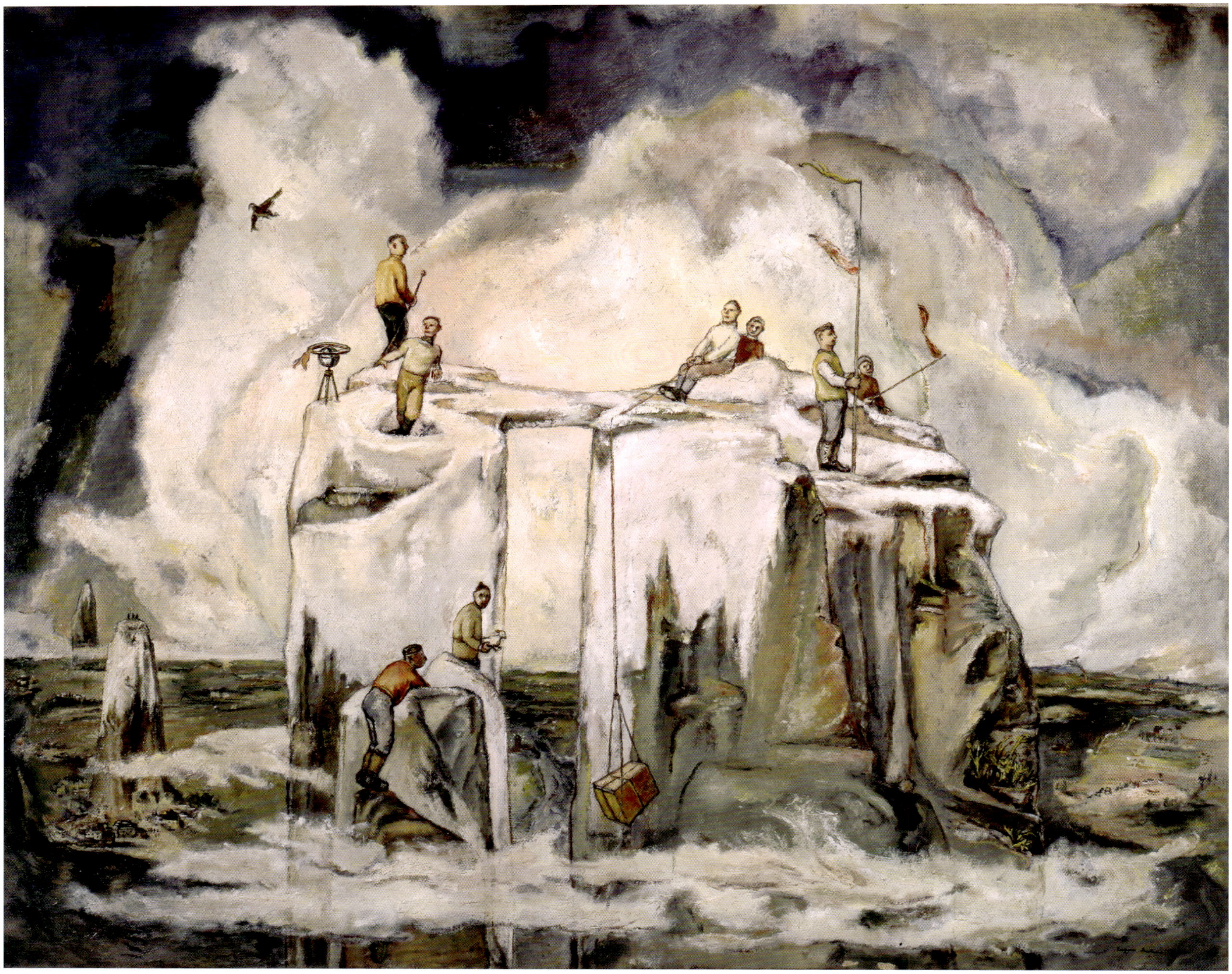

CAT. 19

New Lands

1934, oil on canvas
39¼ x 50¼ in.
Woodstock Artists Association and Museum, gift of Joseph DePaul

CAT. 20

Game of War

1933, oil on canvas
36 x 40 in.
Estate of Eugene Ludins

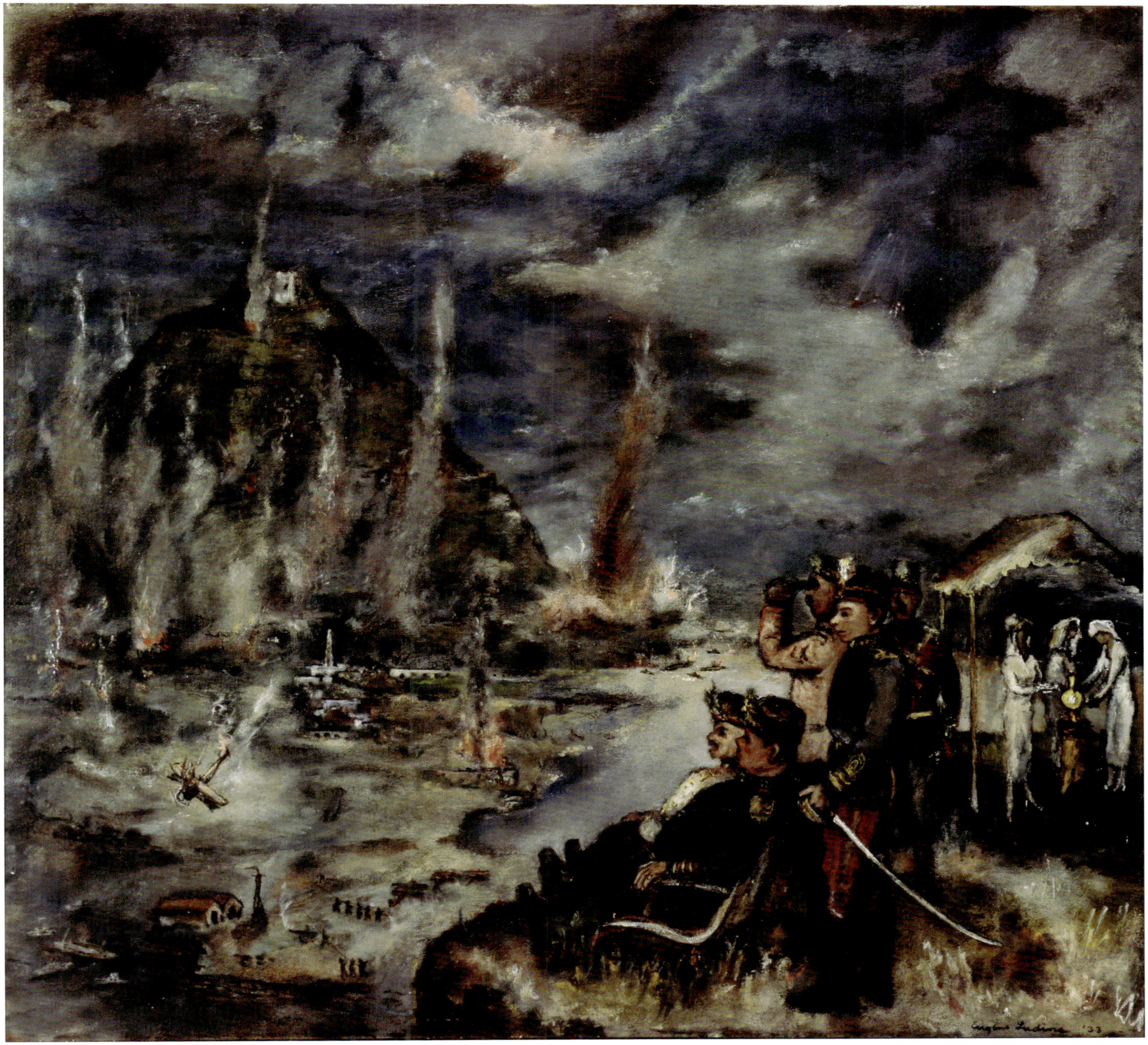

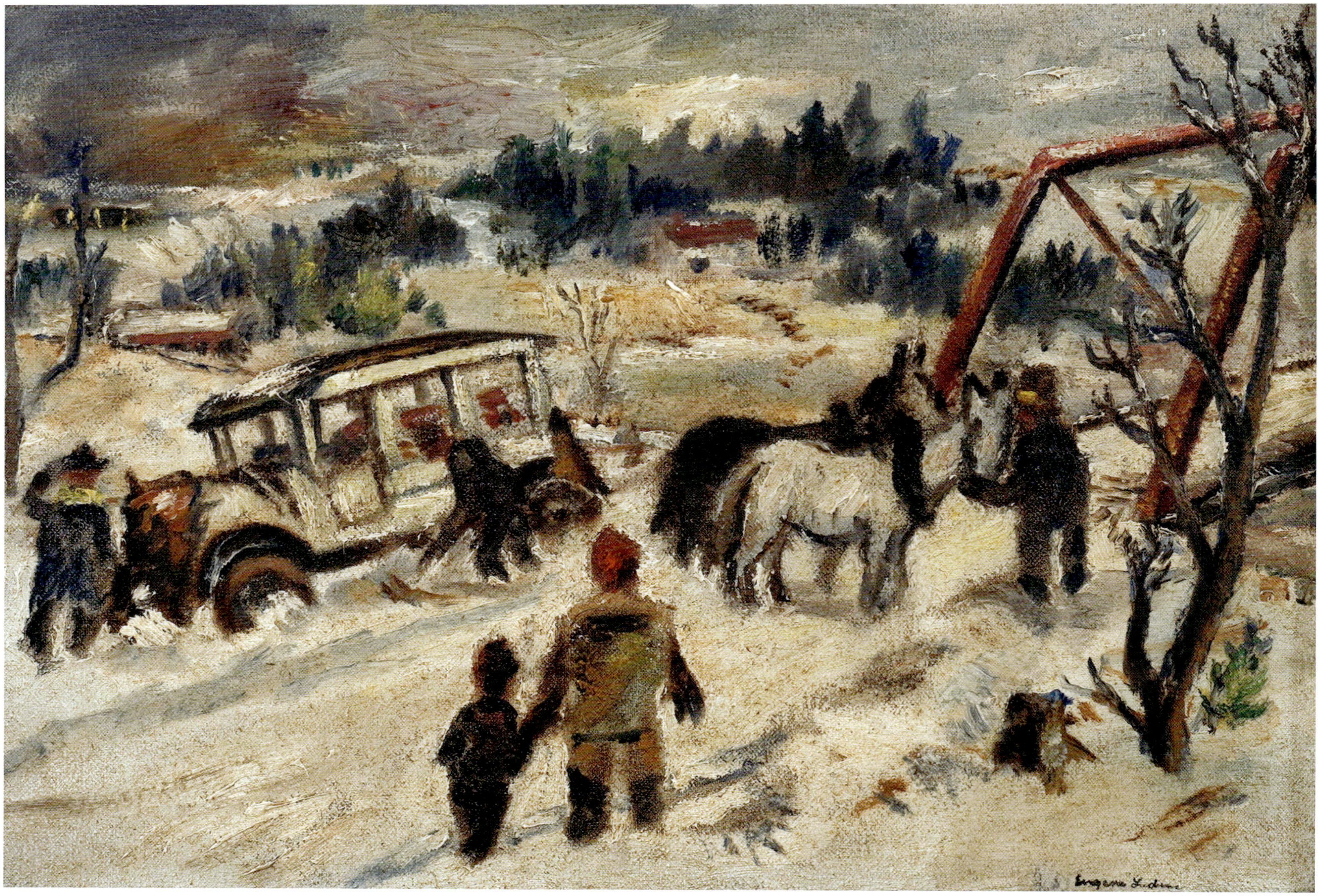

CAT. 21

Winter Scene

c. 1940, oil on canvas
10½ x 16 in.
Private Collection

CAT. 22

Spring Thaw

1932, oil on canvas
34 x 36 in.
Estate of Eugene Ludins

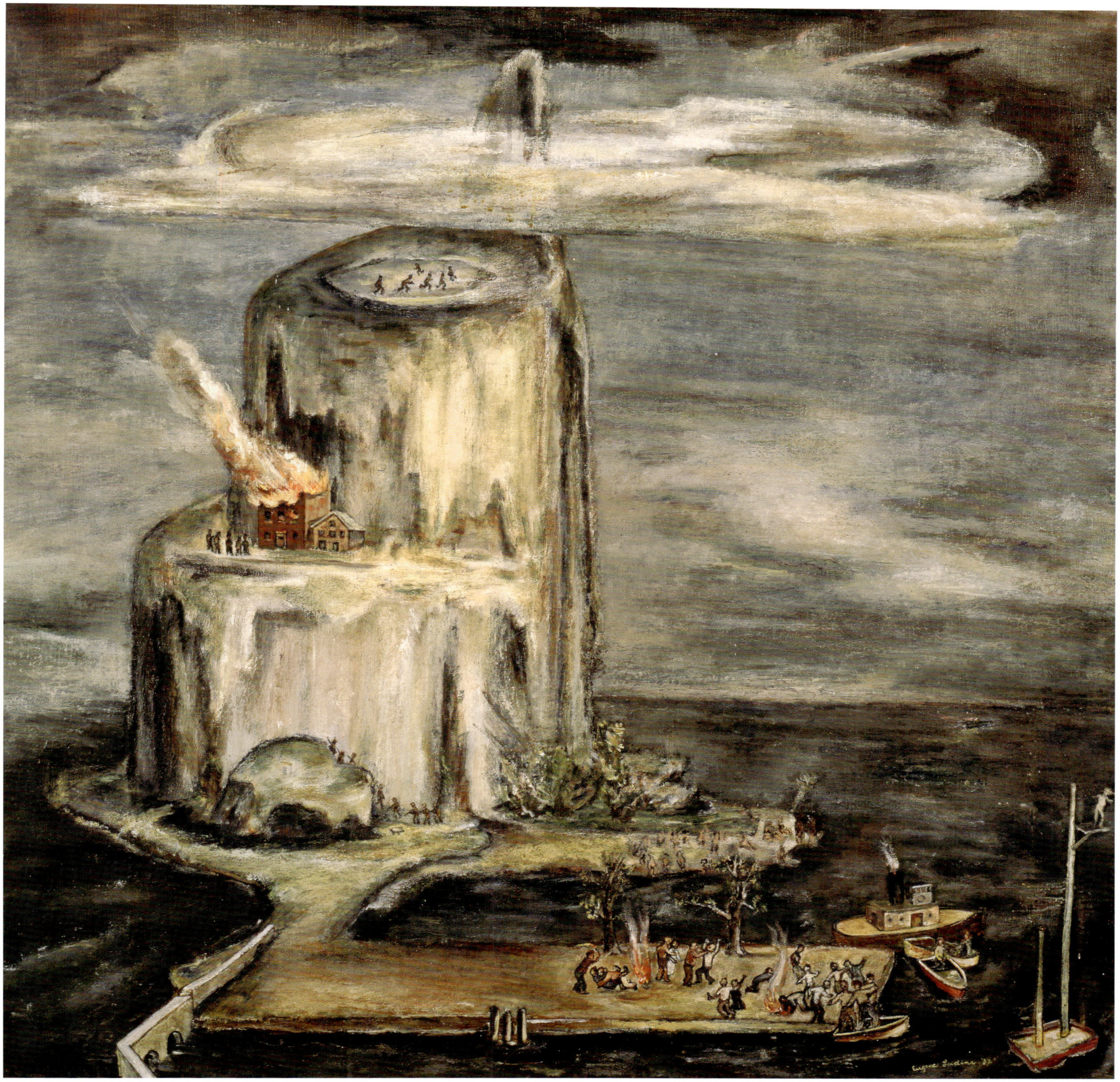

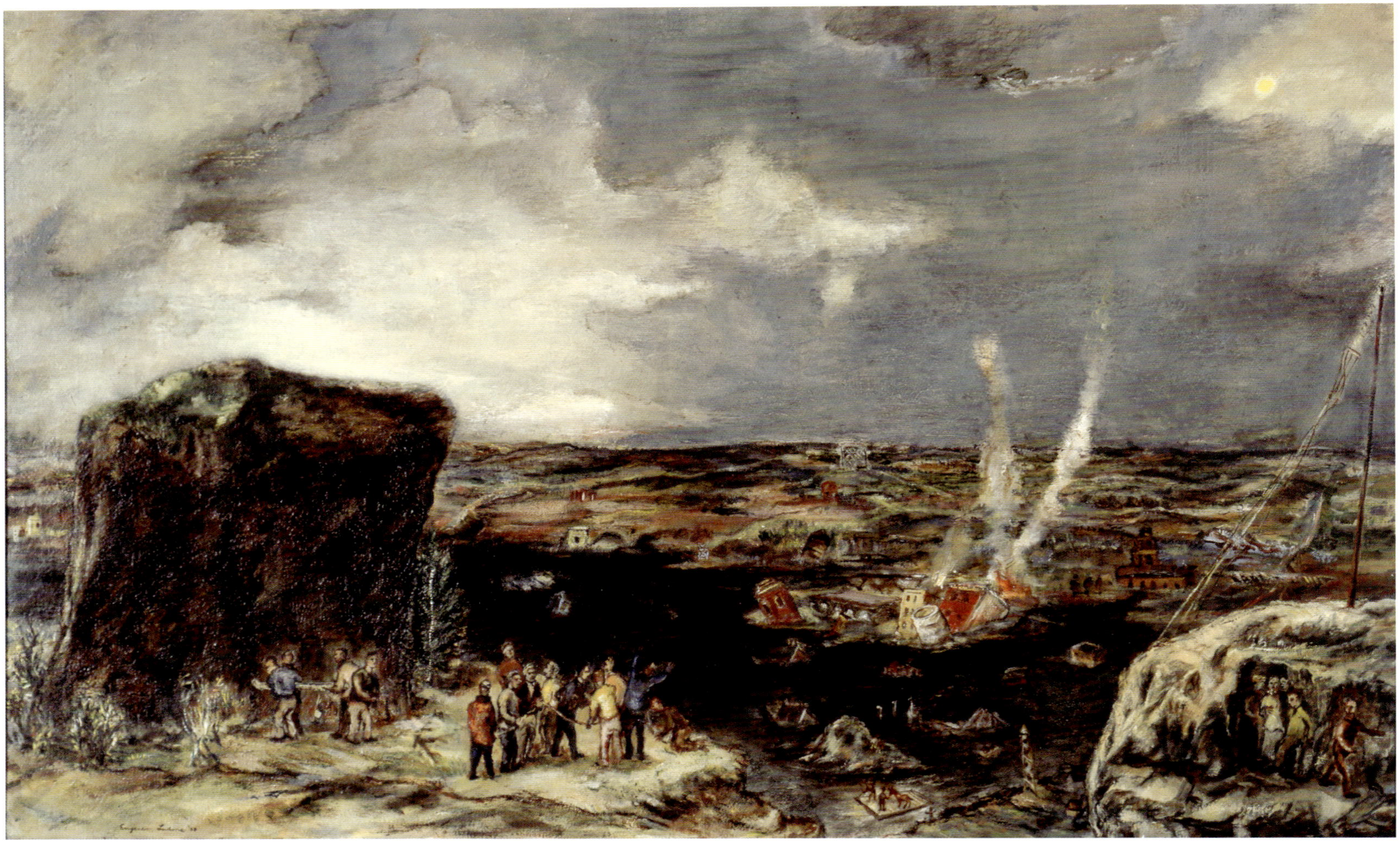

CAT. 23

Rotten Foundations

1938, oil on canvas
30 x 50 in.
Estate of Eugene Ludins

CAT. 24

Interlude

1940, oil on canvas
36 x 48 in.
Collection Abby and Mark Lerner

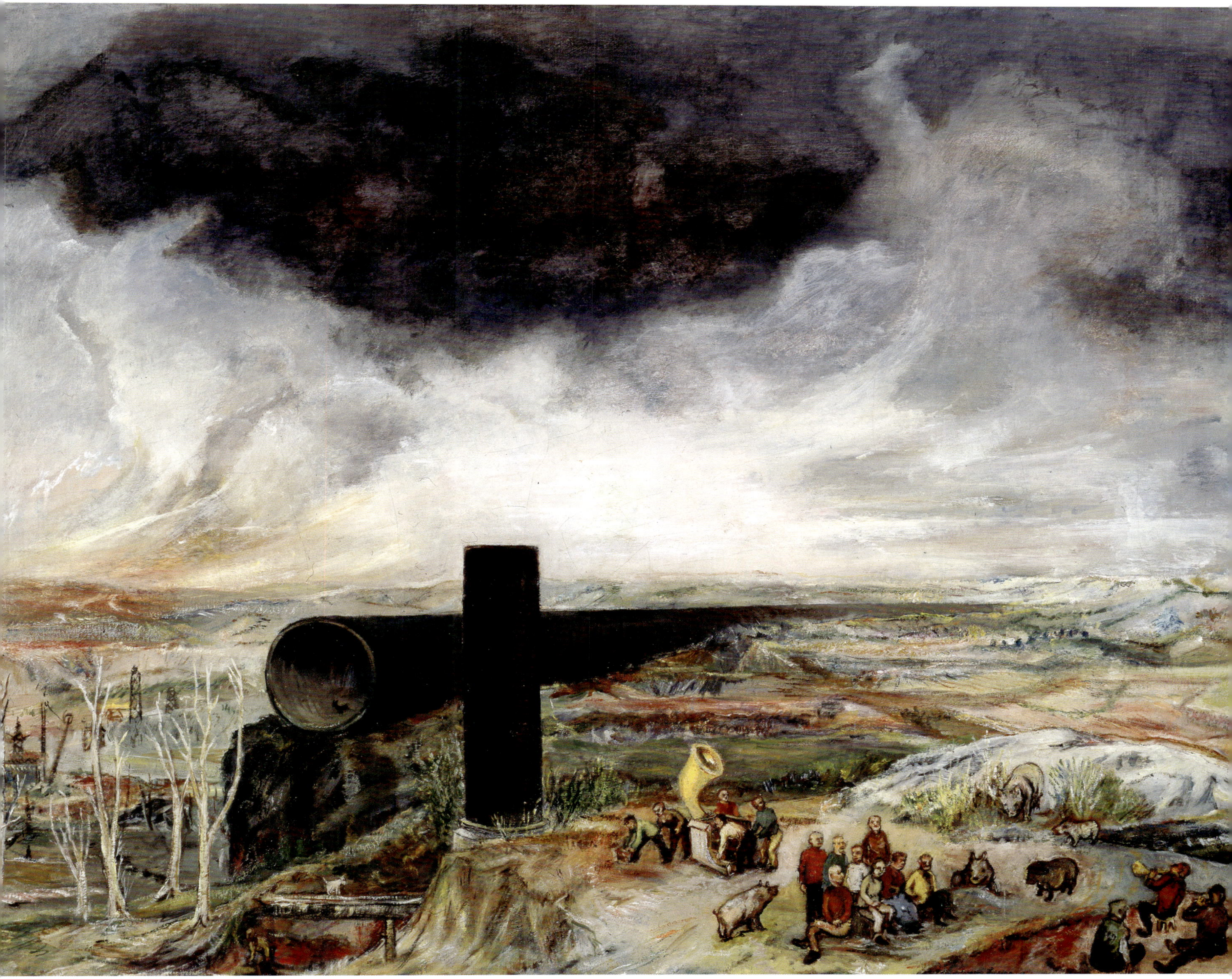

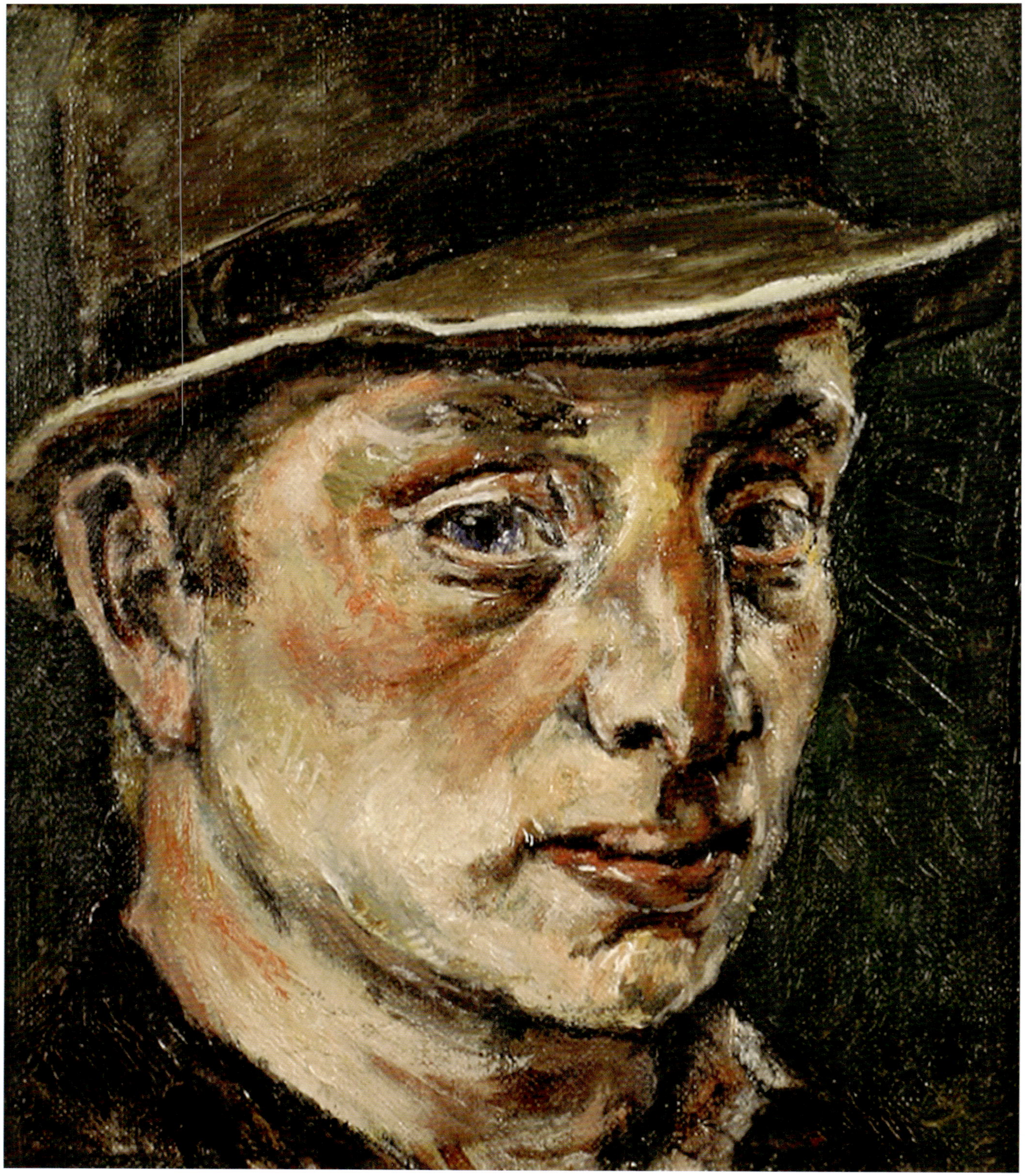

CAT. 25

Self-Portrait

c. 1940, oil on canvas
8½ x 7½ in.
Collection Janis Conner
and Joel Rosenkranz

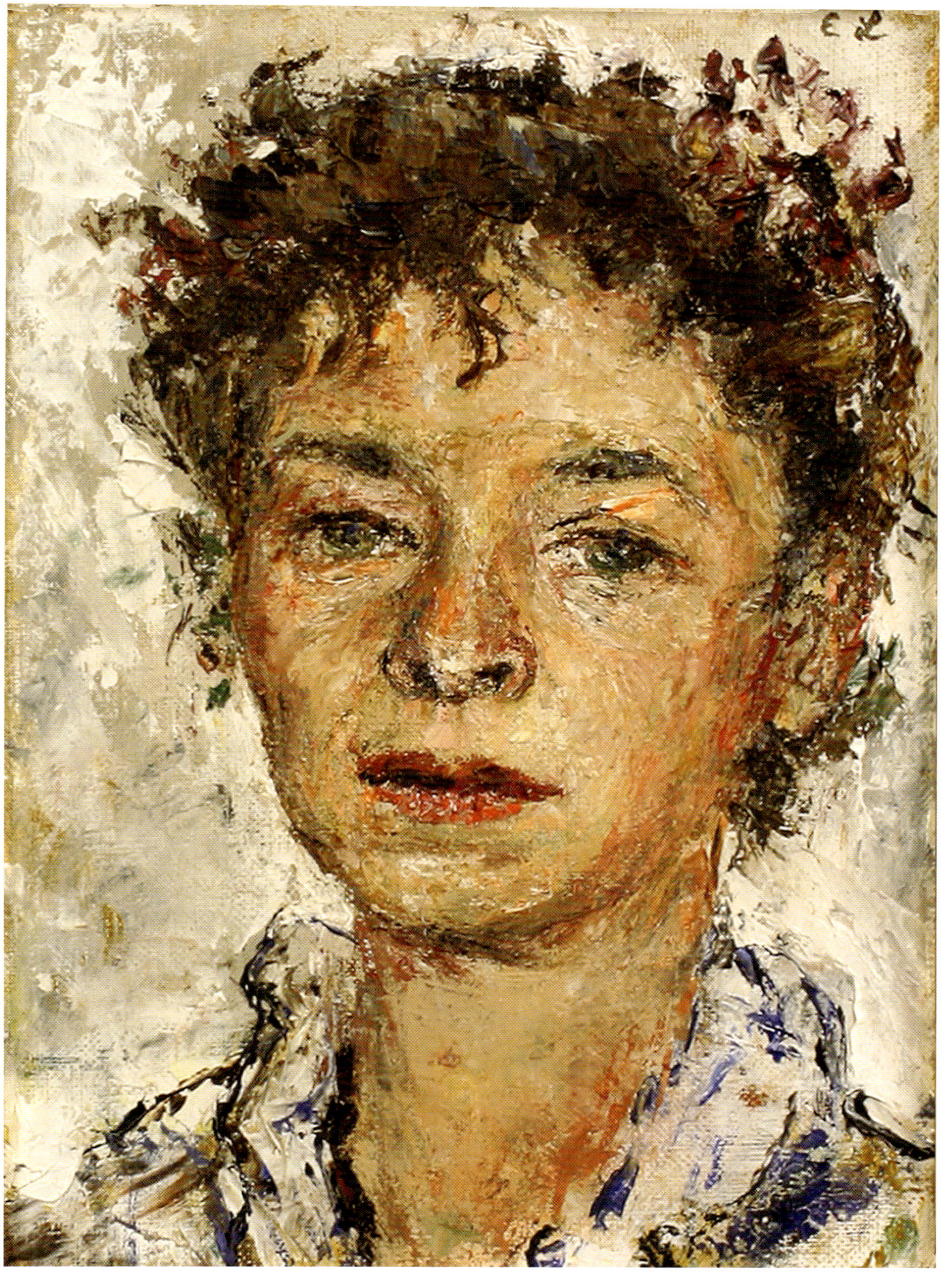

CAT. 26

Portrait of Hannah Small

c. 1940, oil on canvas
8 x 6 in.
Collection Janis Conner and Joel Rosenkranz

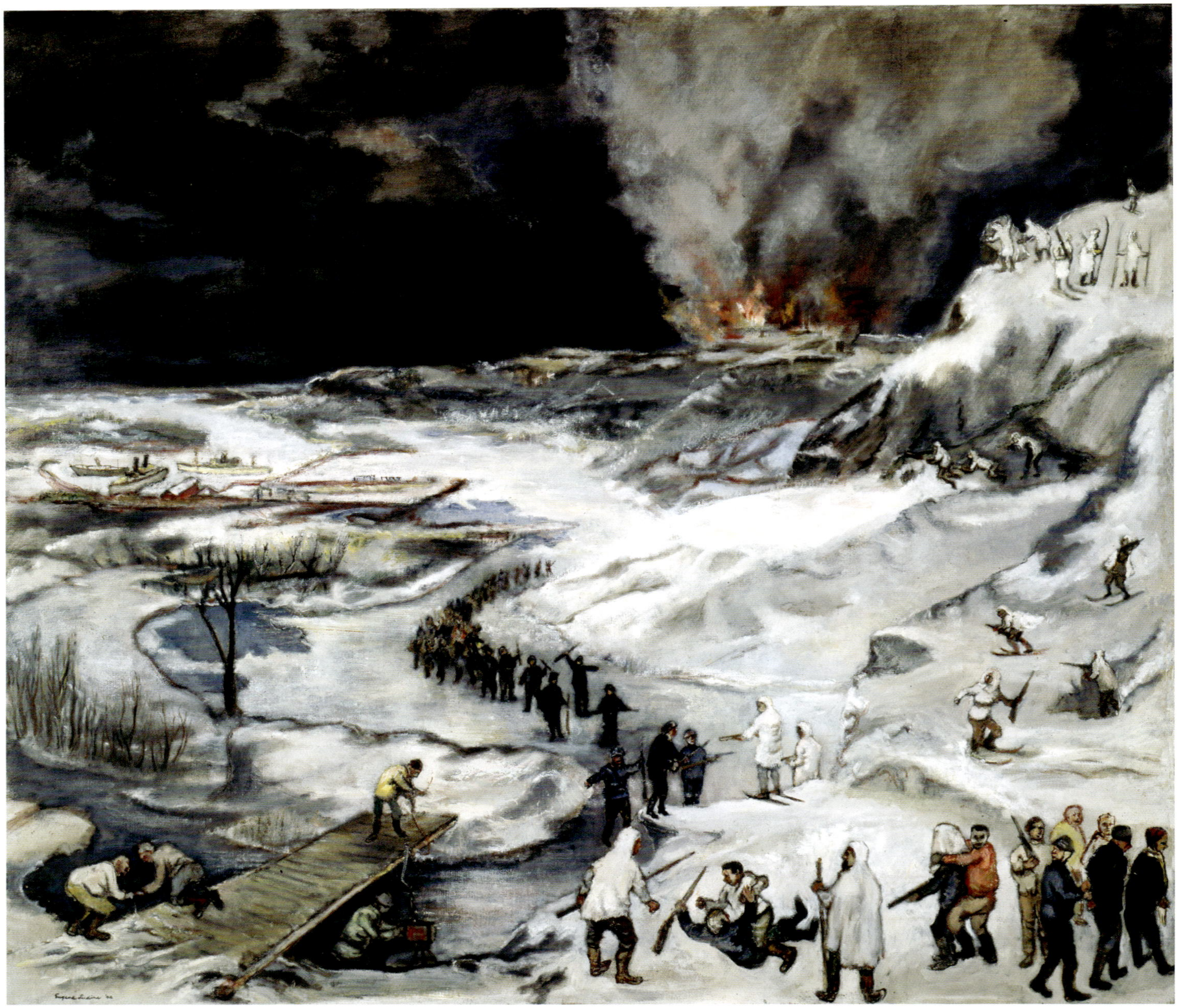

CAT. 27

Guerrillas

1942, oil on canvas
42 x 50 in.
Estate of Eugene Ludins

CAT. 28

Heavy Water

1942, oil on canvas
24 x 36 in.
Private Collection

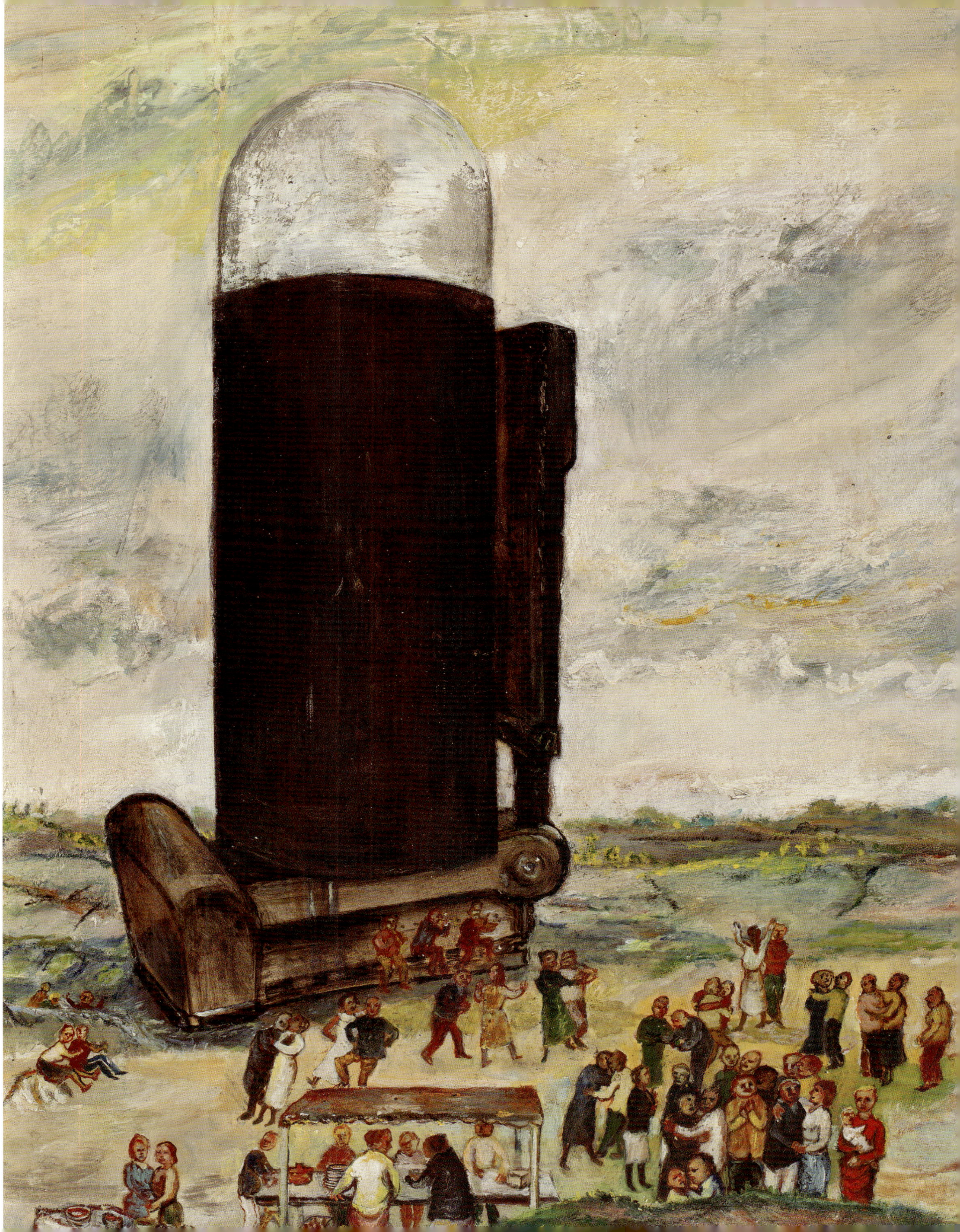

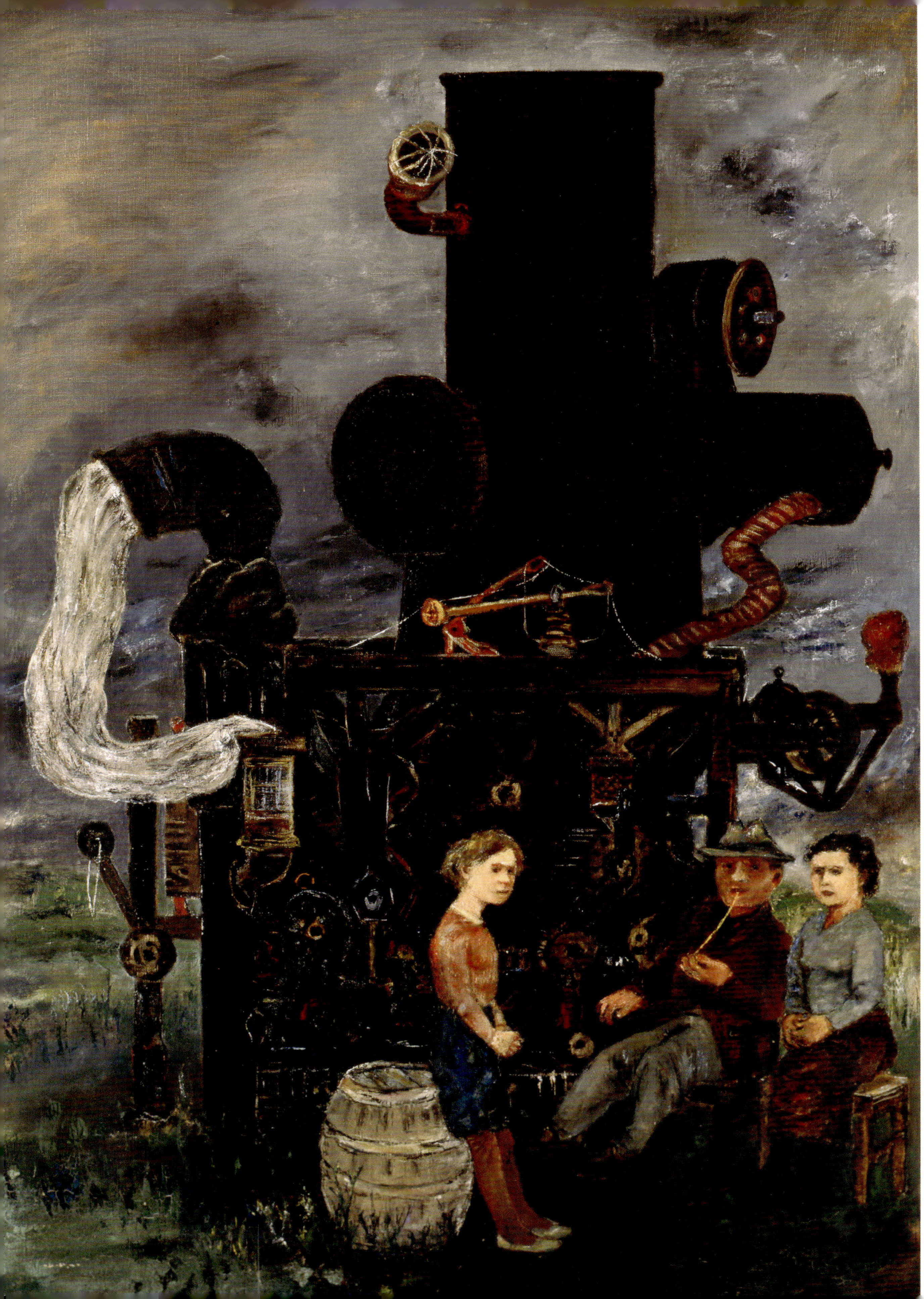

CAT. 29

Faith

1948, oil on canvas
50 x 36 in.
Estate of Eugene Ludins

CAT. 30

The Valley

1947, oil on canvas
48 x 36 in.
Woodstock Artists Association
and Museum, gift of Ira Janow

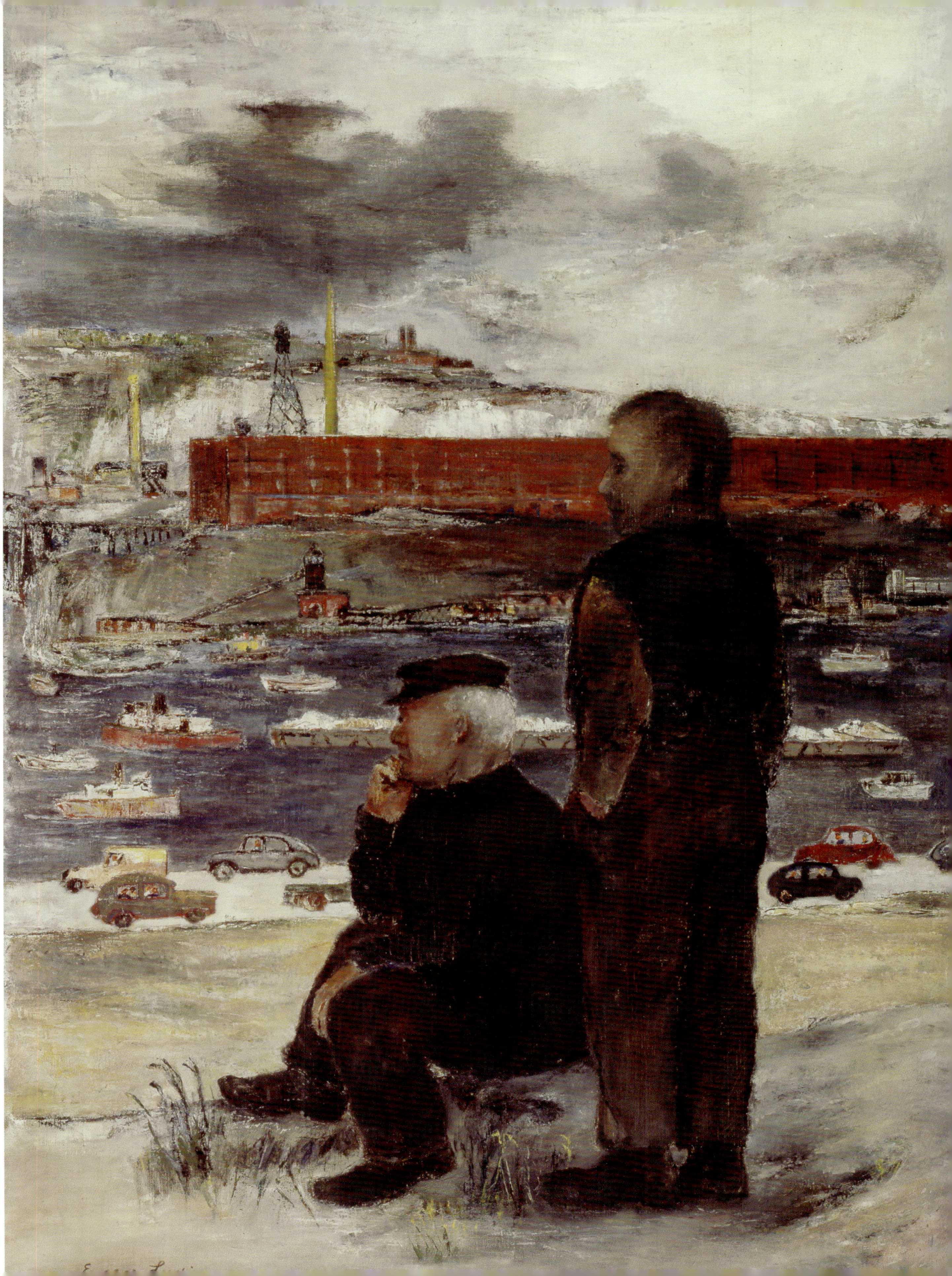

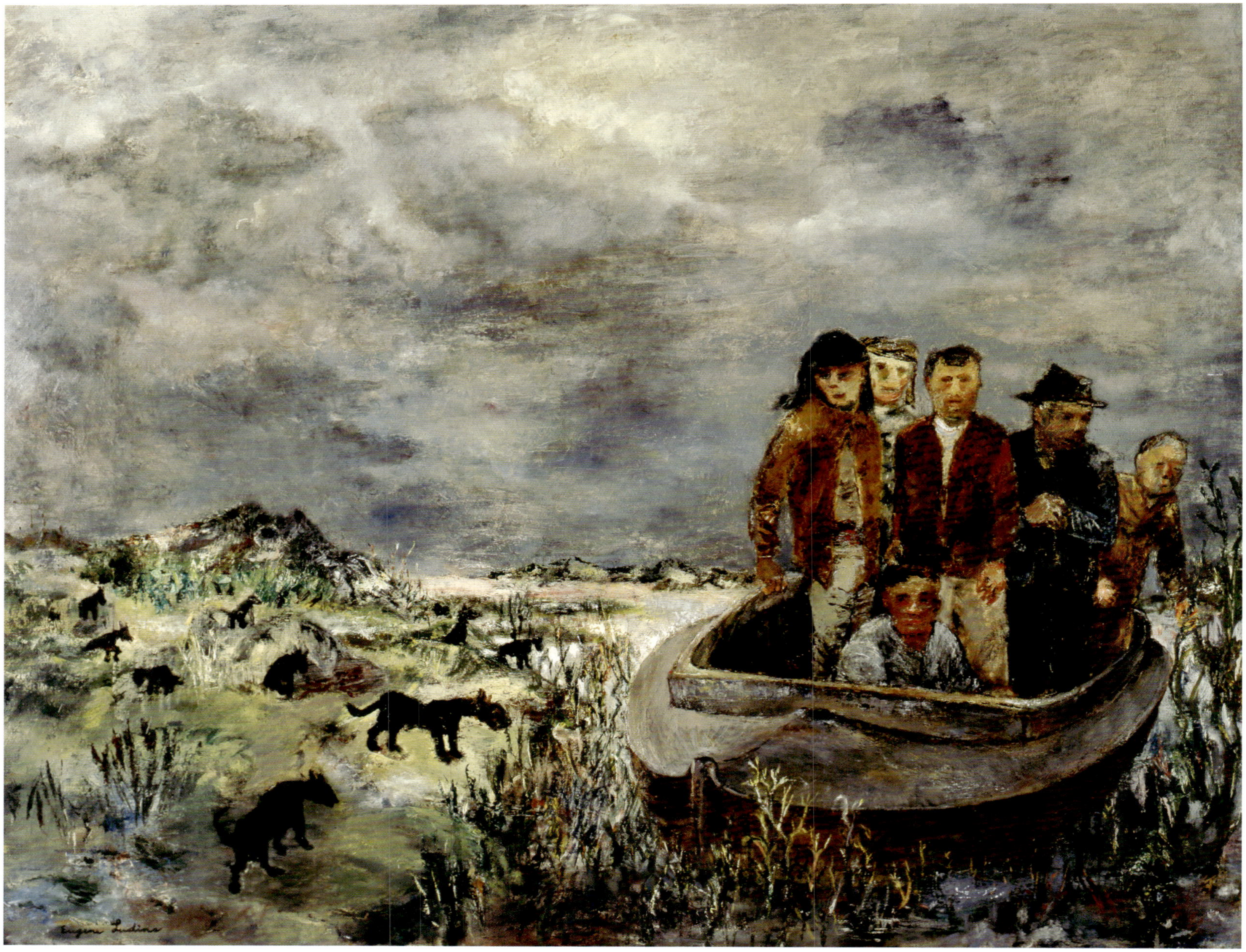

CAT. 31

Intruders

c. 1949, oil on canvas
38 x 50 in.
Estate of Eugene Ludins

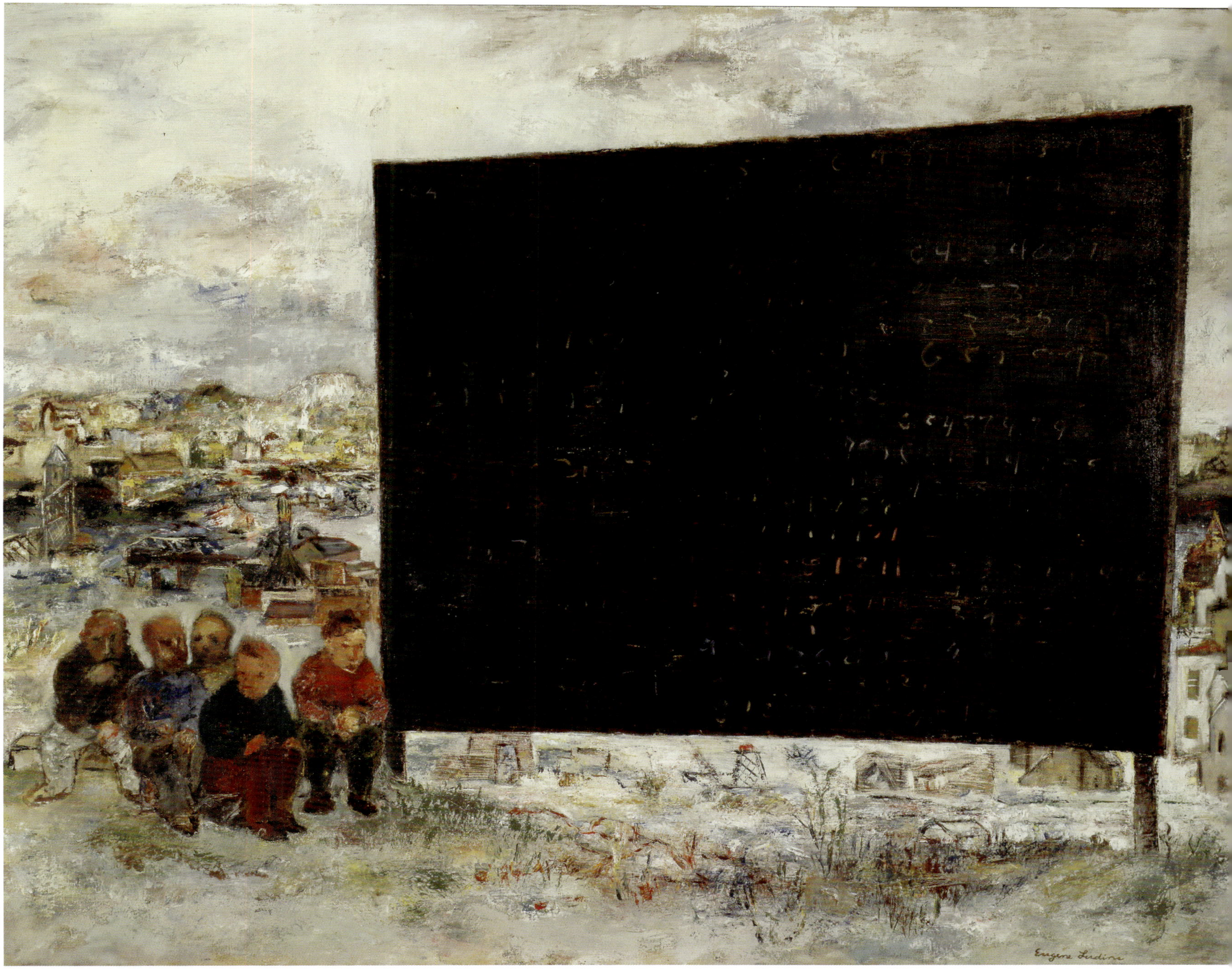

CAT. 32

Sum

c. 1949, oil on canvas
38 x 50 in.
Estate of Eugene Ludins

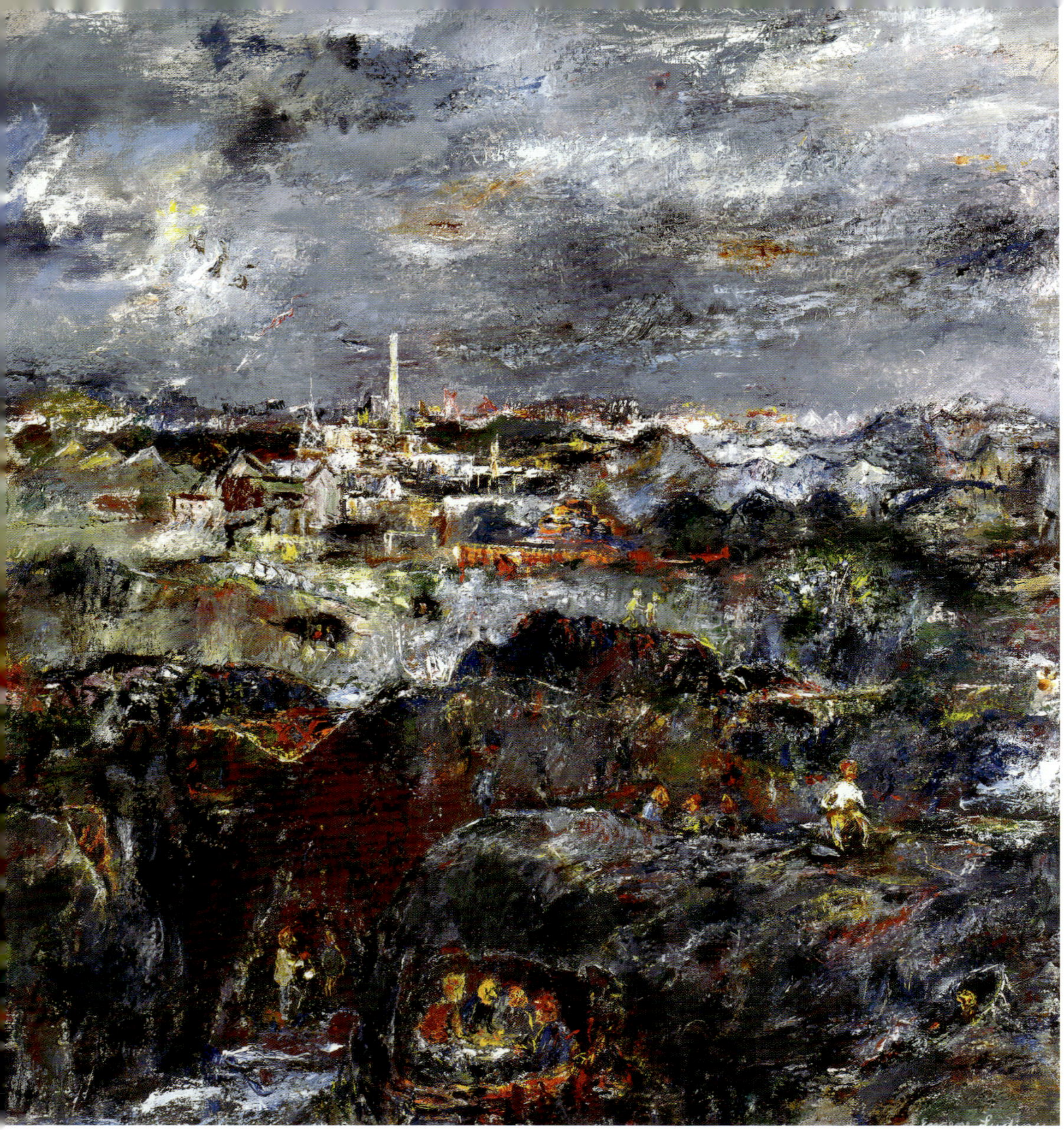

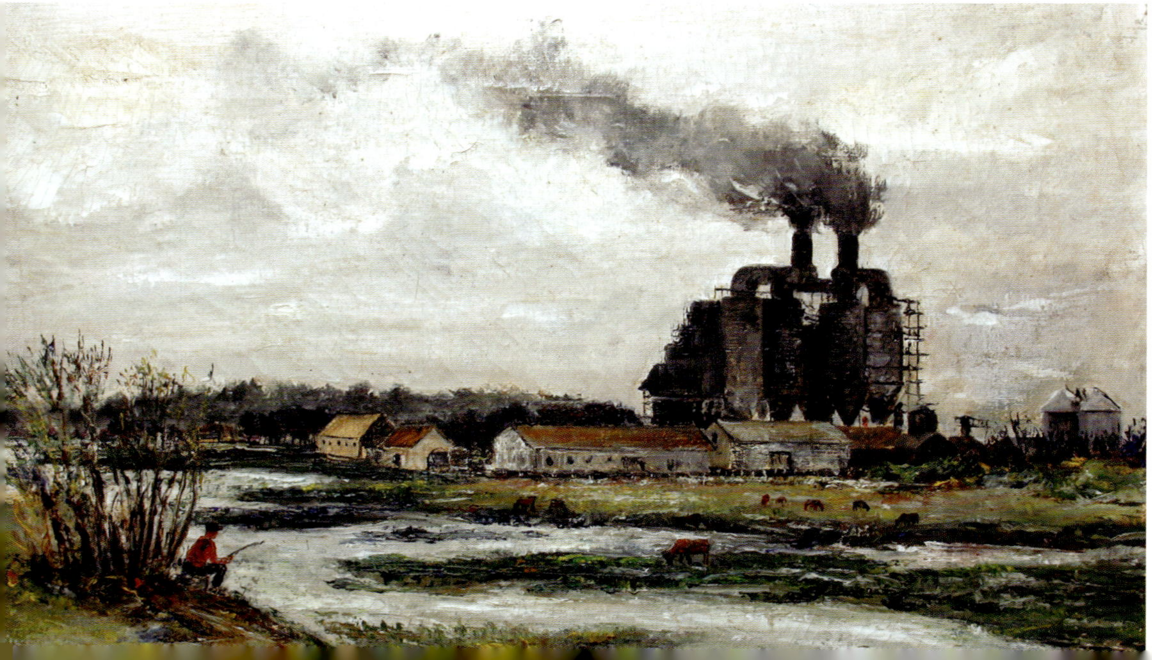

CAT. 33

Hiding Places

c. 1949, oil on canvas
40¾ x 39 in.
Private Collection

CAT. 34

Carbon Black

1946, oil on canvas
14 x 24 in.
Private Collection

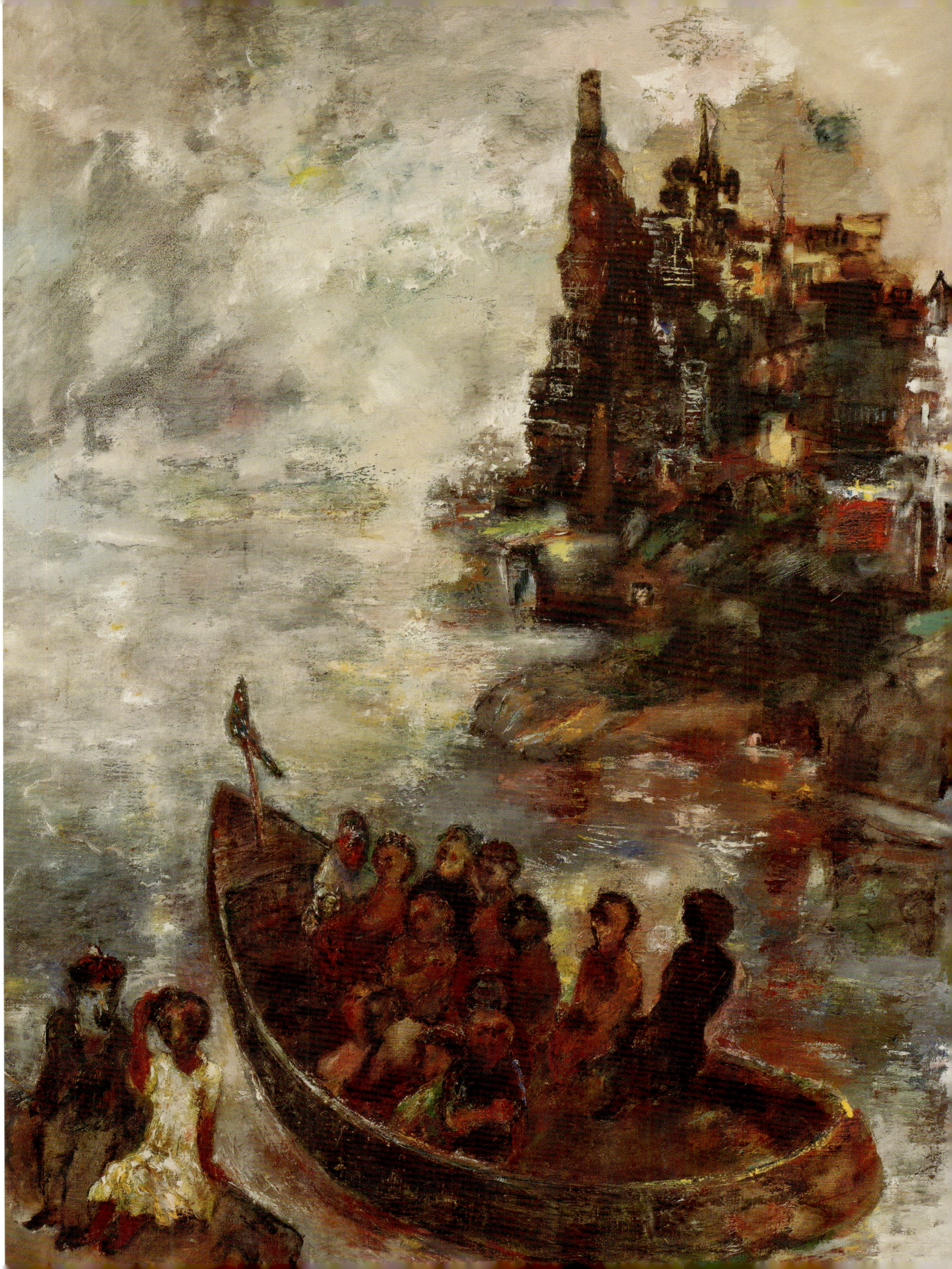

CAT. 35

Excursion

Early 1950s, oil on canvas
50 x 38 in.
Estate of Eugene Ludins

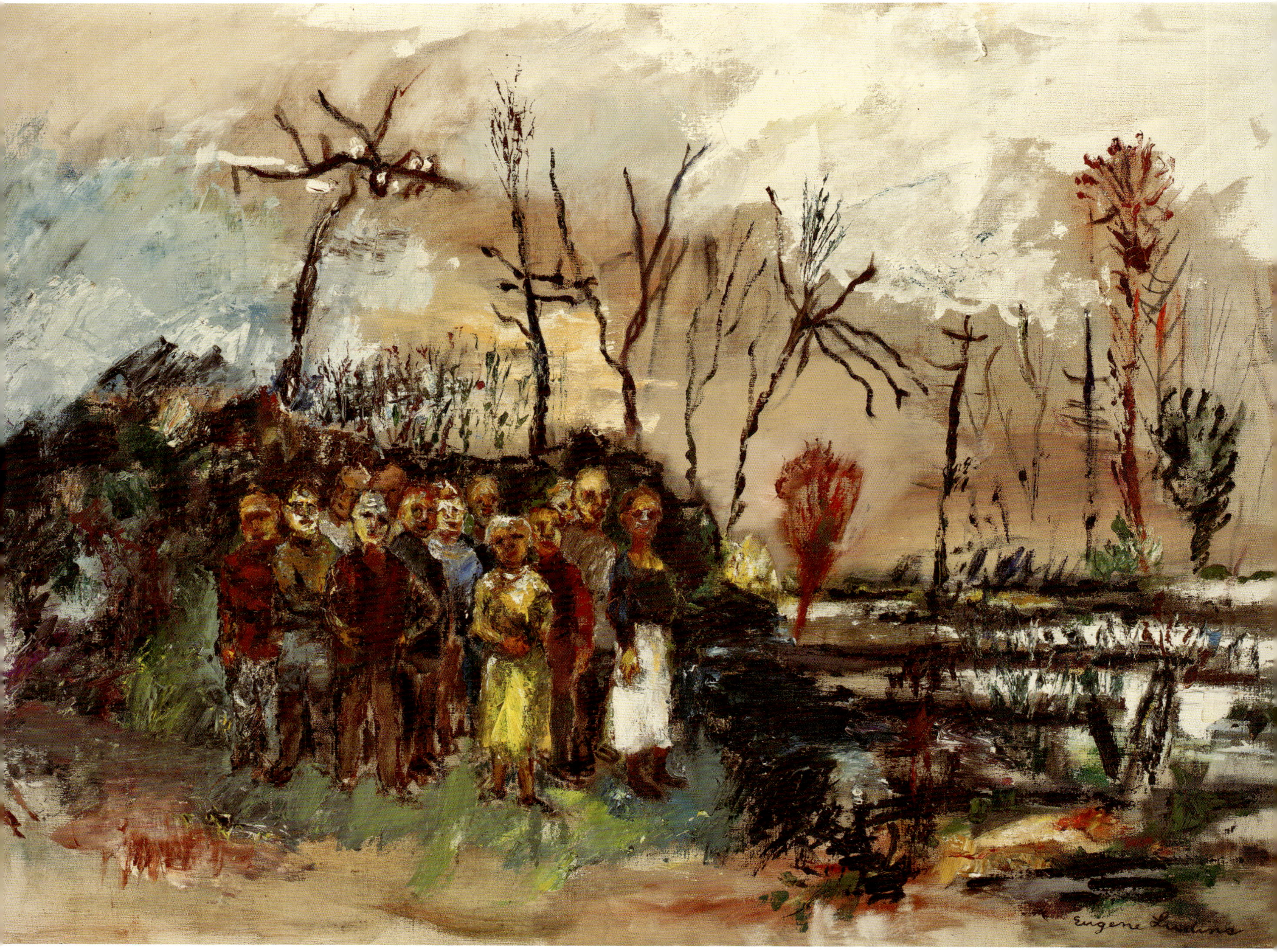

CAT. 36

Suspicion

c. 1951–52, oil on canvas
30 x 43 in.
Estate of Eugene Ludins

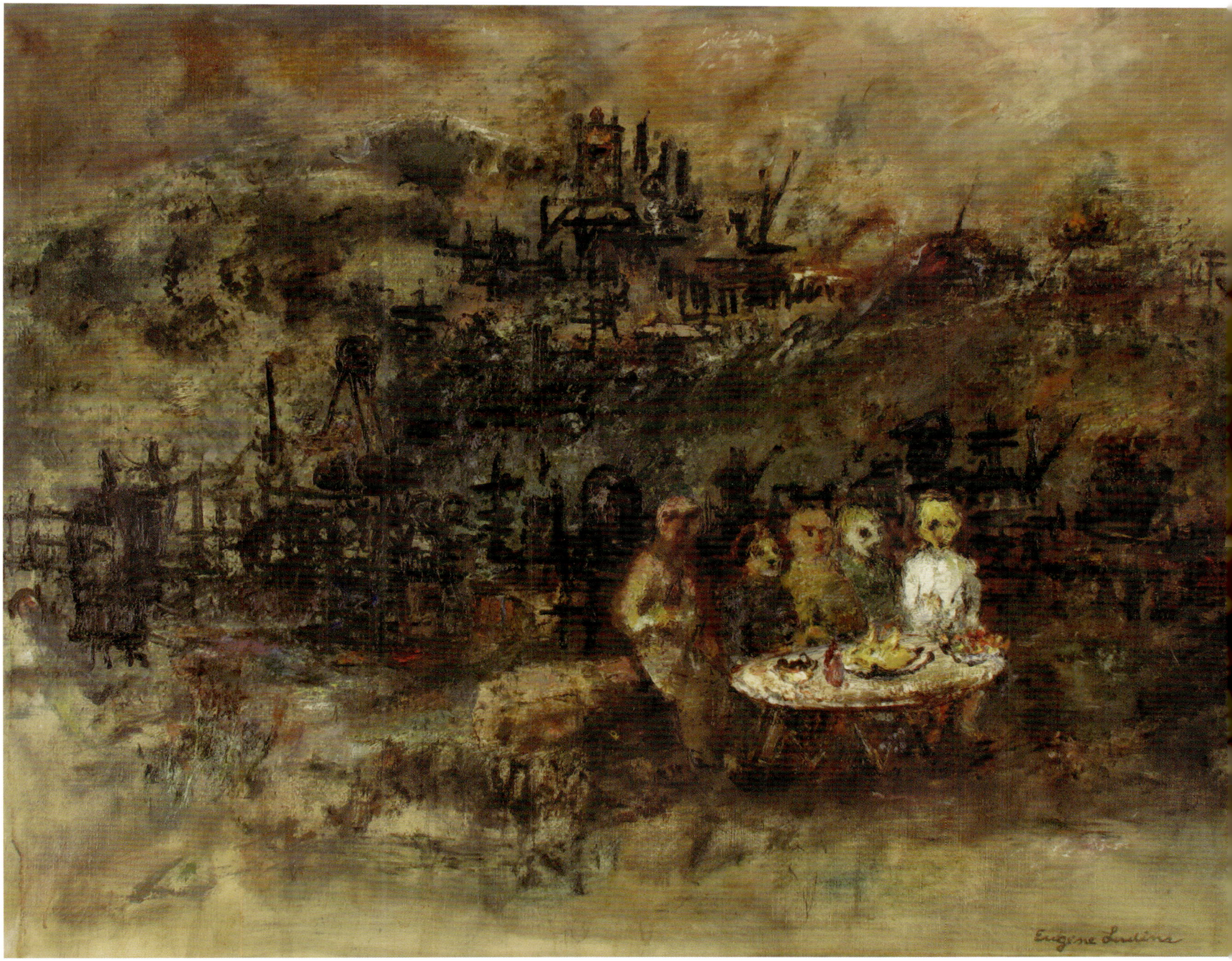

CAT. 37

Al Fresco

1954, oil on canvas
30 x 40 in.
Collection Samuel Dorsky Museum of Art, State University of New York at New Paltz, gift of Petra Cabot

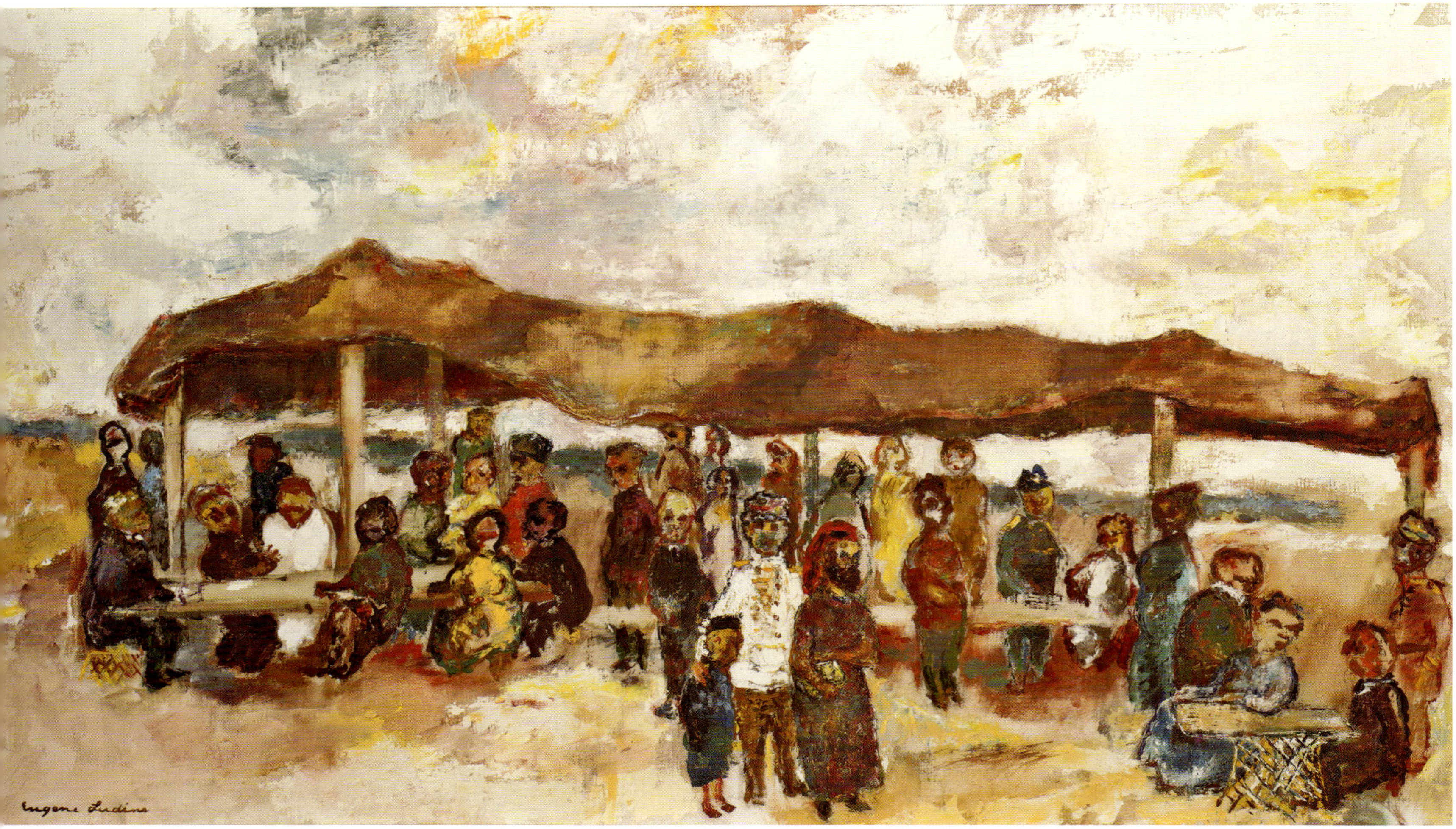

CAT. 38

High-Level Conference

1957, oil on canvas
28 x 50 in.
Estate of Eugene Ludins

CAT. 39

Oil Riches

1961, oil on canvas
50 x 42 in.
Estate of Eugene Ludins

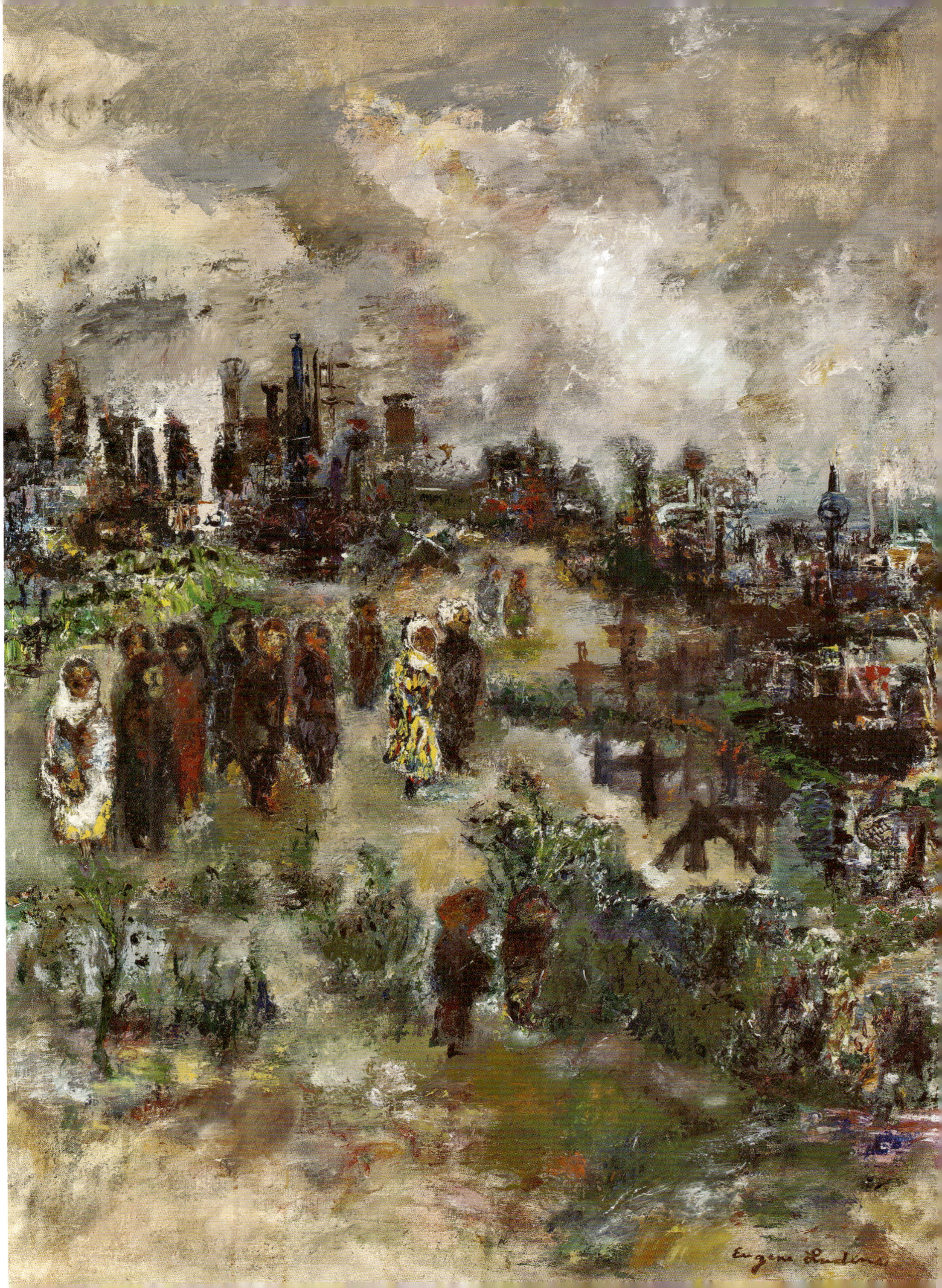
Eugene Ludins

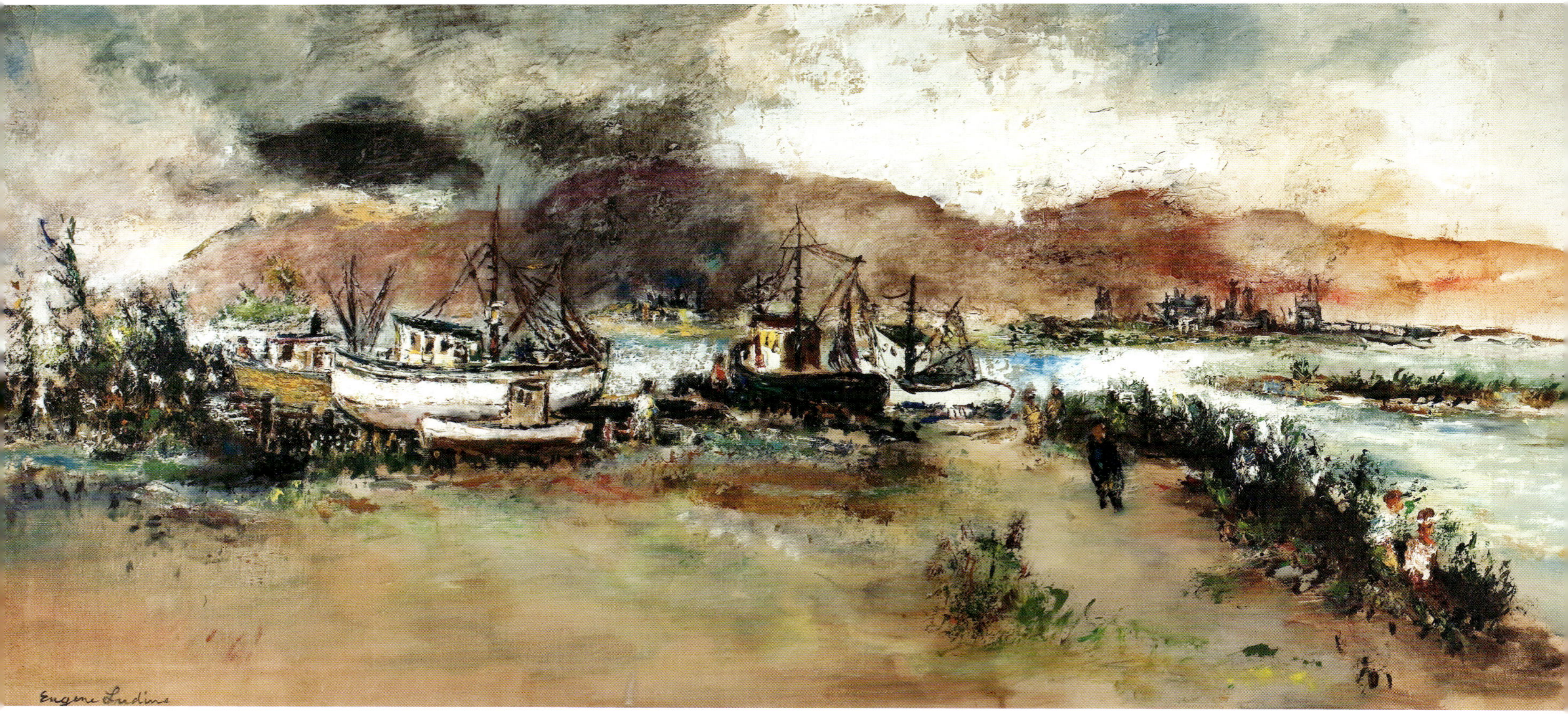

CAT. 40

Aransas Pass

1955, oil on canvas
20 x 44 in.
Private Collection

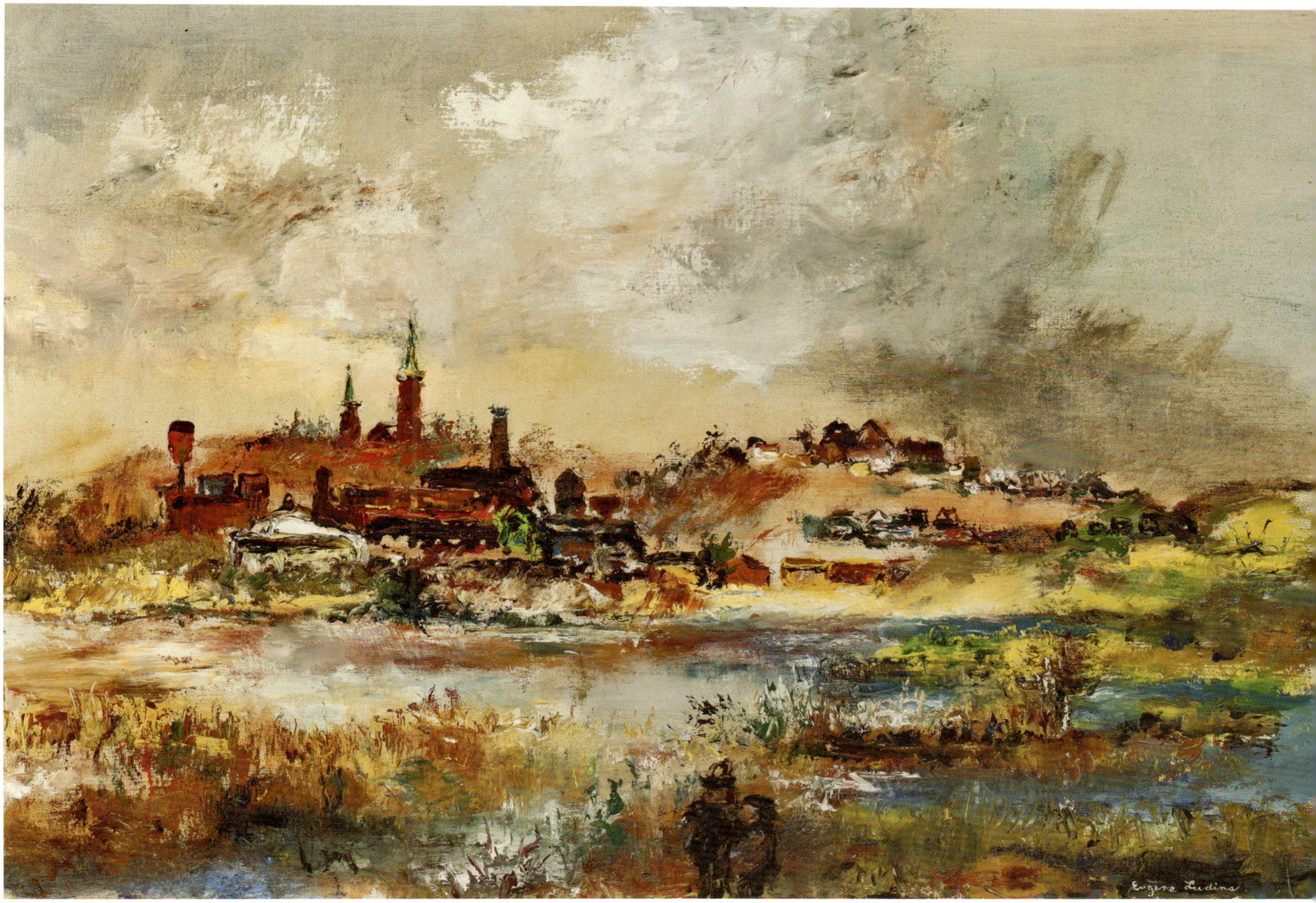

CAT. 41

Dubuque

1962, oil on canvas
20 x 30 in.
Estate of Eugene Ludins

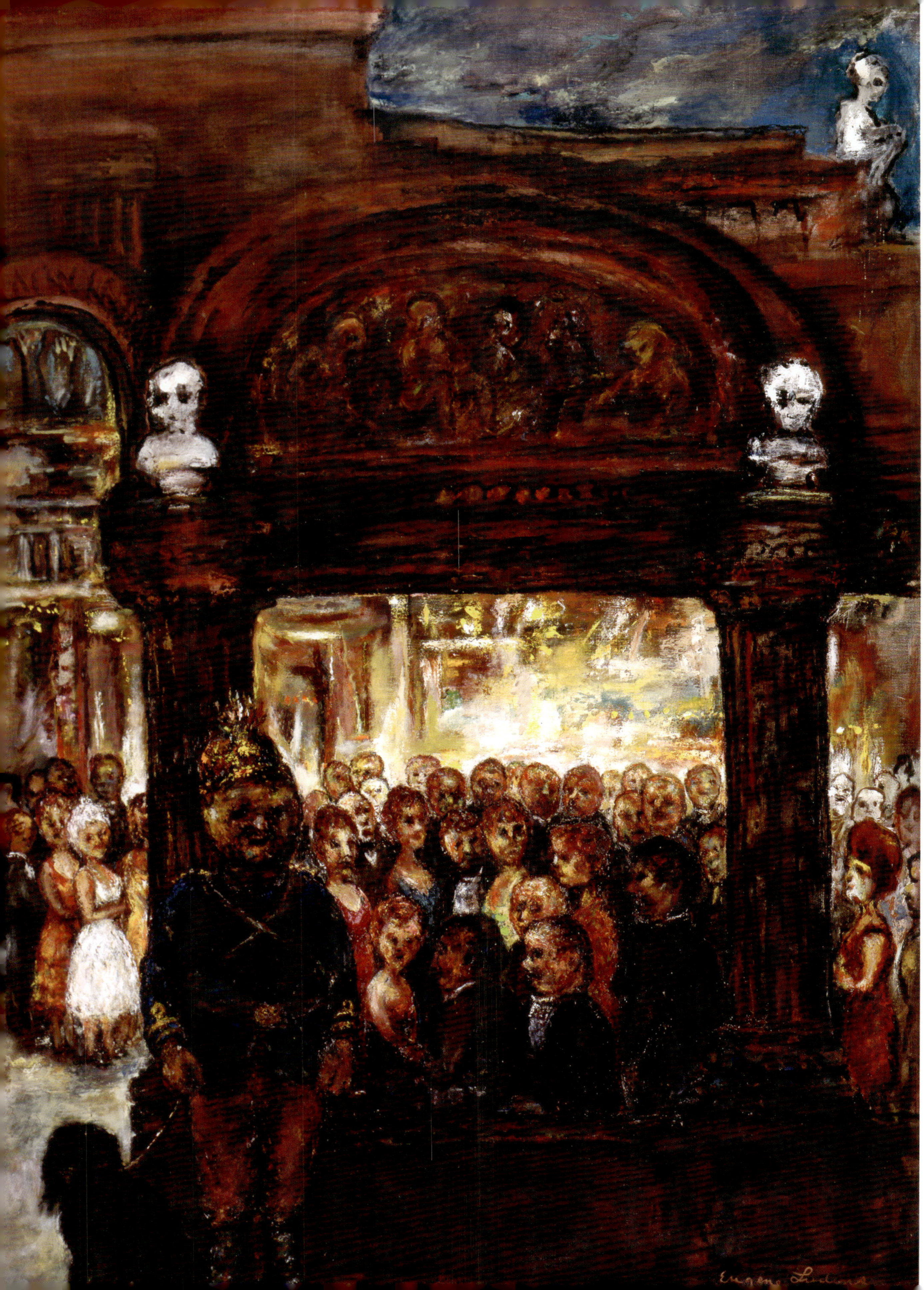

CAT. 42

Near the Summit

1960s, oil on canvas
50 x 36 in.
Estate of Eugene Ludins

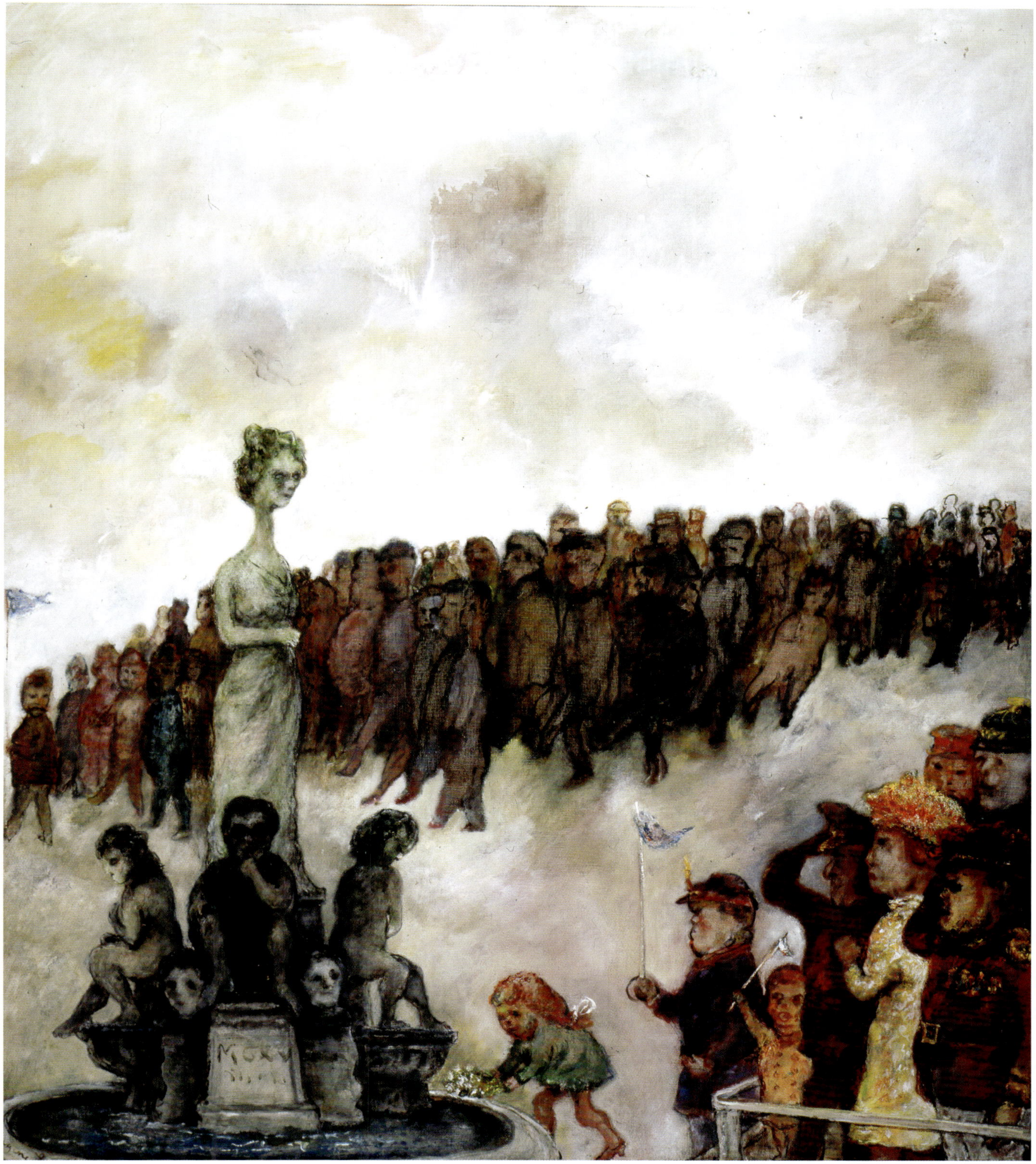

CAT. 43

Veterans of Several Wars

1960s, oil on canvas
55 x 50 in.
Estate of Eugene Ludins

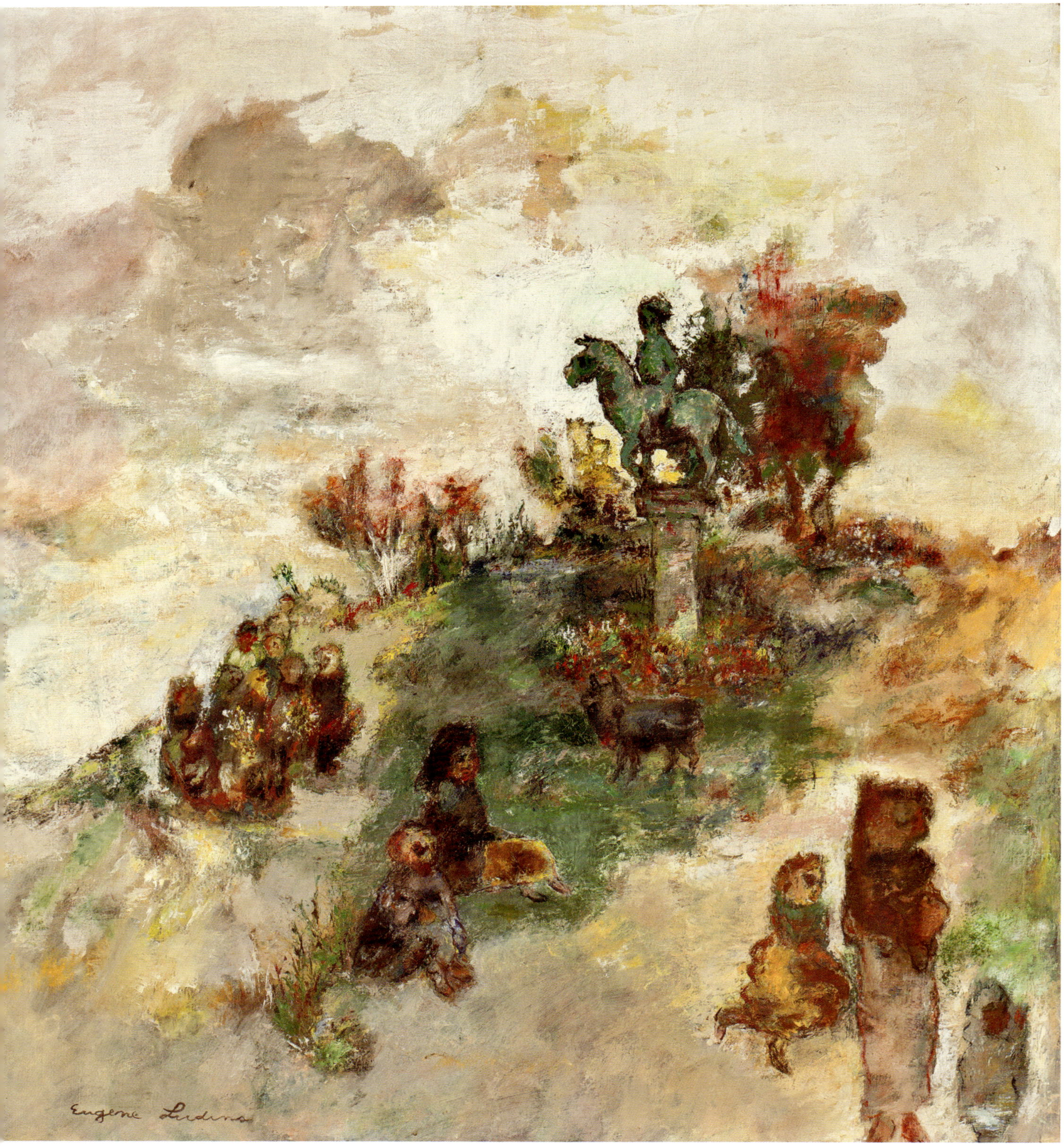

CAT. 44

Monument

1958–60, oil on canvas
40 x 38 in.
Estate of Eugene Ludins

CAT. 45

Crossing

c. 1960, oil on canvas
38 x 50 in.
Estate of Eugene Ludins

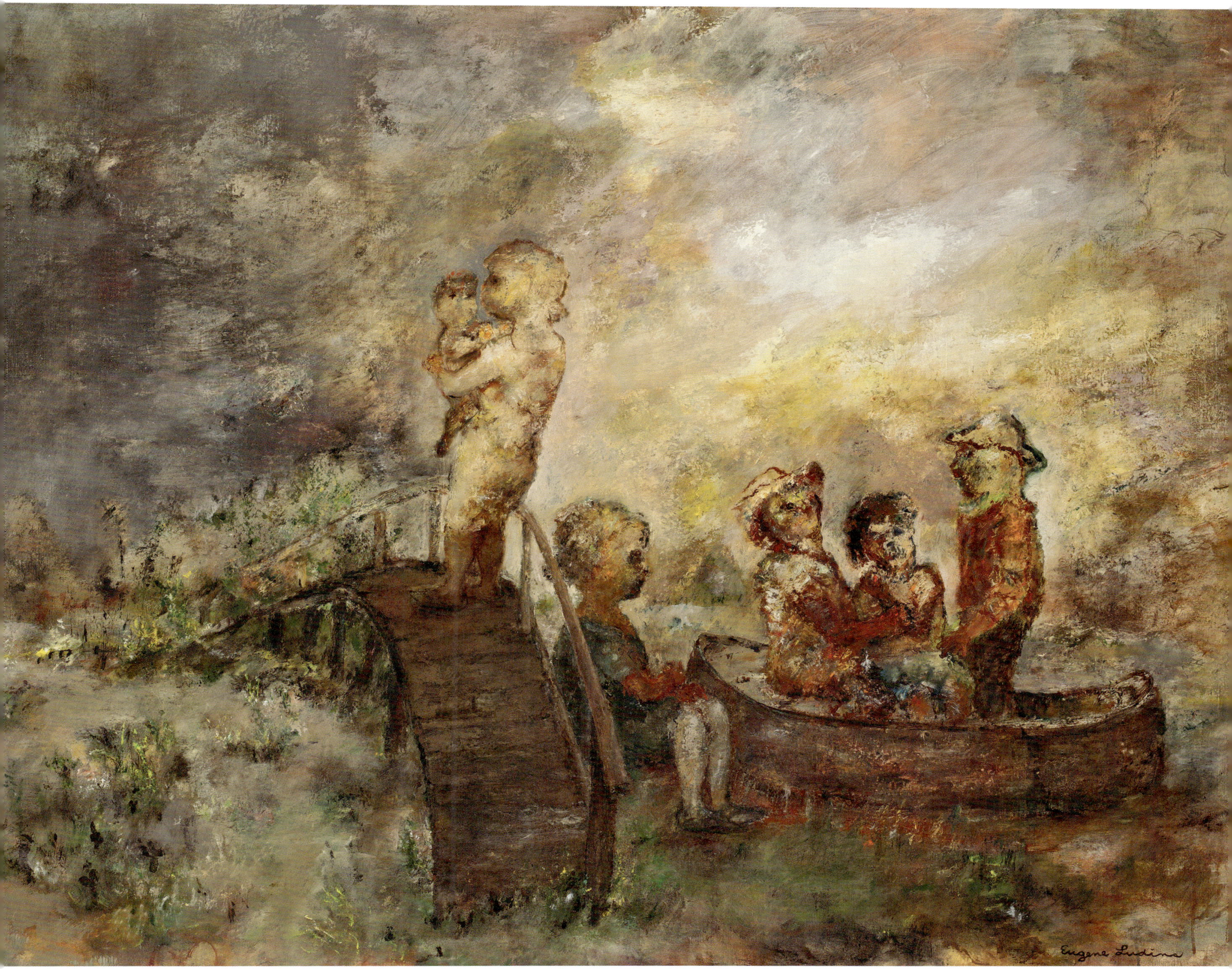
Eugene Ludins

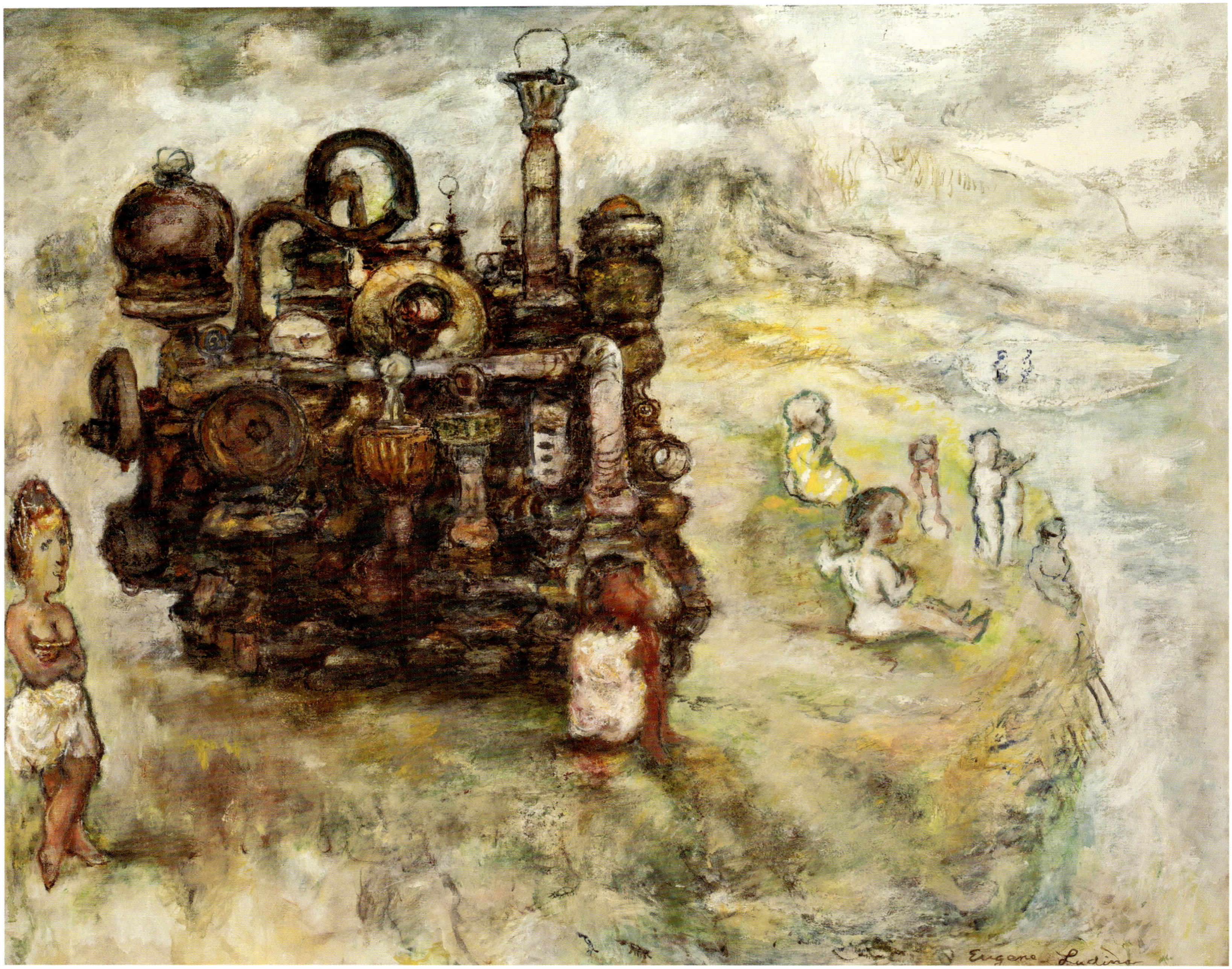

CAT. 46

Regenerator

1965–75, oil on canvas
39 x 50 in.
Estate of Eugene Ludins

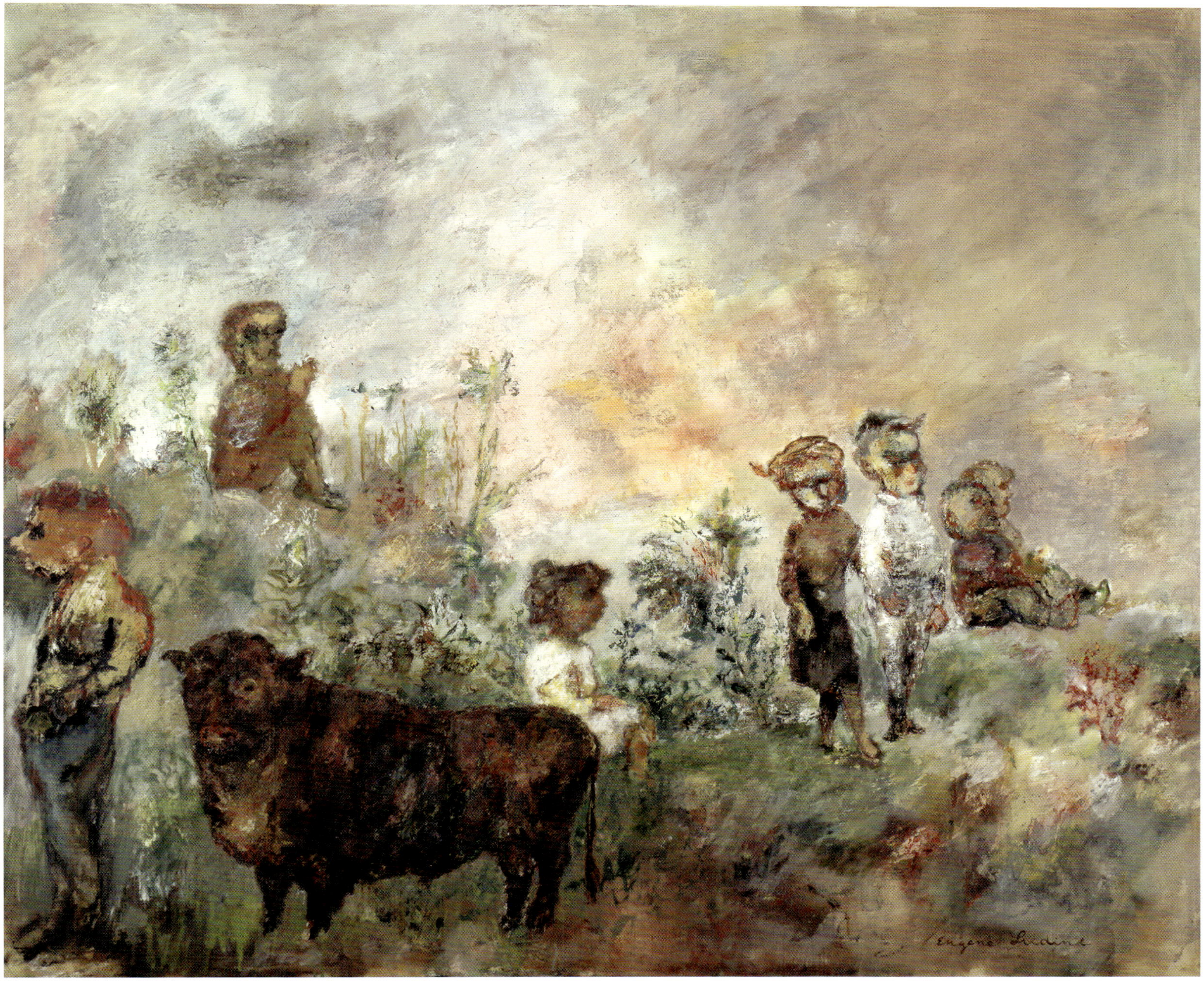

CAT. 47

Meadow

1960s, oil on canvas
40 x 50 in.
Estate of Eugene Ludins

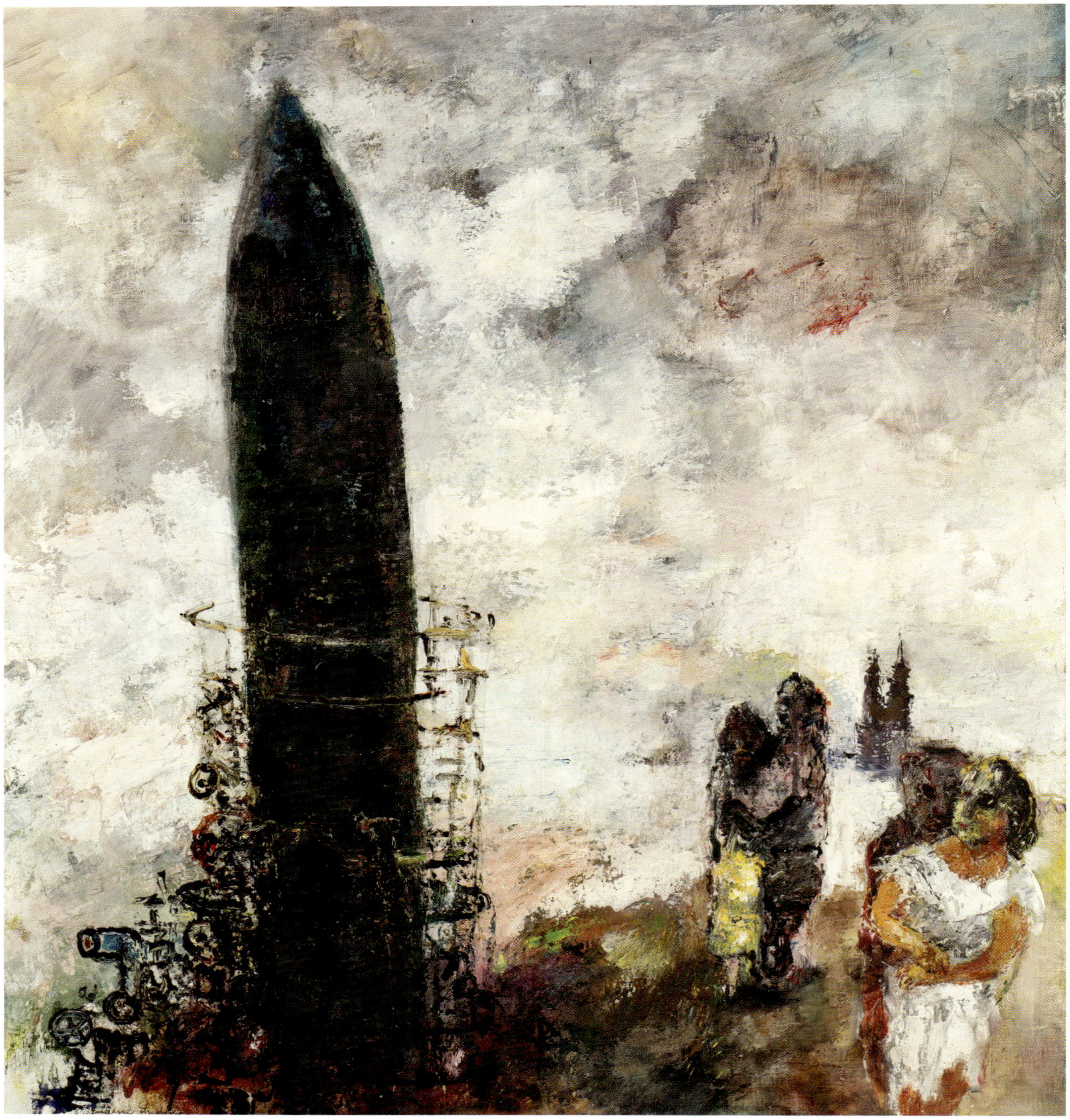

CAT. 48

To Space

1961, oil on canvas
40 x 38 in.
Estate of Eugene Ludins

CAT. 49

Pastoral

1965, oil on canvas
40 x 55 in.
Estate of Eugene Ludins

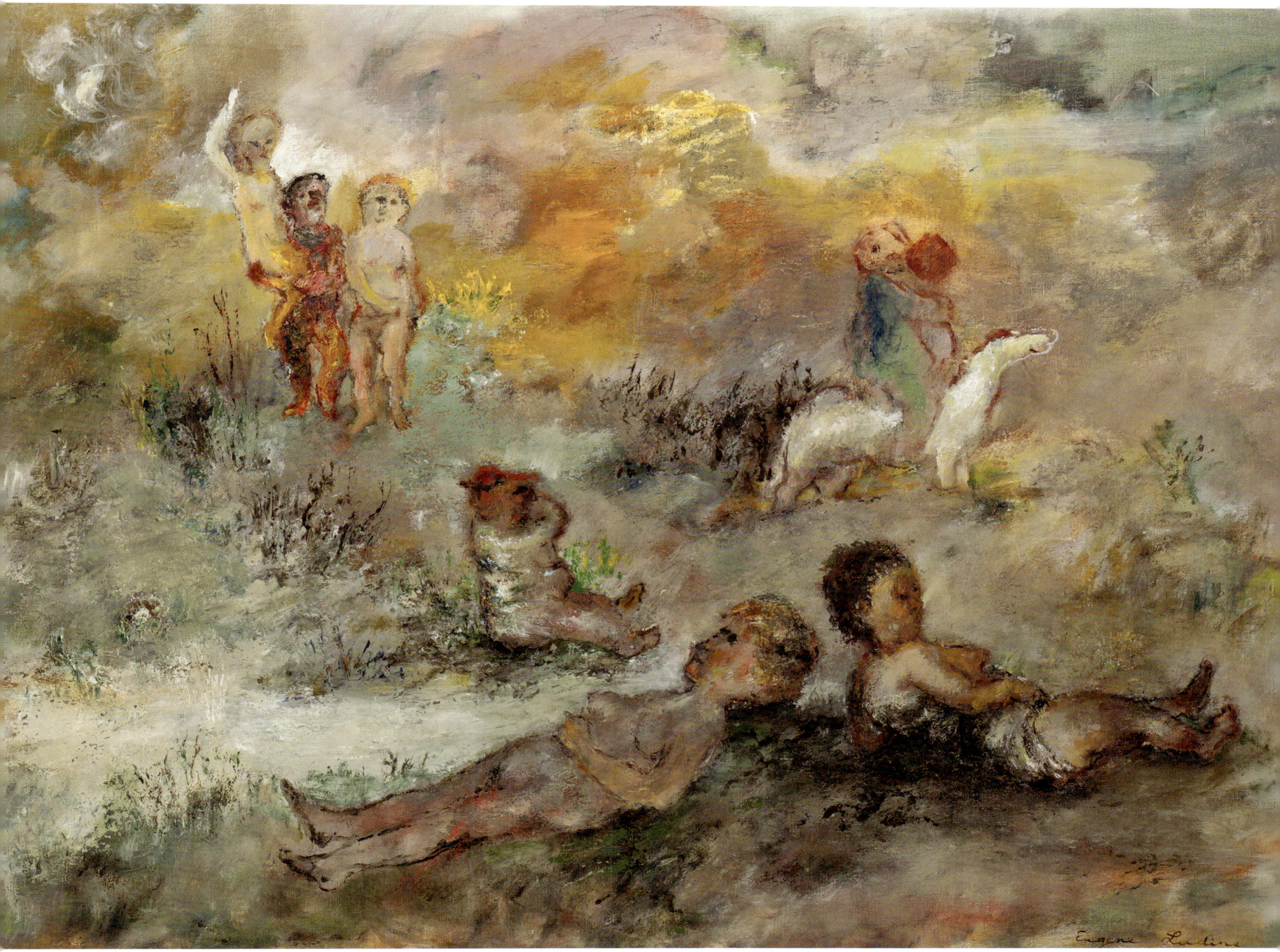

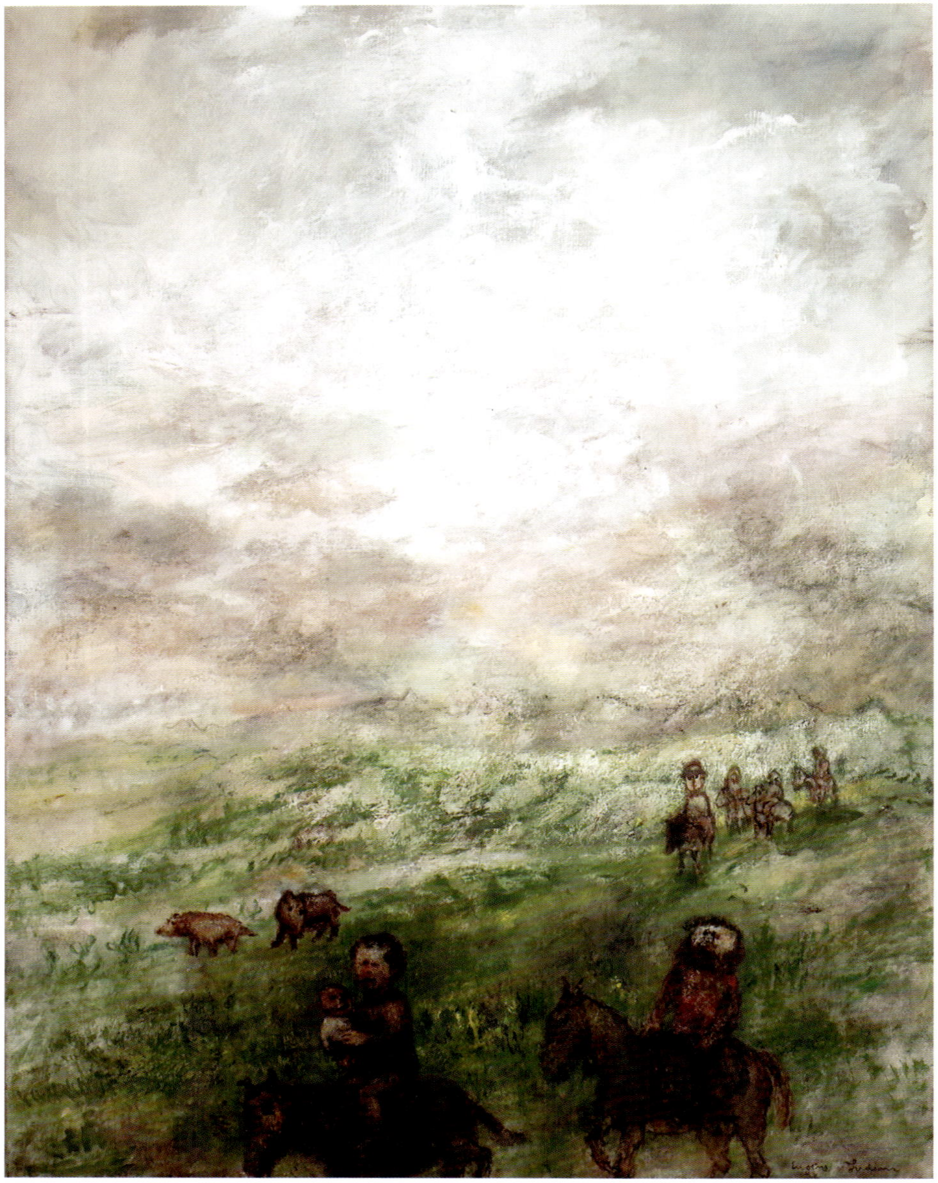

CAT. 50

From the Hills

Late 1970s, oil on canvas
50½ x 40¼ in.
Private Collection

CAT. 51

Red Hills

1977, oil on canvas
16 x 30 in.
Estate of Eugene Ludins

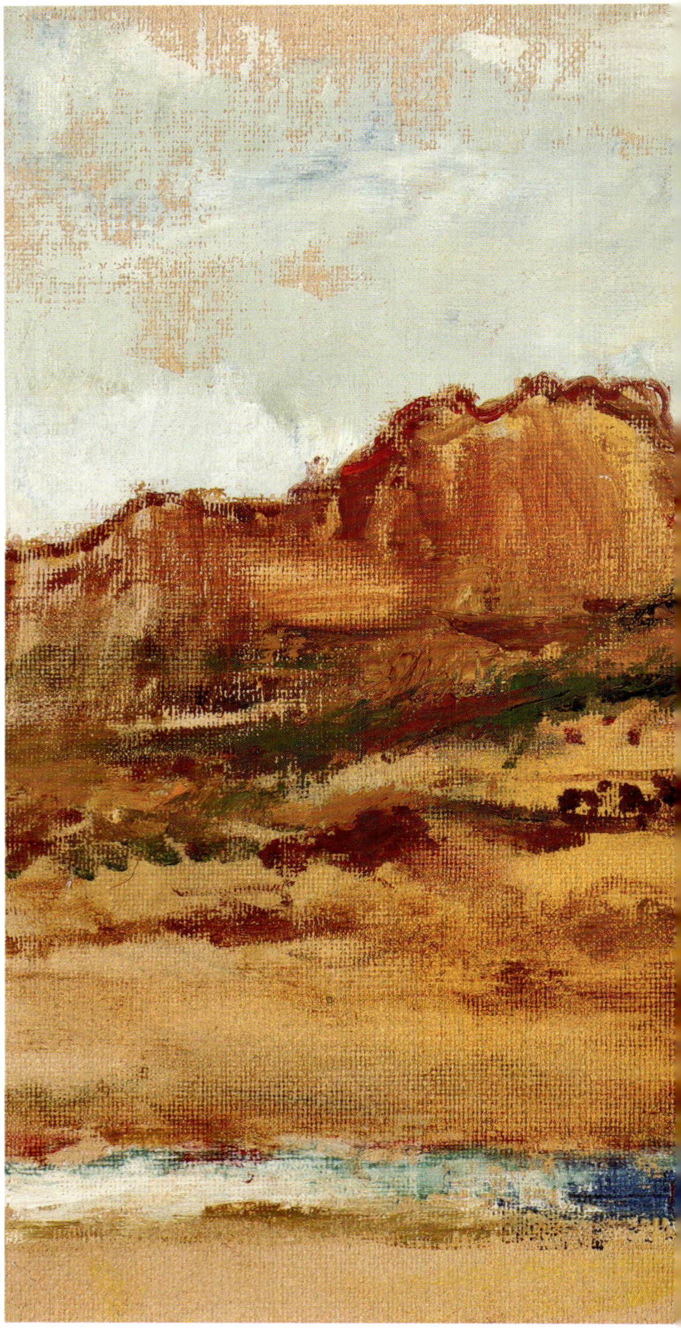

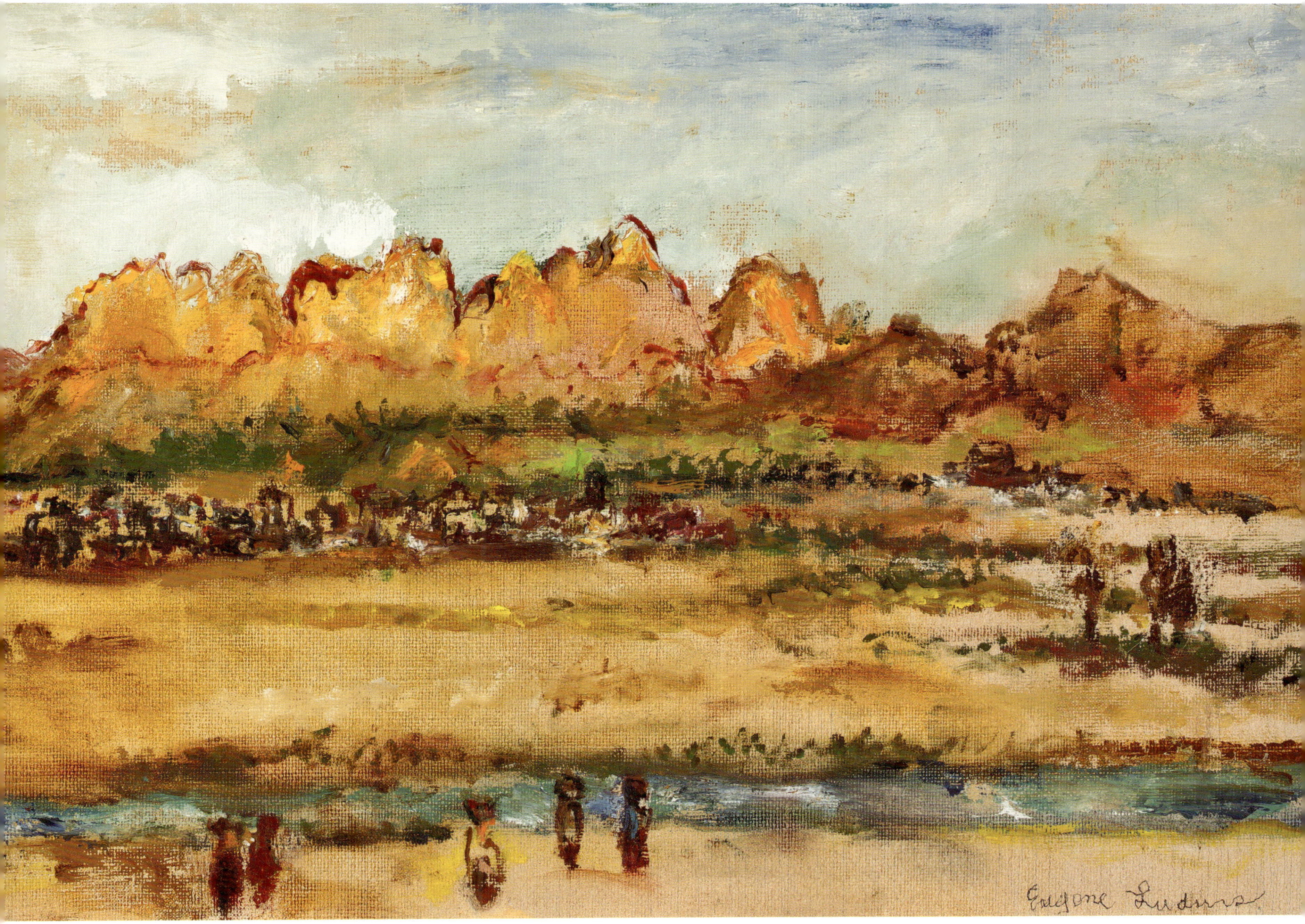
Eugene Ludins

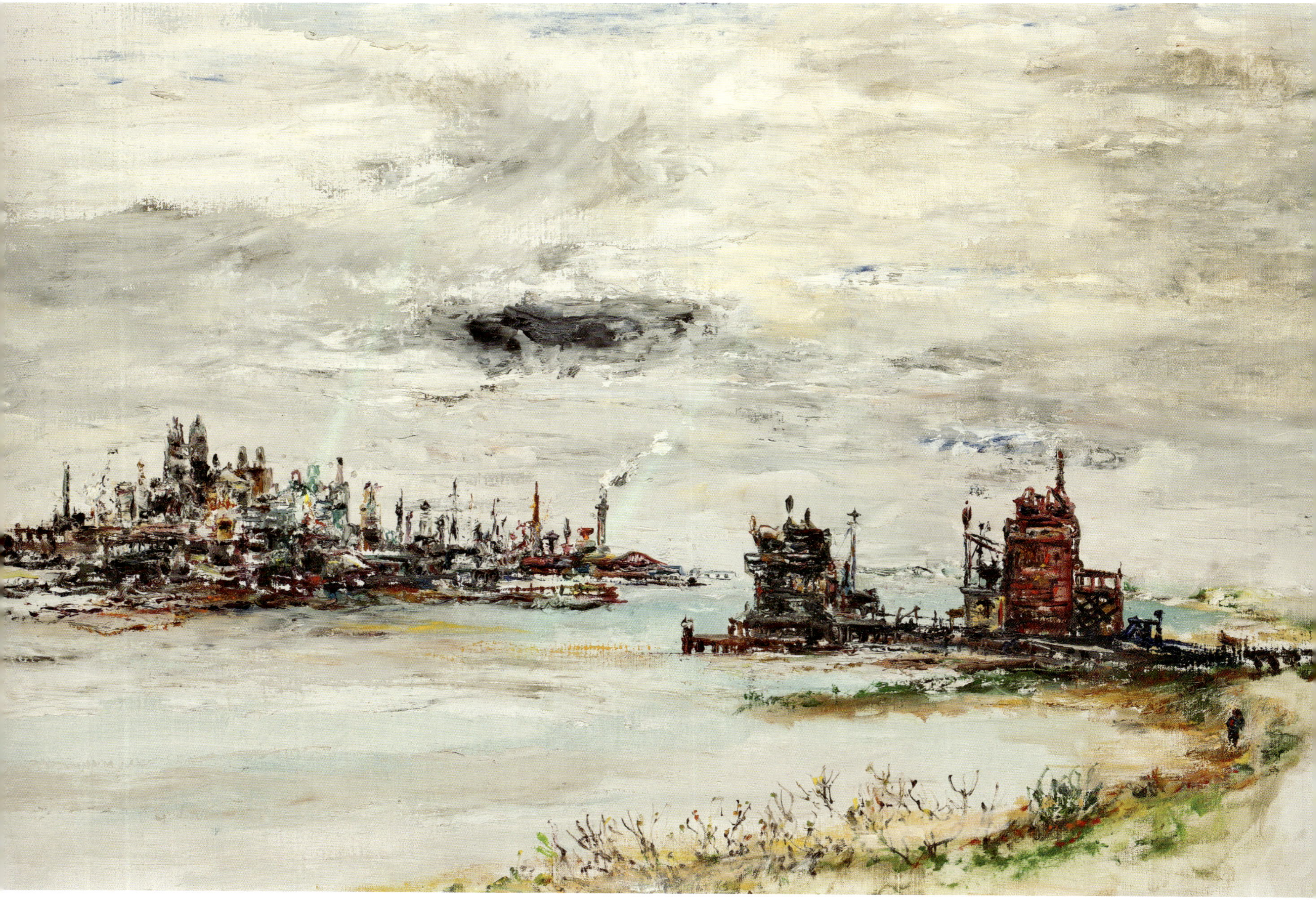

CAT. 52

Navigation Boulevard

1970s, oil on canvas
24 x 36 in.
Estate of Eugene Ludins

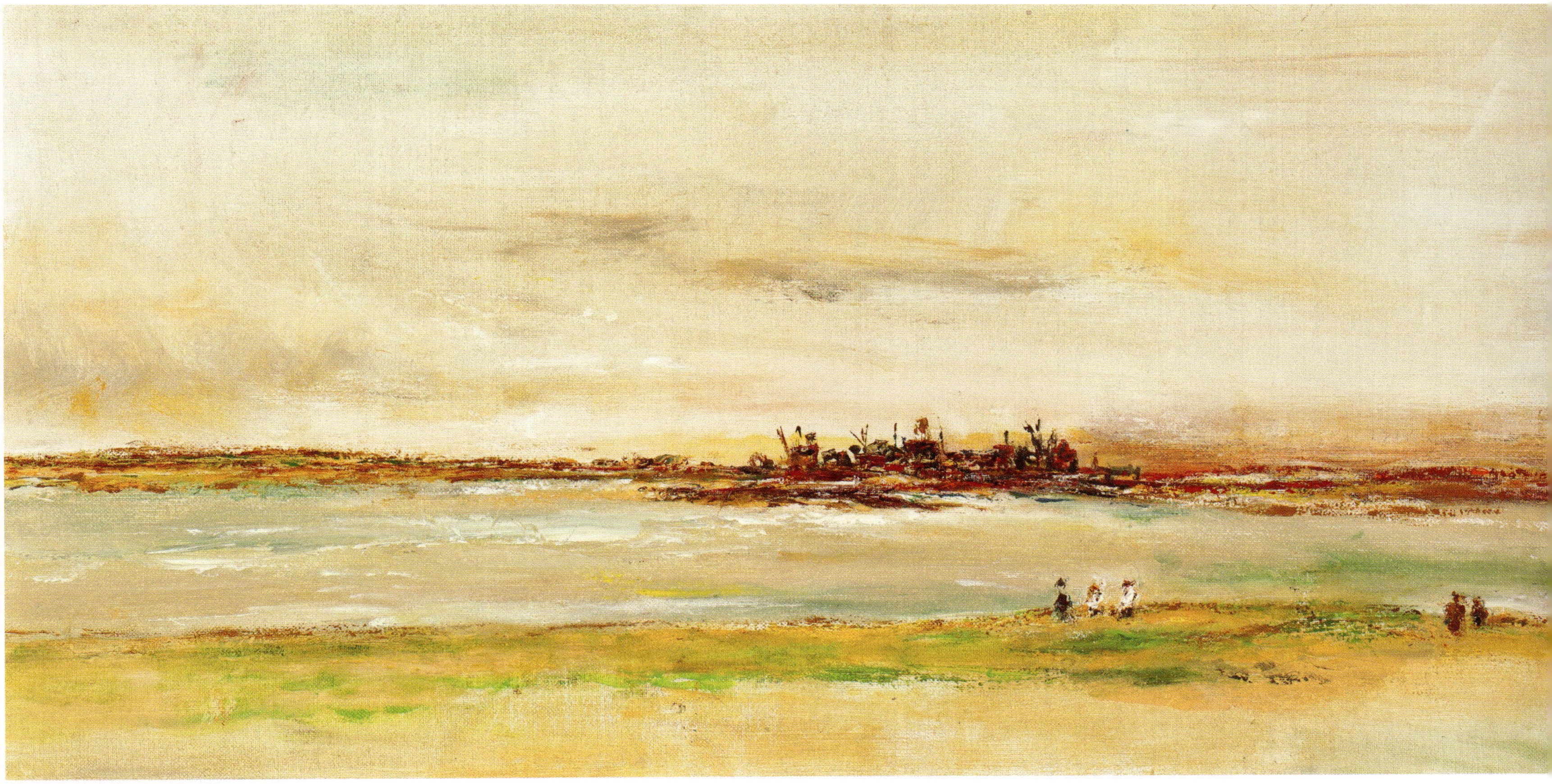

CAT. 53

Aransas

1980s, oil on canvas
12 x 24 in.
Estate of Eugene Ludins

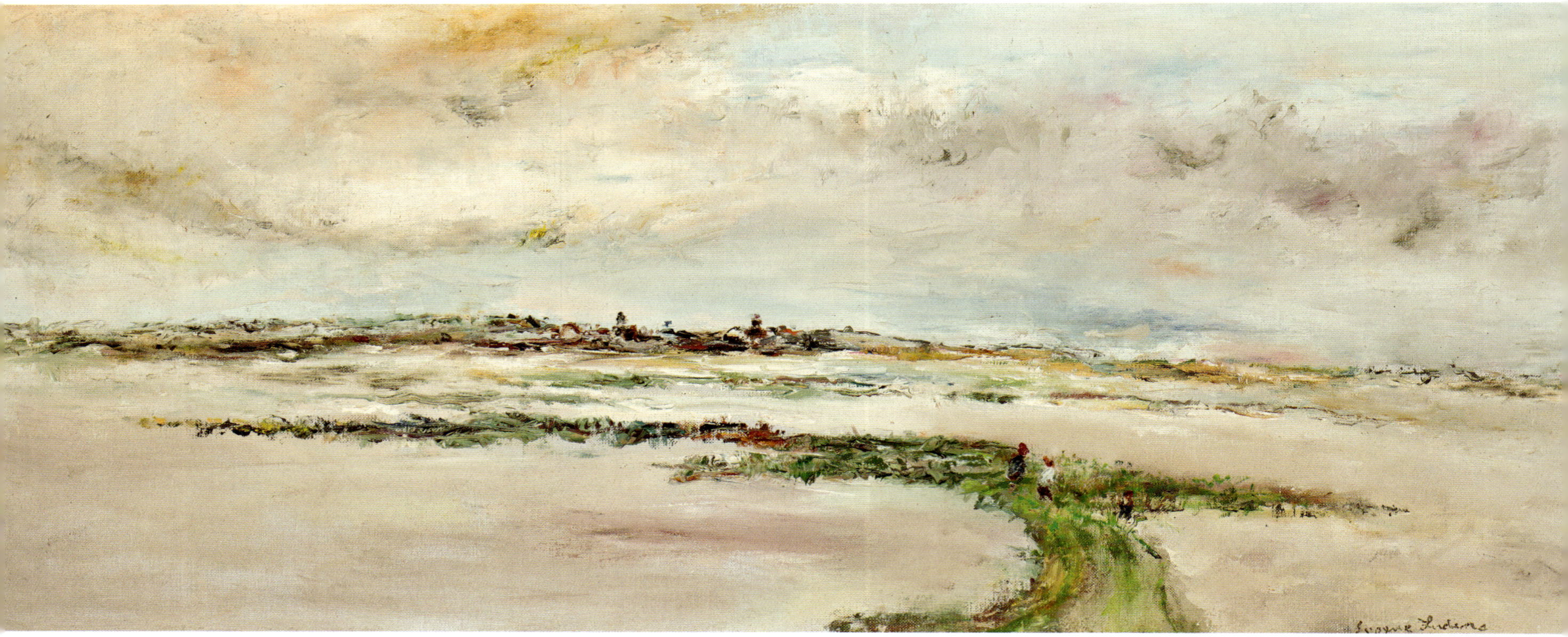

CAT. 54

Coastal Landscape

1983, oil on canvas
12 x 30 in.
Estate of Eugene Ludins

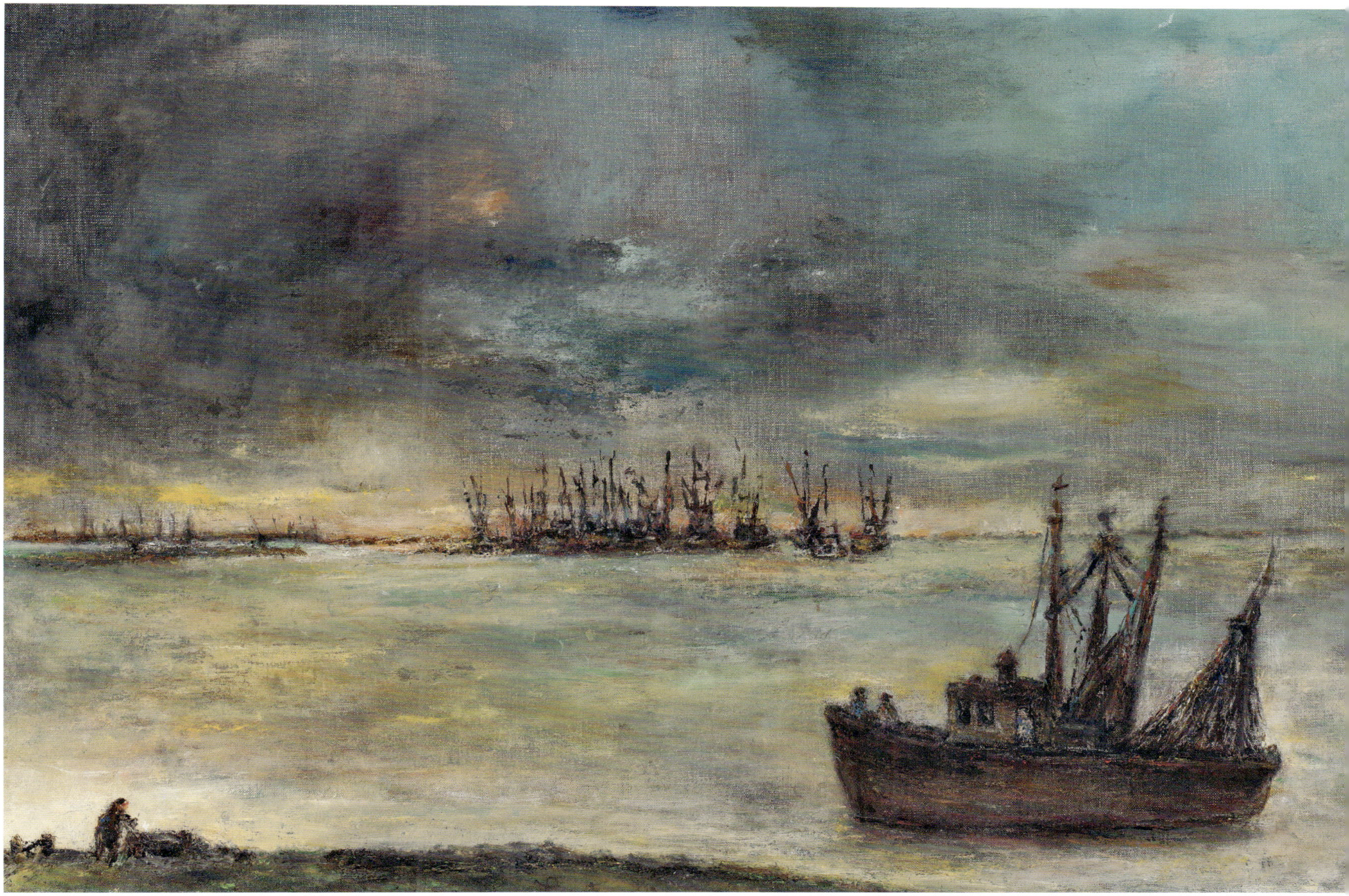

CAT. 55

Fishing Boats

1983–85, oil on canvas
20 x 30 in.
Estate of Eugene Ludins

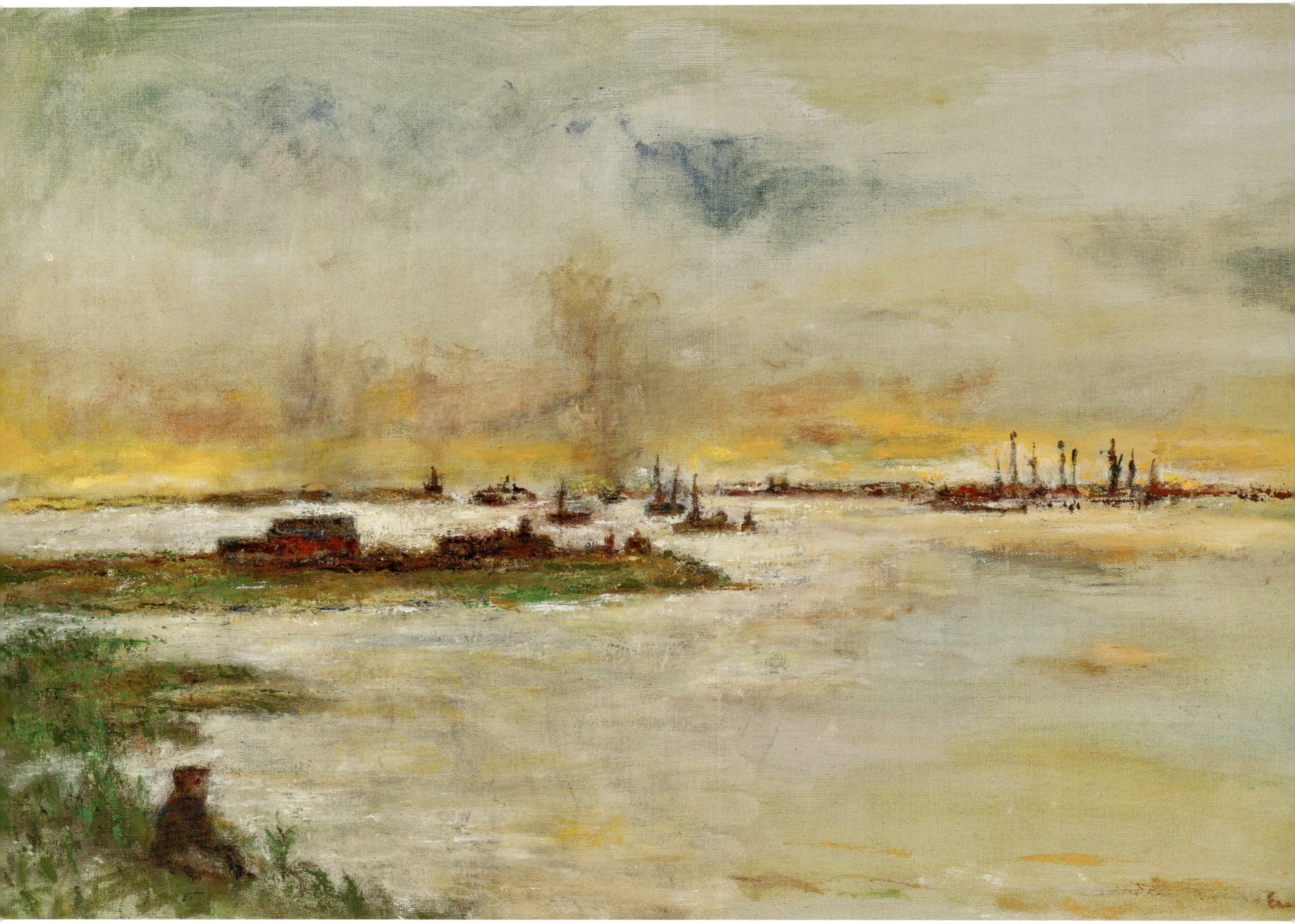

CAT. 56

Gulf Coast Landscape

1985, oil on canvas
18 x 30 in.
Estate of Eugene Ludins

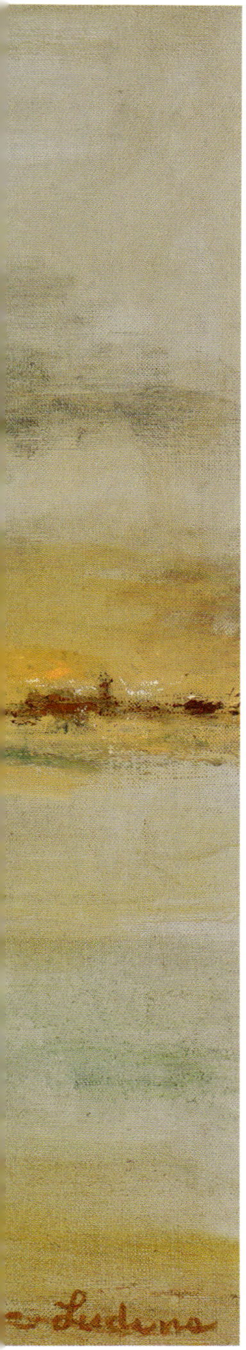

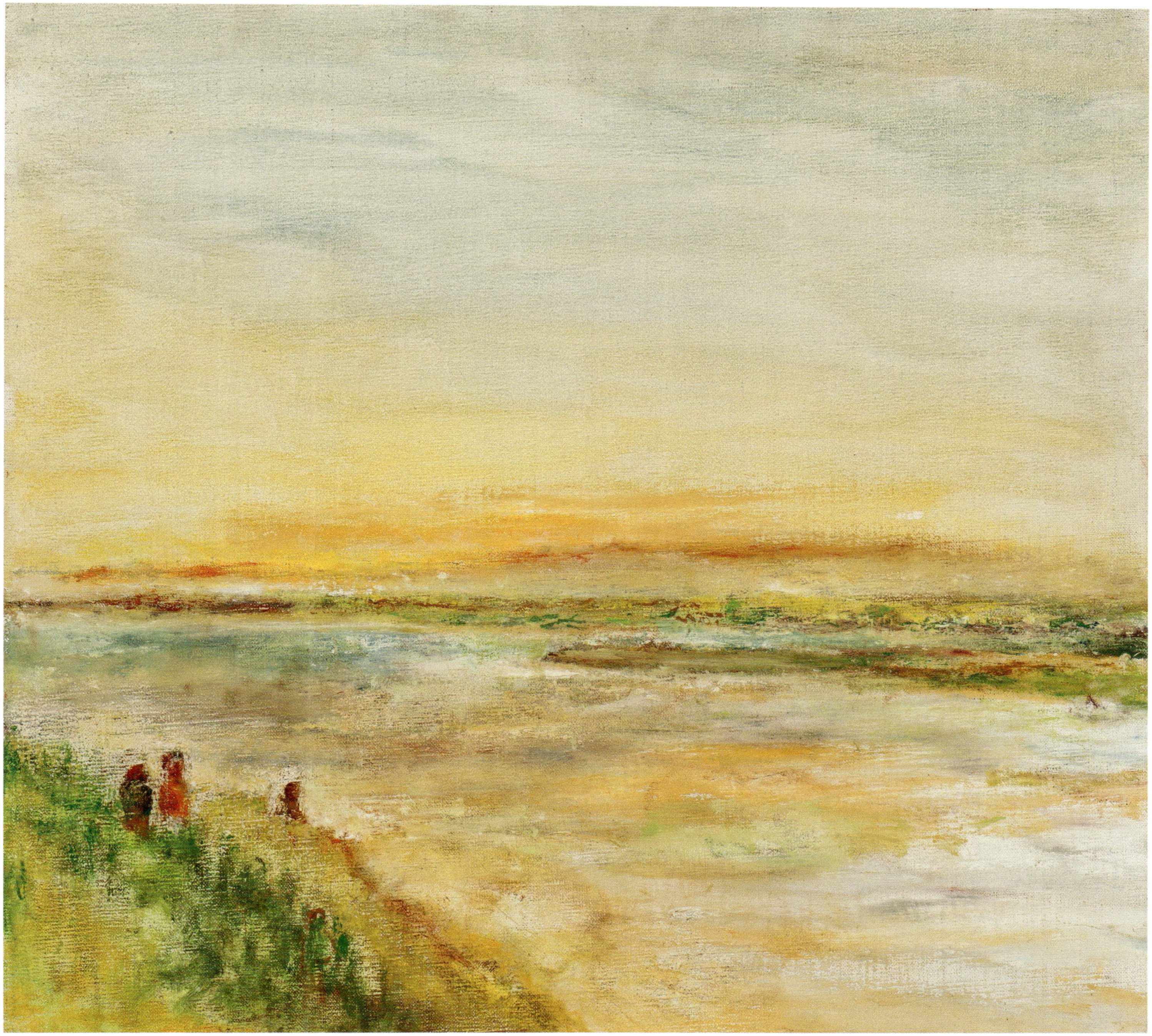

CAT. 57

Wells, Maine

1989, oil on canvas
18 x 20 in.
Estate of Eugene Ludins

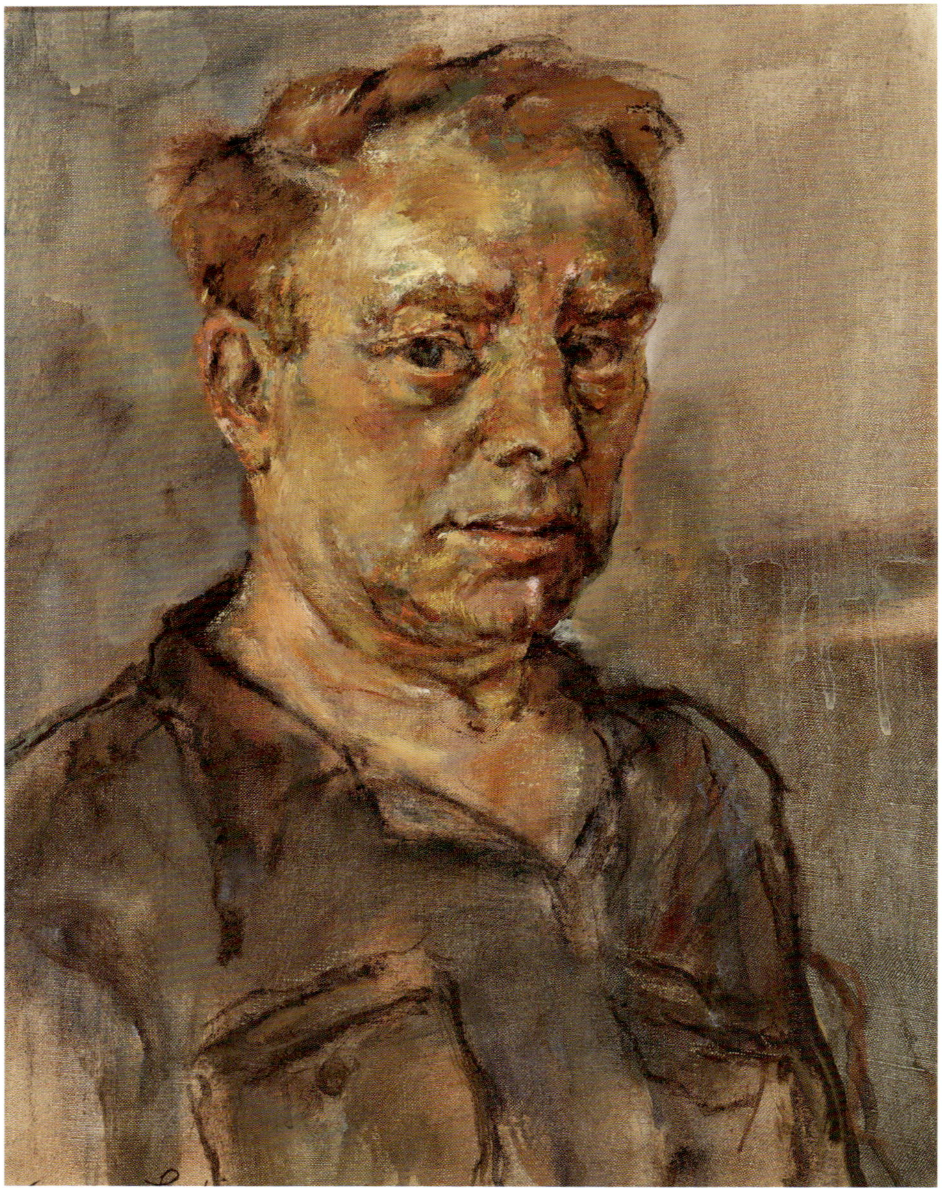

CAT. 58

Untitled Portrait Bust

1950s, oil on canvas
20 x 16 in.
Collection Arthur Anderson

CAT. 59

Self-Portrait

1960s, oil on canvas
8 x 7 in.
Private Collection

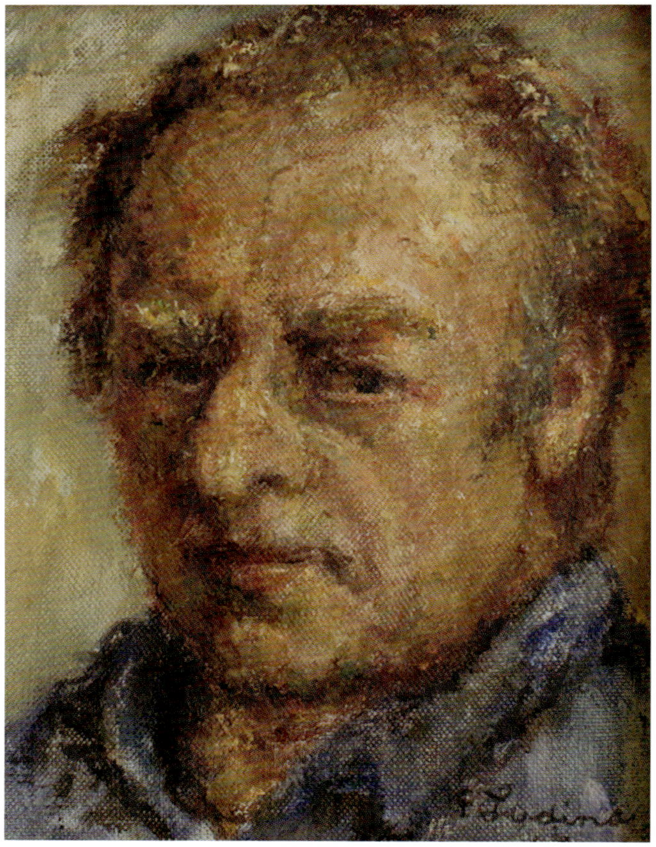

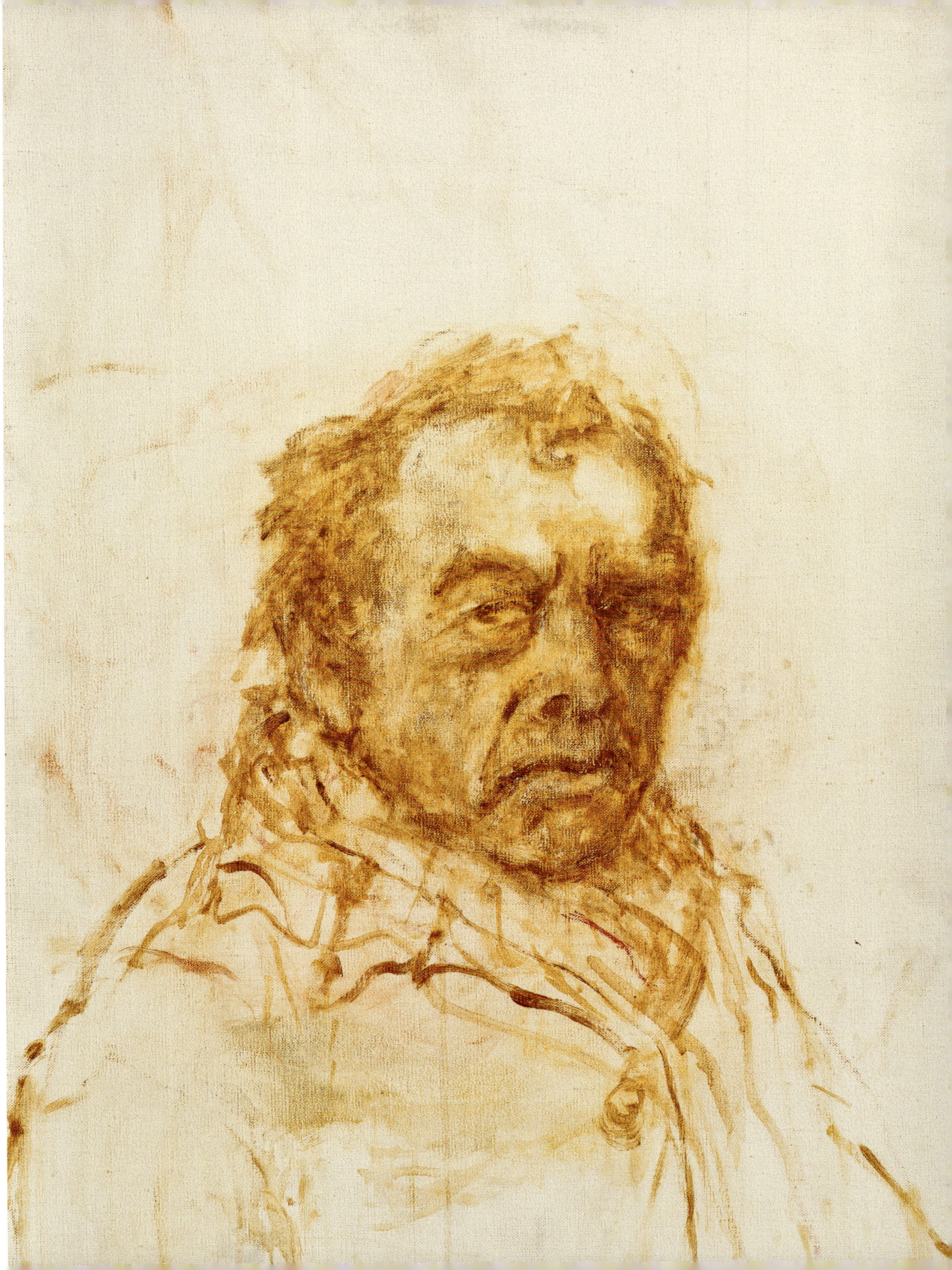

CAT. 60

Self-Portrait

1980s, oil wash on canvas
24 x 18 in.
Estate of Eugene Ludins

DRAWINGS

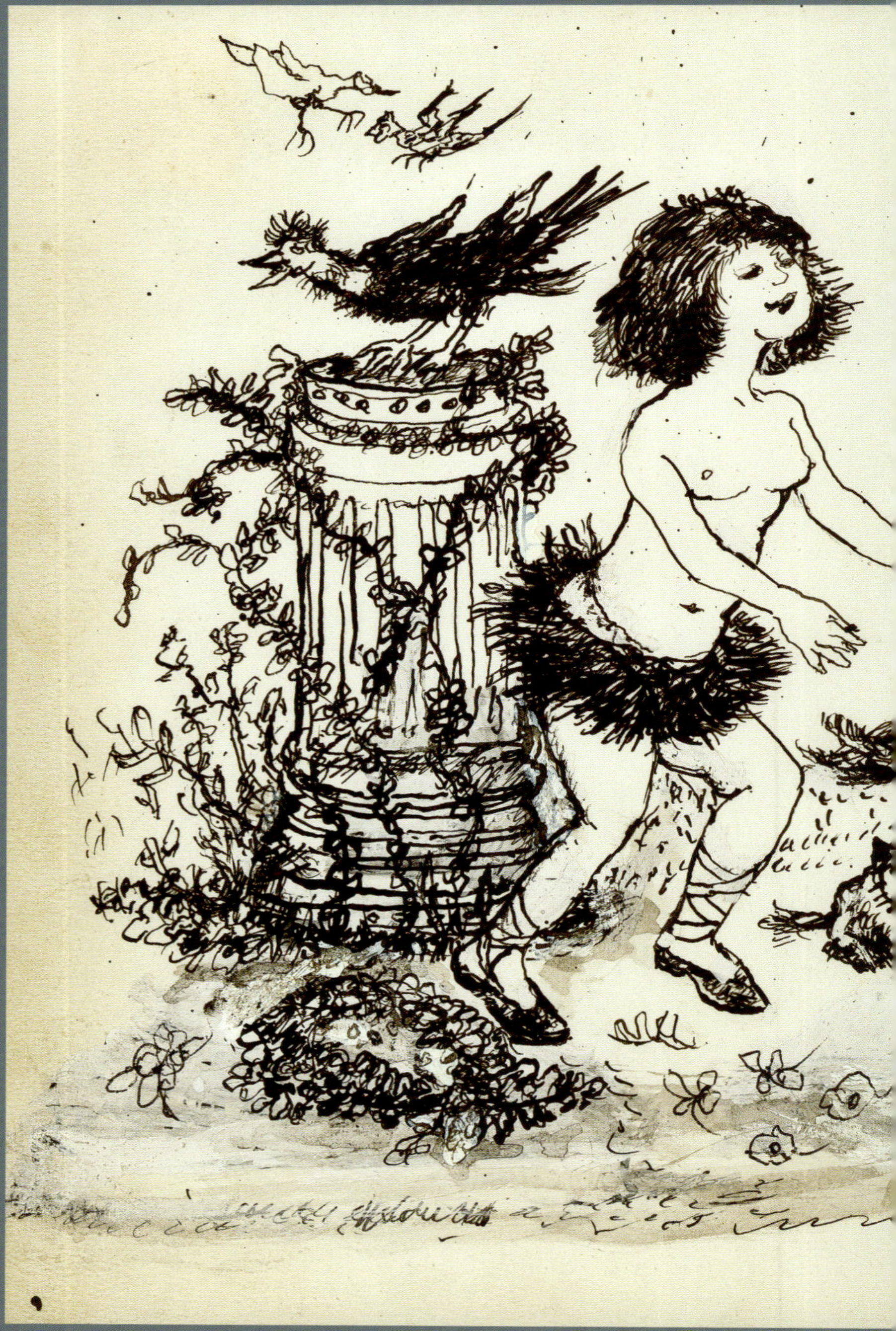

CAT. 61

Mai Fest

February 1979, ink and wash on paper

6¼ x 13¼ in.

Collection Edgar and Cornelia Rosenblum

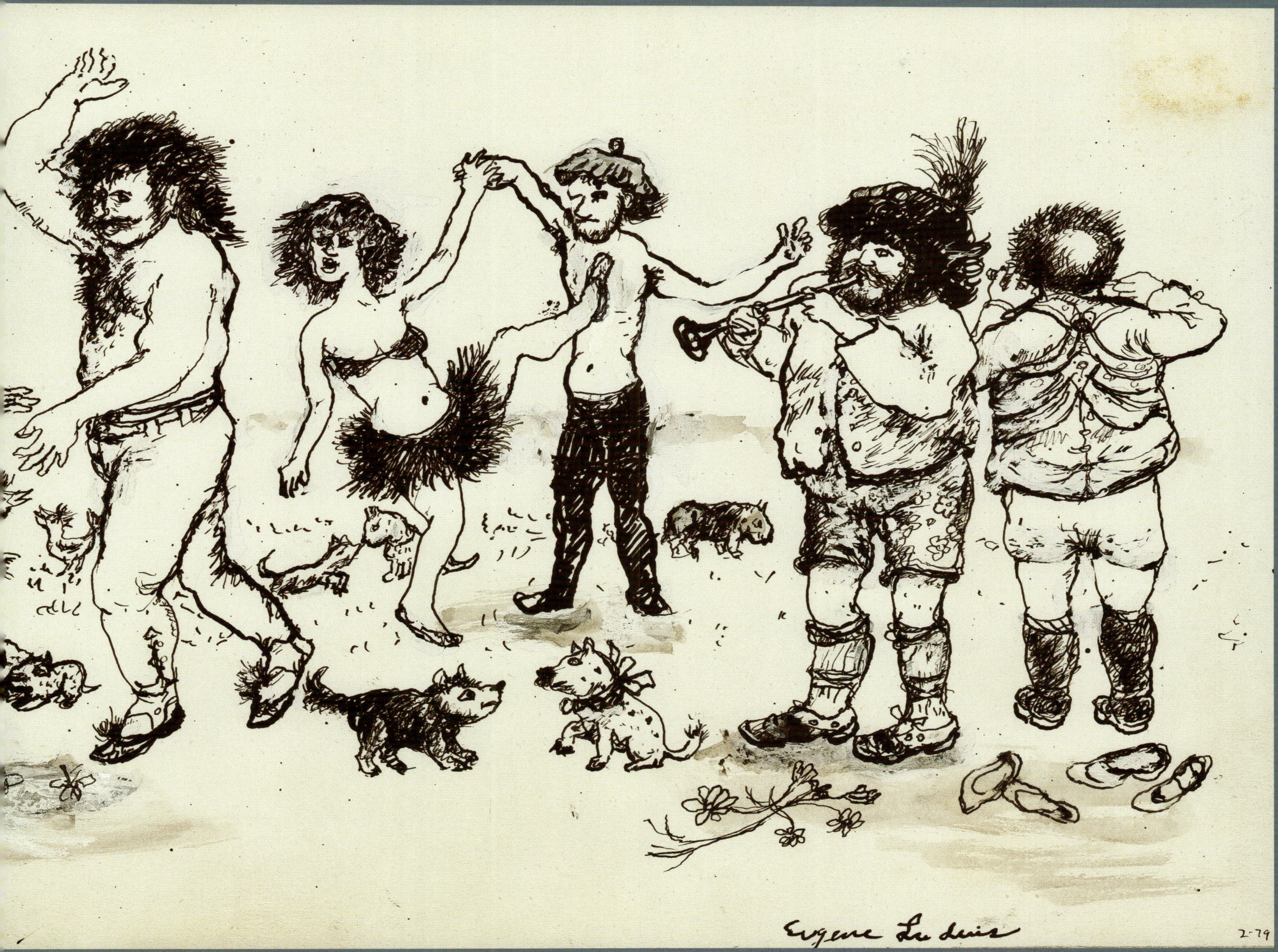
Eugene Ludins
2-79

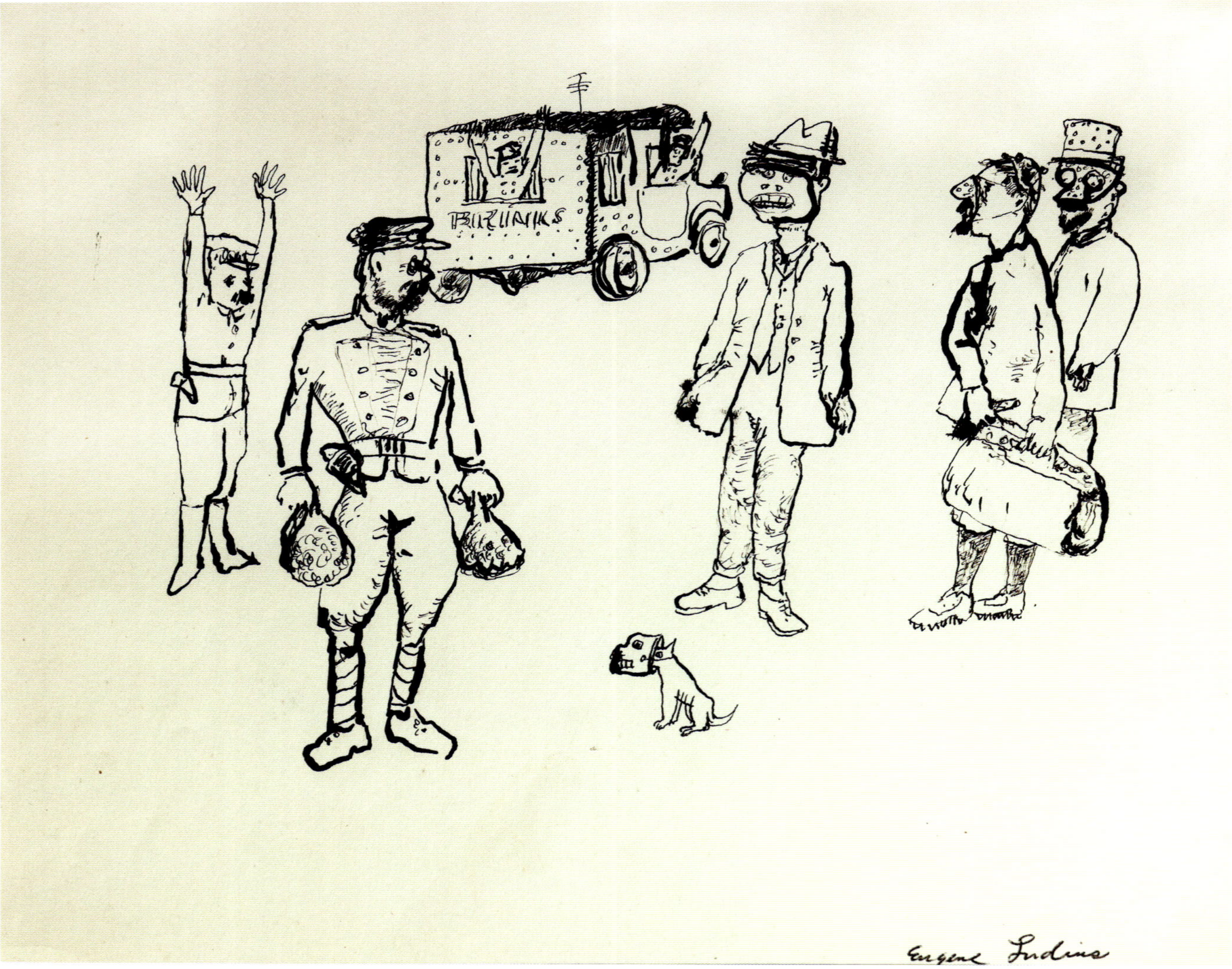

CAT. 62

Stick-up

Undated, ink and wash on paper

8⅜ x 10⅞ in.

Collection Jane Jones

CAT. 63

Live Sculpture with Sculptor

Undated, ink on paper

7¾ x 7¾ in.

Collection Edgar and Cornelia Rosenblum

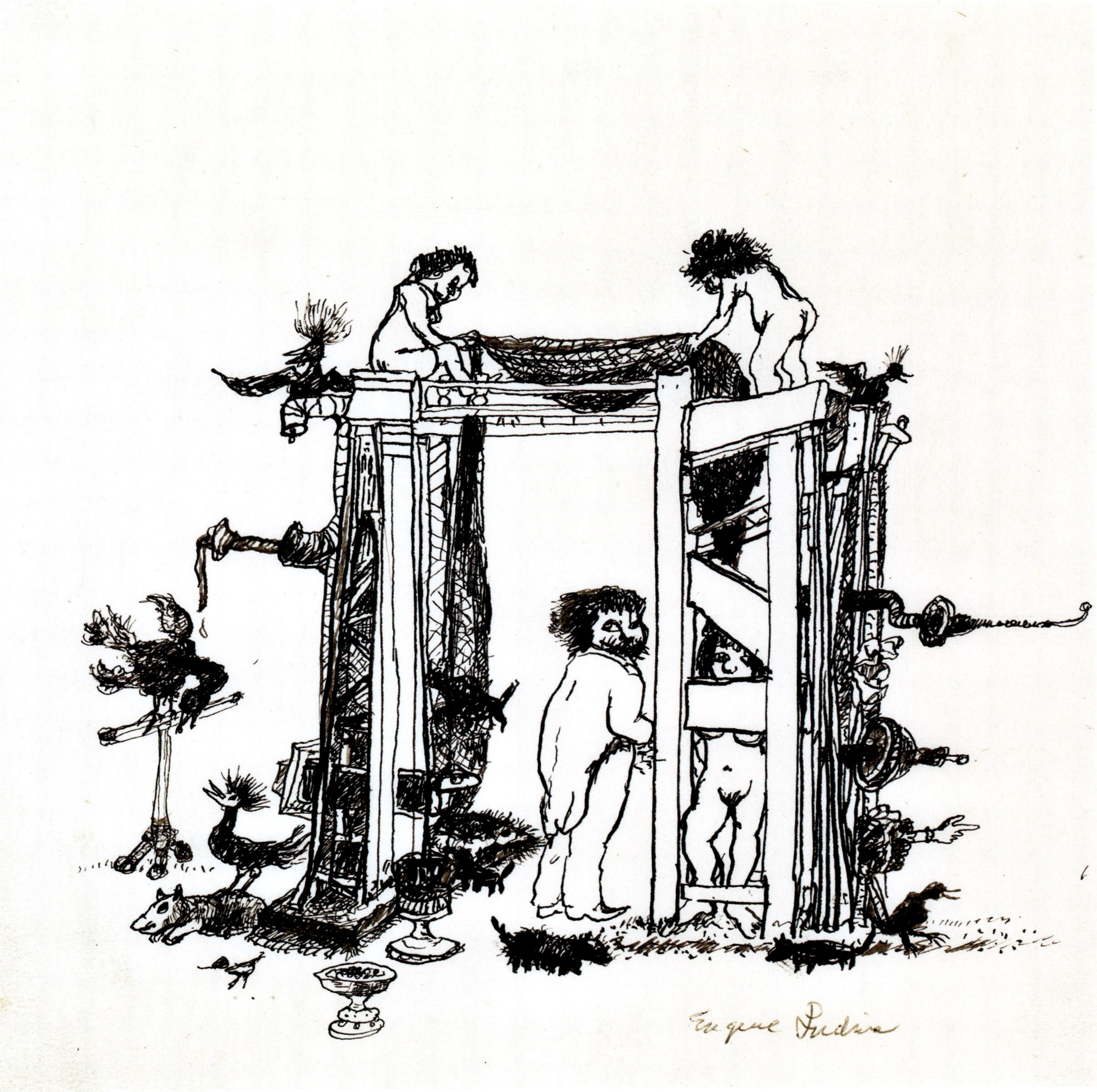
Eugene Ludins

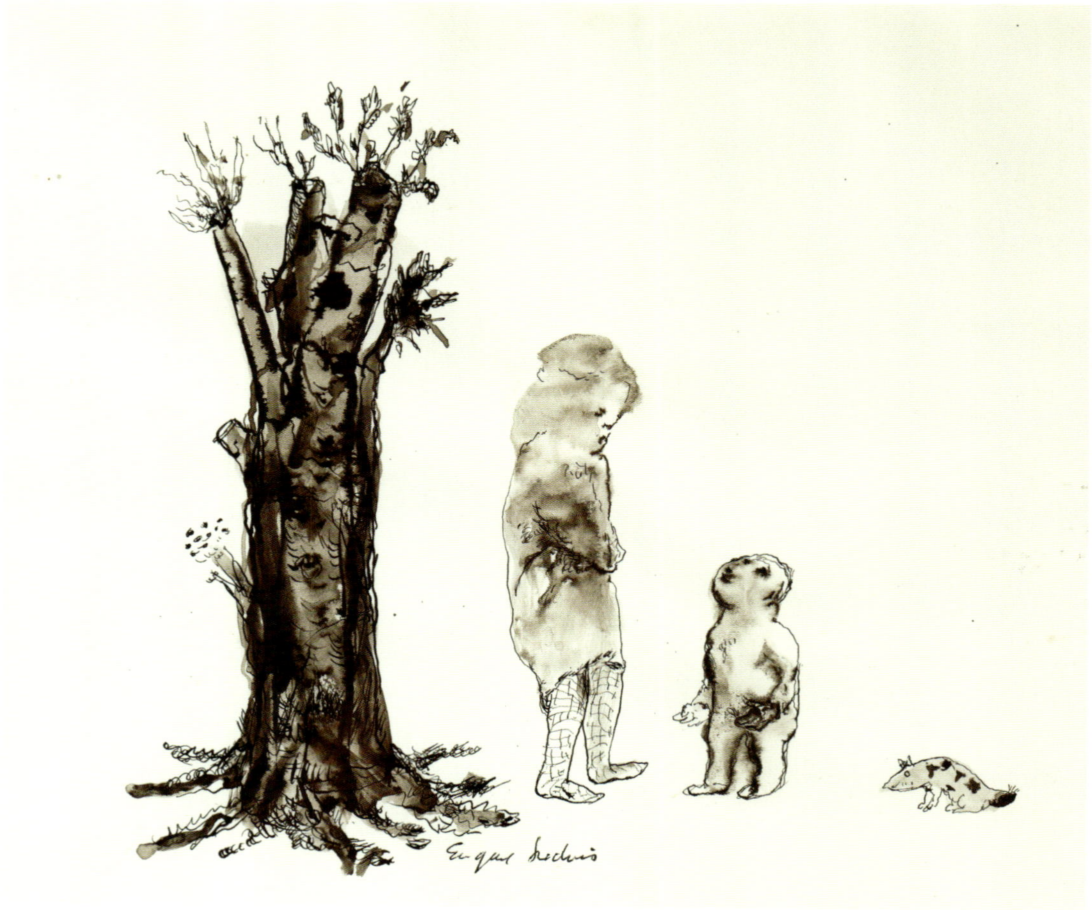

CAT. 64

Untitled Drawing

c. 1950, ink and wash on paper
9½ x 11¾ in.
Collection Peter Mayer

CAT. 65

Bone of Contention

Undated, ink and wash on paper
7 x 10½ in.
Collection Jane Jones

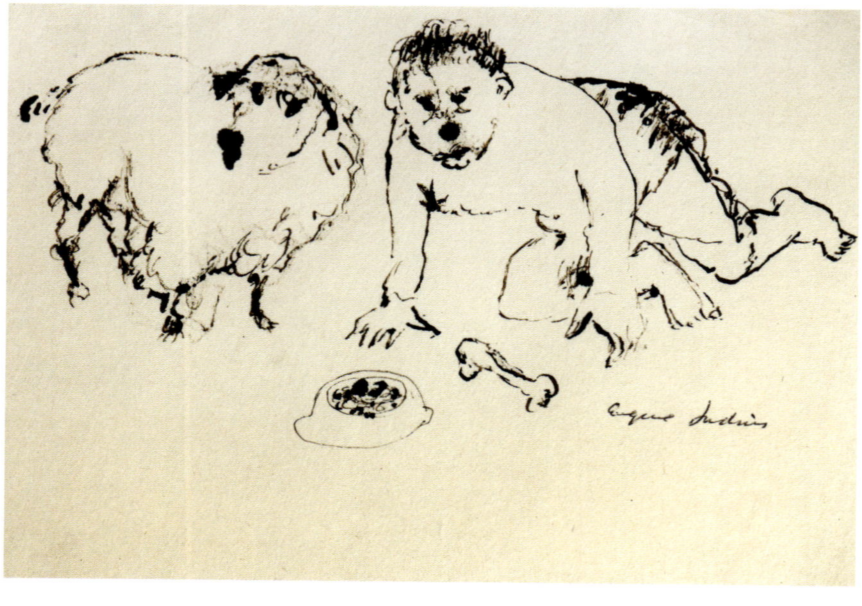

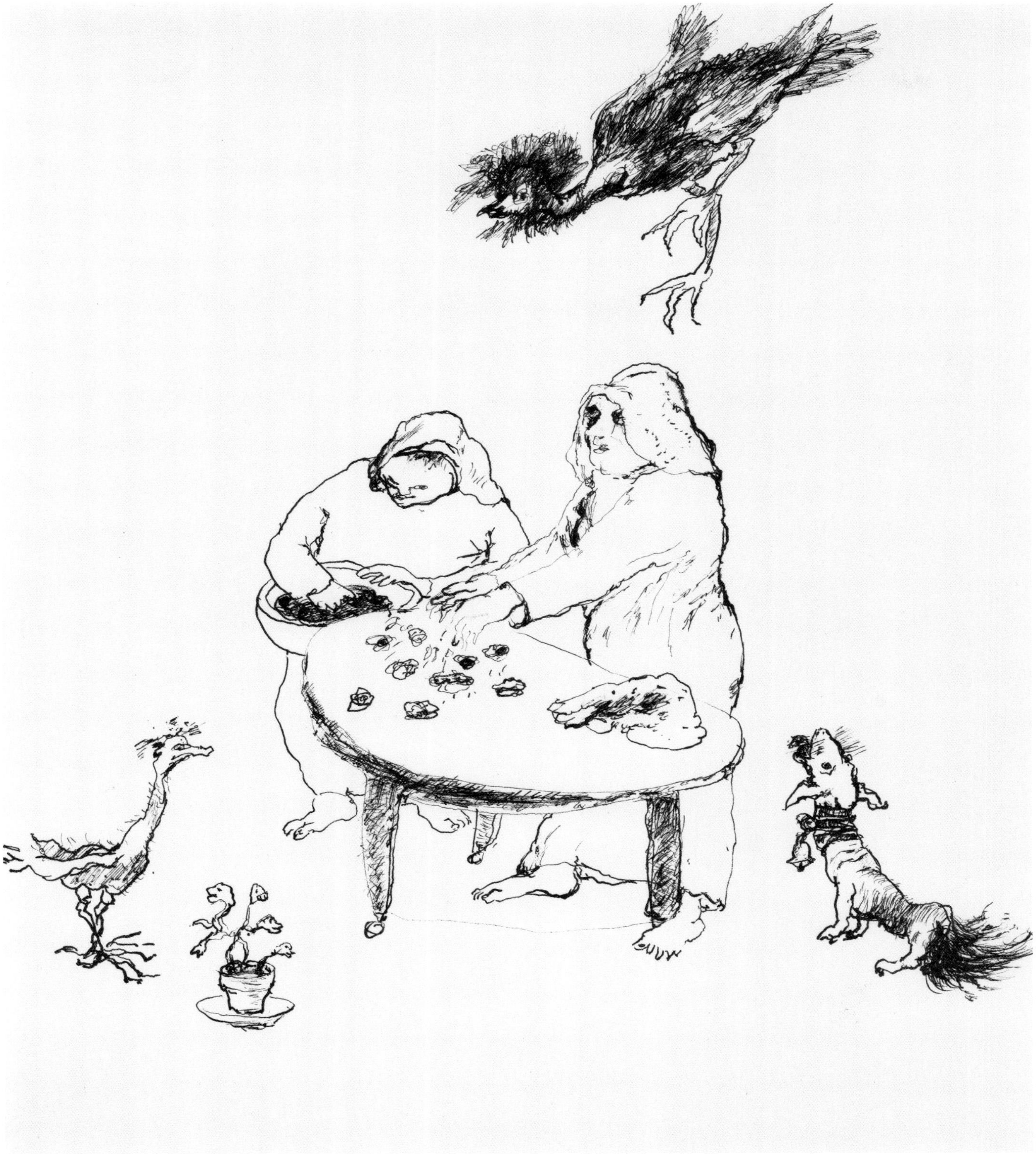

CAT. 66

Sweetbreads

Undated, ink on paper
9¼ x 8¼ in.
Private Collection

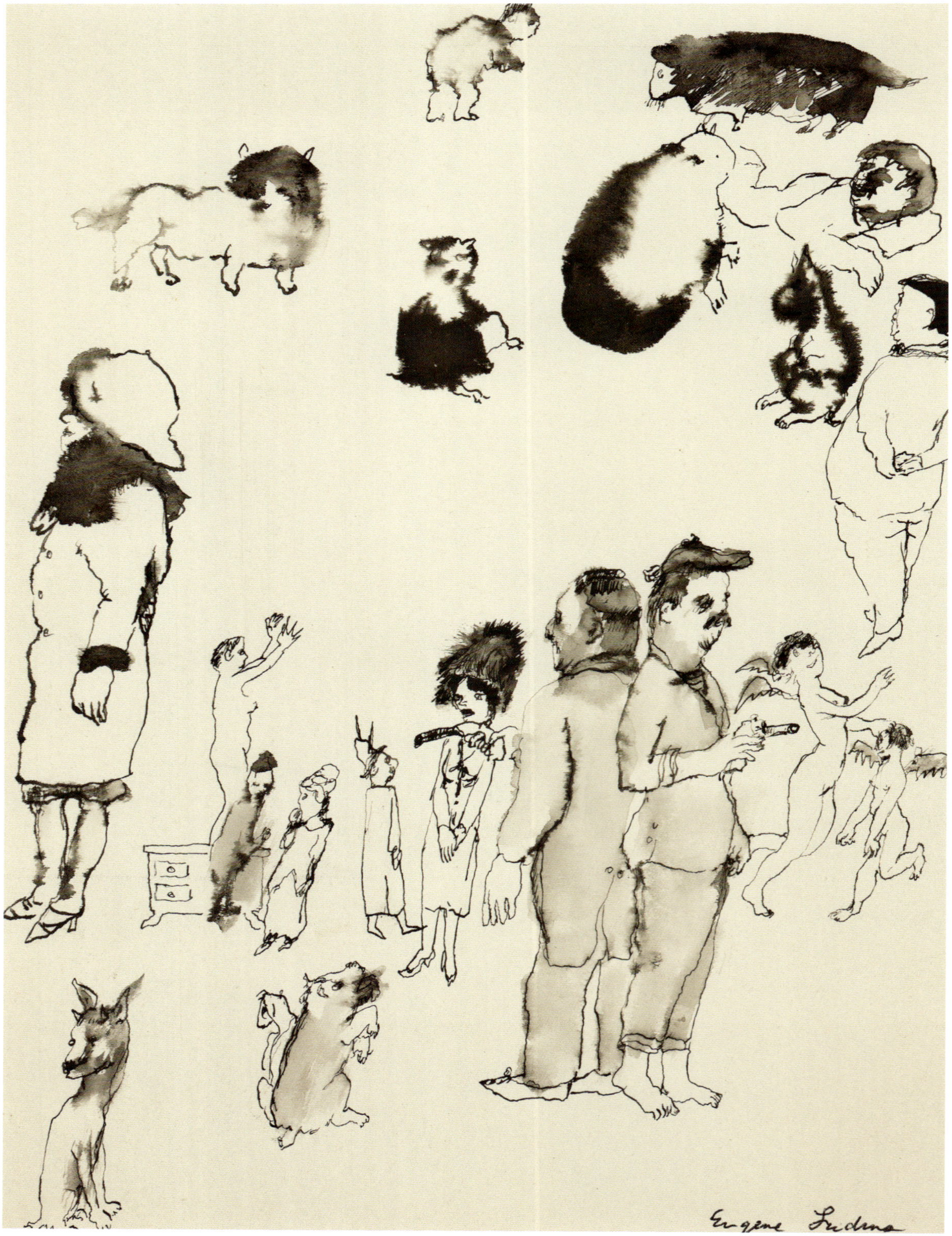

CAT. 67

Honor

Undated, ink and wash on paper

11 x 8¼ in.

Collection Arthur Anderson

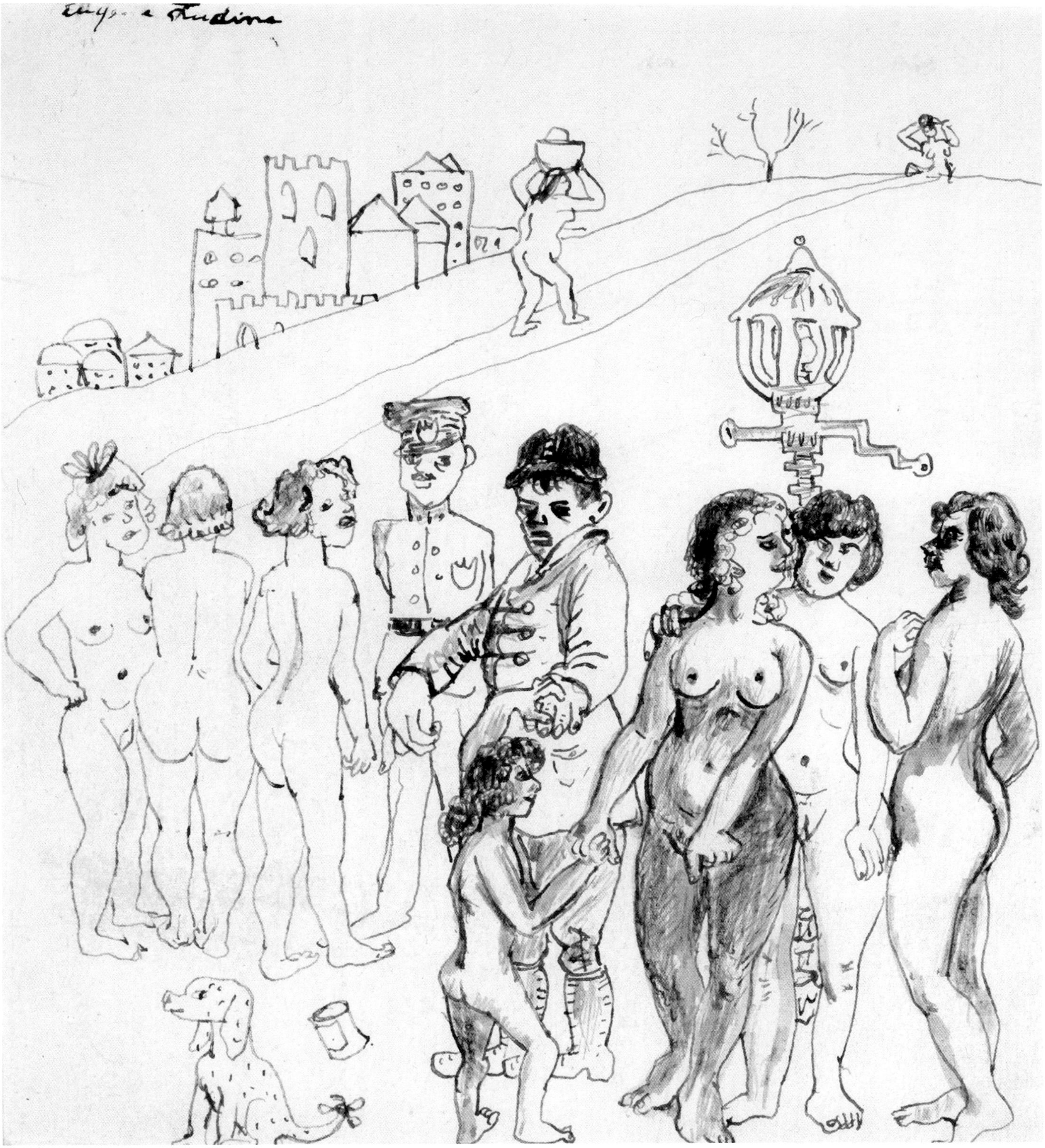

CAT. 68

Foreign Nudes

Undated, ink on paper
14 x 13½ in.
Private Collection

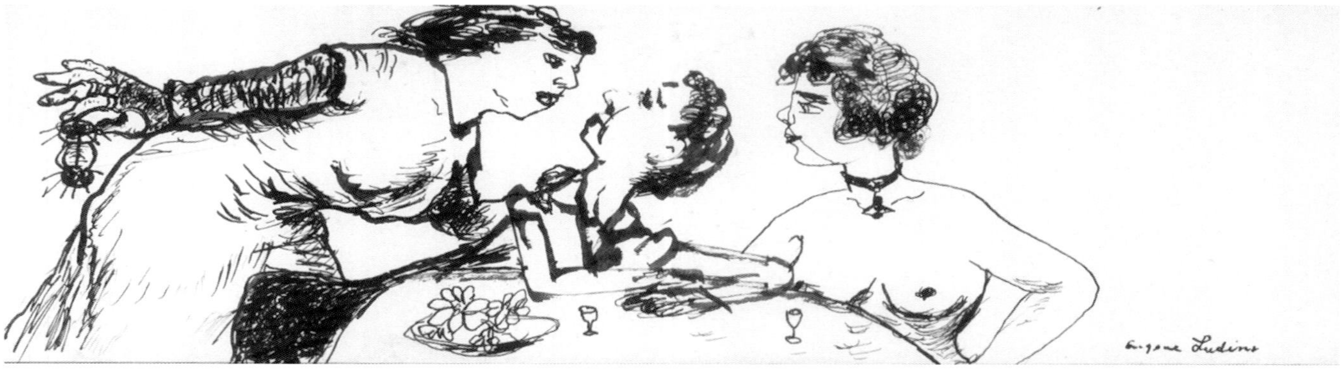

CAT. 69

Showdown

Undated, ink on paper

2 x 9 in.

Collection Nancy Kline

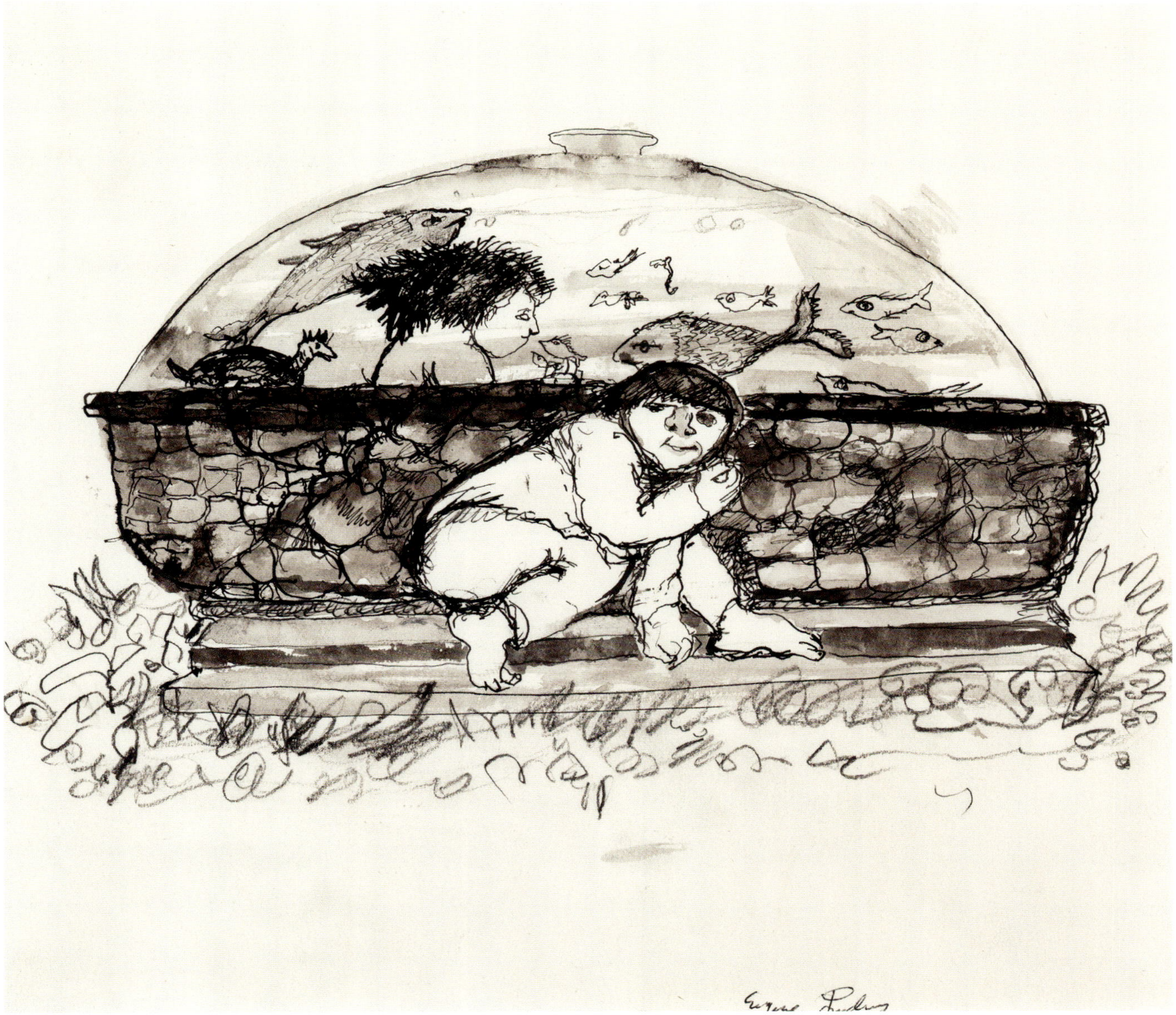

CAT. 70

Untitled Drawing

Undated, ink, wash, and graphite on paper
9 x 10¼ in.
Courtesy of Cornelia Seckel and Raymond J. Steiner from the *Art Times* Collection

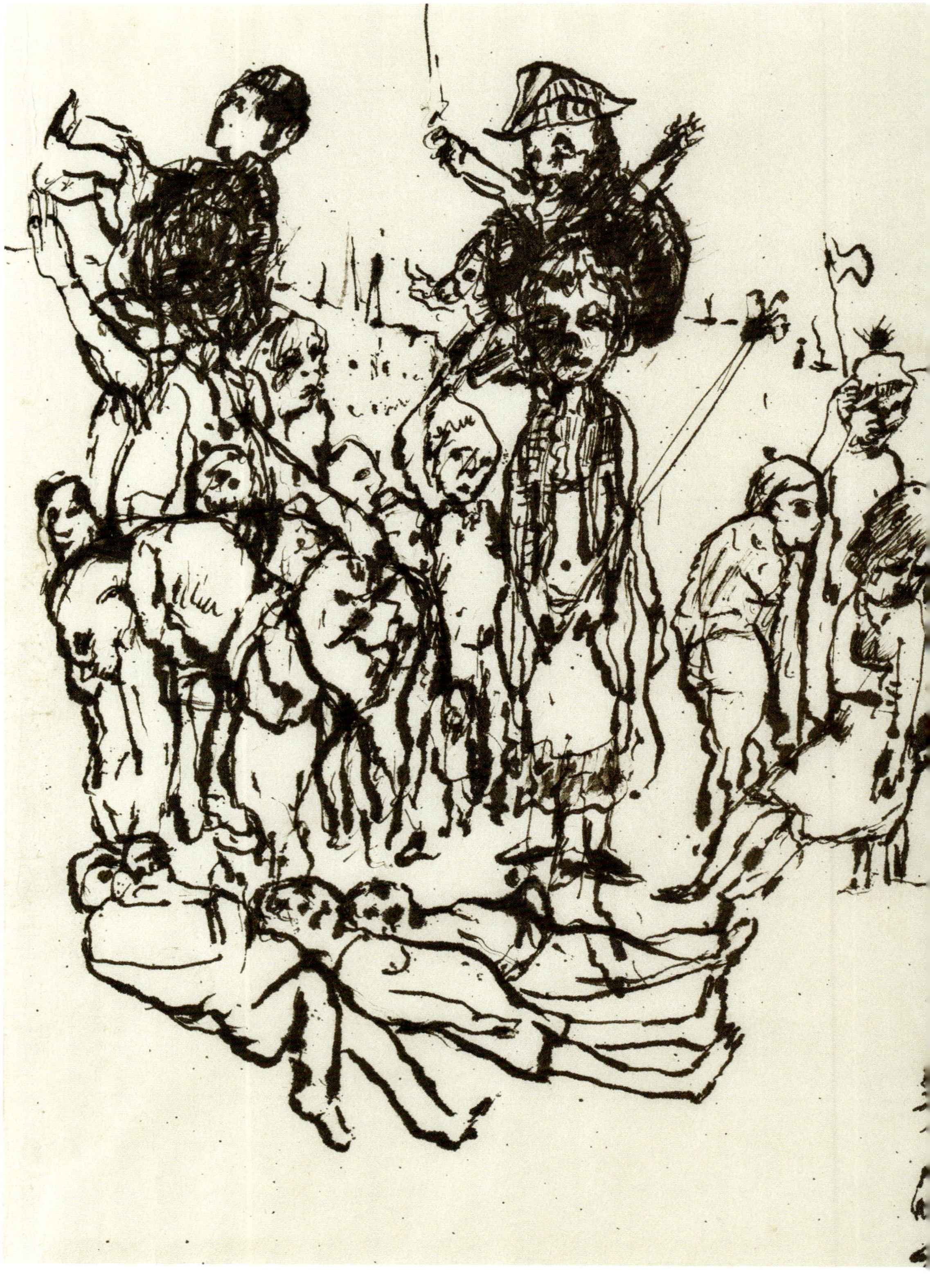

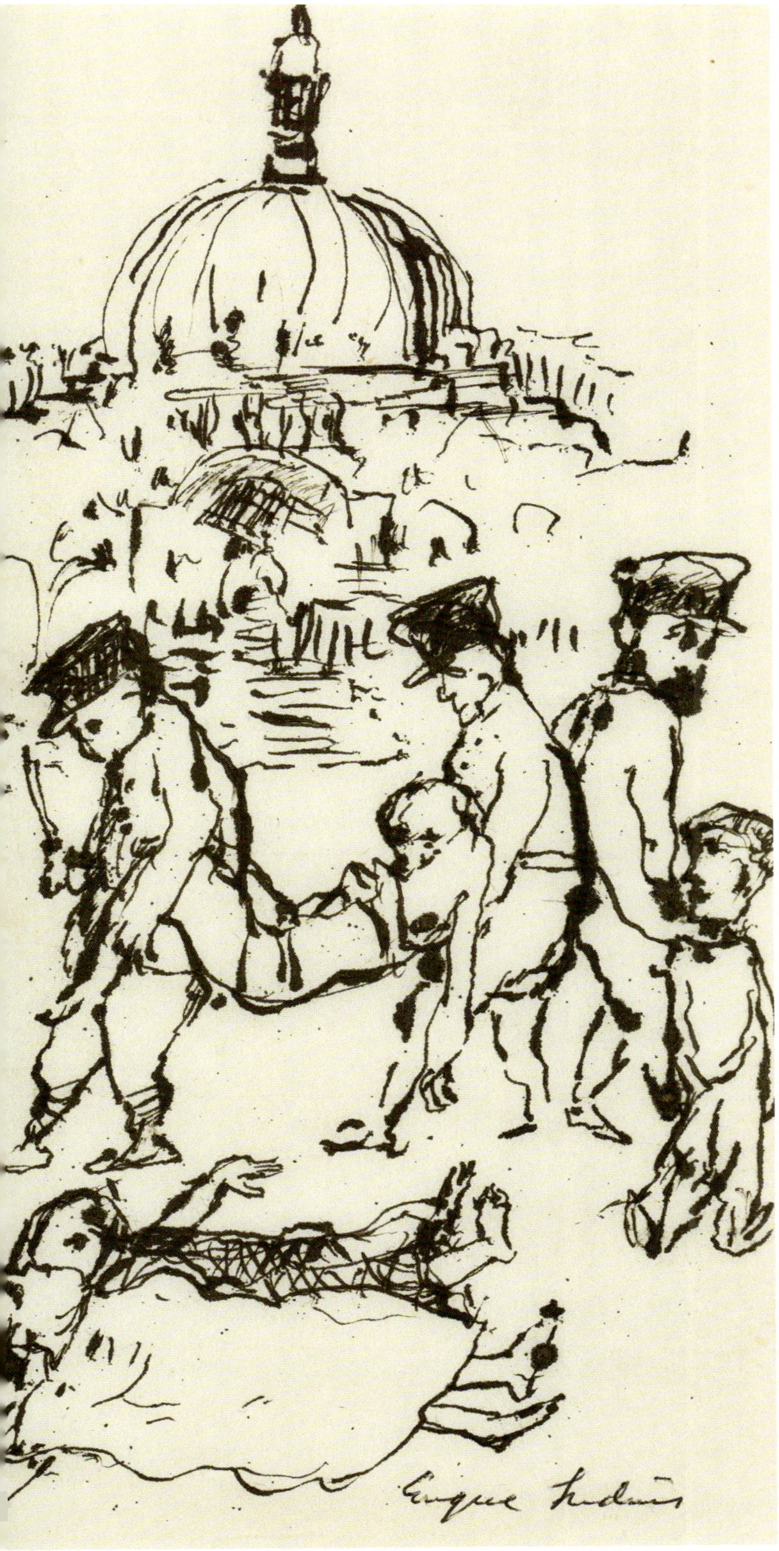

CAT. 71

Putsch

Undated, ink on paper

9½ x 12 in.

Collection Jane Jones

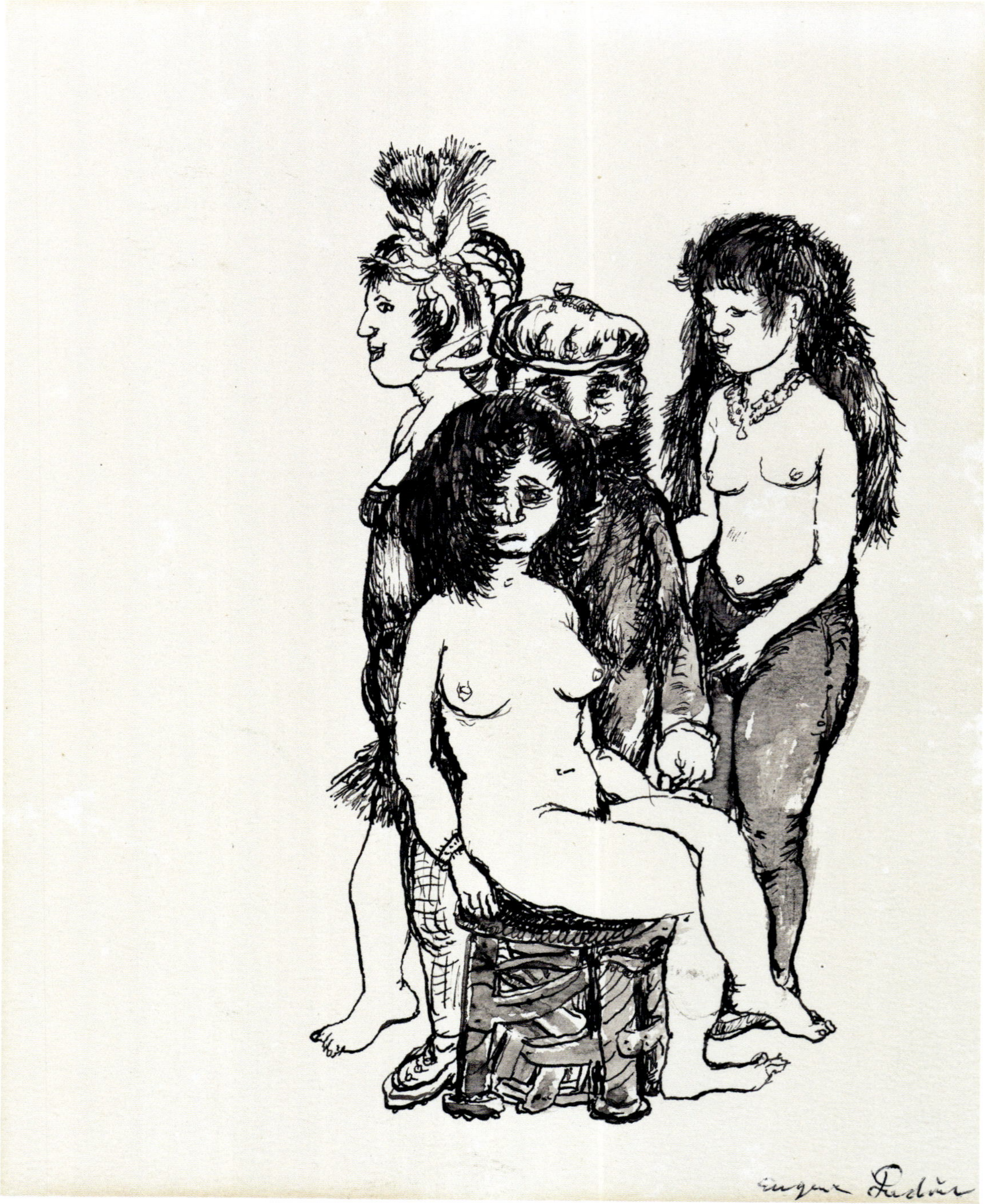

CAT. 72

The Favorite

Undated, ink on paper

8⅝ x 7 5/16 in.

Collection Jane Lyon

CAT. 73

Untitled Drawing

Undated, ink on paper

14¾ x 9¼ in.

Private Collection

CAT. 74

Untitled Drawing

Undated, ink on paper

9½ x 4 9/16 in.

Collection Jane Jones

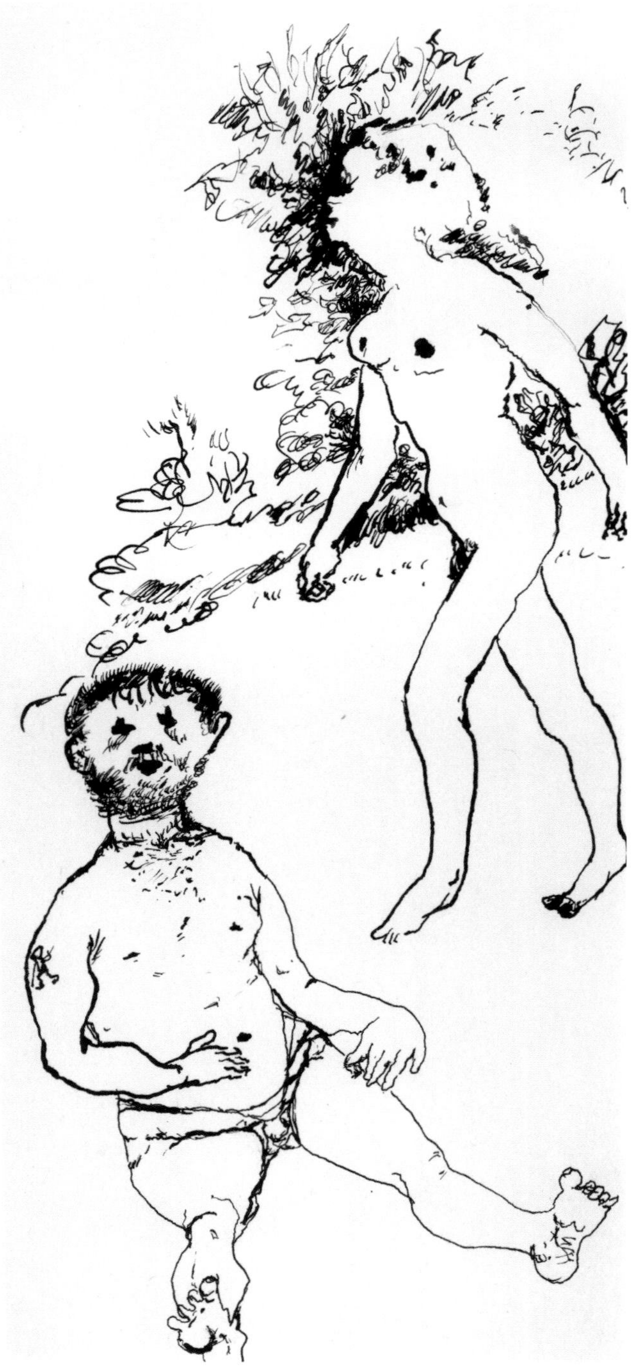

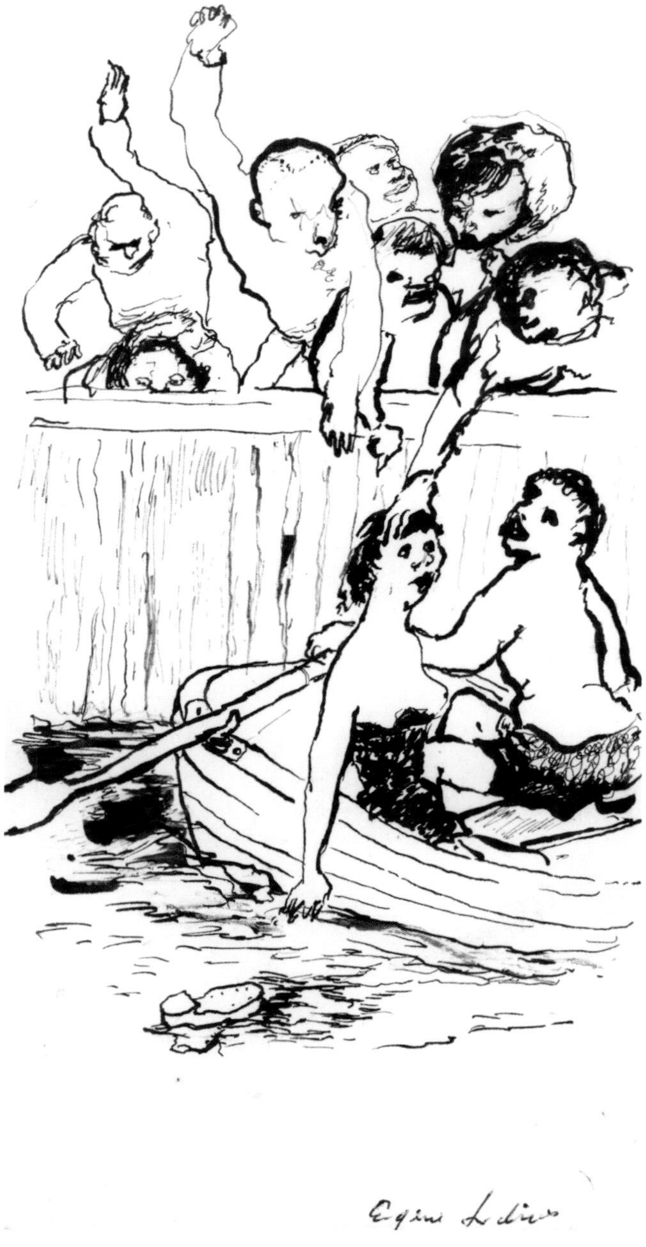

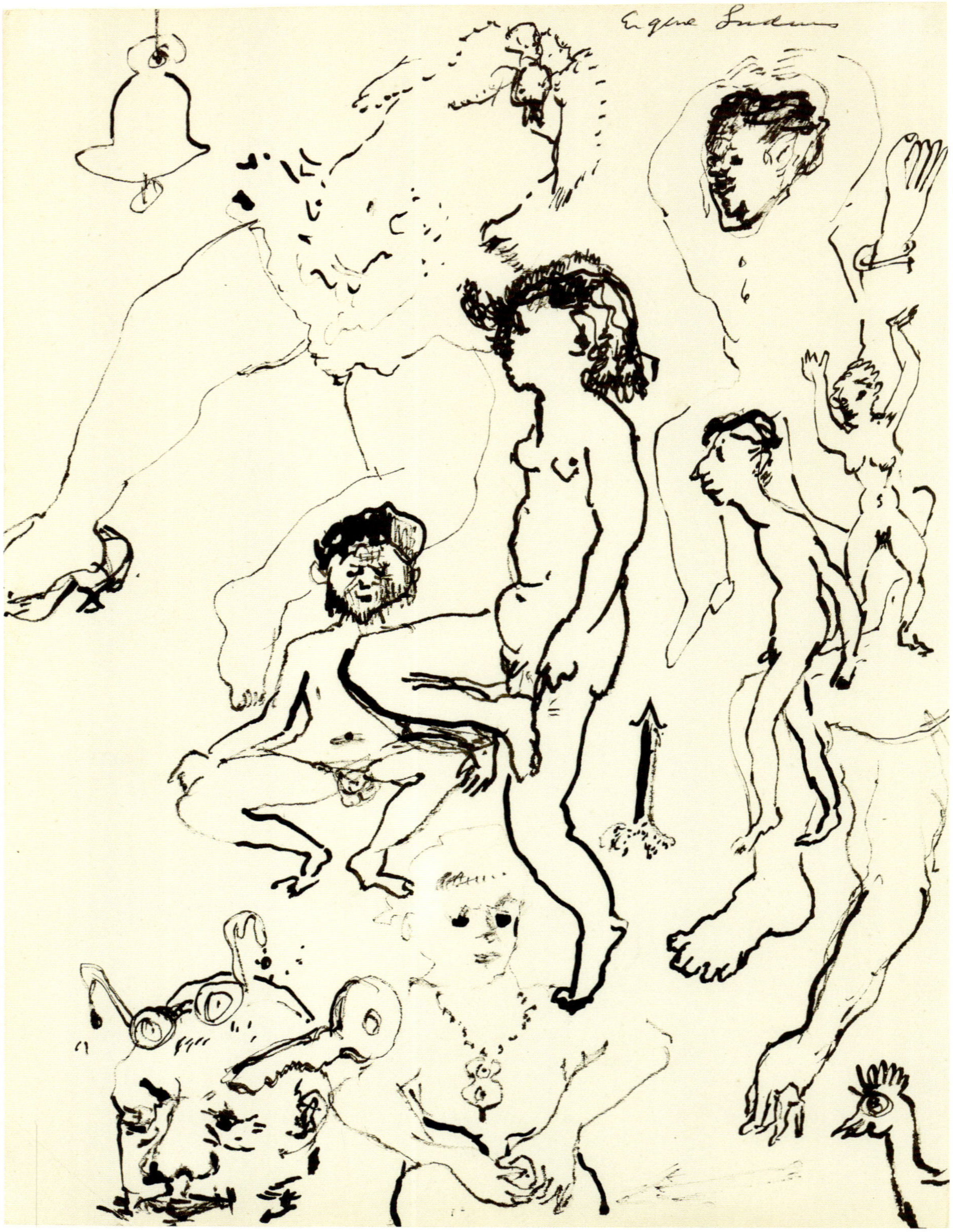

CAT. 75

Sketch

Undated, ink on paper
11 x 8¾ in.
Private Collection

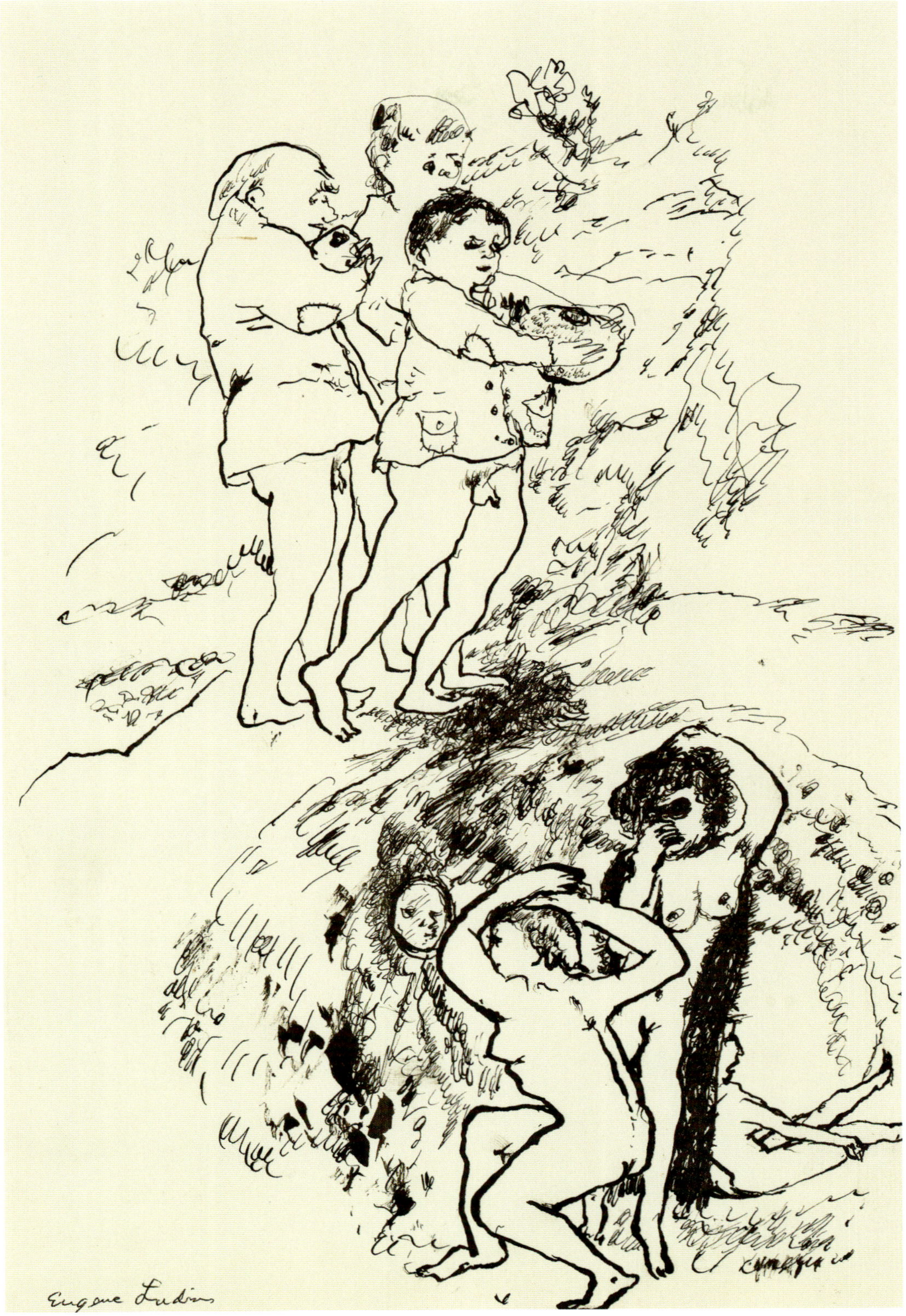

CAT. 76

Six Figures

Undated, ink on paper
10⅝ x 7⅞ in.
Private Collection

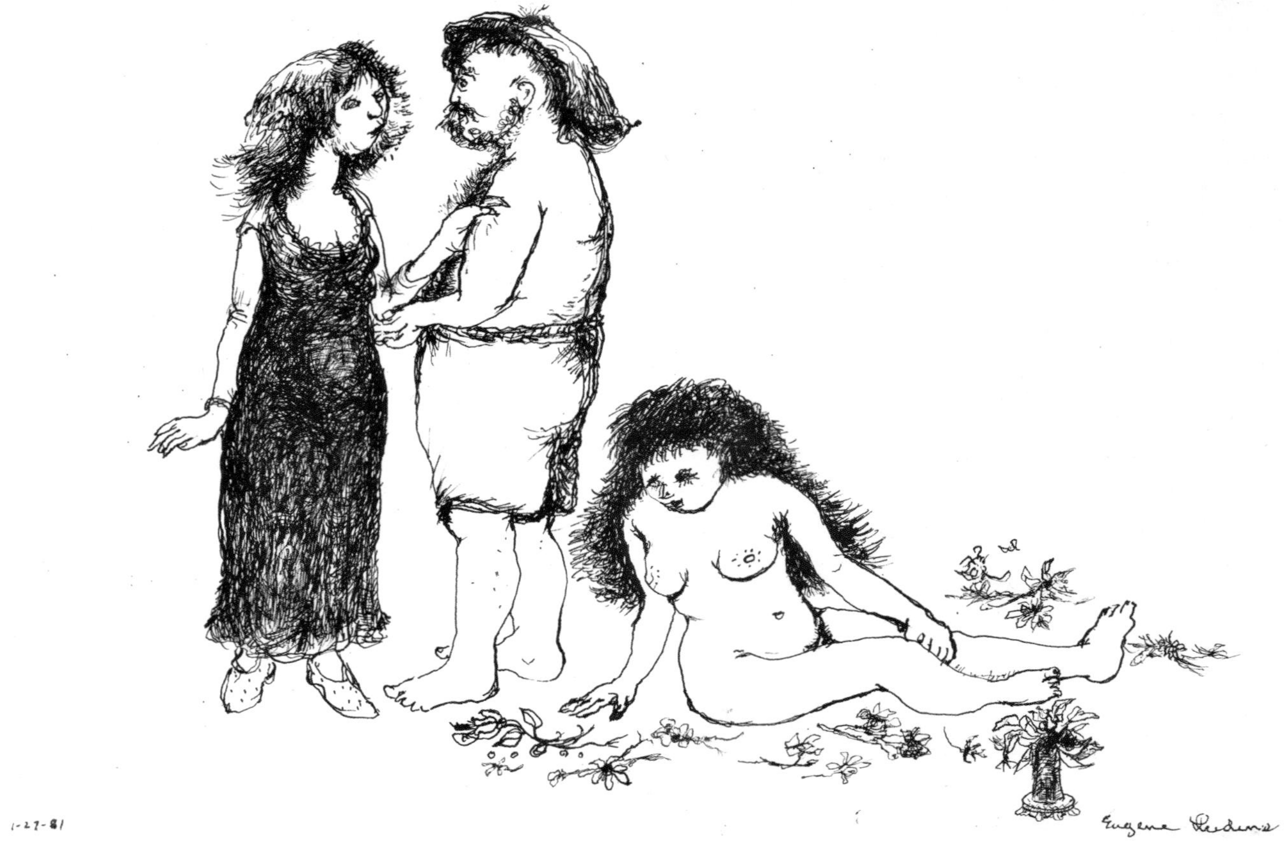

CAT. 77

Untitled Drawing

1981, ink on paper

8½ x 10¾ in.

Collection John Kleinhans and Paula Nelson

CAT. 78

Cosmetics

1982, ink and wash on paper

10½ x 7½ in.

Collection Peter Mayer

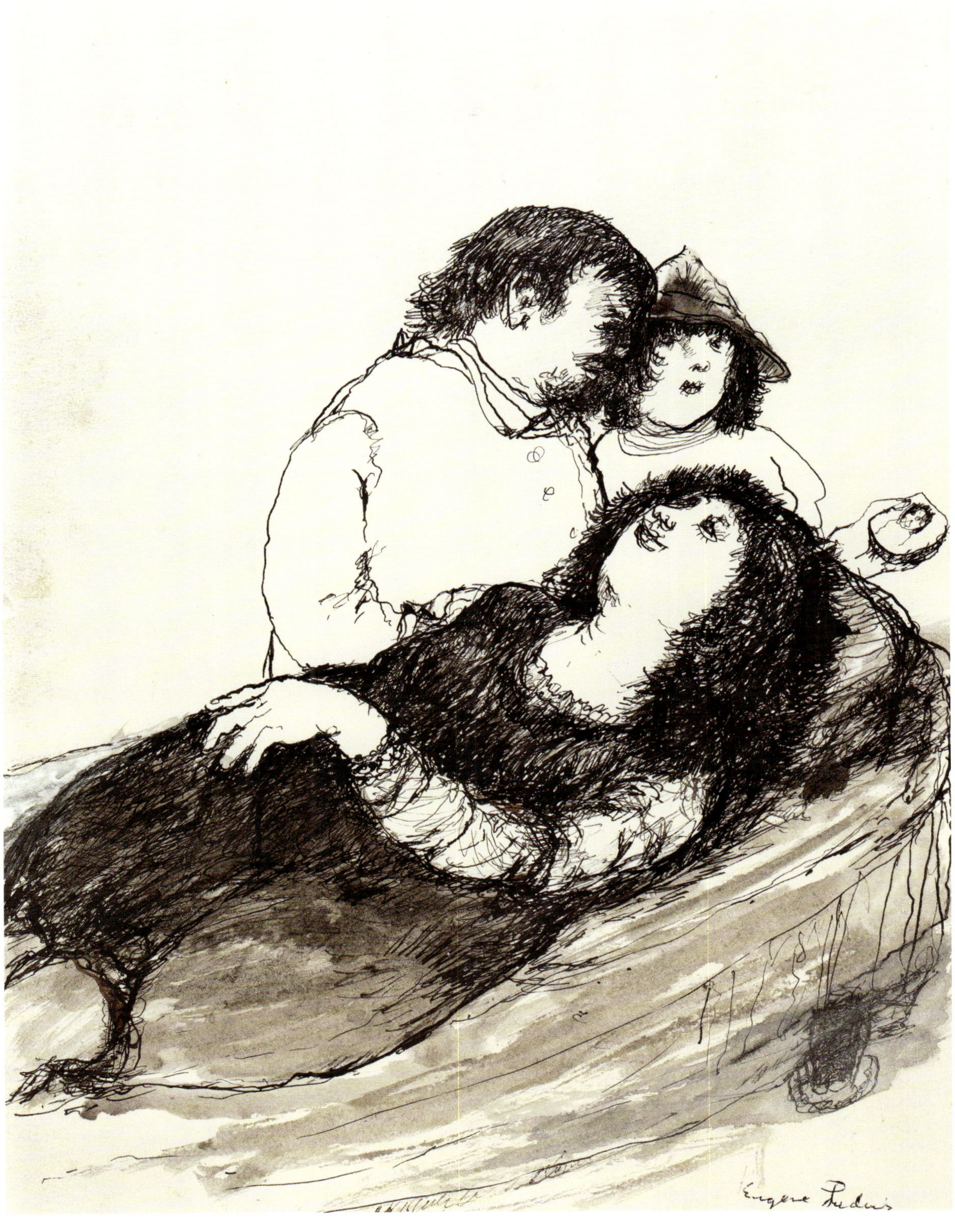

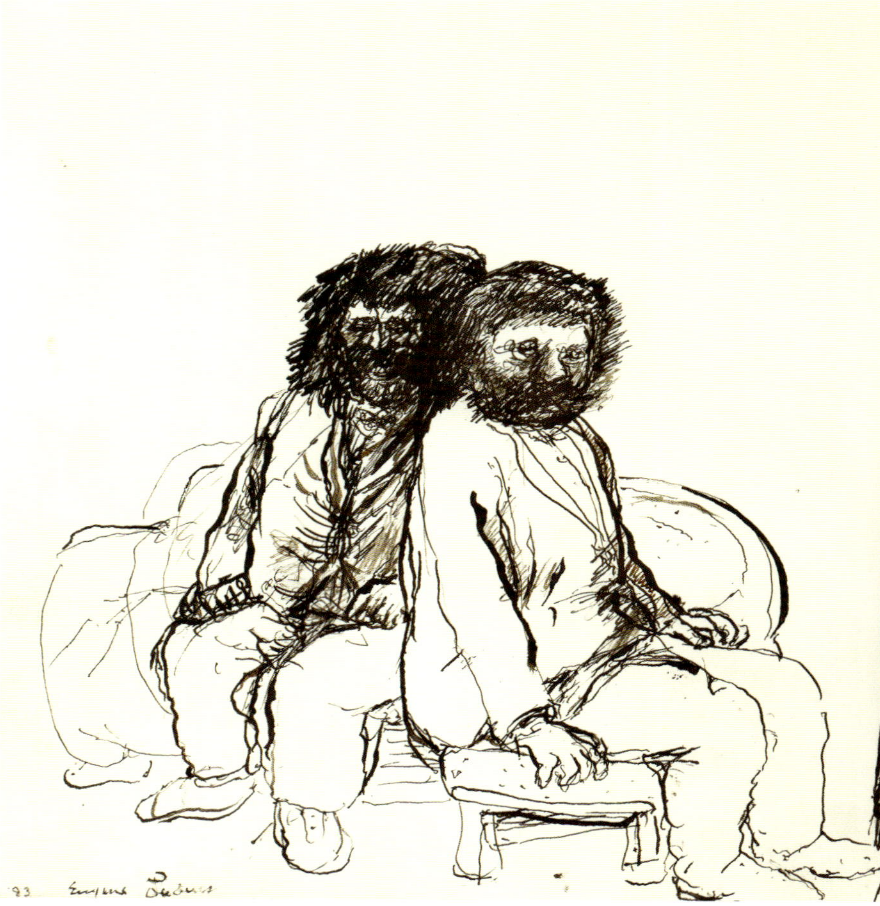

CAT. 79

Untitled Drawing

1983, ink on paper

8½ x 12 in.

Private Collection

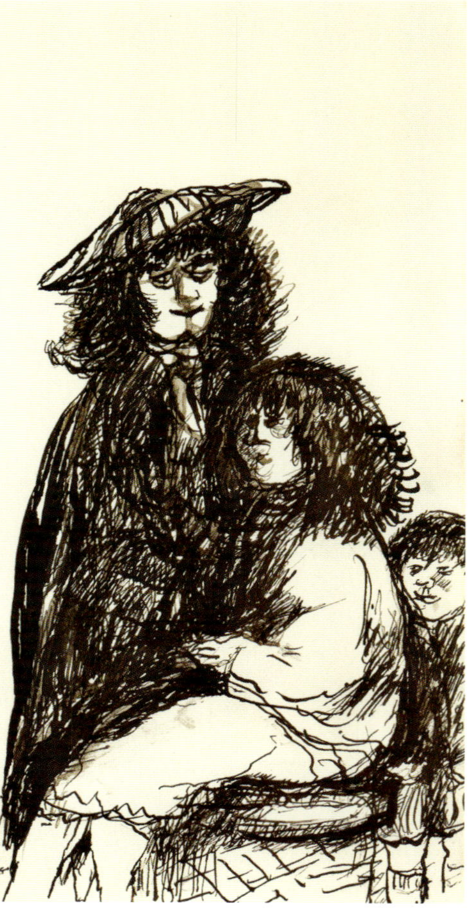

CAT. 80

Untitled Drawing

Undated, ink and wash on paper

7 x 5¼ in.

Courtesy of Cornelia Seckel and Raymond J. Steiner from the *Art Times* Collection

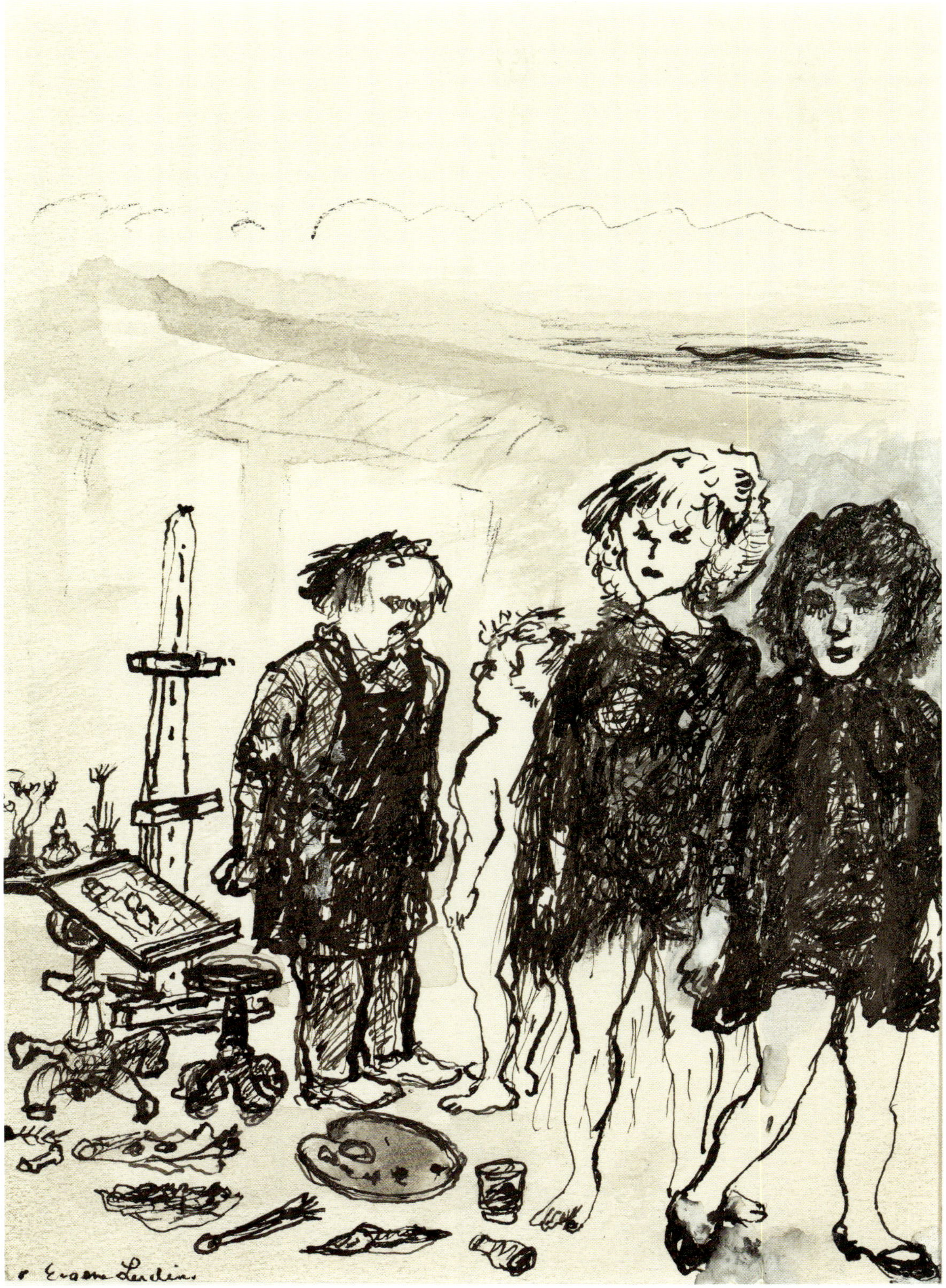

Chronology

Peter R. Jones

Specific dates are supported by primary documents from the Ludins estate, such as letters, including correspondence with his dealers, catalogs, deeds, Camp Jened programs and photos, wedding invitations, Hannah Small's birth certificate, Ludins's certificate of citizenship, and their marriage certificate. Other sources include records from the Art Students League of New York and the Whitney Museum, documents from the archives of the Woodstock Artists Association and Museum, and letters from Wendell Jones to his fiancée, Jane Hays, and to his parents, from the Jane Jones estate. Early family dates are supplied by Kim Klausner in *Tima Ludins, a Life on the Left*. Details and anecdotes are drawn from interviews with Karl Fortess, Raymond Steiner, and Polly Kline, and from stories that Ludins, Small, Petra Cabot, and Jane Jones told to Peter Jones.

1902

Byrdcliffe Colony founded by Ralph Radcliffe and Jane Byrd Whitehead, Bolton Brown, and Hervey White.

1904

March 23. Born Eugene David Ludschinski, Mariupol (Ukraine), Russia.

Sails to New York with family, first class, on *Pretoria*. Father has already changed family name to Ludins.

Family settles on Jennings Street, Bronx, New York. Father works as a contractor.

1905

Maverick Colony founded by Hervey White.

1906

House on Jennings Street burns. Maid rescues older brother George from building. Family moves to Morris Avenue.

Art Students League opens in Woodstock, had summer school in Woodstock till 1922.

c. 1910

Ludins family moves to Charlotte Street near Crotona Park in Bronx.

1911

July 3. Citizenship for Ludins family.

1919

Woodstock Art Association founded. (Changed name in 1933 to Woodstock Artists Association; in 2005, to Woodstock Artists Association and Museum.)

Nov. 1. Morris High plays Commerce High at Polo Grounds in the Bronx as high school football resumes after wartime hiatus. Ludins watches Lou Gehrig drop-kick a 50-yard field goal. Later calls Gehrig the most gifted natural athlete he ever saw.

1920

George Bellows moves to Woodstock. Plays on the Woodstock baseball team.

May 15. Ludins plays against Lou Gehrig as Morris High loses to Commerce High in baseball championship playoff series. (Commerce High wins national championship.)

1921

Graduates from Morris High School.

1923–25

Summers. Works as counselor at Camp Jened, near Hunter, in the Catskills. (Jened and sister camp, Stony Clove, are run by relatives of novelists Howard Fast—*Spartacus*—and Julius Fast.)

1923

April 28. Hannah Workum Small, sculptor, a cousin of Alfred Stieglitz, marries Austin Merrill Mecklem, painter. They settle in the Maverick Colony, among the first artist couples.

While at Camp Jened, visits sisters Tima (a teacher) and Ryah (an artist) in their Woodstock summer rental.

Attends Cornell for one week; decides to go to the Art Students League of New York instead.

1924–27

Studies at the Art Students League of New York. Teachers: Allen Tucker, Boardman Robinson, Kenneth Hayes Miller, Walt Kuhn.

1924

Gets job on *Kroonland*, Panama Pacific Line, as second ass't. pantryman's helper (dishwasher).

Makes round trip to San Francisco through Panama Canal. Fascinated by landscape.

1925–28

Participates in four Whitney Studio Club exhibitions (*Portrait of a Man*, 1925; *Third Inning*, 1928).

1925

Sails on *The Republic* to Bremerhaven, Germany, as seaman, cook's assistant.

George Bellows dies at 42.

1927–29

Spends summers in Woodstock. Plays on baseball team.

1928–29

Rents studio space at Art Students League, October-February (*Skating in Central Park*).

1928

Whitney Studio Club closes. Juliana Force says: "...not only fulfilled its purpose, it has outgrown itself."

May. Moves to Woodstock for summer.

1929

Makes living as a frame maker, trained by John Carroll, who has given him a Marsh miter machine and backsaw. Frames Carroll's 1929 sold-out New York exhibit. After stock market crash, according to Ludins, all Carroll's sales are cancelled. Ludins allowed to keep his payment.

October 29. Moves into Maverick house, becomes year-round Woodstock resident.

1930

Builds garage for Pierce-Arrow automobile given Ludins by his father. Hervey White is offended on principle.

May 10. Letter from Wendell Jones to Jane Hays: "Moved into Gene's. Polly [Rosen?] came alone last night and after supper Gene did a spontaneous pantomime that lasted an hour while he chanted dramatic music nonsense but funny as hell. He loves to show off when the audience is so sympathetic. Wonderful egg. He built an elaborate pyre on the hearth to burn a little piece of celluloid, etc. etc."

1931

Best man at Wendell and Jane Jones wedding, September 19. Joneses settle in Maverick.

American Paintings & Prints, Springfield Art Museum (*Rondout*).

1932

Austin Mecklem and Hannah Small joint show, Ferargil Gallery, New York City.

May. 54th Annual San Francisco Art Association, Palace of the Legion of Honor (*Mr. Patrick* [sic] *Gormley and Mrs. Gormley*).

Exhibits *Mr. Gormley and Mrs. Gormley* at first Whitney Biennial.

Becomes involved with Hannah Small following their participation in a Maverick production of *Scheherazade*.

Fall. Mecklem and Small are separated.

1933–43

National New Deal art programs in effect.

1933

July 31. Hannah Small and Austin Mecklem divorced.

October 9–28. First solo show, Contemporary Arts gallery, New York City (*The Fire*, *Rondout*, *Mr. Gormley and Mrs. Gormley*, *Game of War*).

Ludins and Small leave for California with their new dog, Popey, but stop in Santa Fe, renting a small adobe house.

1934

Wendell and Jane Jones join them in Santa Fe. Ludins joins baseball team and breaks nose during game against team from prison. Doctor setting Ludins's nose receives conflicting suggestions from a sculptor and two painters. Small commissioned by Public Works of Art Project, carves two stone sculptures for old public library.

Summer. Ludins and Small return to Woodstock. Exhibits *Family Portrait* at WAA Annual.

Exhibits *New Lands* at Whitney Biennial.

1935

January 2–3. Hannah Small buys property in Zena, Chestnut Hill Road, with proceeds from sale of her Tea Island (Lake George) property. Previously a summer camp, the new property consists of a year-round house, two summer houses that will be rented, and two buildings that will become studios.

Sawkill Gallery of Painters and Sculptors opens. Catherine Viviano of Pierre Matisse Gallery hired as summer director.

One of 110 artists to sign the flier for the first Exhibition and Call for Membership, American Artists Congress, Stuart Davis foreword.

1936

First American Artists Congress Against War and Fascism.

Elisha Keith Memorial Prize at Woodstock Artists Association for Woodstock's "Most Promising Young Painter (under 35)."

Exhibits *The True Story* at Whitney Biennial.

Fall. Driving new 1937 Ford station wagon, Ludins and Small join Jane and Wendell Jones in Santa Fe. They travel together to Hermosillo, Mexico. Ludins and Wendell Jones paint landscapes.

1937–38

Supervisor WPA/FAP, Woodstock and Ulster County.

1937

June. Magazine of Art article on the Sawkill (Gallery) Experiment, by Nancy Schoonmaker (*Game of War*).

August 9. Ludins and Small married at City Hall, New York. Petra Cabot is one of witnesses.

c. 1938

Sawkill Gallery closes.

1938

September. First tour of WPA Art Caravan.

Honorable Mention, Pennsylvania Academy of Fine Art (*Rotten Foundations*).

American Artists Congress, Third Annual Membership Exhibition.

Small has miscarriage.

May–July. Second tour of WPA Art Caravan.

July–October. State Supervisor for Hudson Valley (one of three regions), WPA, Federal Art Project.

1939

Mrs. Roosevelt dedicates stone building on Route 212 as Craft School, National Youth Administration (now part of Woodstock School of Art).

Allen Tucker dies.

Early 1940s

Travels to Martha's Vineyard with Petra and Blake Cabot. Paints landscapes. Meets writer and humorist S. J. Perelman.

1940

Small receives Logan Award, Art Institute of Chicago.

American Artists Congress, Fourth Annual Membership Exhibition.

1941

Exhibits *Interlude* in Carnegie's "New Directions in American Painting." Jurors: Charles Burchfield, Charles Hopkinson, Kenneth Hayes Miller, Millard Sheets.

1943

Trained as (airplane) recognition officer for the Woodstock Observation Post (*Big Day at the Post*).

May 19–29. Solo show, AAA Galleries, 711 Fifth Avenue (*Rotten Foundations*, *Interlude*, *Guerrillas*).

Exhibits *Rotten Foundations* and *Interlude* in Museum of Modern Art's "Romantic Painting in America."

Artists League of America, "This is Our War," Wildenstein Gallery. Rockwell Kent foreword.

1944

October 20. Hervey White dies.

June. Accepted by Red Cross for service.

July 11. After taking loyalty oath, is issued Certificate of Citizenship "as required by Immigration Act of 1940."

August 25. AAA Gallery writes to end relationship with Ludins. Ludins has already left for the Pacific.

August 1944–May 1946. Service in World War II in Okinawa, captain's rank. Field director for the American Red Cross Ambulance Corps.

1945

February 1–March 4. Exhibits *Big Day at the Post* in Carnegie Institute's "Portrait of America, One Hundred and Fifty paintings selected from the National Pepsi Cola Competition for American Artists. Conducted by Artists for Victory Incorporated."

1946

Painting trip through Southeast, along Gulf Coast to Texas "in celebration of his return from the Pacific theater."

September 23–October 12. Solo show, "Recent Landscapes," Passedoit Gallery, 121 East 57th Street, New York City (*Carbon Black*).

1947, 1948, 1950

Woodstock Art Conferences sponsored by WAA and Artists Equity.

1947–79

Art Students League summer school in Woodstock.

1947

November 24–December 13. Solo show, Passedoit Gallery, landscapes and figure compositions (*The Valley*).

1948–49

Chair, Woodstock Artists Association Board of Directors.

1948–69

Teaches painting, State University of Iowa. Ludins and Small take weekend trips in Mississippi valley and travel to the Gulf Coast and Mexico during vacations to paint landscapes. Small and Ludins rent their "big" Woodstock house, and, adding indoor plumbing to one of their summer houses, continue to summer in Woodstock. Retires as full professor in 1969.

1948

Juliana Force dies.

Temple Medal for "best oil without regard to subject," Pennsylvania Academy of Fine Art (*The Valley*). Prize jury: Peppino Mangravite, Louis Bouche, Bernard Karfiol, Richard Lahey, Walter Stuempfig.

Exhibits *Faith* at Carnegie Institute, Painting in the United States.

Serves on Organizing Committee for Second Woodstock Art Conference.

Appointed visiting assistant professor, State University of Iowa, Iowa City.

c. 1950

English setter dog, Popey (*Family Portrait*) dies in Iowa, age 17.

1950

"Art Conference Show," Woodstock Artists Association (*Sum*).

Whitney Biennial (*Intruders*).

Metropolitan Museum of Art, American Painting Today (*Hiding Places*).

1951

Promoted to associate professor, with tenure.

1952–53

December 15–January 3. Solo show, Passedoit Gallery (*Suspicion*).

1952–56

Participates in Museum of Modern Art art rental program.

1952

Fourth Woodstock Art Conference sponsored by WAA and American Society for Aesthetics.

1953

March 4. Sister Tima Ludins appears before the Senate Internal Security Sub-Committee. Asked about her activities in the teacher's union, she lectures the committee about academic freedom and democracy and refuses to cooperate.

1954

First section of New York Thruway opens, Rochester to Lowell.

1955–56

Chair, Woodstock Artists Association Board of Directors.

1955

March 16–April 17. Solo show, Des Moines Arts Center (*Al Fresco*).

1956

January 27. Wendell Jones dies. Writes tribute for catalogue for his memorial show at WAA in 1957. "From our earliest days at the League and through all our life in Woodstock, Wendell Jones was my dearest friend."

August 31. Final three-mile section through Yonkers opened to complete 426-mile New York City-Buffalo Mainline. Woodstock to New York City trip takes two instead of four hours.

October 29–November 17. Solo show, Passedoit Gallery (*Aransas Pass*).

November. Provides proof of citizenship as Metropolitan Museum considers purchase of *Hill Town* for American collection. Bob Hale, on committee, advocates purchase but sale does not occur.

1957

Exhibits *Hill Town* at Whitney. Last participation in Whitney.

August 30. Sister Ryah Ludins dies.

1958

February 3–15. First one-man drawings show, Passedoit Gallery, New York.

Art USA, Madison Square Garden (*High Level Conference*).

1959

May 9. Receives letter offering representation by Krasner Gallery, 1061 Madison Avenue, New York.

May 20. Small sells Flannagan rosewood sculpture, *Kneeling Figure*, to Weyhe Gallery for $3,000.

Takes one-year leave without pay from Iowa as a trial retirement, intending to paint full time. Sells house at 224 Melrose Court, near football stadium.

1960

Spring. Small and Ludins take trip to Europe. Spend time on ship socializing with Alexander Calder. (Small had studied with Calder's father, Alexander Stirling Calder.)

April 8. Receives grant, National Institute of Arts and Letters. Letter from Peter Blume, chair of Grant Committee of Art, received upon arrival in Rome. Exhibits five paintings.

September 6. His father, David G. Ludins, dies.

Fall. Returns to Iowa, buys back house at 224 Melrose Court.

1961

August 11. Juries 22nd annual Wisconsin State Fair Art Show.

October. Ludins-Small Woodstock summer house is included in book, *The Personal House, Homes of Artists and Writers*, by Betty Alswang and Ambur Hiken.

November 5–27. Solo show, University of Iowa, of works to be shown at Krasner Gallery, New York.

1962
January 29–February 17. Solo show, Krasner Gallery.

Last solo show in New York City (*To Space, Oil Riches*). Reviewed by Robert Coates in the *New Yorker* magazine, February 10, 1962.

1964
February 4. Named research associate professor. Class schedule is arranged to occupy two consecutive full days, with the rest of the week to be spent in the studio.

1968
Woodstock School of Art founded.

American Pavilion at Venice Biennale, selected by Norman Geske of the University of Nebraska, criticized in New York as too conservative. Inclusion of midwestern artists James McGarrell from University of Indiana, and Ludins's colleague Byron Burford pointedly derided by Grace Glueck in the *New York Times.*

1969
Returns to Woodstock full time. Buys Ford van to use instead of station wagon as mobile studio for landscape trips to Gulf Coast, Southwest, Maine, and Nova Scotia. (*Navigation Boulevard*, *Red Hills*, *Coastal Landscape*).

1970–82
Trustee, WAA.

c. late 1970s
Peter Fiolic closes Rudolph Galleries in Woodstock and keeps Florida gallery open.

1974
Exhibits *Oil Riches* (1959), National Academy of Design.

Writes letter about Allen Tucker, in reply to inquiry from Susan Geller, a Mt. Holyoke college student. Calls him "a great person and a most important influence."

1975
Ledger entry: painting trips: April 14–19, Virginia; May 28–June 4, Gaspe, Canada; September 18–29, Nova Scotia.

1976–79
Exhibits landscapes and drawings at Ann Blanch Gallery, Woodstock.

1976
Ledger entry: 11/3/76-11/11/76 (no destination given), 775 miles.

1977
Ledger entry: 2/10/77-3/14/77 (no destination given), $1,127.82.

January 2–March 4. Woodstock, An American Art Colony, 1902-1977, Vassar College Art Gallery, Poughkeepsie, New York. Curated by Karal Ann Marling (*Game of War*).

1978
Ledger entry: 2/10/78-3/18/78, Texas, New Mexico, 6,830 miles, $1,286.06.

1980
Acting chair, WAA Board of Trustees.

Exhibits in National Academy of Design, his final national exhibition (*Rare Birds*, 1952).

1983
January 3–28. Recent Drawings show, Louisiana Tech University, Ruston, Louisiana; Ludins and Small attend opening, and continue on painting trip to Fulton, Texas (*Fishing Boat*).

1984
Drawings exhibition, WAA, Woodstock.

Publication of book on his drawings, foreword by Heywood Hale Broun.

1985
Exhibits in Woodstock Artists and the Federal Art Project of the WPA Era, Historical Society of Woodstock.

1986
Last recorded sale of painting at Rudolph Galleries, Florida.

1987
October 3-31. Joint show with Hannah Small, Petrucci Gallery, Saugerties.

Buys new 1988 Dodge Ram cargo minivan with only two seats, replacing old Ford van; equips for landscape painting (*Wells, Maine*).

1989
Responding to growing interest in artist-made frames, sells group of frames made for his earlier paintings to Julius Lowy.

Petrucci Gallery, Saugerties, sales catalogue: "23 Woodstock Artists." Text by Ray Steiner, foreword by Alf Evers (*War Games*, *Interlude*, *Intruders*, *Birds*, and *Rare Birds* illustrated).

Ledger entry: May 16–May 30, 1989, Belfast, Ogunquit, 1,231 miles.

1990
Silver leaf "artist's frame" illustrated in Julius Lowy catalogue of historic frames.

1991
Ledger entry: June 4–June 11, 1991, sketch trip to Maine, $1,036.27.

1992
April 2. Hannah Small dies.

1993
Last landscape trip to Maine; colored pencil drawings.

1994
Solo show, early work, Fletcher Gallery, Woodstock.

1995
September 2–October 2. Joint Retrospective of Hannah Small and Eugene Ludins at Woodstock Artists Association (WAA).

Two frames, *Cross-Hatched Frame*, silver leaf, c. 1935, and *Whistler Inspired Frame*, gold leaf, c. 1940, shown in The Frame in America, 1860–1960, at Federal Reserve Board Building, Washington, D.C. Catalogue essay by William Adair.

1996
May 20. Eugene Ludins dies. Last studio van has 28,000 miles on odometer.

Exhibitions

NATIONAL EXHIBITIONS

Art Institute of Chicago
1941
Fish Hunt

Carnegie Institute
Painting in the United States, 1941
Interlude
Painting in the United States, 1944
Catfishing
Portrait of America, 1945
Big Day at the Post
Painting in the United States, 1946
Oyster Town
Painting in the United States, 1947
Gulfport
Painting in the United States, 1948
Faith
Pittsburgh International, 1955
Maze

Metropolitan Museum of Art
American Painting Today, 1950
Hiding Places

Museum of Modern Art
Romantic Painting in America, 1943
Interlude

National Academy of Design
Paintings of the Year, 1946
Port Lavaca
Paintings of the Year, 1947
Hunters
Paintings of the Year, 1948
Birds
1974
Oil Riches
1980
Rare Birds

Pennsylvania Academy of Fine Arts
1939
Rotten Foundations
1940
Bon Voyage
1944
Strength Through Joy
1947
The Little Red House
1948
The Valley
1950
The Cove

University of Illinois
Contemporary American Painting, 1951
Quarry
Contemporary American Painting, 1957
Grove

Virginia Museum of Fine Arts
1940
Green Landscape
1941
Rotten Foundations
1954
Rare Birds

Whitney Studio Club
1925
Portrait of a Man
1926
Actor
1927
Landscape
1928
Third Inning

Whitney Museum of American Art
1932
Mr. Gormley and Mrs. Gormley
1934
New Lands
1936
The True Story
1942
Man with Cat
Woman with Bird
Contemporary American Painting, 1944
Strength Through Joy
1946
Oyster Point
1947
Birds
Contemporary American Painting, 1948
Waterworks
1950
Intruders
1951
Working Model
1955
Marquette
1956
The Dance
1957
Hill Town

ONE-MAN EXHIBITIONS

Contemporary Arts
41 West 54th Street, New York
October 9–28, 1933

Associated American Artists
711 Fifth Avenue, New York
May 10–29, 1943

Passedoit Gallery
121 East 57th Street, New York
September 23–October 12, 1946
November 24–December 13, 1947
December 15, 1952–January 3, 1953
October 29–November 17, 1956
Drawings, February 3–15, 1958

Krasner Gallery
1060 Madison Avenue, New York
January 29–February 17, 1962

Checklist of Paintings

CAT. 1
Self-Portrait with Pipe
c. 1929–31, oil on canvas
20 x 16 in.
Private Collection

CAT. 2
Portrait of Hannah
1930s, oil on canvas
10 x 8 in.
Estate of Eugene Ludins

CAT. 3
Art Class
1924–27, oil on canvas
16 x 22 in.
Estate of Eugene Ludins

CAT. 4
Third Inning
1928, oil on canvas
30 x 40 in.
Private Collection

CAT. 5
Skating in Central Park
1928, oil on canvas, screen, three panels
57 x 23½ x 3 in. each
Estate of Eugene Ludins

CAT. 6
MARION GREENWOOD
Portrait of Gene Ludins
1929, oil on canvas
30 x 20 in.
Estate of Marion Greenwood

CAT. 7
Self-Portrait with Pipe
Early 1930s, oil on canvas
16 x 12 in.
Estate of Eugene Ludins

CAT. 8
Self-Portrait in Roadster
Early 1930s, oil on canvas
28 x 32 in.
Estate of Eugene Ludins

CAT. 9
Saugerties Pool
1930, oil on canvas
24 x 30 in.
Private Collection

CAT. 10
Landscape
1930, oil on canvas
30¼ x 33 in.
Whitney Museum of American Art

CAT. 11
Maverick Studio
1931, oil on canvas
36 x 32 in.
Estate of Eugene Ludins

CAT. 12
Maverick Kitchen
c. 1931, oil on canvas
30 x 26 in.
Estate of Eugene Ludins

CAT. 13
View of Kingston
c. 1931, oil on panel
5 x 11 in.
Collection Jane Jones

CAT. 14
Woodstock Landscape
1936, oil on canvas
6½ x 11½ in.
Historical Society of Woodstock

CAT. 15
The True Story
1936, oil on canvas
34 x 42 in.
Estate of Eugene Ludins

CAT. 16
Family Portrait
1934, oil on canvas
54 x 46 in.
Estate of Eugene Ludins

CAT. 17
Mr. Gormley and Mrs. Gormley
1932, oil on canvas
30 x 22 in.
Collection Jean and Jim Young

CAT. 18
Self-Portrait in Winter
c. 1940, oil on canvas
31 x 19 in.
Collection John and Elisabeth Small

CAT. 19
New Lands
1934, oil on canvas
39¼ x 50¼ in.
Woodstock Artists Association and Museum
Gift of Joseph DePaul

CAT. 20
Game of War
1933, oil on canvas
36 x 40 in.
Estate of Eugene Ludins

CAT. 21
Winter Scene
c. 1940, oil on canvas
10½ x 16 in.
Private Collection

CAT. 22
Spring Thaw
1932, oil on canvas
34 x 36 in.
Estate of Eugene Ludins

CAT. 23
Rotten Foundations
1938, oil on canvas
30 x 50 in.
Estate of Eugene Ludins

CAT. 24
Interlude
1940, oil on canvas
36 x 48 in.
Collection Abby and Mark Lerner

CAT. 25
Self-Portrait
c. 1940, oil on canvas
8½ x 7½ in.
Collection Janis Conner and Joel Rosenkranz

CAT. 26
Portrait of Hannah Small
c. 1940, oil on canvas
8 x 6 in.
Collection Janis Conner
and Joel Rosenkranz

CAT. 27
Guerrillas
1942, oil on canvas
42 x 50 in.
Estate of Eugene Ludins

CAT. 28
Heavy Water
1942, oil on canvas
24 x 36 in.
Private Collection

CAT. 29
Faith
1948, oil on canvas
50 x 36 in.
Estate of Eugene Ludins

CAT. 30
The Valley
1947, oil on canvas
48 x 36 in.
Woodstock Artists Association
and Museum, gift of Ira Janow

CAT. 31
Intruders
c. 1949, oil on canvas
38 x 50 in.
Estate of Eugene Ludins

CAT. 32
Sum
c. 1949, oil on canvas
38 x 50 in.
Estate of Eugene Ludins

CAT. 33
Hiding Places
c. 1949, oil on canvas
40¾ x 39 in.
Private Collection

CAT. 34
Carbon Black
1946, oil on canvas
14 x 24 in.
Private Collection

CAT. 35
Excursion
Early 1950s, oil on canvas
50 x 38 in.
Estate of Eugene Ludins

CAT. 36
Suspicion
c. 1951-52, oil on canvas
30 x 43 in.
Estate of Eugene Ludins

CAT. 37
Al Fresco
1954, oil on canvas
30 x 40 in.
Collection Samuel Dorsky Museum
of Art, State University of
New York at New Paltz
Gift of Petra Cabot

CAT. 38
High-Level Conference
1957, oil on canvas
28 x 50 in.
Estate of Eugene Ludins

CAT. 39
Oil Riches
1961, oil on canvas
50 x 42 in.
Estate of Eugene Ludins

CAT. 40
Aransas Pass
1955, oil on canvas
20 x 44 in.
Private Collection

CAT. 41
Dubuque
1962, oil on canvas
20 x 30 in.
Estate of Eugene Ludins

CAT. 42
Near the Summit
1960s, oil on canvas
50 x 36 in.
Estate of Eugene Ludins

CAT. 43
Veterans of Several Wars
1960s, oil on canvas
55 x 50 in.
Estate of Eugene Ludins

CAT. 44
Monument
1958–60, oil on canvas
40 x 38 in.
Estate of Eugene Ludins

CAT. 45
Crossing
c. 1960, oil on canvas
38 x 50 in.
Estate of Eugene Ludins

CAT. 46
Regenerator
1965–75, oil on canvas
39 x 50 in.
Estate of Eugene Ludins

CAT. 47
Meadow
1960s, oil on canvas
40 x 50 in.
Estate of Eugene Ludins

CAT. 48
To Space
1961, oil on canvas
40 x 38 in.
Estate of Eugene Ludins

CAT. 49
Pastoral
1965, oil on canvas
40 x 55 in.
Estate of Eugene Ludins

CAT. 50
From the Hills
Late 1970s, oil on canvas
50½ x 40¼ in.
Private Collection

CAT. 51
Red Hills
1977, oil on canvas
16 x 30 in.
Estate of Eugene Ludins

CAT. 52
Navigation Boulevard
1970s, oil on canvas
24 x 36 in.
Estate of Eugene Ludins

CAT. 53
Aransas
1980s, oil on canvas
12 x 24 in.
Estate of Eugene Ludins

CAT. 54
Coastal Landscape
1983, oil on canvas
12 x 30 in.
Estate of Eugene Ludins

CAT. 55
Fishing Boats
1983–85, oil on canvas
20 x 30 in
Estate of Eugene Ludins

CAT. 56
Gulf Coast Landscape
1985, oil on canvas
18 x 30 in.
Estate of Eugene Ludins

CAT. 57
Wells, Maine
1989, oil on canvas
18 x 20 in.
Estate of Eugene Ludins

CAT. 58
Untitled Portrait Bust
1950s, oil on canvas
20 x 16 in.
Collection Arthur Anderson

CAT. 59
Self-Portrait
1960s, oil on canvas
8 x 7 in.
Private Collection

CAT. 60
Self-Portrait
1980s, oil wash on canvas
24 x 18 in.
Estate of Eugene Ludins

Checklist of Drawings

CAT. 61
Mai Fest
February 1979, ink and wash on paper
6¼ x 13¼ in.
Collection Edgar and Cornelia Rosenblum

CAT. 62
Stick-up
Undated, ink and wash on paper
8⅜ x 10⅞ in.
Estate of Eugene Ludins

CAT. 63
Untitled Drawing
Undated, ink on paper
7¾ x 7¾ in.
Collection Edgar and Cornelia Rosenblum

CAT. 64
Untitled Drawing
c. 1950, ink and wash on paper
9½ x 11¾ in.
Collection Peter Mayer

CAT. 65
Bone of Contention
Undated, ink and wash on paper
7 x 10½ in.
Estate of Eugene Ludins

CAT. 66
Sweetbreads
Undated, ink on paper
9¼ x 8¼ in.
Private Collection

CAT. 67
Honor
Undated, ink and wash on paper
11 x 8¼ in.
Collection Arthur Anderson

CAT. 68
Foreign Nudes
Undated, ink on paper
14 x 13½ in.
Private Collection

CAT. 69
Showdown
Undated, ink on paper
2 x 9 in.
Collection Nancy Kline

CAT. 70
Untitled Drawing
Undated, ink, wash, and graphite on paper
9 x 10¼ in.
Courtesy of Cornelia Seckel and Raymond J. Steiner from the *Art Times* Collection

CAT. 71
Putsch
Undated, ink on paper
9½ x 12 in.
Collection Jane Jones

CAT. 72
The Favorite
Undated, ink on paper
8⅝ x 7 5/16 in.
Collection Jane Lyon

CAT. 73
Untitled Drawing
Undated, ink on paper
14¾ x 9¼ in.
Private Collection

CAT. 74
Untitled Drawing
Undated, ink on paper
9½ x 4 9/16 in.
Collection Jane Jones

CAT. 75
Sketch
Undated, ink on paper
11 x 8¾ in.
Private Collection

CAT. 76
Six Figures
Undated, ink on paper
10⅝ x 7⅜ in.
Private Collection

CAT. 77
Untitled Drawing
1981, ink on paper
8½ x 10¾ in.
Collection John Kleinhans and Paula Nelson

CAT. 78
Cosmetics
1982, ink and wash on paper
10½ x 7½ in.
Collection Peter Mayer

CAT. 79
Untitled Drawing
1983, ink on paper
8½ x 12 in.
Private Collection

CAT. 80
Untitled Drawing
Undated, ink and wash on paper
7 x 5¼ in.
Courtesy of Cornelia Seckel and Raymond J. Steiner from the *Art Times* Collection

Contributors

AVIS BERMAN, an independent writer and art historian, has written extensively on painting, sculpture, photography, design, and museum history for numerous magazines and newspapers, including the *New York Times*, *ARTnews*, *Smithsonian*, *Boston Globe*, *Washington Post*, *Philadelphia Inquirer*, *Antiques*, and *Art & Antiques*. She has contributed essays to encyclopedias, anthologies, and museum catalogues on the Armory Show, Brassaï, Roy Lichtenstein, John Sloan, Edward Hopper, the Addison Gallery of American Art, the Andy Warhol Museum, Elie Nadelman, Ursula von Rydingsvard, and James McNeill Whistler. She is the author of *Rebels on Eighth Street: Juliana Force and the Whitney Museum of American Art*; *James McNeill Whistler*; and *Edward Hopper's New York*, and co-author and editor of Katharine Kuh's memoir, *My Love Affair with Modern Art: Behind the Scenes with a Legendary Curator*. Since 2001, she has directed the oral history program of the Roy Lichtenstein Foundation.

PETER R. JONES is a second-generation Woodstock artist and the executor of the Eugene Ludins estate. His parents, Jane and Wendell Jones, were close friends of Ludins from their earliest days at the Art Students League of New York. He earned a degree in fine arts from Amherst College and studied art history at the Institute of Fine Arts, New York University, before studying under Ludins at the University of Iowa. After receiving his M.F.A. degree in painting, he taught at Sullins College, Virginia, from 1969 to 1973. Following that he spent seven years as art director of *Vermont Life Magazine* before returning to teaching at Louisiana Tech University's School of Art, where he retired with professor emeritus status after thirty-one years on the faculty. Jones has exhibited his paintings, primarily still lifes and landscapes, at two one-man shows in New York as well as in Woodstock, West Virginia, Virginia, South Carolina, and Louisiana. His exhibition profiles on Woodstock artists include essays on Marianne and Austin Mecklem, Carolyn and Reginald Wilson, Petra Cabot, and Betty Sturges. He resides in Ruston, Louisiana, and maintains the Jones family home in Woodstock. He has two children, Emily (Woodstock Artists Association and Museum archivist) and Nicholas, and one grandson, Kai.

SUSANA TORRUELLA LEVAL, curator of the Eugene Ludins exhibition, has been a member of the Woodstock community since 1974. She had the good fortune, through in-laws, to befriend an extraordinary older generation of Woodstock artists. Eugene Ludins and his wife, Hannah Small, were particularly close friends of the Leval family for twenty joyous years. Born in Buenos Aires and raised in Puerto Rico, Susana Torruella Leval has worked in New York City since 1970 as an art historian and curator, specializing in Puerto Rican, Latino, and Latin American contemporary art. She was director of El Museo del Barrio from 1994–2001. She has served also as chair of New York City's Cultural Institutions Group (CIG) and as vice president and president elect of the Association of Art Museum Directors (AAMD). She sits on the boards of the Metropolitan Museum of Art, Dreamyard, and the Aperture Foundation, as well as on the advisory boards of Hunter College's CENTRO, the Center for Puerto Rican Studies, and the Virtual Mirror of Race Project at Suffolk University, Boston. She is married to Judge Pierre N. Leval of the United States Court of Appeals for the Second Circuit. Their daughter India works in fashion.

JUDITH SMALL NASH is the niece of Hannah Small, Eugene Ludins's wife. Her parents were John and Amy Small. She spent summers in Woodstock as a child and teenager, along with her brother, John Jr. They both currently maintain homes in Woodstock. She is an art dealer and well-known expert in pre-Columbian art, having owned galleries in both New York and London. Nash has also organized many exhibitions and lectured and written extensively on her subject and in related fields such as African and American Indian art.

TOM WOLF is a professor of art history at Bard College. He is active as a curator and has written extensively about twentieth-century American art, including publications about Yasuo Kuniyoshi (among them *Yasuo Kuniyoshi's Women* and "Kuniyoshi in the Early 1920s," in *The Shores of a Dream: Yasuo Kuniyoshi's Early Work in America*). He has also published studies of the art colony at Woodstock, New York, and the Byrdcliffe Arts and Crafts colony that preceded it. Recent publications include "The Tip of the Iceberg: Early Asian American Artists in New York," in *Asian American Art, A History, 1850–1970*, and *Peggy Bacon, Cats & Caricatures*.

Index

Page numbers in *italic* refer to illustrations.

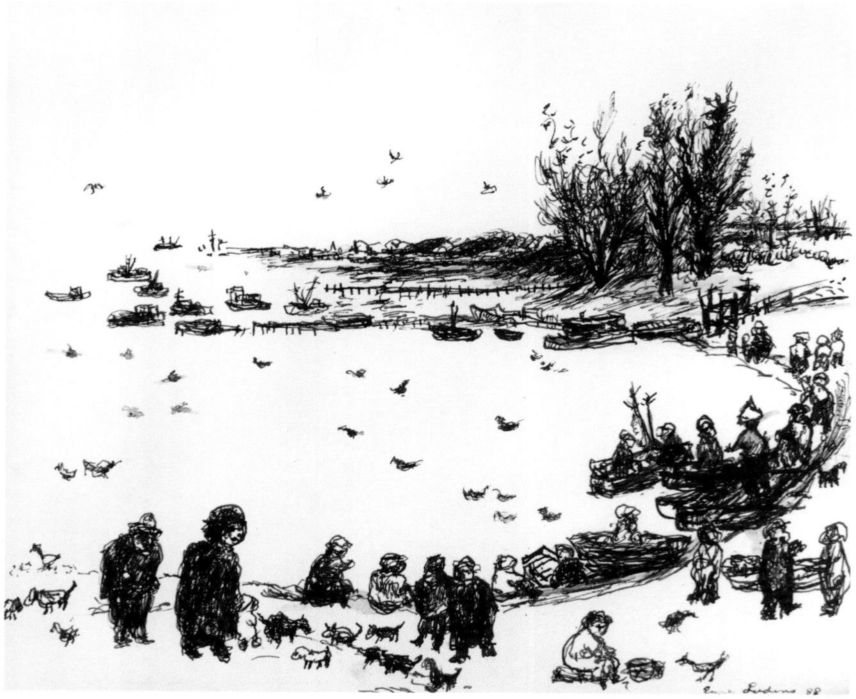

Figures in Landscape

1988, ink and wash on paper
8 x 10 in.
Collection Jane Jones

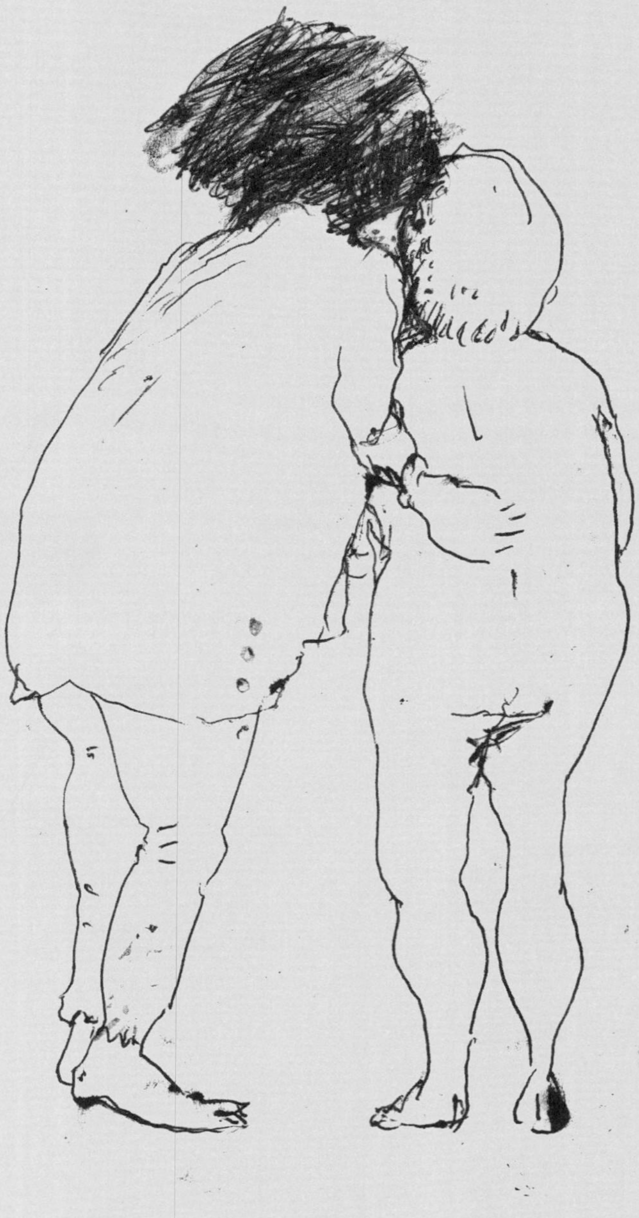